Practical Readings in Financial Derivatives

Practical Readings in Financial Derivatives

Edited by Robert W. Kolb

Copyright © Robert W. Kolb, 1998

First published 1998

2 4 6 8 10 9 7 5 3 1

Blackwell Publishers Inc.
350 Main Street
Malden, Massachusetts 02148
USA

Blackwell Publishers Ltd
108 Cowley Road
Oxford OX4 1JF
UK

Library of Congress Cataloguing-in-Publication Data

Practical readings in financial derivatives / edited by Robert W.
  Kolb.
      p.   cm.
    Includes bibliographical references and index.
    ISBN 1–57718–084–4 (alk. paper)
    1. Derivative securities. I. Kolb, Robert W.
  HG6024.A3P73   1998
  332.64'5—dc21   97–23202
                                                 CIP

British Library Cataloguing in Publication Data

A CIP catalogue record for this book is available from the British Library.

Typeset in 10 on 12 pt Bembo
by Graphicraft Typesetters Ltd, Hong Kong
Printed and bound in Great Britain by MPG Books Ltd, Bodmin, Cornwall

This book is printed on acid-free paper

Contents

Preface   vii

I Instruments and Pricing

Introduction   3

A *Futures and Forwards*   7

1   Determining the Relevant Fair Value(s) of S&P 500 Futures: A Case Study Approach   9
Ira G. Kawaller

2   Cash-and-carry Trading and the Pricing of Treasury Bill Futures   18
Ira G. Kawaller and Timothy W. Koch

B *Options*   27

3   How to Use the Holes in Black-Scholes   29
Fischer Black

C *Swaps*   39

4   Beyond Plain Vanilla: A Taxonomy of Swaps   41
Peter A. Abken

5   The Pricing of Interest Rate Swaps   65
John F. Marshall and Kenneth R. Kapner

6   Over-the-counter Interest Rate Derivatives   85
Anatoli Kuprianov

D *Exotics*   111

7   Path-dependent Options   113
William C. Hunter and David W. Stowe

8   Path-dependent Options: Valuation and Applications   121
William C. Hunter and David W. Stowe

9 An Introduction to Special-purpose Derivatives:
  Path-dependent Options   138
    Gary Gastineau

II Risk Management Applications

Introduction   155

A *Overview*   159

10 Managing Financial Risk   161
    Clifford W. Smith, Jr., Charles W. Smithson,
    and D. Sykes Wilford

B *Debt Markets*   191

11 Improving Hedging Performance Using Interest Rate Futures   193
    Robert W. Kolb and Raymond Chiang

12 Immunizing Bond Portfolios with Interest Rate Futures   205
    Robert W. Kolb and Gerald D. Gay

13 Interest Rate Swaps versus Eurodollar Strips   220
    Ira G. Kawaller

C *Equity Markets*   229

14 The Mechanics of Portfolio Insurance   231
    Thomas J. O'Brien

15 Alternative Paths to Portfolio Insurance   245
    Mark Rubinstein

16 The October Crash: Some Evidence on the Cascade Theory   259
    G. J. Santoni

17 Portfolio Insurance and the Market Crash   279
    Mark Rubinstein

D *Over-the-counter Markets*   293

18 The Role of Interest Rate Swaps in Corporate Finance   295
    Anatoli Kuprianov

19 A Tale of Two Bond Swaps   312
    Andrew Kalotay and Bruce Tuckman

20 Over-the-counter Financial Derivatives: Risky Business?   325
    Peter A. Abken

Sources   356

Preface

Practical Readings in Financial Derivatives presents a blend of articles that are accessible to undergraduate and masters students of financial derivatives. In total, the 20 articles in this reader cover the broad waterfront of theory and practical applications of financial derivatives. As such, *Practical Readings in Financial Derivatives* should be of interest to all students of finance, as well as finance professors and finance professionals. By presenting a thorough selection of articles focusing on pricing and applications, *Practical Readings in Financial Derivatives* is a useful supplement for any course on futures, options, swaps, or financial engineering.

Twenty years ago, there were essentially no financial derivatives – at least not in comparison to the present. In the last two decades, markets for financial derivatives have been founded, and they have flourished. The success of these markets has been so great that we now hear cries that the markets for underlying instruments must be protected from competition with the derivatives that have grown up beside them. For example, the trading of stock index futures and options has been blamed for the Crash of 1987, and critics of financial derivatives claim that the tail (financial derivatives) now wags the dog (the market for underlying financial instruments).

In a limited sense, these critics of financial derivatives are correct, for financial derivatives have become just as important as the markets for the underlying instruments. Further, by many measures, the markets for derivatives are far larger than the markets for the underlying instruments. The greater liquidity and lower transaction costs offered by markets for financial derivatives attract greater trading interest than the markets for the underlying securities, and they promise to grow more rapidly than the markets for underlying instruments. Consistent with the prominent role now captured by derivative markets, many academics and market professionals look first to activity in financial derivatives markets to anticipate the short-term direction of prices on underlying instruments.

Twenty years ago, there were virtually no university courses focusing on financial derivatives. Since that time, spectacular advances in understanding the pricing and uses of financial derivatives has led to a central role for the study of financial derivatives in the finance curriculum.

The 20 readings in this book are organized into two major parts, with a number of sections as follows:

I   Instruments and Pricing
   A   Futures and Forwards
   B   Options

    C Swaps
    D Exotics
II Risk Management Applications
    A Overview
    B Debt Markets
    C Equity Markets
    D Over-the-counter Markets

Part I focuses on the particulars of these instruments and the principles for pricing them. Part II shows how these instruments can be used singly, or in combination, to manage the types of risk encountered in business today. The Sources section at the end of this book shows the original place and date of publication for each article. It is customary to praise others for making a book possible. For this book, such praise has special meaning. The creativity of the authors represented in this text really did make this book possible.

Robert W. Kolb

Acknowledgments and thanks are also due for permissions for the following:

- Gary Gastineau, An Introduction to Special-purpose Derivatives; this copyright material is reprinted with permission from the *Journal of Derivatives*, a publication of Institutional Investor, Inc., 488 Madison Avenue, New York, NY 10022.
- R. Kolb and R. Chiang, Improving Hedging Performance Using Interest Rate Futures, and R. Kolb and G. Gay Immunizing Bond Portfolios with Interest Rate Futures; reprinted by permission of Financial Management Association, College of Business Admin. #3331, University of South Florida, Tampa, FL 33620-5500, tel. (813)974-2084, vol. 10 No. 4.
- Fisher Black, How to Use the Holes in Black and Scholes, 1:4, Winter 1989, pp. 67–73; reprinted with permission from the *Journal of Applied Corporate Finance*, Stern Stewart Management Services, Inc.
- Andrew Kalotay and Bruce Tuckman, A Tale of Two Bond Swaps, 1:3, December 1992, pp. 325–343; with permission from the *Journal of Financial Engineering*, copyright 1992 IAFE.
- Ira G. Kawaller, Determining the Relevant Fair Value(s) of S&P 500 Futures: A Case Study Approach, and Interest Rate Swaps versus Eurodollar Strips; reprinted with permission from Ira G. Kawaller.
- Ira G. Kawaller and T. Koch, Cash-and-carry Trading and the Pricing of Treasury Bill Futures, 4:2, Summer 1984, pp. 115–123. Copyright 1984. Reprinted by permission of John Wiley & Sons, Inc.
- T. O'Brien, The Mechanics of Portfolio Insurance; this copyright material is reprinted with permission from the *Journal of Portfolio Management*, a Publication of Institutional Investor, Inc., 488 Madison Avenue, New York, NY 10022.
- Mark Rubinstein, Portfolio Insurance and the Market Crash, Jan/Feb 88, and Alternative Paths to Portfolio Insurance, Jul/Aug 85; reprinted with permission from *Financial Analysts Journal* (Article 24). Copyrights 1988, 1985, Association for Investment Management and Research, Charlottesville, VA. All rights reserved.

PART I

Instruments and Pricing

Introduction

Part I, Instruments and Pricing, explores the theory and pricing principles that underlie financial derivatives. Without a thorough understanding of the factors that affect prices of derivatives, it is impossible to use these instruments to manage financial risk. The four major types of financial derivatives are: forwards and futures, options, swaps, and exotics. The articles in this part provide a thorough grounding in pricing these instruments. The articles are organized into four sections, one section for each type of derivative.

Futures and Forwards

The basic pricing principles for forward and futures contracts is the no-arbitrage requirement embodied in the "cost-of-carry" model. In essence, the model says that one should not be able to make an arbitrage profit by buying a good and carrying it forward, by storing and financing the good, to deliver on a futures contract. Ira G. Kawaller explores the pricing of stock index futures in his article, "Determining the Relevant Fair Value(s) of S&P 500 Futures: A Case Study Approach." The "fair value" of a stock index futures contract is the price that precludes profits from stock index arbitrage. As Kawaller explains, the idea of fair value must be refined to reflect the goals of the user of futures markets. For example, the concept of the fair value must be adjusted depending on whether the goal is to find profitable arbitrage opportunities or to create synthetic money market instruments.

Turning next to interest rate futures, Ira Kawaller and Tim Koch apply the basic no-arbitrage framework of futures pricing to Treasury bills in their paper, "Cash-and-carry Trading and the Pricing of Treasury Bill Futures." In interest rate futures, no-arbitrage conditions exist that are similar to the idea of a fair value for stock index futures. With Treasury bill futures, the underlying cash market instrument has no cash flows until maturity, thus simplifying the pricing principles. As Kawaller and Koch note, the T-bill futures' market exhibits prices that conform well to the no-arbitrage conditions.

Options

In spite of its widespread acceptance, The Black-Scholes option pricing model does rely on several unrealistic assumptions. In "How to Use the Holes in Black and

Scholes," Fischer Black notes that the model "depends on at least 10 unrealistic assumptions." In this article, Black explores the assumptions and the effects that they have on the adequacy of the model. While improving the assumptions may make the model more exact mathematically, Black points out that it does not necessarily make the model more useful in actual markets. Further, Black considers each of the ten assumptions he has identified and suggests how traders can alter their strategies to reflect adjustments to those assumptions.

Swaps

A swap agreement is a contract in which two parties agree to exchange a series of cash flows over time. As an example, the parties to the contract, called counterparties, may agree for one party to make a series of fixed payments in exchange for a series of payments based on fluctuating interest rates. Generally, the motivation for entering into such an agreement is to reduce an existing risk. For example, one party may be scheduled to receive a series of fixed cash inflows but might prefer that the size of the flows varies with interest rates. The swap just described is the simplest kind of interest rate swap – a "plain vanilla" swap in the jargon of the trade. Other swap agreements include foreign exchange and physical commodities. Starting from a virtually non-existent base a decade ago, the swaps industry has reached enormous proportions. Existing swap agreements cover trillions of dollars of underlying value.

Peter A. Abken provides a survey of the different types of swaps in his article, "Beyond Plain Vanilla: A Taxonomy of Swaps." Starting with a plain vanilla swap, Abken carefully elaborates the various terms of swap agreements that can be altered to allow the swap to deal with more complicated risk exposures. For example, a currency swap normally involves risk dimensions of both interest rates and foreign exchange rates. By systematically explaining the different types of swaps, Abken provides a valuable introduction to the burgeoning world of swap finance.

As with all financial derivatives, the price of the instrument depends upon the underlying asset. John F. Marshall and Kenneth R. Kapner tackle the problem of pricing directly in their article, "The Pricing of Interest Rate Swaps." The swaps market has matured rapidly, with swap brokers and swap dealers coming to have increasing importance. A swap broker facilitates swap agreements by finding and matching potential counterparties, but takes no financial position in the swap itself. By contrast, a swap dealer actually acts as a counterparty to a swap agreement to facilitate the transaction. The swap dealer then normally tries to find another counterparty for a new swap agreement in which the dealer can hedge any risk that may have been assumed in the first agreement. Because the swap dealer occupies such a pivotal role in the process of consummating many swaps, an understanding of swap pricing requires an understanding of the dealer function. In this article, Kapner and Marshall provide an integrated discussion of the swap dealer function and the way the dealer sets prices.

From the early 1970s until the mid-1980s exchange-traded financial futures and options dominated the growth of financial derivatives. In the last decade, over-the-counter derivatives have come to center stage. Anatoli Kuprianov focuses on these newly important instruments in his article, "Over-the-counter Interest Rate

Derivatives." Kuprianov relates these derivatives to futures and options and shows that contemporary swap agreements may include a complex mixture of features found in both futures and options.

Exotics

An exotic option contrasts with a plain vanilla option, such as that priced in the Black-Scholes model. An *exotic option* is one with special features related to one or more of the familiar option parameters: the underlying good, the exercise price, the time until expiration, the volatility of the underlying good, or the risk free rate of interest. For example, the value of a plain vanilla option at any moment depends only upon the current price of the underlying good. For many exotic options, the price depends upon the price history of the underlying good. A *lookback call option*, for example, takes as its exercise price the lowest stock price achieved by the underlying good during a specific period. As with the lookback call, the price of most exotic options depends on the path followed by the price of the underlying good, not just on the value of the underlying good at a specific moment. Thus, a *path dependent option* is an option whose price depends on the price path, not merely the price level, of the underlying good. Path dependency substantially complicates the problem of option valuation. Nonetheless, path dependent options are becoming increasingly popular.

William C. Hunter and David W. Stowe provide an introduction to this topic in their article, "Path-dependent Options." They begin their discussion with the most familiar of path dependent options – the American put. They go on to consider more exotic options such as a lookback option. In a lookback call option, the exercise price is set equal to the lowest price of the underlying good during the life of the option. Therefore, the price of a lookback option depends not on the price of the underlying good today, but it depends on the price path followed by the underlying good over the life of the option. William C. Hunter and David W. Stowe provide a sequel, "Path-dependent Options: Valuation and Applications." In this second paper, the authors show how to value and use lookback and Asian options.

In his article, "An Introduction to Special-purpose Derivatives: Path-dependent Options," Gary Gastineau explores the pricing and uses of several different types of exotic options, including barrier options and average or Asian options. A barrier option has a payout only if the price of the underlying good crosses a particular barrier price. For example, an up-and-in call becomes a plain vanilla call if, and only if, the price of the underlying good goes up to a particular barrier price during the life of the option. If the price of the underlying good does not pierce the barrier, then the up-and-in call expires worthless. A down-and-out option is like a plain vanilla option, but with an additional condition – if the price of the underlying good falls to the barrier the option immediately expires worthless. For an average or Asian option, the option payoff depends on the average price of the underlying good during a particular period. Thus, for an average price call, the payoff equals the average price during the relevant period minus the exercise price. Average price options are quite useful in executive compensation packages.

SECTION A

Futures and Forwards

1

Determining the Relevant Fair Value(s) of S&P 500 Futures: A Case Study Approach

— Ira G. Kawaller

A fundamental consideration for potential users of stock index futures is the determination of the futures' break-even price or fair value. Conceptually, being able to sell futures at prices above the break-even or buy futures at prices below the break-even offers opportunity for incremental gain. This article points out an important, though widely unappreciated caveat. That is, no single break-even price is universally appropriate. Put another way, the break-even price for a given institution depends on the motivation of that firm as well as its marginal funding and investing yield alternatives.

In this article five differentiated objectives are identified, and the calculations of the respective break-even futures prices are provided. The various objectives are (a) to generate profits from arbitrage activities, (b) to create synthetic money market instruments, (c) to reduce exposure to equities, (d) to increase equity exposure, and (e) to maintain equity exposure using the most cost effective instrument via stock/futures substitution. All these alternative objectives have the same conceptual starting point, which relates to the fact that a combined long stock/short futures position generates a money market return composed of the dividends on the stock position as well as the basis[1] adjustment of the futures contract. Under the simplified assumptions of zero transactions costs and equal marginal borrowing and lending rates, the underlying spot/futures relationship can be expressed as follows:

$$F = S\left(1 + (i - d)\frac{t}{360}\right) \tag{1}$$

Where
  F = break-even futures price
  S = spot index price
  i = interest rate (expressed as a money market yield)
  d = projected dividend rate (expressed as a money market yield)
  t = number of days from today's spot value date to the value date of the futures contract.

In equilibrium, the actual futures price equals the break-even futures price, and thus the market participant would either have no incentive to undertake the transactions or be indifferent between competing tactics for an equivalent goal.

Moving from the conceptual to the practical simply requires the selection of the appropriate marginal interest rate for the participant in question, as well as precise accounting for transactions costs. This paper demonstrates that these considerations foster differences between the break-even prices among the alternative goals considered. Each goal is explained more fully, and the respective theoretical futures prices are presented.

I. Generating Profits From Arbitrage Activities

Generally, arbitrage is explained as a process whereby one identifies two distinct marketplaces where something is traded and then waits for opportunities to buy in one market at one price and sell in the other market at a higher price. This same process is at work for stock/futures arbitrage, but these market participants tend to view their activities with a slightly different slant. They will enter an arbitrage trade whenever (a) buying stock and selling futures generates a return that exceeds financing costs, or (b) selling stocks and buying futures results in an effective yield (cost of borrowing) that falls below marginal lending rates. Completed arbitrages will require a reversal of the starting positions, and the costs for both buying and selling stocks and futures must be included in the calculations.[2] Thus, the total cost of an arbitrage trade reflects the bid/ask spreads on all of the stocks involved in the arbitrage, the bid/ask spread for all futures positions, and all commission charges on both stocks and futures.[3]

Table 1 calculates these arbitrage costs under three different scenarios. In all cases, the current starting value of the stock portfolio, based on last-sale prices, is $100 million and the S&P 500 index is valued at 335.00. The hedge ratio is calculated in the traditional manner:[4]

$$H = \frac{V \times \text{Beta}}{\text{S\&P} \times 500}$$

Where
H = hedge ratio (number of futures contracts required)
V = value of the portfolio
Beta = portfolio beta
S&P = spot S&P 500 index price.

The average price per share is estimated to be the S&P 500 index divided by five.

In column A, transactions are assumed to be costless, reflected by zero values for bid/ask spreads as well as zero commissions. In column B, more typical conditions are shown. Commissions on stock are assumed to be $.02 per share; bid/ask spreads on stocks are assumed to be 1/8th ($.125 per share); commissions on futures are assumed to be $12 on a round-turn basis (i.e. for both buy and sell transactions); and bid/ask spreads on futures are assumed to be 1 tick or 0.05, worth $25.[5] Column C assumes the same commission structure as that of column B; but bid/ask spreads are somewhat higher, reflecting a decline in liquidity relative to the former case. This scenario might also be viewed as representing the case where impact costs of trying to execute a stock portfolio were expected to move initial bids or

Table 1 Arbitrage break-evens

Arbitrage costs	A	B	C
Index Value	335.00	335.00	335.00
Size of Portfolio	100,000,000	100,000,000	100,000,000
Average Price Per Share	67	67	67
Number of Shares	1,492,537	1,492,537	1,492,537
Commission Per Share of Stock	0	0.02	0.02
Stock Commissions Per Side	0	29,851	29,851
Stock Commissions (Rnd Trn)	0	59,701	59,701
Bid/Ask Per Unit of Stock	0	0.125	0.5
Bid/Ask Stock	0	186,567	746,269
Contracts	597	597	597
Commissions Per Round Turn	0	12	12
Futures Commissions	0	7,164	7,164
Bid/Ask Per Futures Contract	0.00	0.05	0.50
Bid/Ask Futures	0	14,925	149,250
Dollar Costs	0	268,358	962,384
Index Point Cost	0.00	0.90	3.22
Marginal Borrowing Rate	9.00%	9.00%	9.00%
Marginal Lending Rate	8.00%	8.00%	8.00%
Dividend Rate	3.50%	3.50%	3.50%
Shorter Horizon (Case a):			
Days to Expiration	30	30	30
Upper Bound	336.54	337.43	339.76
Lower Bound	336.26	335.36	333.03
No-Arbitrage Range	0.28	2.08	6.73
Longer Horizon (Case b):			
Days to Expiration	60	60	60
Upper Bound	338.07	338.97	341.29
Lower Bound	337.51	336.61	334.29
No arbitrage range	0.56	2.36	7.01

offers for a complete execution. The index point costs in all cases reflects the respective dollar costs on a per contract basis.

The arbitrageur would evaluate two, independent arbitrage bounds: an upper bound and a lower bound. During those times when futures prices exceed the upper arbitrage boundary, profit could be made by financing the purchase of stocks at the marginal borrowing rate and selling futures. When the futures prices are below the lower bound, profits could be made by selling stocks and buying futures, thus creating a synthetic borrowing, and investing at the marginal lending rate. In both cases, the completed arbitrages would require an unwinding of all the original trades.

The upper bound is found by substituting the arbitrage firm's marginal borrowing rate in equation (1) and adding the arbitrage costs (in basis points) to this calculated value. In the case of the lower arbitrage boundary, the marginal lending rate is used for the variable i in equation (1), and the arbitrage costs are subtracted. The calculations in Table 1 assume marginal borrowing and lending rates of 9% and 8%, respectively, and a dividend rate of 3.5%. The upper and lower arbitrage boundaries are given for the three alternative cost structures. For comparative purposes, two sets of arbitrage boundaries are generated for two different terms.

Most obvious is the conclusion that an arbitrageur with a higher (lower) cost structure or a wider (narrower) differential between marginal borrowing and lending costs would face wider (narrower) no-arbitrage boundaries. In addition, Table 1 also demonstrates the time-sensitive nature of the difference between the two bounds, or the no-arbitrage range. As time to expiration expands, this range increases, monotonically, all other considerations held constant.

II. Creating Synthetic Money Market Securities

The case of the firm seeking to construct a synthetic money market income security by buying stocks and selling futures is a slight variant of the arbitrage case described in the prior section.[6] In this situation, too, the firm will seek to realize a rate of return for the combined long stock/short futures positions, but the relevant interest rate that underlies the determination of the break-even futures price is different. While the arbitrageur who buys stock and sells futures will do so whenever the resulting gain betters his marginal borrowing rate, the synthetic fixed-income trader will endeavor to outperform the marginal lending rate. For both, however, the imposition of transaction costs will necessitate the sale of the futures at a higher price than would be dictated by the costless case.

Not surprisingly, the break-even price for this player is directly related to both transaction costs and time to expiration. What may not be quite as readily apparent is the fact that, at least theoretically, situations may arise that provide no motivation for arbitrageurs to be sellers of futures, while at the same time offering a motivation for a potentially much larger audience of money managers to be futures sellers. Put another way, large scale implementation of the synthetic money market strategy by many market investors could certainly enhance these players' returns but also have the more universally beneficial effect of reducing the range of futures price fluctuations that do *not* induce relative-price-based trading strategies.

Yet another seemingly perverse condition that is highlighted by these calculations is that firms that operate less aggressively in the cash market, and thereby tend to have lower marginal lending rates, will likely have a greater incremental benefit from arranging synthetic securities than will firms that seek out higher cash market returns. For example, assume Firm A has access to Euro Deposit markets while Firm B deals only with lower yielding U.S. domestic banks; and assume further that the difference in marginal lending rates is .25%. Firm B's break-even futures price necessarily falls below that of Firm A. At any point in time, however, the current futures bid is relevant for both firms. Assuming the two firms faced the same transaction cost structures, this futures price would generate the same effective yield for the two firms. Invariably, Firm B will find a greater number of yield enhancement opportunities than will Firm A; and any time both firms are attracted to this strategy simultaneously, B's incremental gain will be greater.

III. Decreasing Equity Exposures

The case of the portfolio manager who owns equities and is looking to eliminate that exposure requires a further determination before the break-even calculation can be made. That is, two different break-evens would result depending on
whether the desired reduction in equity exposure were expected to be permanent
or temporary.

First, consider the case where the shift out of equities is expected to be permanent. Hedging with futures simply defers the actual stock transaction. At the same
time, it introduces futures transactions costs that would otherwise be saved if the
immediate sale of stock were chosen. The determination of this break-even, therefore, requires an evaluation of the return that one could realize by liquidating stock
today and investing the resulting funds in some money market security maturing
at the futures value date, versus the return of hedging the stock portfolio today and
subsequently liquidating it on the futures value date.

In calculating the returns from the traditional sell stocks/buy money market
securities tactic, one should recognize that the liquidation cost effectively "haircuts"
the portfolio. For example, the liquidation of a $100 million portfolio involves
an immediate expense such that some amount *less than* the original $100 million
becomes available for reinvestment. Thus, the portfolio manager realizes a lower
fixed income return than the nominal yield on the proposed money market security. The break-even futures price would be that price which, when including all
transactions costs, generates the same realized yield as the net money market return
available from the shift into money market instruments.

In Table 2, the haircut is estimated to reflect half of the bid/ask spread as well as
the stock commissions. The same commission and bid/ask structure is assumed as
that which faces the firms analyzed in the prior section; and, similarly, the same
marginal investment rate (8%) is incorporated. Under these conditions, the manager who chooses the liquidation of the stock portfolio and the investment of the
proceeds at 8% (rather than hedging) realizes an effective net money market return
of 6.51% for 30 days or 7.25% for 60 days. Respective break-even futures prices
are 336.33 and 337.58.

The case where the decision to reduce exposure is more likely to be temporary involves a minor modification to the above calculations. That is, operating
exclusively in the arena of stocks would add the cost of repurchasing a portfolio,
thereby lowering the net money market return even further. In contrast, the hedging alternative generates no stock charges. As a consequence, the break-evens in
this case are substantially below the break-evens required for the former example.

IV. Increasing Equity Exposure

Perhaps the easiest situation to explain is the choice between buying today at the
spot price versus buying in the future at the futures price. This determination
simply requires calculating the forward value of the index, which, in turn, reflects
the opportunity costs of foregoing interest income of a fixed income investment
alternative as well as an adjustment for transactions costs of futures, alone.[7] For the

Table 2   Reducing equity exposures: permanent adjustment

Short Hedging Considerations

Index Value	335.00
Size of Portfolio	100,000,000
Portfolio Beta	1.0
Average Price Per Share	67
Number of Shares	1,492,537
Commission Per Share	0.02
Commissions Per Side	29,850.74
Bid/Ask Per Stock	0.125
1/2 Bid/Ask Stock	93,283.56
Total Stock Costs	123,134.30
Investable Funds	99,876,865.70
Money Market Return	8.00%
Hedge Calculations	597.0
Number of Futures Contracts	597
Commissions (Rnd Trn)	12.00
Futures Commissions	7,164.00
Bid/ask Per Contract	0.05
Bid/ask Futures	14,925.00
Total Futures Costs	22,089.00
Total Stock Costs	123,134.30
Dollar Costs/Contract	243.26
Index Point Cost	0.49
Dividend Rate	3.50%

Shorter Horizon (Case a):	
Days to End Point	30
Ending Value	100,542,711.47
Net Money Market Return	6.51%
Break-even Futures Price	336.33

Longer Horizon (Case b):	
Days to End Point	60
Ending Value	101,208,557.24
Net Money Market Return	7.25%
Break-Even Futures Price	337.58

case of the same prototype firm discussed in the earlier sections, and given the same portfolio, the opportunity cost is generated using the marginal lending rate of 8.0%. Futures costs total $14,925 or slightly more than seven basis points per contract.

Thus, the portfolio manager would be indifferent between buying stocks now and hedging for a future purchase if the futures were cheaper than the price calculated from equation (1), inputting 8.0% for i. In this case, with the spot S&P 500 index at 335.00 and 30 days to the futures value date, the break-even price is 336.18. For a 60-day horizon, the break-even becomes 337.44.

Table 3 Alternate break-even prices

	Days to expiration	
	30-days	*60-days*
Lower Arbitrage Boundary*/Futures Substitution Break-even	335.36	336.61
Temporary Equity Adjustment (Short Hedge) Break-even	335.50	336.76
Long Hedge Break-even	336.18	337.44
Permanent Equity Adjustment (Short Hedge) Break-even	336.33	337.58
Synthetic Fixed Income Break-even	337.16	338.41
Upper Arbitrage Boundary	337.43	338.97

* Not reflective of costs associated with the uptick rule.

V. Maintaining Equity Exposure in the Most Cost Effective Instrument

Consider the case of the portfolio manager who currently holds equities, with the existing degree of exposure at the desired level. Even this player may find using futures to be attractive if they are sufficiently cheap. At some futures price it becomes attractive to sell the stocks and buy the futures, thereby maintaining the same equity exposure. The break-even price for this trader, then, would be the trigger price. That is, any futures price lower than this break-even would induce the substitution of futures for stocks and generate incremental benefits.

Like the prior case, this strategy rests on the comparison of present versus future values; and again, the firm's marginal lending rate is the appropriate discounting factor. Regarding trading costs, commissions and bid/ask spreads for both stocks and futures must be taken into account, as the move from stocks to futures would be temporary. Thus, the break-even price would be lower than the zero-cost theoretical futures price by the basis point costs of the combined commissions and bid/ask spreads.

For the prototype firm with the marginal lending rate of 8.00%, under the same normal market assumptions used throughout, the break-even price for 30- and 60-day horizons becomes 335.36 and 336.61, respectively.[8]

VI. Consolidation and Summary

The respective break-even prices that are relevant to the various applications discussed in the article are shown in ascending order. All calculations relate to a firm with a marginal borrowing rate of 9.00% and a marginal lending rate of 8.00%. Break-even prices are given for two different time spans for the hedging period: 30-days and 60-days. Further, these calculations reflect the additional assumption of "normal" transactions cost and bid/ask spreads.

The highest price for which it becomes advantageous to take a long futures position is the long hedger's break-even price; and if prices decline sufficiently from this value, such that they fall below the lower arbitrage boundary, additional market participants – namely arbitrageurs – will be induced to buy futures, as well. The lowest price for which it becomes advantageous to sell futures would be the break-even for the temporary short hedger; and, in a similar fashion, if prices rise sufficiently above this level, additional short sellers will be attracted to these markets.

Note that regardless of the time horizon, the lowest price for which buying futures is justified (336.18 or 337.44) is higher than the highest price for which selling futures is justified (335.50 or 336.76). Thus, at every futures price there is at least one market participant who "should" be using this market. Moreover, it is also interesting that if the futures price enables the arbitrageur to operate profitably, at least one other market participant would find the futures to be attractively priced as well. For example, if the futures were below the lower arbitrage bound, aside from the arbitrageur, the long hedger would certainly be predisposed to buying futures rather than buying stocks; and if the futures price were above the upper arbitrage bound, willing sellers would include arbitrageurs, both temporary and permanent short hedgers, and those constructing fixed income securities.

The overall conclusion, then, is that it pays (literally) to evaluate the relevant break-even prices for any firm interested in any of the above strategies – a population that includes all firms that manage money market or equity portfolios. At every point in time, at least one strategy will dictate the use of futures as the preferred transactions vehicle because use of futures in the given situation will add incremental value. Failure to make this evaluation will undoubtedly result in either using futures at inopportune moments or, more likely, failing to use futures when it would be desirable to do so. In either case, neglecting to compare the currently available futures price to the correct break-even price will ultimately result in suboptimal performance.

Notes

This article originally appeared in the August 1991 issue of *The Journal of Futures Markets*, pp. 453–460.
The author appreciates helpful comments from Dan Siegel and two anonymous reviewers.
1.   "Basis" in this paper is defined as the futures price minus the spot index value. Elsewhere, the calculation might be made with the two prices reversed.
2.   If any fees or charges apply to the borrowing or lending mechanisms, these, too, would have to be incorporated in the calculations. Put another way, for the calculations that are presented in this article, the marginal borrowing and lending rates are effective rates, inclusive of all such fees.
3.   Brennan & Schwartz note that the cost of closing an arbitrage position may differ if the action is taken at expiration versus prior to expiration. Thus the appropriate arbitrage bound should reflect whether or not the arbitrageur is expecting (or hoping) to exercise his "early close-out option."
4.   See Kawaller (1985) for a discussion of the justification for this hedge ratio.
5.   In practice, it may be appropriate to assume two different cost structures for the upper- and lower-bound break-even calculations, as costs differ depending on whether the trade starts with long stock/short futures or vice versa. The difference arises because initiating

the short stock/long futures arbitrage requires the sale of stock on an uptick. The "cost" of this requirement is uncertain because the transactions price is not known at the time the decision is made to enter the arbitrage. No analogous uncertainty exists when initiating the arbitrage in the opposite direction.

6. Section III of this article covers the case where the firm already holds the stock.

7. Stock costs would be roughly comparable whether one were to buy now or later, so they do not enter into the calculation. This treatment, admittedly, is not precise. For example, with a significant market move, the number of shares required may vary, as may the average bid-ask spreads; so some differences may arise. Moreover, the statement ignores the fact that although absolute magnitudes may be identical in both the buy-now or buy-later cases, the present values of these charges may differ. This consideration, if taken into account more rigorously, would bias the decision toward a later purchase. For the purposes of this analysis, however, these differences are ignored.

8. This result happens to be identical to that shown for the lower arbitrage bound of the firm operating with the same cost structure. As explained in note 5, however, the arbitrage firm that sells stock short has additional costs that do not apply to the stock/futures substituter. Thus, in practice, the break-even for the substituter is likely to be a higher price than the lower bound for the equivalent firm involved with arbitrage.

Bibliography

Brennan, M. and Schwartz E. (1990): "Arbitrage in Stock Index Futures," *Journal of Business*, 63:S7–S31.

Comell, B. and French, K. (1983, Spring): "The Pricing of Stock Index Futures," *The Journal of Futures Markets*, 3:1–14.

Figlewki, S. (1985, Summer): "Hedging with Stock Index Futures: Theory and Application In A New Market," *The Journal of Futures Markets*, 5:183–199.

Hansen, N. H. and Kopprasch, R. W. (1984): "Pricing of Stock Index Futures," Fabozzi, F. J., and Kipnis, G. M. eds, *Stock Index Futures*, Dow Jones-Irwin, 6:65–79.

Kawaller, I. G. (1985, Fall): "A Comment on Figlewski's Hedging with Stock Index Futures: Theory and Application in a New Market," *The Journal of Futures Markets*, 5:447–449.

Kawaller, I. G. (1987, June): "A Note: Debunking the Myth of the Risk-Free Return," *The Journal of Futures Markets*, 7:327–331.

2

Cash-and-carry Trading and the Pricing of Treasury Bill Futures

— Ira G. Kawaller
and Timothy W. Koch

Ira G. Kawaller and T. Koch, Cash-and-carry Trading and the Pricing of Treasury Bill Futures, 4:2, Summer 1984, pp. 115–123. Copyright 1984. Reprinted by permission of John Wiley & Sons, Inc.

Considerable effort has been devoted to examining whether the Treasury bill futures market is efficient. Most studies have compared futures yields to coincident forward yields implied by the term-structure of spot market bills, and many have found that numerous arbitrage possibilities were available. The existence of statistically significant differences has been attributed to market inefficiency whenever the differences could not be explained, but numerous explanations have been offered.

Early research focused on the impact of differential transactions costs (Poole, 1978; Rendleman & Carrabini, 1979), daily settlement for futures trades (Morgan, 1978), differential tax influences (Arak, 1980), and the cost of guaranteeing performance in futures trades (Kane, 1980). More recently, Chow and Brophy (1982) have argued that futures contracts incorporate a differential "habitat premium" which reflects investors' preferences for the more speculative futures transactions. Regardless of the presumed causal factors incorporated in their analyses, many researchers have concluded that arbitrage opportunities have consistently been available over time.

An entirely different focus on the futures-forward yield relationship was provided by Vignola and Dale (1980). They used Working's theory of storage costs to evaluate the impact of financing costs in establishing equilibrium futures prices under pure arbitrage conditions.[1] Working (1949) originally examined commodity prices and argued that the difference between cash and futures prices could be attributed to carrying charges including transportation, insurance, and warehouse costs as well as interest. Vignola and Dale applied Working's analysis to Treasury bill futures by comparing actual futures prices to equilibrium futures prices constructed under the assumption that arbitragers borrow the deliverable bills when trading futures. They concluded that carrying costs provide a better explanation of futures prices than unbiased expectations and the term-structure.

This study extends recent research concerning the role of carrying costs and Treasury bill futures. In particular, we examine the pricing of nearby Treasury bill futures with regard to pure arbitrage. Variations in the differential between rates on nearby futures contracts and corresponding forward rates are explained in terms of the spread between rates on term and overnight repurchase agreements. The futures to forward differential, which is typically associated with futures market efficiency, reflects trading strategies employed primarily by U.S. government securities dealers. The arbitrage that drives these rates, the cash-and-carry trade, involves comparing a holding period yield with a financing rate. Traders buy a deliverable Treasury bill and short the corresponding futures contract whenever the yield realized from purchasing the bill, holding it to delivery and ultimately surrendering the bill in fulfillment of the short contract exceeds their financing cost. Conversely, they borrow the deliverable bill via a reverse repurchase agreement, sell it, and go long the futures contract whenever the holding period yield is less than the financing cost.[2]

Although the decision rule appears to be straightforward, a variety of financing alternatives reflecting various repurchase agreements (RPs) leads to different trading decisions. It is the purpose of this article to discuss the different approaches to financing the cash-and-carry trade and to demonstrate that prices on nearby Treasury bill futures are set at the margin via this arbitrage. The analysis helps explain much of the seemingly inefficient behavior in the nearby futures markets described in earlier research.

The remainder of the article is structured as follows. Section I describes the arbitrage in more detail and explains why the futures-forward rate differential varies over time. Section II uses daily data to test whether the differential can be explained in terms of speculative arbitrage, and the final section summarizes the results and compares the conclusions with previous studies.

I. Nearby Futures Arbitrage

Market efficiency suggests that traders arbitrage away any differences between the forward rate implied by two spot Treasury bills of different maturities and the futures rate. Inequalities suggest the possibility of arbitrage opportunities. Most studies have thus tested for efficiency by constructing forward rates from yield curve data and comparing these rates with coincident futures rates via mean difference t-tests.

While we accept the theoretical soundness of the approach, the arbitrage implied by the futures-forward rate comparison is not the predominant one in the marketplace. The calculation of forward rates focuses on the period beginning with the futures' delivery date and ending 91 days forward. Instead, professional traders and government securities dealers focus on the period from the present to the delivery date of the nearby futures contract and compare a holding period yield with a financing rate.[3]

Consider the following time chart (Figure 1). The time line identifies the current date $(t = 0)$, the delivery date of the Treasury bill futures contract T days from the present and the maturity date of the cash bill that matures 91 days following the delivery date, $T + 91$ days from the present. Let R represent the discount rate per \$100 of face value and the notations T and $T91$ refer to the underlying instrument with maturity of T and $T + 91$ days from the present. The forward rate (RFOR) on a 91-day contract to begin T days from the present is calculated from the following equation:[4]

$$[1 - \text{RFOR}(91/360)] = [1 - \text{RT91}(T + 91)/360]/[1 - \text{RT}(T/360)] \qquad (1)$$

It is normally argued that if the futures and spot markets are in equilibrium and no inefficiencies exist, the futures rate (RFUT) would equal the forward rate from

Figure 1   Time chart

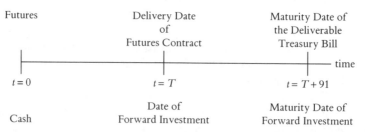

Eq. (1) after adjusting for transactions costs. This comparison suggests that traders focus on 91-day returns available T days from the present. In fact, the true focus of active bill traders covers the interval from the present until the delivery of the nearby futures contract. For example, a trader can effectively lock-in a return by purchasing a cash bill with $T + 91$ days to maturity and simultaneously shorting the nearby future, thus fixing the selling price of the cash bill T days after purchase. This rate of return (RT*) is commonly referred to as the "implied RP rate" and is calculated on a discount basis from Eq. (2):[5]

$$[1 - RT^*(T/360)] = [1 - RT91(T + 91)/360]/[1 - RFUT(91/360)] \qquad (2)$$

Traders compare the implied RP rate with a financing rate that is typically the actual RP rate available when Treasury securities are used as collateral in a re-purchase agreement. Whenever the implied RP rate exceeds the actual RP rate, traders buy the deliverable bill and short the future as characterized above. Whenever the actual RP rate exceeds the implied RP rate, traders reverse the transactions by borrowing the deliverable bill via a reverse repurchase agreement, selling it, and going long the nearby futures contract. At delivery, the deliverable Treasury bill is immediately returned to its lender, thereby satisfying the reverse repurchase agree-ment. In either case any realized difference in the RP rates – implied versus actual – offers a profit opportunity to arbitragers.

With this arbitrage, the futures price is determined at the margin by speculative activity during the three months prior to delivery. Traders buy or sell Treasury bill futures depending on the sign and magnitude of the differential between the im-plied RP rate and the expected financing rate. Traditional tests of efficiency using forward rates ignore this speculative activity. Instead, it is inferred that futures prices are set relative to 91 day returns available at delivery of the futures contract.

It should be noted, however, that the near-term arbitrage is not entirely risk-free. For example, suppose a trader buys a bill with a six-month remaining life and simultaneously sells a three-month future with a delivery date three-months for-ward. If interest rates on both the cash and future bill were to fall by 100 basis points, two things would happen: (1) a variation margin payment would be re-quired of $2500 per futures contract and (2) the cash bill would appreciate in value by $5000. The two to one difference reflects a six-month maturity on the cash bill versus a three-month maturity on the future. The added collateral value on the cash instrument, however, might not be realized by the cash-and-carry trader, as the bill has been used in a term RP agreement and it was not in the possession of the trader. The trader must then find additional financing to cover the margin call.

If rates alternatively increased by 100 basis points, the trader would receive $2500 for each futures contract, but *might* be required to add $5000 of collateral to the RP contract. Whether additional financing is required depends upon the margining practice with the RP contract. As these contracts are principal-to-principal agreements, they may be written in a variety of ways. Some allow for marking the collateral to market on a periodic basis as frequently as daily. For others, the terms require only one way margining. When the value of the bills declines, additional collateral is required, but when the bill appreciates, no "excess collateral" is remitted to the "borrower." When financing overnight the asymmetrical valuation effects between the cash bill and the futures can be managed by ratio hedging; that is, by adjusting the ratio of cash bills to futures, the cash-flow asymmetries can be minimized.[6]

An important element of the arbitrage, therefore, is the time for which financing is arranged. If traders finance the transactions to the delivery date using a term RP, they eliminate the risk that borrowing costs might increase over the life of the arbitrage, but they bear the risk of additional costs for financing margin calls. If they finance on a shorter-term basis, they are effectively speculating on future movements in RP rates; however, this strategy may permit better management of cash flow requirements.

When testing for market efficiency, the standard comparison of futures to forward rates is equivalent to a comparison of the implied RP rate with the term RP rate. Our fundamental proposition, however, is that the futures-forward rate differential largely reflects traders' practices of financing cash positions on an overnight basis as opposed to any market inefficiencies. In essence, the nearby futures price varies with the overnight RP rate. We hypothesize that whenever the term RP rate is greater (less) than the overnight RP rate (RON), the futures-forward rate differential is positive (negative) with the magnitudes directly related.[7]

In addition, the relationship between the two differentials is likely to be time dependent. The further away is delivery at the initiation of the contracts, the greater is the risk that overnight RP rates will vary prior to delivery – and the wider spread it takes between RP rates to induce traders to speculate.

II. Empirical Evidence

The empirical analysis consists of an examination of the relationships between actual Treasury bill futures rates and forward rates constructed using different assumed financing rates in the arbitrage. The forward rates reflect either assumed term financing or overnight financing. First, we duplicate previous work by testing for the equality of nearby futures rates and corresponding forward rates from Eq. (1) calculated from the term-structure of Treasury yields. This is equivalent to testing whether term RP finance can explain the difference in futures and forward rates. We then construct adjusted forward rates (RFOR*) by substituting the compounded value of the overnight RP rate (RON*) for RT in Eq. (1) such that

$$[1 - RFOR^*(91/360)] = [1 - RT91(T + 91)/360]/$$
$$(1 - RON^*(T/360)) \qquad (3)$$

Table I   Summary statistics for arithmetic differences: futures rates minus forward rates calculated from eq. (1); daily data for September 1977 through June 1982[a]

Statistic	Number of days to delivery of futures contract					
	Entire sample	<15	15–29	30–44	45–59	>60
Mean	−0.314	−0.006	−0.166	−0.330	−0.434	−0.484
Standard deviation	0.365	0.232	0.288	0.296	0.316	0.387
Number of observations	1126	189	191	194	207	345
t-value	−28.8[b]	−0.3	−8.0[b]	−15.5[b]	−19.8[b]	−23.2[b]

[a] All variables are measured in percentages.
[b] Significantly different from zero at the 1% level.

and we retest for equality between RFUT and RFOR*.[8] RFOR* represents the forward rate that is consistent with overnight financing of securities dealers' arbitrage. A zero difference provides evidence that the futures contract is priced according to the cash and carry arbitrage. In every instance we segment the analysis in terms of the number of days prior to delivery of the nearby futures contract.

The data employed are daily closing quotations for spot and future rates from September 1977 through June 1982. This period covers 18 different cash/futures combinations. Futures rates are based on closing settlement prices from the *Daily Information Bulletin* provided by the International Monetary Market. Rates on outstanding Treasury bills and repurchase agreements are offered rates provided by the Bank of America via Data Resources, Inc. The calculations of RFOR and RFOR* reflect the practice of next day settlement for Treasury bills such that the daily quoted rate actually applies to the following day's transactions.

Table I presents the results of the mean difference t-tests. Initially, we analyze the arithmetic differences between futures rates on nearby contracts and the associated forward rates calculated from Eq. (1). Summary statistics are provided in the top part of Table I where the t-values reported reflect the hypothesis that the futures rate equals the forward rate. The first column presents the results for the entire sample. The other five columns report similar results for the sample segmented according to the number of days to delivery. Interestingly, the mean difference is zero nearest to delivery, becomes negative after 14 days, and grows increasingly larger in absolute terms farther from delivery. The negative means are not surprising given the inverted yield curve that existed over most of the sample period. During that time, overnight RP rates typically exceeded term RP rates so that futures rates were lower than the forward rates inherent in the term-structure. These results would seem to support earlier work that indicated some evidence of market inefficiency.

Similar data are presented in Table II except that the forward rate (RFOR*) used in the comparison is calculated by substituting the compounded overnight RP rate for RT in Eq. (1). In effect we are examining whether the futures rate is determined by RON* as traders generally finance their positions on a continuous overnight basis. If this is the case, the computed differential between RFUT and RFOR*

Table II   Summary statistics for arithmetic differences: futures rates minus forward rates calculated using the compounded overnight RP rate; daily data for September 1977 through June 1982[a]

Statistic	Number of days to delivery of futures contract					
	Entire sample	<15	15–29	30–44	45–59	>60
Mean	0.030	0.054	0.044	0.013	−0.001	0.037
Standard deviation	0.479	0.212	0.223	0.287	0.309	0.771
Number of observations	1126	189	191	194	207	345
t-value	2.1	3.5[b]	2.7[b]	0.6	−0.1	0.9

[a] All variables are measured in percentages.
[b] Significantly different from zero at the 1% level.

Table III   Summary statistics for arithmetic differences: futures rates minus forward rates calculated using the overnight RP rate; daily data for September 1980 through June 1982[a]

Statistic	Number of days to delivery of futures contract					
	Entire sample	<15	15–29	30–44	45–59	>60
Mean	0.041	0.072	0.037	−0.027	0.028	0.072
Standard deviation	0.640	0.288	0.271	0.351	0.379	1.053
Number of observations	588	100	101	100	109	178
t-value	1.6	2.5	1.4	−0.8	0.8	0.9

[a] All variables are measured in percentages.
[b] Significantly different from zero at the 1% level.

should be much smaller than the differential between RFUT and RFOR. In fact, in all cases the mean differences are much smaller using the overnight RP rate than the term RP rate. Moreover the contention of market efficiency generally is supported by the data. The mean rate differential is not significantly different from zero over the entire sample period, but significant differences do appear when data are restricted to less than 30-days prior to the delivery day of the futures contract. These differences may be due to the time difference between the collection of the cash market rate and the future market rate on any given day (roughly 1½ hours). With compounding, such a temporal difference may be more important near the delivery date but less so as the delivery day extends into the future.

Importantly, when the sample was restricted to the period from September 1980 to June 1982, a period when Federal Reserve policy targeted bank reserves and permitted greater interest rate volatility than previously, our results were stronger. As demonstrated in Table III, the mean differences were not significantly different from zero for the entire sample, as well as for each of the time intervals prior to delivery.[9] The results further suggest that one need not appeal to such considerations as transaction costs, variation margin uncertainty, tax treatment, etc. in order to explain futures prices.[10]

The importance of these results is magnified by recent changes in delivery dates for Treasury Bill futures. Except on rare occasions prior to the March 1983 contract, arbitrage opportunities for specific cash/futures combinations were only available for about 90 days, with a cash market instrument that declined in maturity from, at most, 183 days and the nearby futures contract. Beginning June 1983, the Treasury Bill delivery cycle was altered so that any original one-year bill could satisfy delivery requirements. Thus, the cash-and-carry arbitrage can potentially be extended to nine months. It seems likely that corresponding futures rates on these contracts will come under a greater discipline reflecting this new arbitrage opportunity. Previous studies that have shown significant differences in futures and forward rates on contracts farther from delivery generally have not recognized that the cash and carry trade has not been available.

III. Conclusions

This study examines the cash-and-carry trade employed by U.S. government securities dealers to explain why futures rates on nearby Treasury bill contracts differ from corresponding forward rates implied by the Treasury yield curve. The nearby contract is the only one for which the actual deliverable bill has been available. Mean difference t-tests are used to demonstrate that futures rates are determined largely by overnight carrying costs. Specifically, futures rates calculated on the basis of compounded overnight RP rates do not differ significantly from observed futures rates on nearby contracts. Thus the nearby futures market is efficient. The availability of deliverable bills on more distant futures contracts suggests that corresponding arbitrage activity will foster greater efficiency in these distant-month contracts than has been found by earlier researchers.

Notes

Appreciation is expressed to Robert Klassen for providing computer assistance.
   1.   In pure arbitrage situations a cash position is financed with borrowed funds. This contrasts with quasi-arbitrage transactions which incorporate securities actually owned. Rendleman and Carrabini (1979) and Vignola and Dale (1980) elaborate on this distinction.
   2.   We focus on nearby futures contracts and the 91 days prior to delivery because deliverable Treasury bills are always available in the arbitrage. This provides traders the option to lock-in a profit whenever they finance to term. Prior to the June 1983 Treasury Bill futures cycle, the aribitrage was not always possible farther from delivery. After June 1983, however, the calendar of delivery dates is adjusted to permit the delivery of previously issued one-year bills with 13 weeks remaining life. Vignola and Dale (1980) examine prices beyond 91 days to delivery and do not address the speculative aspects of this pure arbitrage during the time of their investigation. We do not analyze quasi-arbitrage activities or pricing discrepancies in this study.
   3.   Vignola and Dale point out that pure arbitrage is especially applicable to these market participants which, at the time of a 1979 CFTC Survey, held 34% of all outstanding Treasury bill contracts.

4. For consistency, discount rates are used throughout this article even though some rates are typically quoted on a money market basis. We ignore transactions costs and other influences that may alter effective rates.
5. Again, in practice, traders tend to calculate this rate on a money market yield basis, but for simplicity, we have chosen to work with a discount rate construction.
6. For example, taking the six-month cash position against a three-month future, two futures contracts should be used for each million dollars of cash bills. This ratio will decline as the maturity of the cash bill shortens. Thus the cash-and-carry trade becomes an actively managed hedge, where the risks of asymmetrical cash flow considerations can be minimized.
7. Our analysis implicitly assumes that traders expect overnight RP rates to remain constant to term. This treatment is consistent with other studies, such as Hamburger and Platt (1975) which conclude that investors largely act as if they expect future short-term interest rates to equal current short-term rates.
8. The compounded overnight RP rate (RON*) is calculated as:

$$RON^* = (360/T)[1 - (1 - RON/360)^T].$$

9. The results from September 1977 through December 1979 were comparable to those in Table II.
10. Using data from 1976 through 1978, Vignola and Dale (1980) demonstrated that mean price differences between futures prices and similarly constructed forward prices cycled around zero. Their study, in contrast, used the federal funds rate as a proxy for overnight carrying costs. We duplicated their tests for the five contracts that overlapped in our sample and obtained comparable results. Comparing price data, actual December 1977 and March 1978 futures prices exceeded projected prices assuming overnight RP financing by an average of $154 and $22, respectively. For the next three contracts, the actual futures prices were $82, $150, and $151 less than the projected prices. These estimates have the same sign as Vignola and Dale's but differ in magnitude. This reflects significant differences in the Federal funds rate and overnight RP rates during each contract period.

Bibliography

Arak, M. (1980): "Taxes, Treasury Bills, and Treasury Bill Futures," Federal Reserve Bank of New York (March).

Capozza, D., and Cornell, B. (1979): "Treasury Bill Pricing in the Spot and Futures Market," *Review of Economics and Statistics* (November).

Chow, B., and Brophy, D. (1982): "Treasury Bill Futures Market: A Formulation and Interpretation," *The Journal of Futures Markets* (Winter).

Hamburger, M., and Platt, E. (1975): "The Expectations Hypothesis and the Efficiency of the Treasury Bill Market," *The Review of Economics and Statistics* (May).

Kane, E. (1980): "Market-Incompleteness and Divergences Between Forward and Future Interest Rates," *Journal of Finance* (May).

Lang, R., and Rasche, R. (1978): "A Comparison of Yields on Futures Contracts and Implied Forward Rates," *Federal Reserve Bank of St. Louis Review* (December).

Morgan, G. (1978): "Pricing Treasury Bill Futures Contracts," Comptroller of the Currency (June).

Poole, W. (1978): "Using T-Bill Futures to Gauge Interest-Rate Expectations," *Federal Reserve Bank of San Francisco Economic Review* (Spring).

SECTION B

Options

3

How to Use the Holes in Black-Scholes

Fischer Black

The Black-Scholes formula is still around, even though it depends on at least 10 unrealistic assumptions. Making the assumptions more realistic hasn't produced a formula that works better across a wide range of circumstances.

In special cases, though, we can improve the formula. If you think investors are making an unrealistic assumption like one of those we used in deriving the formula, there is a strategy you may want to follow that focuses on that assumption.

The same unrealistic assumptions that led to the Black-Scholes formula are behind some versions of "portfolio insurance." As people have shifted to more realistic assumptions, they have changed the way they use portfolio insurance. Some people have dropped it entirely, or have switched to the opposite strategy.

People using incorrect assumptions about market conditions may even have caused the rise and sudden fall in stocks during 1987. One theory of the crash relies on incorrect beliefs, held before the crash, about the extent to which investors were using portfolio insurance, and about how changes in stock prices cause changes in expected returns.

The Formula

The Black-Scholes formula looks like this:

$$\mathbf{w\ (x,t)} = \mathbf{xN(d_1) - ce^{-r(t^*-t)}N(d_2)}$$

$$\text{where } d_1 = \frac{\ln(x/c) + (r + 1/2v^2)\,(t^* - t)}{v\sqrt{t^* - t}}$$

$$\text{and} \quad d_2 = \frac{\ln(x/c) + (r - 1/2v^2)\,(t^* - t)}{v\sqrt{t^* - t}}$$

In this expression, $\mathbf{w}$ is the value of a call option or warrant on the stock, $\mathbf{t}$ is today's date, $\mathbf{x}$ is the stock price, $\mathbf{c}$ is the strike price, $\mathbf{r}$ is the interest rate, $\mathbf{t^*}$ is the maturity date, $\mathbf{v}$ is the standard deviation of the stock's return, and $\mathbf{N}$ is something called the "cumulative normal density function." (You can approximate $\mathbf{N}$ using a simple algebraic expression.)

The value of the option increases with increases in the stock's price, the interest rate, the time remaining until the option expires, and the stock's volatility. Except for volatility, which can be estimated several ways, we can observe all of the factors the Black-Scholes formula requires for valuing options.

Note that the stock's expected return doesn't appear in the formula. If you are bullish on the stock, you may buy shares or call options, but you won't change your estimate of the option's value. A higher expected return on the stock means a higher expected return on the option, but it doesn't affect the option's value for a given stock price.

This feature of the formula is very general. I don't know of any variation of the formula where the stock's expected return affects the option's value for a given stock price.

How to Improve the Assumptions

In our original derivation of the formula, Myron Scholes and I made the following unrealistic assumptions:

- The stock's volatility is known, and doesn't change over the life of the option.
- The stock price changes smoothly: it never jumps up or down a large amount in a short time.
- The short-term interest rate never changes.
- Anyone can borrow or lend as much as he wants at a single rate.
- An investor who sells the stock or the option short will have the use of all the proceeds of the sale and receive any returns from investing these proceeds.
- There are no trading costs for either the stock or the option.
- An investor's trades do not affect the taxes he pays.
- The stock pays no dividends.
- An investor can exercise the option only at expiration.
- There are no takeovers or other events that can end the option's life early.

Since these assumptions are mostly false, we know the formula must be wrong. But we may not be able to find any other formula that gives better results in a wide range of circumstances. Here we look at each of these 10 assumptions and describe how we might change them to improve the formula. We also look at strategies that make sense if investors continue to make unrealistic assumptions.

Volatility changes

The volatility of a stock is not constant. Changes in the volatility of a stock may have a major impact on the values of certain options, especially far-out-of-the-money options. For example, if we use a volatility estimate of 0.20 for the annual standard deviation of the stock, and if we take the interest rate to be zero, we get a value of $0.00884 for a six-month call option with a $40 strike price written on a $28 stock. Keeping everything else the same, but doubling the volatility to 0.40, we get a value of $0.465.

For this out-of-the-money option, doubling the volatility estimate multiplies the value by a factor of 53.

Since the volatility can change, we should really include the ways it can change in the formula. The option value will depend on the entire future path that we expect the volatility to take, and on the uncertainty about what the volatility will be at each point in the future. One measure of that uncertainty is the "volatility of the volatility."

A formula that takes account of changes in volatility will include both current and expected future levels of volatility. Though the expected return on the stock will not affect option values, expected changes in volatility will affect them. And the volatility of volatility will affect them too.

Another measure of the uncertainty about the future volatility is the relation between the future stock price and its volatility. A decline in the stock price implies a substantial increase in volatility, while an increase in the stock price implies a substantial decrease in volatility. The effect is so strong that it is even possible that a stock with a price of $20 and a typical daily move of $0.50 will start having a typical daily move of only $0.375 if the stock price doubles to $40.

John Cox and Stephen Ross have come up with two formulas that take account of the relation between the future stock price and its volatility.[1] To see the effects of using one of their formulas on the pattern of option values for at-the-money and out-of-the money options, let's look at the values using both Black-Scholes and Cox-Ross formulas for a six-month call option on a $40 stock, taking the interest rate as zero and the volatility as 0.20 per year. For three exercise prices, the value are as follows:

Exercise Price	Black-Scholes	Cox-Ross
40.00	2.2600	2.2600
50.00	0.1550	0.0880
57.10	0.0126	0.0020

The Cox-Ross formula implies lower values for out-of-the-money call options than the Black-Scholes formula. But putting in uncertainty about the future volatility will often imply higher values for these same options. We can't tell how the option values will change when we put in both effects.

What should you do if you think a stock's volatility will change in ways that other people do not yet understand? Also suppose that you feel the market values options correctly in all other respects.

You should "buy volatility" if you think volatility will rise, and "sell volatility" if you think it will fall. To buy volatility, buy options; to sell volatility, sell options. Instead of buying stock, you can buy calls or buy stock and sell calls. Or you can take the strongest position on volatility by adding a long or short position in straddles to your existing position. To buy pure volatility, buy both puts and calls in a ratio that gives you no added exposure to the stock; to sell pure volatility, sell both puts and calls in the same ratio.

Jumps

In addition to showing changes in volatility in general and changes in volatility related to changes in stock price, a stock may have jumps. A major news development may cause a sudden large change in the stock price, often accompanied by a temporary suspension of trading in the stock.

When the big news is just as likely to be good as bad, a jump will look a lot like a temporary large increase in volatility. When the big news, if it comes, is sure to be good, or is sure to be bad, the resulting jump is not like a change in volatility. Up jumps and down jumps have different effects on option values than symmetric jumps, where there is an equal chance of an up jump or a down jump.

Robert Merton has a formula that reflects possible symmetric jumps.[2] Compared to the Black-Scholes formula, his formula gives higher values for both in-the-money and out-of-the-money options and lower values for at-the-money options. The differences are especially large for short-term options.

Short-term options also show strikingly different effects for up jumps and down jumps. An increase in the probability of an up jump will cause out-of-the-money calls to go way up in value relative to out-of-the-money puts. An increase in the probability of a down jump will do the reverse. After the crash, people were afraid of another down jump, and out-of-the-money puts were priced very high relative to their Black-Scholes values, while out-of-the-money calls were priced very low.

More than a year after the crash, this fear continues to affect option values.

What should you do if you think jumps are more likely to occur than the market thinks? If you expect a symmetric jump, buy short-term out-of-the-money options. Instead of stock, you can hold call options or more stock plus put options. Or you can sell at-the-money options. Instead of stock, you can hold more stock and sell call options. For a pure play on symmetric jumps, buy out-of-the-money calls and puts, and sell at-the-money calls and puts.

For up jumps, use similar strategies that involve buying short-term out-of-the-money calls, or selling short-term out-of-the-money puts, or both. For down jumps, do the opposite.

Interest rate changes

The Black-Scholes formula assumes a constant interest rate, but the yields on bonds with different maturities tell us that the market expects the rate to change. If future changes in the interest rate are known, we can just replace the short-term rate with the yield on a zero-coupon bond that matures when the option expires.

But, of course, future changes in the interest rate are uncertain. When the stock's volatility is known, Robert Merton has shown that the zero-coupon bond yield will still work, even when both short-term and long-term interest rates are shifting.[3] At a given point in time, we can find the option value by using the zero-coupon bond yield at that moment for the short-term rate. When both the volatility and the interest rate are shifting, we will need a more complex adjustment.

In general, the effects of interest rate changes on option values do not seem nearly as great as the effects of volatility changes. If you have an opinion on which way interest rates are going, you may be better off with direct positions in fixed-income securities rather than in options.

But your opinion may affect your decisions to buy or sell options. Higher interest rates mean higher call values and lower put values. If you think interest rates will rise more than the market thinks, you should be more inclined to buy calls, and more inclined to buy more stocks and sell puts, as a substitute for a straight stock position. If you think interest rates will fall more than the market thinks, these preferences should be reversed.

Borrowing penalties

The rate at which an individual can borrow, even with securities as collateral, is higher than the rate at which he can lend. Sometimes his borrowing rate is substantially higher than his lending rate. Also, margin requirements or restrictions put on by lenders may limit the amount he can borrow.

High rates and limits on borrowing may cause a general increase in call option values, since calls provide leverage that can substitute for borrowing. The interest rates implied by option values may be higher than lending rates. If this happens and you have borrowing limits but no limits on option investments, you may still want to buy calls. But if you can borrow freely at a rate close to the lending rate, you may want to get leverage by borrowing rather than by buying calls.

When implied interest rates are high, conservative investors might buy puts or sell calls to protect a portfolio instead of selling stock. Fixed-income investors might even choose to buy stocks and puts, and sell calls, to create a synthetic fixed-income position with a yield higher than market yields.

Short-selling penalties

Short-selling penalties are generally even worse than borrowing penalties. On U.S. exchanges, an investor can sell a stock short only on or after an uptick. He must go to the expense of borrowing stock if he wants to sell it short. Part of his expense involves putting up cash collateral with the person who lends the stock; he generally gets no interest, or interest well below market rates, on this collateral. Also, he may have to put up margin with his broker in cash, and may not receive interest on cash balances with his broker.

For options, the penalties tend to be much less severe. An investor need not borrow an option to sell it short. There is no uptick rule for options. And an investor loses much less interest income in selling an option short than in selling a stock short.

Penalties on short selling that apply to all investors will affect option values. When even professional investors have trouble selling a stock short, we will want to include an element in the option formula to reflect the strength of these penalties. Sometimes we approximate this by assuming an extra dividend yield on the stock, in an amount up to the cost of maintaining a short position as part of a hedge.

Suppose you want to short a stock but you face penalties if you sell the stock short directly. Perhaps you're not even allowed to short the stock directly. You can short it indirectly by holding put options, or by taking a naked short position in call options. (Though most investors who can't short stock directly also can't take naked short positions.)

When you face penalties in selling short, you often face rewards for lending stock to those who want to short it. In this situation, strategies that involve holding the stock and lending it out may dominate other strategies. For example, you might create a position with a limited downside by holding a stock and a put on the stock, and by lending the stock to those who want to short it.

Trading costs

Trading costs can make it hard for an investor to create an option-like payoff by trading in the underlying stock. They can also make it hard to create a stock-like payoff by trading in the option. Sometimes they can increase an option's value, and sometimes they can decrease it.

We can't tell how trading costs will affect an option's value, so we can think of them as creating a "band" of possible values. Within this band, it will be impractical for most investors to take advantage of mispricing by selling the option and buying the stock, or by selling the stock and buying the option.

The bigger the stock's trading costs are, the more important it is for you to choose a strategy that creates the payoffs you want with little trading. Trading costs can make options especially useful if you want to shift exposure to the stock after it goes up or down.

If you want to shift your exposure to the market as a whole, rather than to a stock, you will find options even more useful. It is often more costly to trade in a basket of stocks than in a single stock. But you can use index options to reduce your trading in the underlying stocks or futures.

Taxes

Some investors pay no taxes; some are taxed as individuals, paying taxes on dividends, interest, and capital gains; and some are taxed as corporations, also paying taxes on dividends, interest, and capital gains, but at different rates.

The very existence of taxes will affect option values. A hedged position that should give the same return as lending may have a tax that differs from the tax on interest. So if all investors faced the same tax rate, we would use a modified interest rate in the option formula.

The fact that investor tax rates differ will affect values too. Without rules to restrict tax arbitrage, investors could use large hedged positions involving options to cut their taxes sharply or to alter them indefinitely. Thus tax authorities adopt a variety of rules to restrict tax arbitrage. There may be rules to limit interest deductions or capital loss deductions, or rules to tax gains and losses before a position is closed out. For example, most U.S. index option positions are now taxed each year – partly as short-term capital gains and partly as long-term capital gains – whether or not the taxpayer has closed out his positions.

If you can use capital losses to offset gains, you may act roughly the same way whether your tax rate is high or low. If your tax rate stays the same from year to year, you may act about the same whether you are forced to realize gains and losses or are able to choose the year you realize them.

But if you pay taxes on gains and cannot deduct losses, you may want to limit the volatility of your positions and have the freedom to control the timing of gains and losses. This will affect how you use options, and may affect option values as well. I find it hard to predict, though, whether it will increase or decrease option values.

Investors who buy a put option will have a capital gain or loss at the end of the year, or when the option expires. Investors who simulate the put option by trading in the underlying stock will sell after a decline, and buy after a rise. By choosing which lots of stock to buy and which lots to sell, they will be able to generate a series of realized capital losses and unrealized gains. The tax advantages of this strategy may reduce put values for many taxable investors. By a similar argument, the tax advantages of a simulated call option may reduce call values for most taxable investors.

Dividends and early exercise

The original Black-Scholes formula does not take account of dividends. But dividends reduce call option values and increase put option values, at least when there are no offsetting adjustments in the terms of the options. Dividends make early exercise of a call option more likely, and early exercise of a put option less likely.

We now have several ways to change the formula to account for dividends. One way assumes that the dividend yield is constant for all possible stock price levels and at all future times. Another assumes that the issuer has money set aside to pay the dollar dividends due before the option expires. Yet another assumes that the dividend depends in a known way on the stock price at each ex-dividend date.

John Cox, Stephen Ross, and Mark Rubinstein have shown how to figure option values using a "tree" of possible future stock prices.[4] The tree gives the same values as the formula when we use the same assumptions. But the tree is more flexible, and lets us relax some of the assumptions. For example, we can put on the tree the dividend that the firm will pay for each possible future stock price at each future time. We can also test, at each node of the tree, whether an investor will exercise the option early for that stock price at that time.

Option values reflect the market's belief about the stock's future dividends and the likelihood of early exercise. When you think that dividends will be higher than the market thinks, you will want to buy puts or sell calls, other things equal. When you think that option holders will exercise too early or too late, you will want to sell options to take advantage of the opportunities the holders create.

Takeovers

The original formula assumes the underlying stock will continue trading for the life of the option. Takeovers can make this assumption false.

If firm A takes over firm B through an exchange of stock, options on firm B's stock will normally become options on firm A's stock. We will use A's volatility rather than B's in valuing the option.

If firm A takes over firm B through a cash tender offer, there are two effects. First, outstanding options on B will expire early. This will tend to reduce values for both puts and calls. Second, B's stock price will rise through the tender offer premium. This will increase call values and decrease put values.

But when the market knows of a possible tender offer from firm A, B's stock price will be higher than it might otherwise be. It will be between its normal level and its normal level increased by the tender offer. Then if A fails to make an offer, the price will fall, or will show a smaller-than-normal rise.

All these factors work together to influence option values. The chance of a takeover will make an option's value sometimes higher and sometimes lower. For a short-term out-of-the-money call option, the chance of a takeover will generally increase the option value. For a short-term out-of-the-money put option, the chance of a takeover will generally reduce the option value.

The effects of takeover probability on values can be dramatic for these short-term out-of-the-money options. If you think your opinion of the chance of a takeover is more accurate than the market's, you can express your views clearly with options like these.

The October 19 crash is the opposite of a takeover as far as option values go. Option values then, and since then, have reflected the fear of another crash. Out-of-the-money puts have been selling for high values, and out-of-the-money calls have been selling for low values. If you think another crash is unlikely, you may want to buy out-of-the-money calls, or sell out-of-the-money puts, or do both.

Now that we've looked at the 10 assumptions in the Black-Scholes formula, let's see what role, if any, they play in portfolio insurance strategies.

Portfolio Insurance

In the months before the crash, people in the U.S. and elsewhere became more and more interested in portfolio insurance. As I define it, portfolio insurance is any strategy where you reduce your stock positions when prices fall, and increase them when prices rise.

Some investors use option formulas to figure how much to increase or reduce their positions as prices change. They trade in stocks or futures or short-term options to create the effect of having a long-term put against stock, or a long-term call plus T-bills.

You don't need synthetic options or option formulas for portfolio insurance. You can do the same thing with a variety of systems for changing your positions as prices change. However, the assumptions behind the Black-Scholes formula also affect portfolio insurance strategies that don't use the formula.

The higher your trading costs, the less likely you are to create synthetic options or any other adjustment strategy that involves a lot of trading. On October 19, the costs of trading in futures and stocks became much higher than they had been earlier, partly because the futures were priced against the portfolio insurers. The futures were at a discount when portfolio insurers wanted to sell. This made all portfolio insurance strategies less attractive.

Portfolio insurance using synthetic strategies wins when the market makes big jumps, but without much volatility. It loses when market volatility is high, because an investor will sell after a fail, and buy after a rise. He loses money on each cycle.

But the true cost of portfolio insurance, in my view, is a factor that doesn't even affect option values. It is the mean reversion in the market: the rate at which the expected return on the market falls as the market rises.[5]

Mean reversion is what balances supply and demand for portfolio insurance. High mean reversion will discourage portfolio insurers because it will mean they are selling when expected return is higher and buying when expected return is lower. For the same reason, high mean reversion will attract "value investors" or "tactical asset allocators," who buy after a decline and sell after a rise. Value investors use indicators like price-earnings ratios and dividend yields to decide when to buy and sell. They act as sellers of portfolio insurance.

If mean reversion were zero, I think that more investors would want to buy portfolio insurance than to sell it. People have a natural desire to try to limit their losses. But, on balance, there must be as many sellers as buyers of insurance. What makes this happen is a positive normal level of mean reversion.

The Crash

During 1987, investors shifted toward wanting more portfolio insurance. This increased the market's mean reversion. But mean reversion is hard to see; it takes years to detect a change in it. So investors did not understand that mean reversion was rising. Since rising mean reversion should restrain an increase in portfolio insurance demand, this misunderstanding caused a further increase in demand.

Because of mean reversion, the market rise during 1987 caused a sharper-than-usual fall in expected return. But investors didn't see this at first. They continued to buy, as their portfolio insurance strategies suggested. Eventually, though, they came to understand the effects of portfolio insurance on mean reversion, partly by observing the large orders that price changes brought into the market.

Around October 19, the full truth of what was happening hit investors. They saw that at existing levels of the market, the expected return was much lower than they had assumed. They sold at those levels. The market fell, and expected return rose, until equilibrium was restored.

Mean Reversion and Stock Volatility

Now that we've explained mean reversion, how can you use your view of it in your investments?

If you have a good estimate of a stock's volatility, the stock's expected return won't affect option values. Since the expected return won't affect values, neither will mean reversion.

But mean reversion may influence your estimate of the stock's volatility. With mean reversion, day-to-day volatility will be higher than month-to-month volatility, which will be higher than year-to-year volatility. Your volatility estimates for options with several years of life should be generally lower than your volatility estimates for options with several days or several months of life.

If your view of mean reversion if higher than the market's, you can buy short-term options and sell long-term options. If you think mean reversion is lower, you can do the reverse. If you are a buyer of options, you will favor short-term options when you think mean reversion is high, and long-term options when you think it is low. If you are a seller of options, you will favor long-term options when you think mean reversion is high, and short-term options when you think it's low.

These effects will be most striking in stock index options. But they will also show up in individual stock options, through the effects of market moves on individual stocks and through the influence of "trend followers." Trend followers act like portfolio insurers, but they trade individual stocks rather than portfolios. When the stock rises, they buy; and when it falls, they sell. They act as if the past trend in a stock's price is likely to continue.

In individual stocks, as in portfolios, mean reversion should normally make implied volatilities higher for short-term options than for long-term options. (An option's implied volatility is the volatility that makes its Black-Scholes value equal to its price.) If your views differ from the market's, you may have a chance for a profitable trade.

Notes

1. See John Cox and Stephen Ross, *Journal of Financial Economics* (January/March 1976).
2. See John Cox, Robert Merton, and Stephen Ross, *Journal of Financial Economics* (January/March 1976).
3. Robert Merton, *Bell Journal of Economics and Management Science* (1977).
4. John Cox, Mark Rubinstein, and Stephen Ross, "Option Pricing: A Simplified Approach," *Journal of Financial Economics* Vol. 7 (1979), 229–263.
5. For evidence of mean reversion, see Eugene Fama and Kenneth French, "Permanent and Temporary Components of Stock Prices." *Journal of Political Economy* Vol 96 No 2 (April 1988), 246–273, and James Poterba and Lawrence Summers, "Mean Reversion in Stock Prices Evidence and Implications," *Journal of Financial Economics* Vol 22 No. 1 (October 1988) 27–60.

SECTION C

Swaps

4

Beyond Plain Vanilla:
A Taxonomy of Swaps

―――――――――――――――――――――― Peter A. Abken

Since their introduction over a decade ago, swaps have become an important tool for financial risk management. Generally, swaps alter the cash flows from assets or liabilities into preferred forms. Basic swaps have branched into many variants, some more popular and successful than others, each geared toward meeting specific customer needs in various markets. The author describes the features and typical applications of many variants of the four basic swap types — interest rate, currency, commodity, and equity.

Swap contracts of various kinds have become a mainstay of financial risk management since their introduction in the late 1970s. In the most general terms, a swap is an exchange of cash flows between two parties, referred to as counterparties in the parlance of swap transactions. Swaps, which transform the cash flows of the underlying assets or liabilities to which they are related into a preferred form, have been used in conjunction with positions in debt, currencies, commodities, and equity. Most swap agreements extend from one to ten years, although many have been arranged for much longer periods.[1]

The key players responsible for originating and propelling the swaps market are money center banks and investment banks. These institutions benefit from the fee income generated by swaps, which are off-balance-sheet items, and by the spreads that arise in pricing swaps. Innovations in the swaps market, as in other financial services areas, may be characterized as a Darwinian struggle, in which competition heats up and margins narrow as a particular kind of swap becomes accepted and widely used. Such swaps are disparagingly said to be traded "like commodities." That is, little value is added by the dealer in structuring a swap and bringing counterparties together; consequently, little return is realized for the service of intermediation or position taking.

Perhaps the most basic, and most popular, swap involves the conversion of interest payments based on a floating rate of interest into payments based on a fixed rate (or vice versa). Because many variants of interest rate and other swaps have emerged over the years, this most basic type has become known as the "plain vanilla" swap.[2] As swap forms take on plain vanilla status, the firms that originated them are compelled to develop new types of swaps to regain their margins, amounting to monopoly rents, on new products. Some swap variations succeed, while others languish or fail.

In this article the plain vanilla swap is a starting point for a detailed taxonomy of the various species and subspecies of swaps. Swap variants are classified along cladistic principles, categorized and compared in terms of their features and applications. Examples illustrate many of the important types of swaps.

The Market

A brief history

Before taking a detailed look at swaps, an overview of the market will help put their proliferation into perspective. Although some swaps had been arranged in the late 1970s, the first major transaction was a 1981 currency swap between IBM and the World Bank. This deal received widespread attention and stimulated others.

The currency swap actually evolved from a transaction popular in the 1970s, the parallel loan agreement, that produced cash flows identical to a swap's. For example, in one of these agreements a firm in the United States borrows a million dollars by selling a coupon bond and exchanges (swaps) this amount for an equivalent amount of deutsche marks with a German firm, which borrows those deutsche marks in its domestic market. This is the initial exchange of principal. Thereafter, the U.S. firm makes mark-denominated coupon payments and the German firm makes dollar-denominated coupon payments. Upon maturity of the underlying debt, the firms swap principal payments. These firms have effectively borrowed in one another's capital markets, although for a variety of reasons (such as foreign exchange controls or lack of credit standing in foreign markets) they could not borrow directly. As Clifford W. Smith, Charles W. Smithson, and Lee Macdonald Wakeman (1990a) point out, the problems with such an agreement were that default by one firm does not relieve the other of its contractual obligation to make payments and that the initial loans remain on-balance-sheet items during the life of the agreement for accounting and regulatory purposes. The currency swap, on the other hand, stipulates that a default terminates the agreement for both counterparties and, in general, limits credit-risk exposure to the net cash flows between the counterparties, not the gross amounts. This type of currency swap is essentially a sequence of forward foreign exchange contracts.[3]

Following the 1981 currency swap, the first interest rate swap, in mid-1982, involved the Student Loan Marketing Association (Sallie Mae). With an investment bank acting as intermediary, Sallie Mae issued intermediate-term fixed rate debt, which was privately placed, and swapped the coupon payments for floating rate payments indexed to the three-month Treasury bill yield. Through the swap, Sallie Mae achieved a better match of cash flows with its shorter-term floating rate assets.[4] At the end of 1982, the combined notional principal outstanding for interest rate and currency swaps stood at $5 billion. Notional principal is the face value of the underlying debt upon which swap cash flows are based.

The commodity swap made its appearance in 1987, when it was approved by a number of U.S. banking regulators (see Schuyler K. Henderson 1990 and Krystyna Krzyzak 1989b, c). Banks had been prohibited from direct transactions in commodities or related futures and forward contracts. In 1987 the Office of the Comptroller of the Currency permitted Chase Manhattan Bank to act as a broker in commodity swaps between an Asian airline and oil producers. Shortly afterward Citicorp also obtained approval for engaging in commodity swaps through its export-trading subsidiary. Regulations were further relaxed in February 1990 to allow national banks to use exchange-traded futures and options to hedge commodity swap positions. However, much commodity swap activity took place offshore because of uncertainties about the Commodity Futures Trading Commission's (CFTC) view of commodity swaps. The CFTC undertook a study of off-exchange transactions in February 1987 to determine whether they came under the CFTC's regulatory jurisdiction. In July 1989 the CFTC established criteria that would exempt commodity swaps from its regulatory oversight.[5] Since the CFTC's decision commodity swap activity has been increasing in the United States. As of early 1990, commodity swaps outstanding totaled about $10 billion in terms of the value of the underlying commodities (Julian Lewis 1990, 87).

Equity swaps are the newest variety, first introduced in 1989 by Bankers Trust. Based on both domestic and foreign stock indexes, these instruments may take complex forms, such as paying off the greater of two stock indexes against a floating rate of interest. The mechanics of such instruments and their advantages will be discussed below.

The size of the market

As of year-end 1989, the size of the worldwide swaps market, as measured by the dollar value of the notional principal, stood at $2.37 trillion. This figure does not include commodity or equity swaps, but these new types of swap have relatively small amounts outstanding compared with interest rate and currency swaps. The International Swap Dealers Association (ISDA), a trade organization, periodically surveys its members, who include most of the major swap dealers. Table 1 displays the survey results for swaps in various categories. The interest rate swap market, involving swaps denominated in one currency, composed roughly two-thirds of the market, or $1.5 trillion as of year-end 1989. Of that amount, two-thirds consisted of U.S. dollar swaps, the most prevalent kind of swap. The average contract size was $20.35 million and $27.13 million for total and total dollar interest rate swaps, respectively. Currency swap market data are given in Table 2. The U.S. dollar is less dominant among currency swaps, for which it represents 41 percent of the total, compared with its 66 percent share of interest rate swaps. For the years during which the survey has been conducted, swaps of every type have grown rapidly.[6]

In all categories the position of the end users has been a multiple of those of the swap dealers. Interdealer swaps arise mainly in connection with hedging activities. A certain amount of double counting is therefore involved in the aggregate figures because one swap can set up a number of others as counterparties hedge their positions.

The latest ISDA survey reveals that the most active category for new swaps originated during the period January 1 to June 30, 1990, was non-U.S. dollar interest rate swaps, which grew by 26.4 percent. U.S. dollar swaps increased by 8.2 percent in this period. In contrast, total currency swaps rose by 2.9 percent, with U.S. dollar currency swaps contracted increasing by 4.6 percent. These semiannual growth rates show considerable variability over time and thus do not indicate trend movements. Further discussion of the ISDA survey results appears below in the section on currency swaps.

Table 1 U.S. dollar interest rate swaps 1985–89*

Survey period	End user			ISDA user			Total		
	Contracts	Notional principal	Average contract	Contracts	Notional principal	Average contract	Contracts	Notional principal	Average contract
1985	5,918	$141,834	$23.97	1,061	$28,348	$26.72	6,979	$170,182	$24.38
1986	10,752	$235,829	$21.93	3,330	$76,921	$23.10	14,082	$312,750	$22.21
1987	16,871	$379,880	$22.52	7,472	$161,637	$21.63	24,343	$541,517	$22.25
1988	20,381	$484,272	$23.76	8,968	$243,894	$27.20	29,349	$728,166	$24.81
1989	23,324	$622,602	$26.69	13,303	$371,144	$27.90	36,627	$993,746	$27.13
Total interest rate swaps 1987–89									
1987	23,768	$476,247	$20.04	10,359	$206,641	$19.95	34,127	$682,888	$20.01
1988	35,031	$668,857	$19.09	14,529	$341,345	$23.49	49,560	$1,010,203	$20.38
1989	50,193	$955,492	$19.04	23,635	$547,108	$23.15	73,828	$1,502,600	$20.35

* All dollar amounts are in millions of dollars in U.S. dollar equivalents.
Source: International Swap Dealers Association Market Survey.

Table 2 U.S. dollar currency swaps 1987–89*

Survey period	End user			ISDA user			Total		
	Contracts	Notional principal	Average contract	Contracts	Notional principal	Average contract	Contracts	Notional principal	Average contract
1987	4,665	$129,181	$27.69	1,366	$33,425	$24.48	6,031	$162,606	$26.96
1988	6,777	$201,374	$29.71	2,297	$68,103	$29.66	9,074	$269,477	$29.70
1989	9,078	$257,748	$28.39	3,414	$96,418	$28.24	12,492	$354,166	$28.35
Total currency swaps 1987–89									
1987	5,173	$294,608	$28.47	1,439	$71,006	$24.67	6,612	$365,614	$27.65
1988	7,724	$469,092	$30.37	2,547	$164,550	$32.30	10,271	$633,642	$30.85
1989	11,270	$647,516	$28.73	4,015	$222,182	$27.67	15,285	$869,698	$28.45

* All dollar amounts are in millions of dollars in U.S. dollar equivalents.
Source: International Swap Dealers Association Market Survey.

Interest Rate Swaps

Interest rate swaps account for the most volume in the swaps market, as seen in the previous section. The explanation to follow covers many of the numerous features that can modify the plain vanilla swap. Though discussed in detail only in relation to interest rate swaps, these alternate forms actually or potentially apply to currency, commodity, and equity swaps as well; they can be combined in innumerable ways to alter any kinds of cash flows.

The basic fixed-for-floating interest rate swap involves a net exchange of a fixed rate, usually expressed as a spread over the Treasury bond rate corresponding to the swap maturity, for a floating rate of interest. That floating rate is tied or indexed to any of a number of short-term interest rates. The London Interbank Offered Rate (LIBOR) is the most common.[7] Other rates include the Treasury bill rate, the prime rate, the Commercial Paper Composite, the Certificate of Deposit Composite, the federal funds rate, the J. J. Kenney index, and the Federal Home Loan Bank System's Eleventh District cost-of-funds index. The Eleventh District index has been used mainly by thrift institutions in California.[8] The J. J. Kenney index is based on short-term tax-exempt municipal bond yields.

The fixed rate payer (and floating rate receiver) is said to have bought a swap or to have "gone long" a swap. Similarly, the floating rate payer (and fixed rate receiver) is said to have sold a swap or "gone short" a swap. Swaps are quoted by a dealer (or broker) usually in terms of the spread over the Treasury security of comparable maturity. For example, a swap with seven-year time to maturity, or tenor, might be quoted at 65–72. The dealer is offering to buy a swap (pay fixed) at a rate that is 65 basis points above the seven-year Treasury yield, and offering to sell a swap (receive fixed) at 72 basis points over that yield.[9] The dealer is therefore collecting a 7 basis point margin for standing between the counterparties.

Like floating rate notes, the floating rate payments on a swap do not necessarily match the timetable of the floating rate index.[10] The payment may be based on the average of the underlying index during some specified interval. The point at which the floating rate is established, based on the floating rate at that time or over some previous period, is termed the reset date. This date is not necessarily the same as the settlement date, when payment on the swap is made to the other counterparty. If reset and settlement dates do not coincide, the swap is said to be paid in arrears, which is also a common convention for floating rate notes. The floating rate may be reset daily, weekly, monthly, quarterly, or semiannually, while typically the settlement dates fall monthly, quarterly, semiannually, or annually (Anand K. Bhattacharya and John Breit 1991, 1158).

As over-the-counter instruments, interest rate swap terms are open to negotiation. The conventional way to quote a swap rate is relative to the floating rate index "flat." That is, a swap counterparty would pay the fixed rate and receive LIBOR. Swaps can also be arranged to include a spread above or below the floating rate – for example, LIBOR + 10 basis points. In addition, fixed rate payers and floating rate payers can agree to making payments at different periods – quarterly floating rate payments versus semiannual fixed rate payments.[11] However, swap counterparties usually prefer net transactions so that only a difference check passes between them, thereby limiting credit exposure. In the section below the first alteration of the basic plain vanilla structure that is considered encompasses different treatments of a swap's notional principal. The second general variation outlined allows for specially tailored coupon structures, and the discussion includes consideration of option-like features. Third, different types of underlying instruments – in particular, asset swaps and their uses in creating synthetic assets – are examined. Finally, option structures are discussed, including options on swaps, known as swaptions.

Variations on notional principal

The plain vanilla swap is nonamortizing. Nonamortizing swaps, known as "bullet" swaps, have a constant underlying notional principal upon which interest payments are made. This structure is easily modified to accommodate any kind of predictable changes in the underlying principal. Uncertainty about the future amount of the principal, which frequently arises with mortgage-backed securities, is usually better handled using option features, which will be discussed shortly.

Amortizing, annuity, and mortgage swaps   Amortizing swaps are typically used in conjunction with mortgage loans, mortgage-backed securities, and automobile- and credit-card-backed securities. All of these tend to involve repayment of principal over time. In general it is difficult to match the amortization schedule of a swap, which usually cannot be changed after its initiation, against the amortization rate on these assets or liabilities; thus, the swapholder runs the risk of being over- or underhedged. A particular example of an amortizing swap is discussed in more detail in the section below on asset swaps. One specific kind is the mortgage swap, which is simply an amortizing swap on mortgages or mortgage-backed securities. The extreme form of an amortizing swap, in which the notional principal diminishes to zero as the principal of a fixed rate mortgage does, is an annuity swap.

Accreting swaps   The flip side of an amortizing swap is an accreting swap, which, as its name suggests, allows the notional principal to accumulate during the life of the swap. Both amortizing and accreting swaps are sometimes also called sawtooth swaps. The accreting swap arises commonly with construction finance, in which a construction company or developer has a floating rate drawdown facility with a bank. That is, a line of credit may be tapped that would lead to increasing amounts of floating rate borrowing. An accreting swap would convert those floating rate payments into fixed rate payments, although again there is a risk of not exactly matching notional principal amounts at each settlement date. It is possible to create amortizing or accreting swaps from bullet swaps of varying tenor instead of arranging a swap specifically with the desired characteristics.

Seasonal Swaps and Roller Coasters   Finally, amortizing and accreting notional principals can be combined to form a seasonal swap, which allows the notional principal to vary according to a counterparty's seasonal borrowing needs such as those retailers typically experience. A swap that allows for periodic or arbitrary but predictable swings in notional principal is called a roller coaster.

Variations on coupon payments

Altering cash flows of underlying securities is one of the primary functions of swaps. In the following section a number of important types of swaps that accomplish this end are discussed, including those with option-like features.

Off-market swaps   The plain vanilla swap is also characterized as a par value swap. That is, the fixed rate for the swap is established such that no cash payment changes hands when the swap is initiated. The term *par value* derives from the swap's being viewed as a hypothetical exchange of fixed for floating rate bonds. When arranged at market interest rates, both bonds are equal to their face values (par value). Nonpar, or off-market, swaps involve fixed or floating rates that are different from the par value swap rates. Differences in the fixed rate above or below the par value swap rate entail a cash payment to the fixed rate payer from the floating rate payer if the fixed rate coupon is above the par value swap rate, and vice versa if it is below. The payment's amount is the present value of the difference between the nonpar and par value swap fixed rate payments. Swap counterparties commonly perform this kind of calculation in the process of marking an existing swap to market. An existing swap may be terminated (if permitted in the swap agreement) by such a marking to market of the remaining swap payments. High or low coupon swaps, as off-market swaps are alternatively called, are created simply by doing the calculation at the outset and making or receiving the appropriate payment. One reason for engaging in this type of swap is to change the tax exposure of underlying cash flows. Another is that spreads above or below the floating rate index can be introduced. John Macfarlane, Janet Showers, and Daniel Ross (1991) explain the mechanics of this variation.

Basis swaps   A basis swap is an exchange of one floating rate interest payment for another based on a different index. Consider an example in which a bank, First SmartBucks, has invested in two-year floating rate notes that pay the bank one-month LIBOR plus 100 basis points. First SmartBucks has funded this purchase by issuing one-month certificates of deposit. The problem is that LIBOR and the CD rate will not track each other perfectly, exposing First SmartBucks to a so-called basis risk; it may pay more on its CDs than it receives from its floating rate notes. The problem is solved by entering into a basis swap with a swap dealer, who will pay the one-month CD rate in exchange for LIBOR. Chart 1 illustrates the transaction. Aside from the initial fee for the swap, the cost of this hedging transaction manifests itself as a 10 basis point spread under the CD rate received from the dealer. This hedge may also be less than perfect, however, because the dealer probably would use the Certificate of Deposit Composite, which may not track First SmartBucks's CD rate perfectly, to index his payments. Nevertheless, the swap is likely to mitigate the original basis risk.

Yield curve swaps   The yield curve swap, a variant of the basis swap, typically is an exchange of interest payments indexed to a short-term rate for ones tied to a long-term rate. For example, a counterparty could contract to make semiannual floating rate payments based on six-month LIBOR and receive floating rate payments indexed to the prevailing thirty-year Treasury bond yield, less a spread to the swap

Chart 1 A basis swap

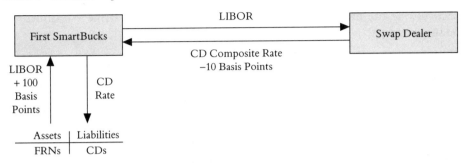

First SmartBucks transforms LIBOR interest coupons into CD composite rate payments via a basis swap.

dealer.[12] The ten-year Treasury bond yield has also been used for yield curve swaps on the long end, as well as three-month LIBOR on the short end.

Yield curve swaps gained popularity in early 1988 when the yield curve began to flatten – that is, when long rates fell relative to short rates (Krzyzak 1988, 29). Savings and loan institutions were major users of this new swap because they found it useful for adjusting the interest rate exposures of their portfolios (see asset swaps below). These swaps were also well suited to speculating on shifts in the yield curve while hedging against changes in its level. Finally, these instruments were combined with a new kind of floating rate debt, called FROGs (floating rate on governments), to transform the FROG's coupon into LIBOR. The coupon was reset semiannually and tied to the yield on newly issued Treasury bonds.[13] This strategy reportedly achieved a lower cost of funding than a standard LIBOR floating rate issue.

Caps, floors, and collars   A floating rate payer can combine option contracts with a swap to tailor the maximum size of potential swap payments. Interest rate caps, floors, and collars are instruments closely related to swaps that can alter swap cash flows.[14] As an example, consider a plain vanilla swap with a fixed rate of 8 percent (the swap rate). At a reset date, a rise in the floating rate above 8 percent would obligate the floating rate payer to pay the counterparty the net amount of the notional principal outstanding times the difference between the actual floating rate – say, 10 percent – and the swap rate. By buying a 9 percent cap of the same maturity as the swap the user would never pay more than one percentage point above the swap rate. The cap could be obtained from another counterparty, or it could be bundled with the swap in one transaction. However, buying a cap from another counterparty introduces an additional credit risk.

A counterparty who sells (or writes) a cap is obligated to pay the excess over the cap's strike rate (9 percent in this example). The purchaser in return pays a cap "premium" up front. In fact, caps are sequences of interest rate options with maturities that match the schedule of floating rate payments. Analogous to caps, interest rate floors pay off whenever the floating interest rate falls below the prespecified floor level. To defray some or all of the cost of buying a cap, the floating rate payer could sell a floor with a strike rate less than the swap rate. Such a sale would create an interest rate collar. Thus, rather than paying for the protection of the cap outright, the floating rate payer could give up part of the payments from the swap resulting from large declines in the floating rate below the swap rate. That is, the maximum possible payment from the other swap counterparty would effectively be the difference of the swap rate and the floor strike rate times the notional principal.

Synthetic swaps   The "collaring" of a swap suggests that a floating rate payer could completely offset a swap by buying a cap and selling a floor that both have strike rates equal to the swap rate. Similarly, a fixed rate payer could nullify a swap by selling a cap and buying a floor with strike rates equal to the swap rate. In these cases the floating rate payer would, in effect, be buying a "synthetic" swap and the fixed rate payer would be selling one. However, swaps are not usually unwound in this way because it is generally cheaper simply to buy or sell the corresponding swap; caps and floors may not be sufficiently liquid at the desired strike rates to execute these transactions at reasonable prices. (That is, an illiquid – infrequently traded – cap or floor would be quoted with large spreads.) Nevertheless, arbitrage between the swap and cap/floor markets is possible and does occur if rates for these instruments get too far out of line.

Participating swaps   A hybrid version of the fixed rate swap and interest rate cap allows a counterparty to benefit partially from declining rates while not requiring any up-front payment as with a cap. Consider an example using LIBOR. The counterparty would receive LIBOR to pay its floating rate debt. In turn, instead of paying a fixed interest rate as for a plain vanilla swap, a higher fixed rate is established (above the swap rate), which is the maximum rate the counterparty would pay if LIBOR rises above that level. However, if LIBOR falls below this maximum rate, the counterparty's payment would decline less than one-for-one with LIBOR. For example, the swap terms could stipulate that a one percentage point drop in LIBOR would reduce the swap payment by one-half percentage point. The so-called participation rate in this case is 50 percent. In other words, the counterparty would participate in 50 percent of any decline in LIBOR below the maximum rate. The maximum rate and the participation rate are set to price the swap at zero cost upon initiation. The price of this swap's option feature is paid by giving up part of the gains from falling rates.

   The participating swap can also be structured to have the counterparty pay LIBOR and receive payments indexed to a fixed schedule. That is, a minimum rate would be specified in the swap, with payments above that minimum determined by the product of the prevailing LIBOR multiplied by the participation rate. A counterparty might want to use such a swap in conjunction with its floating rate assets. Participating swaps can be structured for any interest rates and are also used for currencies and commodities.

Reversible swaps and roller coasters   Reversible swaps and roller coasters are a couple of exotic variants on swap structures. A reversible swap allows a counterparty to change status from floating rate payer to fixed rate payer or vice versa at some point during the life of the instrument. The roller coaster takes this concept a step further by having the counterparties reverse roles at each settlement date. Distinct from the earlier type of roller coaster involving variations in notional principal, this one has been used in only a limited number of transactions.

Zero coupon swaps   As its name implies, all payments on one side of the swap come at the end in one "balloon" payment, while the other side makes periodic fixed or floating rate payments. One use of zero coupon swaps is to transform the cash flows from zero coupon bonds into those of fixed coupon bonds or floating rate bonds, or vice versa.

Asset swaps

Asset swaps are precisely what their name suggests. They effectively transform an asset into some other type of asset, such as the conversion of a fixed rate bond into a floating rate bond. The conversion results in synthetic securities because of the swap's effects. The analysis of asset swaps actually contains nothing new. The earlier example of First SmartBucks's use of a basis swap, exchanging LIBOR for the CD Composite rate, was a type of asset swap. Asset swaps are usually considered in connection with portfolio management and are low-cost tools for changing the characteristics of individual securities or portfolios.

Bhattacharya (1990) discusses an interesting application of asset swaps to a particular kind of mortgage-backed security. The collateral behind mortgage-backed securities is subject to prepayment. For example, homeowners may pay off their mortgage principals early in the event they move or mortgage rates drop sufficiently. Collateralized Mortgage Obligations (CMOs) repackage mortgage cash flows into a variety of securities that carry different prepayment risks. Planned Amortization Class (PAC) bonds are structured to have amortization schedules more predictable than those of other CMO classes. However, the risks are nevertheless sufficient to make PAC bonds trade at fairly wide spreads over corresponding Treasury securities. PAC bonds have been popular candidates for amortizing asset swaps that convert the bonds' fixed coupons into floating rate payments tied to any index. These asset swaps have the potential to make PAC bonds attractive to a broader class of investors and consequently channel more funds to the mortgage market. Such swaps may be a more cost-effective means of altering the characteristics of mortgage-backed securities than having an even broader array of such securities being issued.

As a tool for bond portfolio management, asset swaps can change a portfolio's exposure to interest rate risk. The value of a portfolio, and of any bonds within it, fluctuates with shifts in interest rates, tending to fall as market rates rise and vice versa. The sensitivity to interest rate risk is measured by a portfolio's duration, which is based on the future timing and size of its cash flows.[15] A portfolio manager can extend a portfolio's duration, increasing its volatility with respect to interest rate movements, by entering into asset swaps to receive fixed rate cash flows and to pay floating rate cash flows. Conversely, a portfolio can be protected or "immunized" against interest rate movements by contracting to make fixed rate cash flows and receive floating rate. The intuition here is that the more a portfolio's (or security's) cash flows move with current market rates, the closer its value will stay to face value. Money market funds, for example, experience little change in asset value because they have very short duration. In contrast, a fund consisting of long-term zero coupon bonds, which have durations equal to their maturities, would have extremely volatile asset values.

Asset swaps are particularly useful for adjusting a portfolio when securities sales would result in capital losses. For example, a portfolio manager would be reluctant to change the portfolio's duration by selling off bonds that are "under water" (currently valued below par). As just discussed, an asset swap is ideal for this kind of adjustment.[16] As another example, some bonds cannot be traded because they were purchased from an underwriter through a private placement to avoid registration and other costs associated with public issues. Using an asset swap obviates the need to trade the underlying security to alter interest rate exposure.

Forward and extension swaps

Forward swaps are analogous to forward or futures contracts as hedging instruments. The difference is that forward or futures contracts hedge cash flows at a single point in the future whereas forward swaps (and swaps generally) hedge streams of cash flows. Extension swaps are an application of forward swaps.

Forward swaps   Financial managers, such as corporate treasures, often want to hedge themselves against rising interest rates when considering a future debt issue. For example, selling a new issue of bonds may be necessary to refund outstanding corporate bonds that mature in one year. The yield on that issue is unknown today but could be locked in using a forward or deferred swap. If rates have risen when the outstanding bonds mature, the firm sells the swap, realizing a gain equal to the present value of the difference between the cash flows based on the current swap rate and those based on the lower fixed rate of the forward swap. This gain would offset the higher coupon payments on the newly issued fixed rate bond; the effective rate paid would be the same as the forward swap rate.

However, a fall in rates would translate into a loss on the forward swap upon sale, although the newly issued fixed rate bond would itself carry a lower rate. The effective rate on the fixed rate issue would again be the forward swap rate, neglecting differences in transactions costs. The forward swap in this example is used as a hedging tool, establishing a certain fixed rate today instead of an unknown fixed rate at the future date for debt issuance.

Extension swaps   An extension swap is merely a forward swap appended to an existing swap before its term ends to extend it by some additional period (Jeffry Brown 1991, 127). If the forward swap is arranged based on current forward interest rates, the extension swap would be obtained at no cost. However, if a counterparty wants the forward swap rate to match an outstanding swap's rate, an up-front cash payment (or receipt) might be necessary to compensate for the change in market rates since the outstanding swap's origination. The extension swap in this case would be a type of off-market swap.

Swaptions

The earlier discussion of amortizing swaps and the example of an asset swap involving a PAC bond emphasized the risk inherent in mismatches of principal with notional principal. The amount of principal is not always perfectly predictable, especially for many new types of asset-backed securities. Option contracts are designed to handle contingencies of this kind, and, not surprisingly, a market has developed for options on swaps, known as swaptions. (There is also a market for options on caps and floors, which, as one might guess, are called captions and floortions.)

Like any option, swaptions entail a right and not an obligation on the part of the buyer. Unfortunately, the nomenclature for swaptions is confusing, so the details are often simply spelled out in talking about them. A call swaption (a call option on a swap or payer swaption) is the right to buy a swap – pay a fixed rate of interest and receive floating. A put swaption (put option on a swap or receiver swaption) is the right to sell a swap – pay floating and receive fixed. The swaption on the plain vanilla swap is the most common, although swaptions can be written on more complicated swaps. Both the maturity of the swaption and the tenor of the underlying swap, which commences at a stipulated future date, must be specified. Also like options, swaptions come in both American and European varieties. The European swaption, which accounts for about 90 percent of the market, may be exercised only upon its maturity date, whereas the American swaption may be exercised at any time before maturity (Robert Tompkins 1989, 19). Only European swaptions will be considered in this discussion, unless otherwise noted.

A call swaption would be exercised at maturity if the swaption strike rate – the fixed rate specified in the contract – is lower than the prevailing market fixed rate for swaps of the same tenor. The swaption could be closed out by selling the low fixed rate swap obtained through the swaption for a gain, rather than entering into that swap. Similar reasoning applies to the decision to exercise a put swaption.

Swaptions are quite different from caps and floors, although these instruments are frequently used in similar situations. A swaption involves one option on a swap, while a cap (or floor) represents a series of options expiring at different dates on a floating interest rate. In addition, cap prices depend partly on the volatility of near-term forward rates, whereas swaption prices reflect the volatility of future swap rates, which in turn are averages of more distant, less volatile forward rates. Consequently, swaptions are much cheaper than caps or floors. Like options, swaptions require up-front payments, but these have recently fallen in the range of 20–40 basis points as compared with 200–300 basis points for caps or floors (Krzyzak 1989a, 13). American swaptions would be slightly more costly than European swaptions because of the additional right to exercise the instrument before maturity.

Callable, puttable, and reversible swaps For hedging applications, perhaps the swaption's most basic use is to give a swap counterparty the option to cancel a swap, at no further cost beyond the initial swaption premium. A fixed-for-floating swap bundled together with a put swaption is known as a callable swap. The swap can be canceled upon the maturity of the embedded swaption if, for example, interest rates have fallen. Exercising the swaption creates an offsetting floating-for-fixed swap. A floating-for-fixed swap combined with a call swaption is called a puttable swap. The swap can be terminated if interest rates have risen – that is, if a higher fixed rate could be received from a new swap.

Another example of a swaption application involves the PAC bond considered earlier. The amortizing swap to pay fixed and receive floating could be hedged against the possibility that the rate of amortization is faster than that structured in the swap. A put swaption purchased along with the original fixed-for-floating swap would (partially) hedge this risk. The purchaser would buy a swaption(s) in the amount necessary to partially offset the underlying swap in order to cover the potential additional amortization of principal. An American swaption would be appropriate for this application.

The reversible swap described earlier can be synthesized by a fixed-for-floating plain vanilla swap combined with put swaptions for twice the notional principal of the underlying swap. Assuming a swaption has the same notional principal amount as the swap, the first swaption cancels the exising swap and the second creates a floating-for-fixed swap upon maturity, running for the remaining term of the original swap.

Extendable swaps   As the name suggests, an extendable swap contains the option to lengthen its term at the original swap rate. Such a swap simply amounts to an ordinary swap with a swaption expiring at the end of the swap's tenor. Note the difference between an extendable swap and an extension swap. The former gives the holder the option to extend a swap; the latter is a commitment. The same distinction applies to swaptions and forward swaps.

Leveraged buyout hedging   Another application of swaptions has been in leveraged buyouts, in which a firm's management takes on large amounts of debt to "take a firm private." Lenders, such as commercial banks, often require the firm to hedge its debt, which typically is floating rate. A call swaption with a strike rate at a level the firm could safely meet would accomplish this end. Should the floating rate rise sharply, the swaption would be exercised, converting the remaining floating rate payments to manageable fixed rate payments. However, lenders involved in leveraged buyout financing often prefer to sell caps because a swaption, if exercised, makes its writer a counterparty to a highly leveraged (and often low-rated) firm. A cap writer faces no credit risk from the cap buyer.

Synthetic straight debt   A final example of swaption usage is in stripping callable debt. This strategy has been popular in the swaption market's brief history. Corporate bonds are frequently issued with options allowing the issuer to refinance the debt issue at a lower coupon if interest rates fall before the bonds mature. The issuer usually cannot exercise the embedded call until after some prespecified date. The callable debt's buyer has effectively written a call option on the price of the bond to the issuer, the firm. If bond prices rise above the strike price of the calls (implying that interest rates have fallen sufficiently), the issuer has the right to call the bonds away after paying the strike price.

Because many participants in these markets have believed that the calls attached to these bonds are undervalued, the following arbitrage strategy developed. Firms wanting fixed rate debt issued callable bonds and "stripped" the embedded call options by selling call swaptions, with the net result of creating synthetic noncallable or "straight' bonds at a lower yield than that prevailing on comparable fixed rate bonds. The yield reduction stemmed from selling the undervalued bond market calls at a profit in the swap market.[17]

As an illustration of the basic strategy, assume the bond is callable at par. That is, if at the call date the relevant interest rate is at or below the original coupon rate, the bond will be called. To strip the call option, the issuer writes a put swaption, which, if exercised, obligates the firm to pay fixed and receive floating on a swap

Table 3   Interest rate swaps as of December 31, 1989*

Currency	U.S. dollar equivalent	End-user counterparty (percent)	ISDA counterparty (percent)	Currency as percentage of total ($1,502.6 billion)
U.S. Dollar	$993,746	62.65	37.35	66.14
Yen	$128,022	52.25	47.75	8.52
Sterling	$100,417	60.13	39.87	6.68
Deutsche Mark	$84,620	61.46	38.54	5.63
Australian Dollar	$67,599	84.35	15.65	4.50
French Franc	$42,016	89.92	10.08	2.80
Canadian Dollar	$29,169	87.66	12.34	1.94
Swiss Franc	$28,605	55.65	44.35	1.90
European Currency Unit	$18,988	58.51	41.49	1.26
Dutch Guilder	$5,979	65.14	34.86	.40
Hong Kong Dollar	$2,149	60.12	39.88	.14
Belgian Franc	$835	79.16	20.84	.06
New Zealand Dollar	$444	82.66	17.57	.03

* All dollar amounts are in millions of dollars in U.S. dollar equivalents.
Source: International Swap Dealers Association Market Survey.

commencing on the bond's first call date and ending at the bond's maturity date. In this example the swaption strike would be set to the bond's coupon rate. If interest rates fall, the put swaption is exercised. In turn, the firm would call its debt and simultaneously issue floating rate debt, whose coupon payments would be met by the floating rate payments coming from the swap counterparty. On balance, the firm would continue to make fixed rate payments, though to the swap counterparty instead of to the bondholders. There are many variations on this strategy. Also, embedded put options can be stripped from bonds in a similar way.[18]

The size of the swaption market   As of year-end 1989, $79.7 billion in U.S. dollar and non-U.S. dollar swaptions was outstanding, as measured by the value of the underlying notional principal.[19] The market grew 118 percent compared with the figure for year-end 1988, the first year the survey included swaptions. The size of the caps, collars, and floors market was considerably larger. For year-end 1989, the total U.S. dollar and non-U.S. dollar value of the notional principal for caps, collars, and floors was $457.6 billion, representing a 57 percent increase over the previous year's figure.

Non-U.S. dollar denominated interest rate swaps

The interest rate swap market is active worldwide. About one-third of interest rate swaps outstanding involved currencies other than the U.S. dollar. Table 3 reports the latest International Swap Dealers Association survey results for year-end 1989 reflecting swaps involving a single currency. The dollar equivalent of the notional principal outstanding is shown, ranked by currency. The Japanese yen is a distant number two to the U.S. dollar, accounting for 8.5 percent of the market. The British pound and deutsche mark are next in order, with the New Zealand dollar ranking last.

Currency Swaps

Basic currency swaps were described earlier in connection with their evolution from parallel loan agreements. The fixed-for-fixed currency swap is the most rudimentary type of swap and is roughly equivalent to a series of forward foreign exchange contracts. For example, a firm could borrow yen at a fixed interest rate and swap its yen-dominated debt for fixed rate dollar-denominated debt. The exchange rate for converting cash flows throughout the life of the swap would be established at the outset. Forward foreign exchange contracts, if they were available in long-dated maturities, could also lock in the exchange rate for future cash flows.

All of the features enumerated for interest rate swaps can be applied singly or in combination to swaps involving different currencies. A number of applications of currency swaps are discussed below.

Currency coupon swaps

One of the currency swap's early variants is the currency coupon swap, otherwise known as the cross-coupon swap. This swap is like a plain vanilla swap in which the fixed interest rate is paid in one currency while the floating rate is paid in another. However, the principal involved in the transaction is usually exchanged as well.

An example   Consider a hypothetical transaction between a U.S. firm, USTech, and a British bank, BritBank. A U.S. swap dealer intermediates the transaction, in part because this institution has the relevant credit information about the swap counterparties that they lack individually. USTech is setting up a British subsidiary and issuing dollar-denominated floating rate bonds tied to LIBOR to finance this operation. USTech wants to hedge itself on two counts, though: first, it wants protection against foreign exchange rate fluctuations because the subsidiary's sales revenue will be in sterling but will be needed to service the dollar-denominated floating rate debt; second, USTech prefers to make fixed rate payments. A currency coupon swap would enable the firm to make sterling-denominated fixed rate payments while receiving dollar-denominated LIBOR, which it would pass to its floating rate bondholders. On the other hand, BritBank would like sterling-denominated fixed rate cash flows instead of dollar-denominated LIBOR payments from floating rate notes that it holds in a portfolio within its trust department. The bank wants the fixed rate sterling cash flows to extend the duration of its portfolio.

As is typical of currency swaps, this one involves exchanges of principal at the beginning and end of the swap. The dealer collects his margin on the fixed rate side of the swap. Like the fixed rate currency swap, the exchange rate for the currency coupon swap is established at the outset and prevails at each of the subsequent settlement dates. Payments at those dates are for the gross amounts of the cash flows, not the net amount as with interest rate swaps, although some swaps stipulate that net amounts be exchanged.

European Currency Unit swaps The European Currency Unit (ECU) has become an increasingly important "currency" in the Eurobond market. If progress is made toward monetary union of the European Community (EC), the ECU may become European markets' official unit of account. It currently is valued as a weighted average of twelve EC currencies. Although growing rapidly, the number of outstanding ECU-denominated bonds constitutes only about 4 percent of the outstanding amount of publicly issued Eurobonds (Graham Bishop 1991, 72.) Cross-coupon ECU swaps have been used to transform both principal and coupon payments denominated in the ECU into other currencies and vice versa.

Terry Shanahan and Jim Durrant (1990) discuss an example in which a U.S. multinational firm needed to finance subsidiaries in France, Belgium, and the Netherlands. The firm borrowed in the Eurobond market by floating ECU-denominated fixed rate debt and converted the issue via a cross-coupon swap into floating rate debt with payments in French francs, Belgian francs, and Dutch guilders. The firm exchanged the principal, consisting of a basket of currencies in proportion to each currency's share in the ECU, raised from the bond buyers. In return, the firm received an equivalent value of the three currencies from the swap counterparty. During the life of this five-year swap, the firm received annual ECU coupon payments from the counterparty, which the firm passed on to the bondholders, and it made annual floating rate payments in guilders and Belgian francs and semiannual floating rate payments in French francs to the counterparty. Upon maturity of the swap, the initial transfer of principal was reversed. The counterparty exchanged ECU principal for repayment in the three currencies from the U.S. firm. In turn, the firm redeemed its bonds with the ECU payment from the counterparty.

Swapping illiquid bonds and private placements

A major impetus for the growth of currency swaps has been and continues to be the portfolio management of illiquid securities. The earlier discussion of portfolio duration adjustment showed a basic rationale for using swaps, which holds particularly true in the Eurobond market, where many bonds lack the liquidity to be traded readily. In addition, for internationally diversified portfolios, bond trading may be desired to change portfolios' exposures to exchange rate fluctuations. Currency swaps fulfill portfolio managers' needs for such risk management.

Currency (and interest rate) swaps have been especially useful in managing portfolios of privately placed bonds. In terms of a number of costs to the issuer, these bonds are significantly cheaper than publicly placed bonds. Use of privately placed bonds avoids the public disclosure and registration requirements as well as compliance with U.S. accounting regulations; it also minimizes legal costs, reduces underwriting costs, and speeds placement. Yet such securities appeal to a much narrower class of investors because of their illiquidity.

In April 1990 the Security and Exchange Commission approved Rule 144A, which greatly simplifies disclosure requirements for private placement issuers (Franklin Chu 1991, 55). Non-U.S. corporations that need to fund their U.S. subsidiaries will find it much easier to raise capital through private placements. The disadvantages of holding these relatively illiquid securities is expected to be lessened both by the use of swaps in portfolio management and by the growth of a secondary market for private placements (Brady 1990, 86).

Table 4   Currency swaps as of December 31, 1989*

Currency	U.S. dollar equivalent	End-user counterparty (percent)	ISDA counterparty (percent)	Currency as percentage of total ($869.7 billion)
U.S. Dollar	$354,166	72.78	27.22	40.72
Yen	$201,145	71.83	28.17	23.13
Swiss Franc	$64,823	77.42	22.58	7.45
Australian Dollar	$61,768	70.77	29.23	7.10
Deutsche Mark	$53,839	79.93	20.07	6.19
European Currency Unit	$39,948	83.06	16.94	4.59
Sterling	$33.466	74.11	25.89	3.85
Canadian Dollar	$32.580	81.72	18.28	3.75
Dutch Guilder	$10.132	82.53	17.47	1.17
French Franc	$8,435	88.74	11.26	.97
New Zealand Dollar	$5,818	81.90	18.10	.67
Belgian Franc	$2,997	86.89	13.11	.34
Hong Kong Dollar	$583	90.39	9.61	.07

* All dollar amounts are in millions of dollars in U.S. dollar equivalents.
Source: International Swap Dealers Association Market Survey.

The size of the market

The U.S. dollar is the preeminent currency in the currency swaps market. Table 4 shows that the dollar has a 41 percent share in the currency swaps market, followed by the Japanese yen with a 23 percent share. The Swiss franc, Australian dollar, and German mark occupy the next ranks, with the Hong Kong dollar taking the smallest share of the market for the surveyed currencies.

Commodity Swaps

Commodity swaps are straightforward extensions of financial swaps, though a number of institutional factors make commodity swapping much riskier than the financial variety. As mentioned earlier, only about $10 billion in notional value has been transacted in this relatively new market. However, commodity prices historically have been much more volatile than financial asset prices, and volatility tends to promote the development and use of hedging instruments. Commodity swaps' volume has reportedly doubled in the past year and is expected to do so again in 1991 (Janet Lewis 1990, 207). Another impetus is likely to be the resolution of some regulatory uncertainties, as discussed above. Energy-related commodities hedged via swaps to date include crude oil, heating oil, gasoline, naphtha, natural gas, jet fuel, maritime diesel fuel, and coal. Swap maturities have ranged from one month to five years. A relatively smaller number of swaps have been arranged for gold and for base metals, mainly copper and aluminum, as well as a few in nickel and zinc (Brady 1990, 87).

Chart 2 Commodity swaps

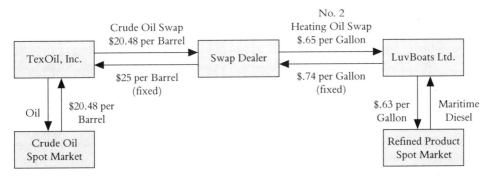

TexOil receives $25 per barrel and pays the spot price for crude oil. LuvBoats receives the spot price for No. 2 heating oil and pays a fixed price for heating oil. LuvBoats in turn buys maritime diesel at the spot price for diesel. There are 42 gallons in a barrel.

The most popular commodity swap has been the plain vanilla fixed-for-floating swap, very much akin to the plain vanilla interest rate swap. End users turn to swaps for hedging for essentially the same reasons that they take positions in commodity futures contracts. Their pricing decisions can be based on a known future cost of inputs or revenue from outputs, allowing the appropriate margins to be built in. The end users avail themselves of hedging instruments to transfer the risk to others who specialize in managing that risk.[20] Exchange-traded futures and options contracts tend to be liquid for contracts with time to maturity of only a few months. Hedging large positions farther out in time would cause the futures prices to move against the hedger, raising the cost of the hedge. In contrast, over-the-counter oil swaps are well suited to hedging intermediate-term risks that cannot be handled by simple positions in futures having relatively short maturity. At the same time, the implication is that swap intermediaries face greater risks because of difficulties they encounter in hedging their swap positions (see Janet Lewis 1990). Oil trading firms have an advantage in acting as dealers because they also carry out transactions in the underlying commodities, giving them additional flexibility in hedging.

A commodity swap may be important as a hedge for a firm that is considering financing a project using debt.[21] The same is true for interest rate and currency swaps as well, but commodity prices are notoriously volatile, giving lenders ample reason to require a commodity swap hedge.[22] In other words, swaps can increase a firm's ability to borrow.

An example

A U.S. producer of oil, TexOil, Inc., sells oil at the spot price but wants to hedge against any large drops in the price of oil that would make production uneconomical. Another counterparty, a charter luxury liner company, LuvBoats Ltd., wants to hedge the proceeds from advanced ticket sales for the coming year. Maritime diesel fuel, purchased at the spot price, is a major operating cost for LuvBoats's ships. Chart 2 depicts a pair of pain vanilla swaps with a swap dealer intermediating the transaction.

As with any kind of swap transaction, a dealer does not necessarily need an offsetting counterparty to enter into a swap with another counterparty. The swap involving LuvBoats Ltd. is actually tied to the price of No. 2 heating oil, which is a more actively traded commodity than maritime diesel. The spread to the counterparty is lower because the swap dealer can better hedge its position, for example by using No. 2 heating oil futures contracts. LuvBoats is willing to bear some basis risk – the risk that maritime diesel and heating oil price movements will be less than perfectly correlated – to avoid paying the dealer a larger spread to index a swap to the price of maritime diesel. TexOil receives a fixed price of $25 per barrel of crude from the swap dealer, while LuvBoats pays a fixed amount of 74 cents per gallon of heating oil. Since the swap's origination, oil and refined product prices have declined, resulting in a $4.52 per barrel net payment to Texoil and a 9 cent per gallon net payment from LuvBoats at the current payment date.

Oil swaps can assume more complex forms. For example, they can be combined with currency and interest rate swaps to convert uncertain, dollar-denominated spot market purchases of oil into fixed deutsche mark payments. To meet regulatory guidelines, commodity swaps require the inclusion of caps and floors, although these are usually set at prices far from the prevailing commodity price and thus are unlikely to be reached. Caps, collars, floors, participating swaps, swaptions, and many other instruments have been adapted to the commodity markets. Also, oil and other commodity swaps typically reset based on daily averages of spot market prices for the underlying commodity. Averaging tends to make the floating side of a swap have a better correspondence with actual spot market purchases by the counterparties. A swap reset based on a single day's price would be less likely to be representative of such purchases.

Equity Swaps

Equity swaps are the newest type of swap and are a subset of a new class of instruments known as synthetic equity.[23] Equity swaps generally function as an asset swap that converts the interest flows on a bond portfolio into cash flows linked to a stock index. The stock indexes that have been used include the Standard and Poor's (S&P) 500, the Tokyo Stock Price Index (TOPIX) and Nikkei 225 (Japan), the Chambre des Agents de Change (CAC) 240 (France), the Financial Times Stock Exchange (FTSE) 100 (United Kingdom), the Toronto Stock Exchange (TSE) 300 (Canada), as well as others (see Salomon Brothers, Inc. 1990; Saul Hansell 1990; and Richard Metcalfe 1990, 40). Linking portfolio performance to an index means that dividends are not received as with actual equity ownership; the portfolio tracks only the capital gain component of the underlying stocks.

One of the advantages of using a synthetic swap is that transactions costs are mitigated, especially in dealing with less liquid foreign stock markets (Hansell 1990, 56). On the other hand, such swaps are also illiquid, which implies that their use be predicated on a buy-and-hold strategy for an investment portfolio. Equity swaps have been structured to have one- to five-year tenors and usually have quarterly or semiannual reset dates.

The mechanics of an equity swap are similar to the workings of other kinds of swaps. Typically, an investor will swap either fixed or floating rate interest payments for payments indexed to the performance of a stock index such as the S&P 500. If the index appreciates during the interval between settlement dates, the investor receives a payment from the counterparty equal to the rate of appreciation times the swap's notional principal. At the same time, the investor pays, for example, LIBOR less a spread representing the margin to the dealer. Actual settlement would involve only the difference between these bases. In the event the S&P 500 falls, the investor would pay the rate of depreciation times notional principal and LIBOR less a spread. Of course, the investor is receiving LIBOR or another floating rate from his or her investment portfolio. The net result of the swap is that the portfolio's income behaves like that of an index equity portfolio.

A variation of the basic equity swap – the asset allocation swap – links the equity side of the swap to the maximum of two indexes. For example, the swap agreement could stipulate that the counterparty receive the maximum of the rate of appreciation (or pay the maximum rate of depreciation) on the S&P 500 or Nikkei 225 at each settlement date. This kind of swap effectively swaps a portfolio into a foreign stock portfolio or domestic stock portfolio instantly, without transactions costs (apart from those associated with the swap). There are many other possibilities for asset allocation swaps. As another example, the swap could be indexed to the maximum of the S&P 500 or a bond index. Index options could be embedded in the swaps to trade away upside exposure in exchange for downside protection from index moves.

Conclusion

Swaps are but one kind of instrument that has been spawned in the profusion of financial innovation during the last two decades.[24] In the most general terms, swaps are contracts that transform cash flows from underlying assets or liabilities. They have been designed to incorporate great flexibility in that task and hence are frequently described as instruments that tailor cash flows. This article encompasses the four basic types of swap: interest rate, currency, commodity, and equity. Each group in turn branches into a variety of forms that can accommodate virtually any application. However, novelty does not guarantee success. The most successful swaps have frequently been the simplest, plain vanilla variety.

Swaps integrate credit markets. By the nature of their function, swaps can link money markets (short-term financing) and capital markets (long-term financing). Swaps also play a significant role in the so-called globalization of financial markets because they obviate the need for many investors to carry out transactions in underlying foreign securities, thereby contributing to the international diversification of portfolios. International arbitrage of securities and swaps markets is left to those participants who have the lowest transactions costs, increasing global market efficiency.

Swaps are an important tool for simplifying financial transactions that cross national borders. At the same time, they pose potential risks to the stability of financial markets. Recent concern about the strength of both banks and investment banks has focused the attention of swap market participants on counterparties' creditworthiness, upon which the financial obligations contracted through a swap agreement depend.[25]

However, part of the reason that swaps evolved was to reduce the credit exposure of counterparties involved in similar financial arrangements. Swaps generally confine credit risk to exposure to the net difference in cash flows, not the gross amounts or exposure of underlying principal, and defaults have been rare occurrences.[26] The implementation of the Basle Agreement in 1992 will establish more uniform capital standards for the world's commercial banks and should help to further reduce credit risks in the swap market.[27]

Notes

1. Shirreff (1989) reports that swaps with thirty-year maturities or "tenors" have been arranged. Such long-lived swaps typically involved counterparties with top credit ratings or relied on third-party credit enhancements.
2. Wall and Pringle (1988) discuss the plain vanilla swap in detail and consider the reasons for using swaps.
3. A forward contract commits the buyer to purchase the underlying asset at a prespecified price (the forward price) upon maturity of the contract. A call option gives the buyer the right, but not the obligation, to purchase an underlying asset at a prespecified price on or sometime before the maturity date of the option. The put gives the corresponding right to sell at a prespecified price. These instruments will be described further at appropriate places in the exposition.
4. See McNulty and Stieber (1991) for a more detailed account.
5. See Henderson (1990) for details about the CFTC's criteria.
6. The growth may be exaggerated by these figures because the number of survey respondents, not reported in the tables, has also been increasing. However, the ISDA points out that the major swap dealers have consistently participated in their surveys.
7. See Kuprianov (1986) for a background discussion of Eurodollar futures and LIBOR.
8. See McNulty and Stieber (1991, 100–101) for information about the Eleventh District cost-of-funds rate.
9. A basis point is a hundredth of a percentage point.
10. Ramaswamy and Sundaresan (1986) analyze floating rate securities and discuss the characteristics of such securities.
11. See Macfarlane, Showers, and Ross (1991) for a discussion of nonstandard swap terms. This article gives a detailed account of swap terminology and conventions.
12. Ordinarily, comparisons of yields along the yield curve are made using instruments of comparable default risk. Yield curve swaps exchange floating payments on debt bearing different default risks. Because the underlying three-month Eurodollar time deposit is default risky, LIBOR is greater than the riskless three-month Treasury bill yield. The swap therefore exchanges credit spreads as well as yield curve spreads.
13. See Goodman (1991, 160–61) for details about this strategy.
14. See Abken (1989) for an introduction to these instruments.
15. See Bodie, Kane, and Marcus (1989) for an introduction to duration analysis.
16. This example is cited by Bhattacharya (1990, 56).
17. Goodman (1991) and Brown and Smith (1990) discuss call monetization using several strategies. Forward swaps may also be used for this purpose. Brown and Smith discuss many subtleties of these strategies.
18. Krzyzak (1988, 29; 1989a, 9) reports that the embedded calls were overvalued and that call monetization was used to undo the expensive call. In this case, call monetization would not be an arbitrage.
19. Chew (1991) discusses recent activity in the non-U.S. dollar swaptions markets, particularly deutsche mark instruments.
20. This point of view is not universal or uncontroversial. Williams (1986) argues that risk aversion has nothing to do with the use of futures. Rather, futures contracts reduce transactions costs in dealing with underlying commodities. His model assumes that all futures market participants are risk neutral.

21. Also, Smith, Smithson, and Wilford (1990) discuss a conflict between stockholders and bondholders of a corporation, known as the underinvestment problem, that swaps can mitigate.

22. See Spraos (1990) for a case study of a complex copper swap required in part for this reason.

23. Other examples of synthetic equity include over-the-counter equity options, public warrant issues, and bonds containing equity options. See Hansell (1990). Index-linked certificates of deposit were a retail form of synthetic equity offered by a number of commercial banks and savings and loans in 1987.

24. See Finnerty (1990) for a comprehensive survey of financial innovations since the 1970s.

25. Krzyzak (1990) and Brady (1991) describe the concerns and difficulties experienced by low-rated swap dealers in dealing with higher-rated counterparties. See Abken (1991) for a model of swap valuation in which swaps are subject to default by the participating counterparties.

26. Aggarwal (1991) reports several sources giving a figure of $35 million in write-offs resulting from swap defaults as of year-end 1988. The collapse of Drexel, Burnham, Lambert in 1989 brought with it potential defaults on its swap book. Most of these swaps were closed out or rearranged with other swap dealers, avoiding defaults that would have shaken the swaps market. See Perry (1990) for an account of the Drexel collapse and its aftermath on the swaps market. Evans (1991) reports that U.S. and foreign banks face potential defaults of up to $1 billion because of a British court ruling that nullifies swap contracts with about 80 British municipalities.

27. See Wall, Pringle, and McNulty (1990) for a discussion of the Basle Agreement and its treatment of swaps under the new capital standards. Levis and Suchar (1990) give further discussion and detailed examples.

References

Abken, Peter A. "Interest-Rate Caps, Collars, and Floors." Federal Reserve Bank of Atlanta *Economic Review* 74 (November/December 1989): 2–24.

——— . "Valuation of Default-Risky Interest-Rate Swaps." Federal Reserve Bank of Atlanta working paper, 1991.

Aggarwal, Raj. "Assessing Default Risk in Interest Rate Swaps." In *Interest Rate Swaps*, edited by Carl R. Beidleman, 430–448. Homewood, Ill.: Business One Irwin, 1991.

Bhattacharya, Anand K. "Synthetic Asset Swaps." *Journal of Portfolio Management* 17 (Fall 1990): 56–64.

——— , and John Breit. "Customized Interest-Rate Risk Agreements and Their Applications." In *The Handbook of Fixed Income Securities*, 3d ed., edited by Frank J. Fabozzi, 1157–1189. Homewood, Ill.: Business One Irwin, 1991.

Bishop, Graham. "ECU Bonds: Pioneer of Currency Union." *Euromoney* (January 1991): 71ff.

Bodie, Zvi, Alex Kane, and Alan J. Marcus. *Investments*. Homewood, Ill.: Richard D. Irwin, Inc., 1989.

Brady, Simon. "How to Tailor Your Assets." *Euromoney* (April 1990): 83–89.

——— . "Time Runs Out for Low-Rated Swappers." *Euromoney* (February 1991): 9–10.

Brown, Jeffry P. "Variations to Basic Swaps." In *Interest Rate Swaps*, edited by Carl R. Beidleman, 114–129. Homewood, Ill.: Business One Irwin, 1991.

Brown, Keith, and Donald J. Simith. "Forward Swaps, Swap Options, and the Management of Callable Debt." *Journal of Applied Corporate Finance* 2 (Winter 1990): 59–71.

Chew, Lillian. "Strip Mining." *Risk* 4 (February 1991): 20ff.

Chu, Franklin J. "The U.S. Private Market for Foreign Securities." *Bankers Magazine* (January/February 1991): 55–60.

Evans, John. "British Court Rules Swaps by Municipalities Illegal." *American Banker*, January 25, 1991, 13.

Finnerty, John D. "Financial Engineering in Corporate Finance: An Overview." In *The Handbook of Financial Engineering*, edited by Clifford W. Smith and Charles W. Smithson, 69–108. Grand Rapids, Mich.: Harper Business, 1990.

Goodman, Laurie S. "Capital Market Applications of Interest Rate Swaps." In *Interest Rate Swaps*, edited by Carl R. Beidleman, 147–174. Homewood, Ill.: Business One Irwin, 1991.

Hansell, Saul. "Is the World Ready for Synthetic Equity?" *Institutional Investor* (August 1990): 54–61.

Henderson, Schuyler K. "A Legal Eye on Hedging's Newest Club." *Euromoney* (May 1990): 95–96.

Krzyzak, Krystyna. "Don't Take Swaps at Face Value." *Risk* 1 (November 1988): 26–31.

——. "Swaptions Deciphered." *Risk* 2 (February 1989a): 9–17.

——. "From Basis Points to Barrels." *Risk* 2 (May 1989b): 8–12.

——. "Copper-Bottomed Hedge." *Risk* 2 (September 1989c): 35–39.

——. "Swaps Survey: Around the Houses." *Risk* 3 (September 1990): 51–57.

Kuprianov, Anatoli. "Short-Term Interest Rate Futures." Federal Reserve Bank of Richmond *Economic Review* (September/October 1986): 12–26.

Levis, Mario, and Victor Suchar. "Basle Basics." *Risk* 3 (April 1990): 38–39.

Lewis, Janet. "Oil Price Jitters? Try Energy Swaps." *Institutional Investor* (December 1990): 206–208.

Lewis, Julian. "The Bandwagon Starts to Roll." *Euromoney* (May 1990): 87–94.

Macfarlane, John, Janet Showers, and Daniel Ross. "The Interest-Rate Swap Market: Yield Mathematics, Terminology, and Conventions." In *Interest Rate Swaps*, edited by Carl R. Beidleman, 233–265. Homewood, Ill.: Business One Irwin, 1991.

McNulty, James E., and Sharon L. Stieber. "The Development and Standardization of the Swap Market." In *Interest Rate Swaps*, edited by Carl R. Beidleman, 97–113. Homewood, Ill.: Business One Irwin, 1991.

Metcalfe, Richard. "Out of the Shadows." *Risk* 3 (October 1990): 40–42.

Perry, Phillip M. "Drexel Redux? Credit Quality Is a Hot Topic." *Corporate Risk Management* (May/June 1990): 27–29.

Ramaswamy, Krishna, and Suresh M. Sundaresan. "The Valuation of Floating-Rate Instruments: Theory and Evidence." *Journal of Financial Economics* 17 (December 1986): 251–272.

Salomon Brothers, Inc. "Equity-Linked Index Swaps." Sales brochure, 1990.

Shanahan, Terry, and Jim Durrant. "Driving Factors." *Risk* 10 (November 1990): 14ff.

Shirreff, David. "Where Others Fear to Tread." *Risk* 2 (September 1989): 11–16.

Smith, Clifford W., Charles W. Smithson, and Lee Macdonald Wakeman. "The Evolving Market for Swaps." In *The Handbook of Financial Engineering*, edited by Clifford W. Smith and Charles W. Smithson, 191–211. Grand Rapids, Mich.: Harper Business, 1990.

Smith, Clifford W., Charles W. Smithson, and D. Sykes Wilford. "Financial Engineering: Why Hedge?" In *The Handbook of Financial Engineering*, edited by Clifford W. Smith and Charles W. Smithson, 126–137. Grand Rapids, Mich.: Harper Business, 1990.

Spraos, Paul B. "The Anatomy of a Copper Swap." *Corporate Risk Management* 2 (January/February 1990): 8, 10.

Tompkins, Robert. "Behind the Mirror." *Risk* 2 (February 1989): 17–23.

Wall, Larry D., and John J. Pringle. "Interest Rate Swaps: A Review of the Issues." Federal Reserve Bank of Atlanta *Economic Review* 73 (November/December 1988): 22–37.

Wall, Larry D., John J. Pringle, and James E. McNulty. "Capital Requirements for Interest-Rate and Foreign-Exchange Hedges." Federal Reserve Bank of Atlanta *Economic Review* 75 (May/June 1990): 14–27.

Williams, Jeffrey. *The Economic Function of Futures Markets*. New York: Cambridge University Press, 1986.

5

The Pricing of Interest Rate Swaps

John F. Marshall
and Kenneth R. Kapner

5.1 Overview

In earlier chapters we discussed how swap dealers quote swap prices. For example, in the case of interest rate swaps, we indicated that indicative swap pricing schedules are typically stated as a spread over Treasuries of equivalent average life. In the case of currency swaps, the dealer typically quotes a mid rate and then adds or subtracts some number of basis points. These two methods of quoting prices are equivalent. That is, we can take an average of the swap coupon on a dealer-pays-fixed-rate interest rate swap and the swap coupon on a dealer-receives-fixed-rate interest rate swap to obtain the dealer's mid rate.

Despite our description of how swap dealers quote swap prices as a mid rate plus or minus some number of basis points, we have not yet addressed what is really the key issue. That is, we have not yet discussed how swap prices are determined. This is really the heart of the matter. Swap pricing refers to the setting of the fixed rate, called the **swap coupon**, against a floating **reference rate**. For our purposes, this means setting the mid rate.

We will focus our discussion here on the pricing of interest rate swaps. This is reasonable for, as shown by Yaksick (1992), there is an identity in the pricing of interest rate swaps and currency swaps. Similarly, as shown by Marshall, Sorensen, and Tucker (1992), the logic underlying the pricing of equity swaps follows directly from the logic underlying the pricing of interest rate swaps.

The pricing of interest rate swaps requires us to distinguish between short-dated interest rate swaps and long-dated interest rate swaps. In the early days of swaps, short-dated swaps were described as swaps with tenors out to about a year. This was gradually extended to two years. Today, we define short-dated interest rate swaps as any swap that can be priced off a series of successive Eurodollar futures contracts. In market parlance, a sequential series of forward contracts or futures contracts is called a **strip** and the strip of Eurodollar futures is often called a Eurodollar strip or a **Eurostrip**. The latter term, Eurostrip, could also apply to a Euroyen strip, a Eurodeutschemark strip, etc. As we will use the term in this chapter, Eurostrip is always understood to refer to a Eurodollar futures strip. The maximum tenor for a swap to qualify as a short-dated swap is then defined by the most forward Eurodollar futures contract that is considered liquid. The point then is that the distinction between short-dated and long-dated interest rate swaps depends on the availability of a precise pricing vehicle, i.e., Eurodollar futures.

In this chapter we will first look at the pricing of short-dated swaps. Next, we will look at the pricing of long-dated swaps. Finally, we will extend the pricing discussion to look at the pricing of forward swaps of any tenor. Forward swaps are swaps in which (1) the swap coupon is fixed at the time of contracting, and (2) the swap does not commence (i.e., begin accruing interest) until a later date. We assume throughout that we are pricing plain vanilla interest rate swaps in which the swap coupon is quoted on a semiannual bond basis against six-month LIBOR flat. We have already discussed how the pricing would be adjusted to fit all sorts of special cases including different payment frequencies, different amortization assumptions, off-market pricing requirements, and so on, once the pricing of the plain vanilla form had been determined. The reader is forewarned that this chapter is the most difficult in the book. Read it slowly and carefully and take the extra time to work through each example we present to be certain that you fully understand it before moving on.

Because Eurodollar futures play such a key role in pricing interest rate swaps, it would perhaps be beneficial to say a few words about the structure of these futures. A Eurodollar futures contract is a cash settled contract written on a Eurodollar deposit. **A Eurodollar deposit** refers to dollars on deposit at a bank outside the United States. These deposits are lent between banks at an interest rate called the London Interbank Offered Rate or **LIBOR**. These futures contracts may be regarded as contracts for the later delivery (taking the form of a cash settlement) of three-month Eurodollar deposits. The contracts are priced at 100 less the three-month LIBOR rate which the market, in its collective wisdom, has determined to be the best estimate of the rate that will prevail at the time the contract settles. The point in time when a Eurodollar deposit begins accruing interest is called the **value date**. The point in time when it stops accruing interest is called the **maturity date**.

5.2 Short-dated Swaps

The swap coupons for short-dated fixed-for-floating interest rate swaps are routinely priced off the Eurodollar futures strip (Eurostrip). This method of pricing can only work to the extent that (1) Eurodollar futures exist, and (2) the futures are liquid. As of June 1992, three-month Eurodollar futures are traded in quarterly cycles (March, June, September, and December) with delivery (final settlement) dates as far forward as five years. However, they are only liquid out to about four years.

5.2.1 Using Eurodollar futures of price swaps

The Eurostrip is a series of successive three-month Eurodollar futures contracts. While identical contracts trade on a number of futures exchanges, the International Monetary Market (IMM) is the most widely used.[1] At present, these Eurodollar futures contracts are the most heavily traded of any futures contract anywhere in the world. This is a consequence of swap dealers' transactions in these markets for purposes of synthesizing short-dated swaps to hedge unmatched swap books and/or to arbitrage between real and synthetic swaps. Kapner and Marshall (1992) document this link between the trading volume of Eurodollar futures and the size of the interest rate swap market.

The key to pricing the swap coupon is to equate the present values of the fixed-rate leg and the floating-rate leg of the swap. Eurodollar futures contracts provide a way to do that. The prices of these contracts imply unbiased estimates of three-month LIBOR expected to prevail at various points in the future.[2] The swap coupon that equates the present value of the fixed leg with the present value of the floating leg based on these unbiased estimates of future values of LIBOR is then the dealer's mid rate. The estimation of the fair mid rate is, however, complicated a bit by the facts that (1) the convention is to quote swap coupons for generic swaps on a semiannual bond basis, and (2) the floating leg, if pegged to LIBOR, is usually quoted money market basis. (Note, on very short-dated swaps the swap coupon is often quoted on a money market basis. For consistency, we will assume throughout that the swap coupon is quoted bond basis.)

The procedure by which the dealer would obtain an unbiased midrate for pricing the swap coupon involves three steps.[3] The first step is to use the implied three-month LIBORs from the Eurostrip to obtain the *implied* annual effective LIBOR for the *full-tenor* of the swap. The second step is to convert this full-tenor LIBOR to an effective rate quoted on an annual bond basis. The final step is to restate this effective bond basis rate on the actual payment frequency of the swap.

For purposes of notation, if the swap is to have a tenor of m months ($m/12$ years) and is to be priced off three-month Eurodollar futures, then pricing will require n sequential futures series, where $n = m/3$ or, equivalently, $m = 3n$.

Step 1: Calculate the implied effective annual LIBOR for the full-tenor of the swap from the Eurodollar strip. This is denoted $r_{0,3n}$ and is obtained using Equation 5.1.

$$r_{0,3n} = \left(\prod_{t=1}^{n} \left[1 + \left(r_{3(t-1),3(t)} \frac{A(t)}{360} \right) \right] \right)^{\tau} - 1 \qquad (5.1)$$

where $\tau = 360/\Sigma A(t)$

where $A(t)$ denotes the actual number of days covered by the tth Eurodollar futures and $\Sigma A(t)$ is the actual number of days covered by the swap, which is equal to the sum of the actual number of days in the succession of Eurodollar futures (the specific example developed in this paper assumes that the swap is using IMM settlement dates). The upper case *pi* (Π) in the formula denotes successive multiplication in the same sense that an upper case *sigma* would denote successive addition.

Step 2:[4] Convert the full-tenor LIBOR, which is quoted on a money market basis, to its fixed-rate equivalent $FRE_{0,3n}$, which is stated as an effective annual rate (annual bond basis). This is accomplished with Equation 5.2 and simply reflects the different number of days underlying bond basis and money market basis.

$$FRE_{0,3n} = r_{0,3n} \times \frac{365}{360} \qquad (5.2)$$

Table 5.1   Eurodollar futures settlement prices June 7, 1991

Contract	Price	Implied 3-M LIBOR	Notation	Number of days covered
JUN 91	93.76	6.24	0 × 3	92
SEP 91	93.43	6.57	3 × 6	91
DEC 91	92.83	7.17	6 × 9	90
MAR 92	92.63	7.37	9 × 12	92
JUN 92	92.22	7.78	12 × 15	92
SEP 92	91.91	8.09	15 × 18	91
DEC 92	91.65	8.35	18 × 21	91
MAR 93	91.65	8.35	21 × 24	92
JUN 93	91.54	8.46	24 × 27	92
SEP 93	91.41	8.59	27 × 30	91
DEC 93	91.20	8.80	30 × 33	90
MAR 94	91.18	8.82	33 × 36	92
JUN 94	91.08	8.92	36 × 39	92
SEP 94	91.01	8.99	39 × 42	91

Under the notation column, the first month represents the starting month and the second month represents the ending month, both referenced from the current month which is treated as month zero. Eurodollar futures contracts assume a deposit of 91 days even though any actual three-month period may have as few as 90 days and as many as 92 days. For purposes of pricing swaps, the actual number of days in a three-month period is used in lieu of the 91 days assumed by the futures. This can introduce a very small discrepancy between the performance of a real swap and the performance of a synthetic swap created from a Eurostrip.

Step 3:   Restate the fixed-rate equivalent on the same payment frequency as the floating leg of the swap. The result is the swap coupon SC. This adjustment is given by Equation 5.3.

$$SC = [(1 + FRE_{0,3n})^{1/f} - 1] \times f \tag{5.3}$$

where f denotes payment frequency.

An example

In order to have a set of prices and rates with which to illustrate the concepts discussed in this chapter, we will employ Eurodollar futures settlement prices from June 7, 1991. These are depicted in Table 5.1. These contracts imply the three-month (3-M) LIBOR rates expected to prevail at the time of the Eurodollar futures contracts' final settlement, which is the third Wednesday of the contract month. By contract construction, the implied rate for three-month LIBOR is found by deducting the price of the contract from 100.

   Three-month LIBOR for JUN 91 is a spot rate, but all the others are forward rates implied by the Eurodollar futures price.[5] Thus, the contracts imply the 3-M LIBOR expected to prevail three months forward, the 3-M LIBOR expected to prevail six months forward, and so on. The contracts themselves are denoted 3 × 6, 6 × 9, etc., where the first subscript indicates the month of commencement (i.e., the month that the underlying Eurodollar deposit is lent) and the second subscript indicates the month of termination (i.e., the month that the underlying Eurodollar deposit is repaid). Both dates are measured in months forward. The corresponding forward rates are denoted $r_{3,6}$, $r_{6,9}$, and so on. Spot 3-M LIBOR is denoted $r_{0,3}$. A plot of these rates would constitute a three-month constant maturity yield curve.

Suppose that we want to price a one-year fixed-for-floating interest rate swap against 3-M LIBOR. The fixed rate will be paid quarterly and, therefore, is quoted quarterly bond basis. We need to find the fixed rate that has the same present value (in an expected value sense) as four successive 3-M LIBOR payments. First we calculate the implied LIBOR rate corresponding to the tenor of the swap using Equation 5.1. This is depicted below. Since the swap has a tenor of twelve months, n is 4. The implied one-year LIBOR is, therefore:

$$r_{0,12} = \left[\left(1 + .0624\frac{92}{360}\right) \times \left(1 + .0657\frac{91}{360}\right) \times \right.$$
$$\left.\left(1 + .0717\frac{90}{360}\right) \times \left(1 + .0737\frac{92}{360}\right)\right]^{360/365} - 1$$

$$= 7.0125 \text{ percent (money market basis).}$$

Next, we need to convert this money market rate to its effective equivalent stated on an annual bond basis. This requires Equation 5.2.

$$FRE_{0,12} = 7.0125 \times \frac{365}{360}$$

$$= 7.1099 \text{ percent (annual bond basis)}$$

Finally, since the coupon payments are to be made quarterly, $f = 4$, we must restate this effective annual rate on an equivalent quarterly bond basis. The result is the swap coupon.

$$SC = [(1.071099)^{1/4} - 1] \times 4$$

$$= 6.9278 \text{ percent (quarterly bond basis)}$$

The swap is depicted in Exhibit 5.1.

Suppose now that, instead of requiring quarterly payments against 3-M LIBOR, the swap is to require semiannual payments against 6-M LIBOR. The first two steps are exactly the same. Only the final step is different (f is 2 instead of 4).

$$SC = [(1.071099)^{1/2} - 1] \times 2$$

$$= 6.9878 \text{ percent (semiannual bond basis)}$$

The corresponding swap is depicted in Exhibit 5.2.

This simple procedure allows a dealer to quote swaps having tenors out to the limit of the liquidity of Eurodollar futures on any payment frequency desired and to fully hedge those swaps in the Eurostrip. The latter is accomplished by purchasing the components of the Eurostrip to hedge a dealer-pays-fixed-rate swap or selling the components of the Eurostrip to hedge a dealer-pays-floating-rate swap.

Exhibit 5.1   Eurostrip-based swap 1

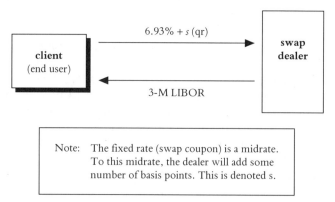

Exhibit 5.2   Eurostrip-based swap 2

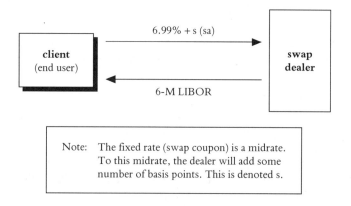

For example, suppose that a dealer wants to price a three-year swap with a semi-annual coupon when the floating leg is six-month LIBOR. Three years is 36 months requiring 12 separate Eurodollar futures (therefore $n = 12$). The payment frequency is 2 ($f = 2$), and the actual number of days covered by the swap is 1,096 ($\Sigma A(t) = 1096$). Step 1 provides an implied LIBOR rate for the period of the swap of 8.1159 percent ($r_{0,36} = 8.1159$ percent). Step 2 provides an equivalent effective annual bond basis of 8.2287 percent ($FRE_{0,36} = 8.2287$ percent pa). And, finally, Step 3 provides an equivalent semiannual swap coupon of 8.0661 percent ($SC = 8.0661$ percent sa). The dealer can hedge the swap by buying or selling, as appropriate, the 12 contracts in the Eurostrip.

The full set of swap tenors out to three and one-half years, having semiannual payments (fixed-rate against 6-M LIBOR), that can be created from the Eurostrip are listed in Table 5.2. The swap coupon would represent the dealer's mid rate. To this the dealer can be expected to add several basis points if fixed-rate receiver, and deduct several basis points if fixed-rate payer. The par swap yield curve out to three and one-half years is depicted in Exhibit 5.3.

Table 5.2   Implied swap pricing schedule out to three and one-half years June 7, 1991

Tenor of swap (in months)	Swap coupon mid rate (semiannual bond basis)
6	6.5427%
12	6.9878
18	7.3655
24	7.6615
30	7.8752
36	8.0661
42	8.2246

All swaps above are priced against 6-M LIBOR flat and assume that notional principal is nonamortizing.

Exhibit 5.3   The short-dated swap yield curve (mid rates)

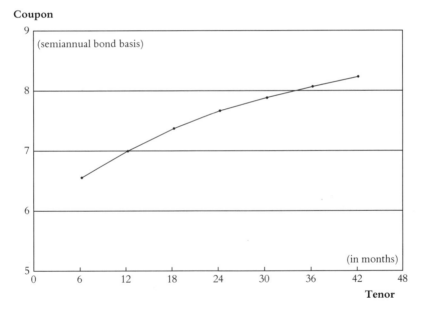

5.3 Long-dated Swaps

The pricing of long-dated swaps is a more complex undertaking than the pricing of short-dated swaps because a precise pricing vehicle is lacking. However, just as the pricing of short-dated swaps hinges on arbitrage relationships, the pricing of long-dated swaps also hinges on arbitrage relationships. In this case, however, the arbitrage is between better credits and poorer credits in the fixed- and floating-rate corporate debt markets. The essence of the argument is that if swaps are in fact motivated by an effort to exploit comparative borrowing advantages, as is so often touted, then market pressures should drive the swap mid rate and the borrowing costs in the fixed- and floating-rate markets to an equilibrium in which arbitrage profits are no longer possible.

While this argument seems logical, observers have long pointed out that apparent cost savings persist and, therefore, it seems that arbitrage opportunities persist. In fact, the issue is far more complex than it first appears and the measurement of the gains from swaps is not nearly as simple as we have led the reader to believe in earlier chapters. *The key to achieving equilibrium pricing for long-dated swaps is accounting for all the costs involved, not just the obvious ones that we have heretofore described.* The analysis that follows is based on the work of Bansal, Bicksler, Chen, and Marshall (1992).

Importantly, because many swaps are explained by objectives other than comparative borrowing advantages, deviations from equilibrium pricing can be expected to occur. At the very least, interest-rate expectations, the absolute level and shape of the yield curve, the volume of asset-based swaps, and numerous technical factors that affect dealers will all play a role. For example, a firm with an existing floating-rate liability which concludes that interest rates are far more likely to rise than to fall may wish to convert its floating-rate liability into a fixed-rate liability before rates rise. If this view is widely enough held, such trading can have a significant, although generally short-lived, effect on swap pricing. Similarly, a desire to convert the interest-rate character of existing assets can have the same effect. We would also note that the significant lags associated with debt issuance in the U.S. markets introduce potential for significant deviations from equilibrium pricing.[6] We begin with the conventional view and then we introduce the complications in a stepwise fashion.

5.3.1 Swap pricing: the conventional view

As one would expect, the key to understanding the pricing of long-dated swaps is arbitrage. The arbitrage is between corporate borrowing costs for better credits and corporate borrowing costs for poorer credits. While better credits (borrowers with a top investment grade rating) will have an absolute borrowing advantage in *both* the fixed-rate and the floating-rate markets, they tend to enjoy a comparative borrowing advantage in the fixed-rate markets. At the same time, poorer credits tend to enjoy a comparative advantage in the floating-rate market even though they are at an absolute borrowing disadvantage in both the fixed-rate market and the floating-rate market.[7] It is often noted that the comparative advantage of poorer credits in the floating-rate market is at a maximum when the floating rate is achieved by a commercial paper, denoted CP, or certificate of deposit, rollover strategy.[8] We will assume throughout that the poorer credit is a CP issuer and that the expected CP rate (CPR) can be expressed in terms of LIBOR ($CPR = $ LIBOR $+ X$ basis points (bps), where X may be positive or negative).

At any given point in time, there is a measurable cost difference between the borrowing costs of poorer credits and the borrowing costs of better credits for each debt maturity and each interest-rate character. This difference in borrowing costs is called a **quality spread**. While the quality spread varies over time, at any point in time it is a measure of the market-perceived quality of the borrower. Importantly, the quality spread differs at different maturities and for different interest-rate characters (fixed versus floating). For example, we might observe that better-credits

Table 5.3 Sample calculation of a quality spread differential

	A Credit		AAA Credit		Quality spread
Five Years	10.55%	−	8.95%	=	160 bps
Six Months	LIBOR + 60 bps	−	(LIBOR − 30 bps)	=	90 bps
			QSD	=	70 bps

Exhibit 5.4 Explaining the quality spread differential

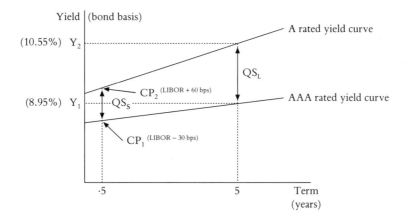

(AAA rated) can borrow for six months at LIBOR less 30 basis points (LIBOR − 30 bps) and for five years at a fixed rate of 8.95 percent.[9] At the same time, we might observe that poorer credits (A rated) can borrow for six-months at LIBOR plus 60 basis points (LIBOR + 60 bps) and for five years at a fixed rate of 10.55 percent. In the six-month market, the quality spread is 90 basis points. In the five-year market, the quality spread is 160 basis points. From these quality spreads, a **quality spread differential** (QSD) is obtained. In this specific case, the QSD is 70 basis points. The calculations are summarized in Table 5.3. (Throughout, we state all rates and rate differentials, including LIBOR, on a bond basis in order to make different rates directly comparable.)

The quality spread differential exists because the slope of the yield curve for poorer credits is somewhat steeper than the slope of the yield curve for better credits.[10] This difference in slopes is illustrated in Exhibit 5.4.

It is generally argued that the QSD represents the source of the comparative advantage and it is the exploitation of this differential which is the source of the cost savings for the counterparties to a swap. Under this argument, the better credit, henceforth denoted as Counterparty 1, is the floating-rate paying counterparty on the swap and the poorer credit, henceforth denoted as Counterparty 2, is the fixed-rate paying counterparty on the swap. The purported savings (QSD) from a matched pair of swaps is then given by Equation 5.4.

$$QSD = Y_2 - Y_1 - (LIBOR + X_2) + (LIBOR + X_1) \qquad (5.4)$$

Where Y_1 and Y_2 denote the at-par fixed-rate coupons (yields) of Counterparties 1 and 2, respectively; and X_1 and X_2 denote the premium over (if $X > 0$) or under (if $X < 0$) LIBOR for short-term debt for Counterparties 1 and 2, respectively.

The logic of Equation 5.4 follows from the reduction in costs achieved by the poorer credit when it creates fixed-rate debt synthetically (as opposed to issuing fixed-rate debt directly), and the reduction in costs achieved by the better credit when it creates floating-rate debt synthetically (as opposed to issuing floating-rate debt directly). That is, if we denote the gains to the poorer credit by G_2 and the gains to the better credit by G_1, then the QSD is given by $G_1 + G_2$:

where G_1 = cost of synthetic floating − cost of real floating
and G_2 = cost of synthetic fixed − cost of real fixed

5.3.2 Swap pricing: a more complete model

The preceding analysis, while a good starting point, is incomplete. It ignores (1) the real cost of issuing debt, (2) the cost of transacting in a swap, and (3) any qualitative differences that might exist between a real (or direct) financing of the desired type and a synthetic financing of the desired type.

Let's begin with the real cost of issuing debt. While the yield on debt securities is typically stated as the yield-to-maturity on the instruments, this does not represent the *true* cost to the issuer of those instruments − even at the moment of issue when the coupon and yield are the same.[11] To ascertain the true cost, we must also consider the flotation costs of the issue, the administrative costs of managing the issue, the cost of the trustee, and so on. The *real* cost is the *all-in* cost of the issue. This is true for both the fixed-rate financing and the floating-rate financing. Clearly, the ancillary expenses associated with debt issuance and debt administration contribute positively to the all-in cost. Denote the difference between the all-in cost of a direct fixed-rate financing and the par yield by a. Similarly, denote the difference between the all-in cost of a direct floating-rate financing and the floating-rate yield by f. Thus the all-in cost of fixed-rate debt is $Y + a$ and the all-in cost of floating-rate debt is LIBOR $+ X + f$.

Next, consider the cost of transacting in the swap. This cost consists of the dealer's pay-receive spread, any front-end fees that might be charged for special financial engineering, and miscellaneous administrative and accounting costs introduced by the greater complexity of the structure. Denote the dealer's midrate swap coupon for *best-credit* counterparties by S. Denote the dealer's spread above or below its mid rate, including the amortized value of any front-end fees, by s. That is, the dealer's pay rate is $S − s$, and the dealer's receive rate is $S + s$. Importantly, the pay-receive rates are only indicative because they are for swaps with counterparties that are best credits. Not all counterparties will be best credits, so it is necessary to subscript s to distinguish among credits. Denote the additional administrative and accounting costs associated with the greater complexity by c.

The final consideration is the qualitative differences between different financial structures. That is, even if two financing structures give rise to the same pattern of cash flows, there can be considerable qualitative differences between them. For example, in the case of a synthetic fixed-rate financing formed by a six-month commercial paper rollover strategy coupled with a fixed-for-floating interest rate

Exhibit 5.5 A direct (real) floating-rate financing

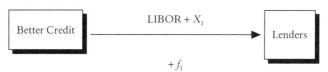

Exhibit 5.6 A synthetic floating-rate financing

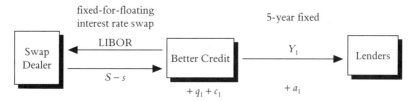

swap, the fixed rate is not fully assured because the issuer's CP rate will change if the issuer's credit quality changes. Second, the CP-LIBOR spread may change, even without a change in the issuer's credit quality, because the CP rate and LIBOR are not perfectly correlated (a manifestation of basis risk).

Finally, long-term debt issues are usually callable. This call feature, which represents an embedded option, can have considerable value to the issuer. A plain vanilla interest rate swap, on the other hand, is not callable. If we fail to consider the value of the embedded option, which is not replicated in the swap, we may overlook a significant part of the explanation for the quality spread differential. To make synthetic fixed-rate debt equivalent to real fixed-rate debt requires that the fixed-rate payer on the swap purchase a call feature. That is, the swap must be a callable swap. The call feature will add to the cost of the swap.

Although it is difficult to assess, qualitative differences have a monetary value. Let's assume that we can assign a monetary value of q, expressed as an annual percentage rate in basis points, to these qualitative differences. Thus, a counterparty that desires fixed-rate financing would require a minimum savings of q basis points to compensate for the qualitative differences on the rollover-with-swap strategy before even considering this alternative for achieving fixed-rate financing. Importantly, the value of the qualitative differences can be positive or negative depending upon whether or not the synthetic structure is preferred to the direct structure. As a general rule, q will be positive for a synthetic fixed rate and negative for a synthetic floating rate. With these pieces in place, the conditions under which synthetic financings that produce real benefits for a better credit (seeking floating-rate financing) and a poorer credit (seeking fixed-rate financing) can be defined.

As can be seen in Exhibit 5.5, if the better credit issues floating-rate debt directly, its cost is $LIBOR + X_1 + f_1$. And, as illustrated in Exhibit 5.6, if it creates floating-rate debt synthetically, its cost is $Y_1 + a_1 - (S - s_1) + LIBOR + q_1 + c_1$. The necessary condition then for the better credit to enter into a swap is given by Equation 5.5a.

cost of synthetic floating ≤ *cost of direct floating*
$$Y_1 + a_1 - (S - s_1) + LIBOR + q_1 + c_1 \le LIBOR + X_1 + f_1 \tag{5.5a}$$

By the same logic, the poorer credit, in need of fixed-rate financing, will find the synthetic attractive if and only if Equation 5.6a is satisfied.

cost of synthetic fixed ≤ cost of direct fixed
$$\text{LIBOR} + X_2 + f_2 - \text{LIBOR} + (S + s_2) + c_2 + q_2 \leq Y_2 + a_2 \qquad (5.6a)$$

Cancelling LIBOR, and rearranging terms, it becomes clear that the conditions for the synthetic financing to be viable are given by Equations 5.5b and 5.6b.

$$Y_1 + a_1 + s_1 + q_1 + c_1 - X_1 - f_1 \leq S \qquad (5.5b)$$

$$S \leq Y_2 + a_2 - X_2 - f_2 - s_2 - c_2 - q_2 \qquad (5.6b)$$

Since both conditions must be satisfied simultaneously in order to have a pair of matched counterparties (or, equivalently, to avoid an imbalance in the dealer's book), the range of allowable swap coupons for sustained swap activity motivated by comparative advantage is given by Equation 5.7.

$$Y_1 + a_1 + s_1 + q_1 + c_1 - X_1 - f_1 \leq S \leq Y_2 + a_2 - X_2 - f_2 - s_2 - c_2 - q_2 \qquad (5.7)$$

5.3.3 Comparative statics

Equation 5.7 provides a number of useful insights. First, the greater the dealer's spread s_1 or s_2, the less likely the synthetic financing will be preferred to the direct financing. Second, the greater the all-in cost of direct fixed-rate financing, relative to the yield, for the better (poorer) credit, a_1 (a_2), the less (more) likely the synthetic structure will be preferred. Third, the greater the all-in cost of a direct floating-rate financing, relative to the nominal cost, f_1 (f_2), the more (less) likely the synthetic will be preferred. Fourth, the greater the CP spread over LIBOR, X_1 (X_2), the more (less) likely that the synthetic will be preferred. Fifth, the greater the additional administrative and accounting costs induced by the complexity of the synthetic financing, c_1 and c_2, the less likely the synthetic will be preferred. Finally, the greater the qualitative benefits from a synthetic financing, q_1 (when $q_1 < 0$), and the less the qualitative costs of a synthetic financing, q_2 (when $q_2 > 0$), the more likely the synthetic will be preferred.

To condense the notation, let:

$$v_1 = a_1 + s_1 + q_1 + c_1 - f_1$$

and

$$v_2 = a_2 - f_2 - s_2 - c_2 - q_2$$

Equation 5.7 then becomes Equation 5.8, which represents boundary conditions for ongoing swap activity motivated by comparative advantage.

$$Y_1 - X_1 + v_1 \leq S \leq Y_2 - X_2 + v_2 \qquad (5.8)$$

5.3.4 Pressure toward an equilibrium

Equation 5.8 suggests a number of important things. First, if $Y_1 - X_1 + v_1 \leq S > Y_2 - X_2 + v_2$, then there would be losses to the poorer credit from entering swaps but there would be gains to the better credit. Under such conditions, dealers will attract more activity to the dealer-pays-fixed-rate side of the swap book than to the dealer-receives-fixed-rate side of the swap book and the book would become badly out of balance. Similarly, if $Y_1 - X_1 + v_1 > S \leq Y_2 - X_2 + v_2$, then there would be losses to the better credit from entering swaps but there would be gains to the poorer credit. Again, the dealer's book would become badly out of balance. Clearly, the dealer has an incentive to set the coupon such that Equation 5.8 is satisfied. Second, if Equation 5.8 is satisfied, the better credits will have a greater incentive to borrow fixed – driving Y_1 ever higher as long as arbitrage profits remain. At the same time, the poorer credits will have an incentive to decrease fixed-rate borrowing – causing Y_2 to drift progressively lower as long as arbitrage profits remain. In the end, arbitrage drives the yield curves for better credits, for poorer credits, and for swaps until Equation 5.8 reduces to Equation 5.9.[12]

$$Y_1 - X_1 + v_1 = S = Y_2 - X_2 + v_2 \tag{5.9}$$

For any given values of v_1, v_2, X_1, and X_2 then, Y_1, S, and Y_2 are jointly determined such that no arbitrage profits will remain. Importantly, Equation 5.9 is a testable condition. Those studies that have ignored the ancillary costs associated with issuing debt, servicing debt, entering a swap, accounting for debt, or failed to value the qualitative differences between direct financing of a desired type and synthetic financing of that same type (all of which are embodied in v_1 and v_2) could easily conclude that persistent large arbitrage opportunities exist when, in fact, they do not. Also, issuers of debt that fail to recognize or to incorporate these ancillary costs when making financing decisions could easily make financing choices that are not cost minimizing, even though they may appear to be.

To see that this can indeed be the case, consider a hypothetical example. Suppose that the par-yield for the better credit for five-year fixed rate is 8.95 percent and that six-month CP for the better credit is LIBOR less 30 bps. Suppose further that the par-yield five-year fixed rate for the poorer credit is 10.55 percent and the six-month CP rate is LIBOR + 60 basis points. Then, the *QSD* is 70 basis points and these are the perceived savings from a swap. (This is the same example employed earlier.) If the five-year swap coupon is 9.45 percent, then we would conclude that the better credit would derive a 20 basis point gain from the swap and that the poorer credit would derive a 50 basis point gain from the swap. This accounts for the full 70-basis point gain, as represented by the *QSD*. It would appear that at least one of the markets is inefficient.

Now suppose that the components of v_1 and v_2, which were overlooked in the earlier example, are as given in Table 5.4. It becomes clear that the markets are efficient after all, relative to one another, and that there are no gains to be derived from arbitrage.

The point of this exercise is *not* to suggest that the values employed in the hypothetical example are realistic, or that the corporate debt markets or the swap markets are efficiently priced. Rather, the point is to illustrate the forces that should

Table 5.4   Hypothetical ancillary expenses in basis points

Better credit			Poorer credit		
a_1 =	30	(+)	a_2 =	35	(+)
s_1 =	5	(+)	s_2 =	8	(−)
q_1 =	−25	(+)	q_2 =	35	(−)
c_1 =	25	(+)	c_2 =	25	(−)
f_1 =	15	(−)	f_2 =	17	(−)
v_1 =	20		v_2 =	−50	(−)

drive the markets to an equilibrium and the often overlooked ancillary costs and benefits that play a role in determining that equilibrium. Only by fully appreciating and assessing these costs can (1) a user of the interest rate swap product determine the true benefits, if any, to be derived from a synthetic financing vis-a-vis a real financing; and (2) the empiricist conduct a thorough analysis and assessment of market efficiency.

5.3.5 Swap futures

In June of 1991, the Chicago Board of Trade introduced two swap futures contracts. The first was a futures written on a three-year constant maturity generic swap and the second was a futures contract written on a five-year constant maturity generic swap. The three-year swap was largely redundant in that it was easily replicated with existing products. Five-year swap futures were not redundant at the time they were introduced. But the recent extension of Eurodollar futures on the IMM from four years to five years has served to lessen the need for a five-year swap futures product. Nevertheless, the fact that five-year swap futures can be written as far forward as several years suggests that they are not entirely redundant. The three-year swap futures product ceased trading in early 1992 and trading volume in the five-year contract has largely disappeared. The CBOT has recently announced plans to introduce ten-year swap futures which stand a much better chance of being accepted as a swap hedge than did either the three-year or five-year varieties because there is no way to replicate ten-year swaps in the Eurostrip.[13]

While only time will tell, it is possible that these futures contracts, and others like them, will do for long-dated swap pricing what Eurodollar futures have done for short-dated swap pricing.

5.4 Implied Forward Pricing

The logic of pricing short-dated swaps in which implied three-month forward rates are obtained from the Eurodollar futures market to generate a swap yield curve can just as easily be used to obtain forward yield curves. For example, if we modify Equation 5.1 to begin the index t at 2 rather than at 1 and end at $n + 1$ rather than at n, then we will generate a forward par swap yield curve for swaps that begin in three months; if we start the index t at 3 and end at $n + 2$, then we generate a forward par swap yield curve for swaps that commence in six months; and so on. We can generate as many such forward swap yield curves as we like by simply varying the starting point as indicated by the index t. Forward par swap yield curves generated in this way are useful for pricing forward swaps and for pricing swaptions[14] and other specialty features.

A forward swap yield curve can also be generated from the par swap yield curve. For example, if we denote the effective full-tenor LIBOR rate applicable to the swap that begins at time b and ends at time e by $r_{b,e}$, then the value $r_{b,e}$ can be obtained from the values $r_{0,e}$ and $r_{0,b}$ by Equation 5.10:

$$r_{b,e} = \left(\frac{(1 + r_{0,e})^{A(0,e)/360}}{(1 + r_{0,b})^{A(0,b)/360}} \right)^{360/A(b,e)} - 1 \qquad (5.10)$$

where $A(0,e)$ denotes the actual number of days from today (0) to the end of the forward swap; $A(0,b)$ denotes the actual number of days from today to the beginning of the forward swap; and $A(b,e)$ is the difference between $A(0,e)$ and $A(0,b)$. The forward full-tenor LIBOR rate $r_{b,e}$ is then converted to a bond basis swap coupon having the appropriate payment frequency by way of Equations 5.2 and 5.3.

An example
Suppose that we want to obtain the implied swap coupon for a two-year swap one-year forward with semiannual payments. That is, we want to price a swap having a two-year tenor but which does not commence until one year from now. We could obtain this from $r_{0,36}$ and $r_{0,12}$. From our earlier calculations, we know that $r_{0,12}$ = 7.0125 percent and $r_{0,36}$ = 8.1159 percent. We also know that $A(0,12)$ = 365, and $A(0,36)$ = 1096. This implies that $A(12,36)$ = 731. Plugging these values into Equation 5.10, we find that $r_{12,36}$ is 8.6712 percent. The calculation is depicted as follows:

$$r_{b,e} = \left(\frac{(1.081159)^{1096/360}}{(1.070125)^{365/360}} \right)^{360/731} - 1$$

$$= 8.6712 \text{ percent}$$

Step 2 converts this money market rate to an annual bond basis of 8.7916 percent, and Step 3 converts this annual bond basis rate to the desired swap coupon (semi-annual bond basis) of 8.6065 percent.

The implied swap coupons with a forward one-year start date, covering swaps from 12 × 18 (6-month swap one-year forward) through 12 × 42 (30-month swap one-year forward) are provided in Table 5.5. The short-dated portion of the one-year forward swap yield curve is depicted in Exhibit 5.7.

Importantly, when forward swap coupons are determined from par swap yields, as in the preceding example, we are not limited to pricing short-dated forward swaps. We can just as easily calculate coupons for long-dated forward swaps. All that is required is knowledge of the current par yields. These are then used to imply the full-tenor LIBORs, which, in turn, are used to calculate fair forward coupons.

Table 5.5   Swap coupons: one-year-forward June 7, 1991

Tenor of swap (in months)	Swap coupon mid rate (semiannual bond basis)
6	8.1206%
12	8.3354
18	8.4672
24	8.6065
30	8.7204

All swaps above are priced against 6-M LIBOR flat and assume that notional principal is nonamortizing.

Exhibit 5.7   Implied forward swap yield curve starting in one year

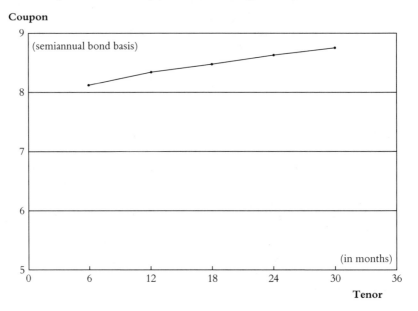

5.5 A Final Note on Spreads Over Treasury

It should be clear from the discussion thus far that swap coupons are determined without reference, at least not direct reference, to the yields on Treasury securities. Nevertheless, once a swap coupon has been determined, the coupon is re-expressed as a spread over Treasuries. For example, in an earlier case, we found the three-year swap coupon to be 8.0661 percent (Table 5.2, 36 months), which we will round to 8.07 percent. Suppose that, at that time, the three-year Treasury note yield was quoted at 7.84 percent. Then we can, and probably would, quote the three-year swap coupon mid rate as 3-year T-note + 23 bps.

It seems reasonable to consider why we would bother to re-express the swap coupon as a spread over Treasuries. The answer is simple. When a swap dealer quotes a swap coupon, the potential counterparty will usually need a little time to check around and compare other dealers' rates and/or to get back to his or her superiors to get an approval to enter the swap. Consequently, some time might elapse between the quotation of the coupon and the actual transaction, assuming that it occurs at all. In the interim, swap coupons might change in response to volatile interest rates. Suppose, for example, that over the course of a few hours, the dealer's three-year mid rate swap coupon drops to 8.05 percent and 3-year T-note yields drop to 7.82 percent. If the dealer had quoted a price of 8.07 percent with the stipulation that the quote is good for two hours, the dealer would be stuck. But, if it quoted 3-year T-note plus 23 basis points with the stipulation that the quote is good for two hours, it is protected. Thus, pricing as a spread over Treasuries helps to protect the dealer from interest rate risk.

5.6 Summary

This chapter has considered the current practice of pricing short-dated interest rate swaps off the Eurodollar strip. It has also considered the many factors which are all too often overlooked in pricing long-dated interest rate swaps. It has shown that the quality spread differential, most often used to explain the gains from interest rate swaps, may seriously overstate the potential gains because the quality spread differential overlooks the true cost of issuing debt, the cost of administering debt, accounting costs, and any qualitative differences between real and synthetic structures. The basic pricing mathematics was extended to consider the pricing of forward swaps and it was shown that forward swap pricing is a straightforward extension of spot swap pricing. Finally, swap futures were described and the merits of quoting swap prices as a spread over Treasuries was discussed.

Review Questions

1. If a three-month Eurodollar futures contract is priced at 95.42, what is the implied 3-M LIBOR rate for the Eurodollar deposit having a term that corresponds to that underlying the futures contract?
2. What is a Eurodollar futures strip? Briefly, in words, what is the fundamental logic involved in pricing a swap coupon off a Eurodollar strip?
3. Why do we distinguish between the pricing of short-dated swaps and the pricing of long-dated swaps? What is the basis for distinguishing between them?
4. What are the three steps involved in pricing short-dated swaps off the Eurostrip?
5. Which step in Question 4 can be skipped if the swap coupon is quoted money market basis rather than bond basis? Why?
6. Suppose that the swap priced in the example in Section 5.2.1 was to be priced with a monthly coupon against one-month LIBOR. What would the swap coupon be?
7. Use the Eurodollar futures prices in Table 5.1 to obtain a swap coupon for a (6 × 18) forward swap having a semiannual coupon against six-month LIBOR. This would be a swap with a tenor of 12 months which takes value in six months.

8.   Summarize the factors that distort the potential gains on a matched pair of swaps relative to what the authors have called the "conventional view."

9.   Why are the slopes of the yield curves for different quality credits different and, specifically, why would we expect the poorer credit to have a steeper yield curve?

10.   Is it possible for a quality spread differential (*QSD*) to be positive and for there to still be no potential gains to either party to a swap? Why or why not?

11.   Why might swap market pricing deviate from a state of no-gains-from-arbitrage? (In other words, what market imperfections could lead to temporary disequilibrium in swap pricing?)

Notes

1.   Technically, the contracts trade on the International Monetary Market (IMM) Division of the Chicago Mercantile Exchange (CME). Identical or nearly identical contracts trade on the Tokyo International Financial Futures Exchange, the Singapore International Monetary Exchange, and the London International Financial Futures Exchange. The Singapore contracts are linked, for purposes of offset, to the IMM contracts.

2.   Barring some very minor differences between forward prices and futures prices induced by the daily marking-to-market of the latter, a swap may also be viewed as a strip of forward rate agreements (FRAs). Indeed, FRAs are priced off the Eurodollar strip in the same manner that swaps are priced off the Eurodollar strip. There is one important difference, however, between single-period FRAs and multiperiod swaps. FRAs cash settle on the contract's value date (i.e., at the front end of the hypothetical Eurodollar deposit) while swaps cash settle on the maturity date for each settlement period (i.e., at the back end of the hypothetical Eurodollar deposit). For this reason, swaps are often described as a strip of in-arrears forward contracts.

3.   This represents an application of the generalized risk-neutral valuation procedure developed by Cox, Ross, and Rubinstein (1979).

4.   While the fixed-rate leg of an interest rate swap is usually quoted bond basis, swaps that are priced off IMM futures contracts *and* which use IMM settlement dates *and* which are called IMM swaps quote the fixed-rate on a money market basis rather than on a bond basis. In these cases, the rate we have obtained for the fixed leg by way of Step 1 (full-tenor LIBOR, denoted $r_{0,3n}$) is the annual fixed rate and we can skip Step 2 entirely. In these cases, we substitute $r_{0,3n}$ for $FRE_{0,3n}$ in Step 3. As a general rule, the fixed rates on swaps with tenors less than one year are usually stated on a money market basis. The final determinant of whether the fixed rate is stated money market basis or bond basis will be the choice of the end user.

5.   Calling the implied three-month rate on the June Eurodollar contract "spot LIBOR" in June is technically incorrect unless we are writing a swap that will employ IMM settlement dates (called IMM swaps). At any given point in time, spot LIBOR, for any given deposit term, is the current LIBOR quote set in London at 11:00 AM London time and does not change until the next day. The June Eurodollar futures contract's implied three-month LIBOR is the market's consensus of the spot rate which will prevail at the time of the futures contract's final settlement. This difference is important for non-IMM swaps. In these cases, the further the near Eurodollar contract is from its final settlement, the more poorly its implied three-month LIBOR rate approximates the current spot rate and, therefore, the greater the influence of spot LIBOR on the swap yield curve. For this reason, traders will often use the London spot rate (from the current date through the near Eurodollar futures contract), in lieu of the rate implied

by the near Eurodollar futures contract, for the first observation on LIBOR. (Recently, one-month Eurodollar futures have been introduced and these can also be used for the same purpose.) An adjustment must also be made for the final period covered by the swap since the final settlement date would fall between two Eurodollar futures settlement dates. The latter adjustment is a simple interpolation between the two implied Eurodollar yields. For example, suppose that a two-year swap with quarterly payments commences on April 10, 1992, and terminates on April 10, 1994. Suppose that the next IMM date is June 17, 1992, and the last two IMM dates that are applicable to this swap (i.e., between which April 10, 1994 falls) are March 16, 1994, and June 15, 1994. The LIBOR quote from April 10, 1992, through June 17, 1992, is the London spot rate for that period. From June 17, 1992, through March 16, 1994, we use the Eurodollar futures. For the final period from March 16, 1994, through April 10, 1994, we interpolate a rate from the March 1994 and the June 1994 futures. The point of this note is that we want to be clear that our treatment of the rate implied by the near Eurodollar futures contract as spot LIBOR is for expositional convenience only.

6. In general, public offerings having a maturity of more than 270 days must be registered with the Securities and Exchange Commission. Registration is a time-consuming and costly undertaking. To some degree, both the cost of registration and the issuance lag have been reduced by the introduction of shelf registration and the rapid development of offshore markets.

7. Comparative borrowing advantages are sometimes called relative advantages.

8. The explanation for the lower cost of the CP with rollover, as opposed to floating rate achieved with a floating rate note (FRN) issue, is explained by (1) the lower issuance costs of short-term CP relative to long-term FRNs – the latter must be registered with the SEC while the former does not; and (2) the CP purchaser possesses an embedded put option relative to the FRN purchaser in the sense that the CP holder may elect not to accept the rollover – an option the FRN holder does not enjoy.

9. The ability of the better credit to borrow floating rate below LIBOR is often described as **sub-LIBOR financing**.

10. Lenders in the short-term debt market have the option not to renew the debt contracts. This option has relatively greater value for holders of poorer quality debt than for holders of better quality debt and, hence, the difference in the slopes of the yield curves.

11. The yield is based on the market price of the debt and the future cash flows to the holder. The all-in cost is based on the proceeds to the issuer and the costs of servicing the issue.

12. As noted earlier in the chapter, the swap coupons on dollar interest rate swaps are most often stated as a spread over Treasuries of comparable average life. If Equation 5.9 was expressed as a spread over Treasuries, it would appear as Equation 5.9b below.

$$p_1 - X_1 + v_1 = p_s = p_2 - X_2 + v_2 \qquad (5.9b)$$

where:

$$Y_1 = T + p_1, \; S = T + p_s, \; Y_2 = T + p_2$$

and where T denotes the N-year Treasury yield (five years in our example). Then, p_1 denotes the better credit's risk premium over Treasuries, p_2 denotes the poorer credit's risk premium over Treasuries, and p_s denotes the spread over Treasuries for the swap coupon – defined as the difference between the indicative mid rate coupon S and the Treasury yield T.

13. The CBOT's swap futures and their uses are described in Marshall and Bansal (1992).

14. Swaptions are options on swaps.

References and Suggested Reading

Bansal, V. K., J. L. Bicksler, A. H. Chen, and J. F. Marshall, "The Pricing of Long-Dated Interest Rates Swaps," working paper, St. John's University, 1992.

Cox, J. C., S. A. Ross, and M. Rubinstein, "Option Pricing: A Simplified Approach," *Journal of Financial Economics*, 7:3, 1979, pp. 229–64.

Evans, E. and G. Parente, "What Drives Interest Rate Swap Spreads," Salomon Brothers, Inc., 1987.

Kapner, K. R. and J. F. Marshall, *The Swaps Handbook*, New York: New York Institute of Finance, 1990.

Kapner, K. R. and J. F. Marshall, "1991–92 Market Update," in *The Swaps Handbook: 1991–92 Supplement*, K. R. Kapner and J. R. Marshall, eds., New York: New York Institute of Finance, 1992.

Liaw, T., "Interest Rate Swaps and Interest Rate Savings," in *The Swaps Handbook: 1991–92 Supplement*, K. R. Kapner and J. F. Marshall, eds., New York: New York Institute of Finance, 1992.

Marshall, J. F. and V.K. Bansal, "Hedging Swaps," in *The Swaps Handbook: 1991–92 Supplement*, K. R. Kapner and J. F. Marshall, eds., New York: New York Institute of Finance, 1992.

Marshall, J. F., E. H. Sorensen, A. L. Tucker, "Equity Derivatives: The Plain Vanilla Equity Swap and Its Variants," *Journal of Financial Engineering*, 2:1, September 1992.

Smith, D. J., "Measuring the Gains from Arbitraging the Swap Market," *Financial Executive*, 4:2, Mar/Apr 1988, pp. 46–9.

Sundaresan, S., "The Pricing of Swaps," First Boston working paper series, 1990.

Sundaresan, S., "Futures Prices on Yields, Forward Prices, and Implied Forward Prices from Term Structure," *Journal of Financial and Quantitative Analysis*, 26:3, September 1991, pp. 409–24.

Yaksick, R., "Swaps, Caps, and Floors: Some Parity and Price Identities," *Journal of Financial Engineering*, 1:1, June 1992, pp. 105–15.

6

Over-the-counter Interest Rate Derivatives

Anatoli Kuprianov

Over-the-counter (OTC) interest rate derivatives include instruments such as forward rate agreements (FRAs), interest rate swaps, caps, floors, and collars. Broadly defined, a derivative instrument is a formal agreement between two parties specifying the exchange of cash payments based on changes in the price of a specified underlying item or differences in the returns to different securities. Like exchange-traded interest rate derivatives such as interest rate futures and futures options, OTC interest rate derivatives set terms for the exchange of cash payments based on changes in market interest rates. An FRA is a forward contract that sets terms for the exchange of cash payments based on changes in the London Interbank Offered Rate (LIBOR); interest rate swaps provide for the exchange of payments based on differences between two different interest rates; and interest rate caps, floors, and collars are option-like agreements that require one party to make payments to the other when a stipulated interest rate, most often a specified maturity of LIBOR, moves outside of some predetermined range.

The over-the-counter market differs from futures markets in a number of important respects. Whereas futures and futures options are standardized agreements that trade on organized exchanges, the over-the-counter market is an informal market consisting of dealers, or market makers, who trade price information and negotiate transactions over electronic communications networks. Although a great deal of contract standardization exists in the over-the-counter market, dealers active in this market custom-tailor agreements to meet the specific needs of their customers. And unlike futures markets, where futures exchange clearinghouses guarantee contract performance through a system of margin requirements combined with the daily settlement of gains or losses, counterparties to OTC derivative agreements must bear some default or credit risk.

The rapid growth and energized pace of innovation in the market for interest rate derivatives since 1981, the date of the first widely publicized swap agreement, has proven truly phenomenal. The advent of trading in interest rate swaps was soon followed by FRAs, caps, floors, collars, as well as other hybrid instruments such as forward swaps, options on swaps (swaptions), and even options on options (captions).

This article offers an introduction to OTC interest rate derivatives. The first five sections describe some of the most common types of OTC derivatives: FRAs, interest rate swaps, caps, floors, and collars. The final section discusses policy and regulatory concerns prompted by the growth of the OTC derivatives market.

1. Forward Rate Agreements

FRAs are cash-settled forward contracts on interest rates traded among major international banks active in the Eurodollar market. An FRA can be viewed as the OTC equivalent of a Eurodollar futures contract. Most FRAs trade for maturities corresponding to standard Eurodollar time deposit maturities, although nonstandard maturities are sometimes traded (Grabbe 1991, Chap. 13). Trading in FRAs began in 1983 (Norfield 1992).

Banks use FRAs to fix interest costs on anticipated future deposits or interest revenues on variable-rate loans indexed to LIBOR. A bank that sells an FRA agrees to pay the buyer the increased interest cost on some "notional" principal amount if some specified maturity of LIBOR is above a stipulated "forward rate" on the contract maturity or settlement date. The principal amount of the agreement is termed "notional" because, while it determines the amount of the payment, actual exchange of the principal never takes place. Conversely, the buyer agrees to pay the seller any decrease in interest cost if market interest rates fall below the forward rate. Thus, buying an FRA is comparable to selling, or going short, a Eurodollar or LIBOR futures contract.

The following example illustrates the mechanics of a transaction involving an FRA. Suppose two banks enter into an agreement specifying:

- a forward rate of 5 percent on a Eurodollar deposit with a three-month maturity;
- a $1 million notional principal; and
- settlement in one month.

Such an agreement is termed a 1 × 4 FRA because it fixes the interest rate for a deposit to be placed after one month and maturing four months after the date the contract is negotiated. If the three-month LIBOR is 6 percent on the contract settlement date, the seller would owe the buyer the difference between 6 and 5 percent interest on $1 million for a period of 90 days. Every 1 basis point change in the interest rate payable on a principal of $1 million for a 90-day maturity changes interest cost by $25, so that the increase in the interest cost on a three-month Eurodollar deposit over the specified forward rate in this case is $25 × 100 basis points = $2,500. But the interest on a Eurodollar deposit is paid upon maturity (at the end of the term of the deposit), whereas FRAs are settled on the contract maturity date (which would correspond to the date the underlying hypothetical deposit would be placed). Therefore, to make the cash payment on the FRA equivalent to the extra interest that would have been earned on a Eurodollar deposit paying 6 percent, the $2,500 difference in interest costs calculated above is discounted back three months using the actual three-month LIBOR prevailing on the settlement date. Thus, if 90-day LIBOR turns out to be 6 percent on the contract maturity date the buyer would receive

$$\$2,463.05 = \$2,500/[1 + 0.06(90/360)].$$

More generally, final settlement of the amounts owed by the parties to an FRA is determined by the formula

$$Payment = \frac{(N)(LIBOR - FR)(dtm/360)}{1 + LIBOR(dtm/360)},$$

where

> N = the notional principal amount of the agreement;
>
> $LIBOR$ = the value of LIBOR for the maturity specified by the contract prevailing on the contract settlement date;
>
> FR = the agreed-upon forward rate; and
>
> dtm = maturity of the forward rate, specified in days.

If $LIBOR > FR$ the seller owes the payment to the buyer, and if $LIBOR < FR$ the buyer owes the seller the absolute value of the payment amount determined by the above formula.

2. Interest Rate Swaps

A swap is a contractual agreement between two parties to exchange, or "swap," future payment streams based on differences in the returns to different securities or changes in the price of some underlying item. Interest rate swaps constitute the most common type of swap agreement. In an interest rate swap, the parties to the agreement, termed the swap counterparties, agree to exchange payments indexed to two different interest rates. Total payments are determined by the specified notional principal amount of the swap, which is never actually exchanged. Financial intermediaries, such as banks, pension funds, and insurance companies, as well as nonfinancial firms use interest rate swaps to effectively change the maturity of outstanding debt or that of an interest-bearing asset.[1]

Swaps grew out of parallel loan agreements in which firms exchanged loans denominated in different currencies. Although some swaps were arranged in the late 1970s, the first widely publicized swap took place in 1981 when IBM and the World Bank agreed to exchange interest payments on debt denominated in different currencies, an arrangement known as a currency swap. The first interest rate swap was a 1982 agreement in which the Student Loan Marketing Association (Sallie Mae) swapped the interest payments on an issue of intermediate-term, fixed-rate debt for floating-rate payments indexed to the three-month Treasury bill yield. The interest rate swap market has grown rapidly since then. Figure 1 displays the year-end total notional principal of U.S. dollar interest rate swaps outstanding from 1985 to 1991. Based on market survey data published by the International Swap Dealers Association (ISDA), U.S. dollar interest rate swaps comprise about one-half of all interest rate swaps outstanding: the notional principal amount of U.S. dollar interest rate swaps outstanding as of the end of 1991 was just over $1.5 trillion, compared to almost $3.1 trillion for all interest rate swaps.

Swap dealers

Early interest rate swaps were brokered transactions in which financial intermediaries with customers interested in entering into a swap would seek counterparties for the transaction among their other customers. The intermediary collected a brokerage

Figure 1   U.S. dollar interest rate swaps

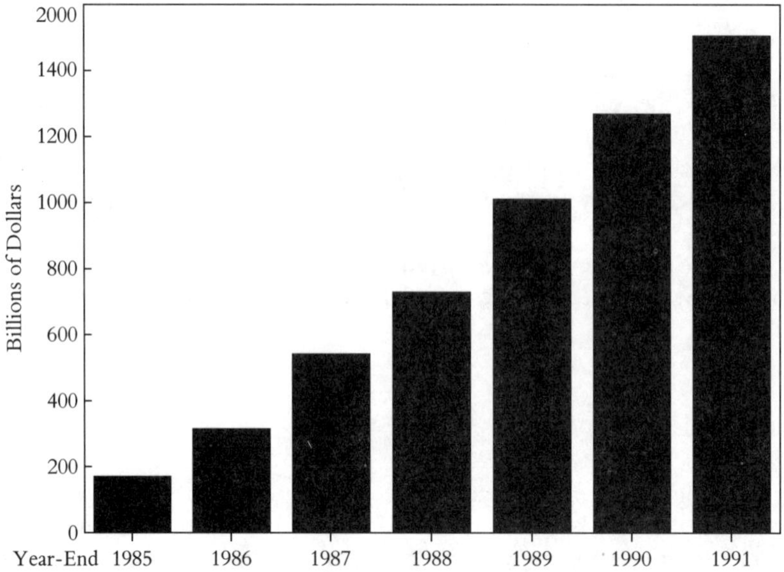

Source: Market Survey Highlights, Year End 1991, International Swap Dealers Association, Inc.

Figure 2   The dealer market for interest rate swaps

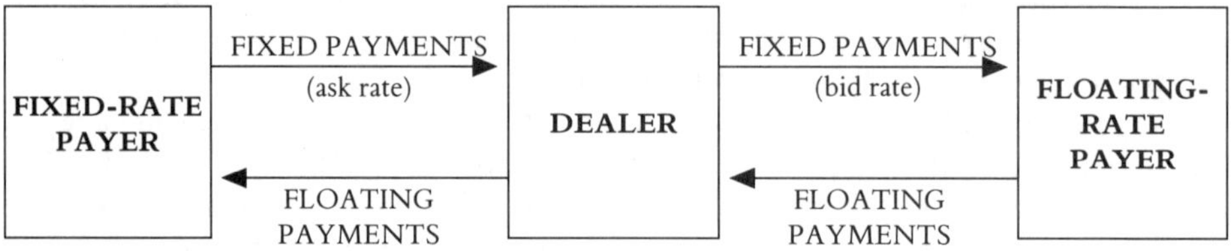

fee as compensation, but did not maintain a continuing role once the transaction was completed. The contract was between the two ultimate swap users, who exchanged payments directly.

Today the market has evolved into more of a dealer market dominated by large international commercial and investment banks. Dealers act as market makers that stand ready to become a counterparty to different swap transactions before a customer for the other side of the transaction is located. A swap dealer intermediates cash flows between different customers, or "end users," becoming a middleman to each transaction. The dealer market structure relieves end users from the need to monitor the financial condition of many different swap counterparties. Because dealers act as middlemen, end users need only be concerned with the financial condition of the dealer, and not with the creditworthiness of the other ultimate end user of the instrument (Brown and Smith 1990).

Figure 2 illustrates the flow of payments between two swap end users through a swap dealer. Unlike brokers, dealers in the over-the-counter market do not charge a commission. Instead, they quote two-way "bid" and "asked" prices at which they stand ready to act as counterparty to their customers in a derivative instrument. The quoted spread between bid and asked prices allows an intermediary to receive a higher payment from one counterparty than is paid to the other.

Swap market conventions

There are many different variants of interest rate swaps. The most common is the fixed/floating swap in which a fixed-rate payer makes payments based on a long-term interest rate to a floating-rate payer, who, in turn, makes payments indexed to a short-term money market rate to the fixed-rate payer. A fixed/floating swap is characterized by:

- a fixed interest rate;
- a variable or floating interest rate which is periodically reset;
- a notional principal amount upon which total interest payments are based; and
- the term of the agreement, including a schedule of interest rate reset dates (that is, dates when the value of the interest rate used to determine floating-rate payments is determined) and payment dates.

The fixed interest rate typically is based on the prevailing market interest rate for Treasury securities with a maturity corresponding to the term of the swap agreement. The floating rate is most often indexed to three- or six-month LIBOR, in which case the swap is termed a "generic" or "plain vanilla" swap, but can be indexed to almost any money market rate such as the Treasury bill, commercial paper, federal funds, or prime interest rate. The maturity, or "tenor," of a fixed/floating interest rate swap can vary between 1 and 15 years. By convention, a fixed-rate payer is designated as the buyer and is said to be long the swap, while the floating-rate payer is the seller and is characterized as short the swap.

Timing of payments
A swap is negotiated on its "trade date" and takes effect two days later on its initial "settlement date." If the agreement requires the exchange of cash at the outset, as in the case of a "nonpar" swap, the transaction takes place on the initial settlement date. Interest begins accruing on the "effective date" of the swap, which usually coincides with the initial settlement date. (Forward swaps, in which the effective date of the swap is deferred, are an exception to this rule.) Floating-rate payments are adjusted on periodic "reset dates" based on the prevailing market-determined value of the floating-rate index, with subsequent payments made on a sequence of payment dates (also known as settlement dates) specified by the agreement. Typically, the reset frequency for the floating-rate index is the term of the interest rate index itself. For example, the floating rate on a generic swap indexed to the six-month LIBOR would, in most cases, be reset every six months with payment dates following six months later. The floating rate can be reset more frequently, however, as in the case of swaps indexed to Treasury bill rates, which are reset weekly.

Fixed interest payment intervals can be three months, six months, or one year. Semiannual payment intervals are most common because they coincide with the intervals between interest payments on Treasury bonds. Floating-rate payment intervals need not coincide with fixed-rate payment intervals, although they often do. When payment intervals coincide, it is common practice to exchange only the net difference between the fixed and floating payments.

Price quotation

The price of a fixed/floating swap is quoted in two parts: a fixed interest rate and an index upon which the floating interest rate is based. The floating rate can be based on an index of short-term market rates (such as a given maturity of LIBOR) plus or minus a given margin, or set to the index "flat" – that is, the floating interest rate index itself with no margin added. The convention in the swap market is to quote the fixed interest rate as an All-In-Cost (AIC), which means that the fixed interest rate is quoted relative to a flat floating-rate index.

The AIC typically is quoted as a spread over U.S. Treasury securities with a maturity corresponding to the term of the swap. For example, a swap dealer might quote a price on a three-year generic swap at an All-In-Cost of "72–76 flat," which means the dealer stands ready to "buy" the swap (that is, enter into the swap as a fixed-rate payer) at 72 basis points over the prevailing three-year interest rate on U.S. Treasuries while receiving floating-rate payments indexed to a specified maturity of LIBOR with no margin, and "sell" (receive fixed and pay floating) if the other party to the swap agrees to pay 76 basis points over Treasury securities.

Bid-asked spreads in the swap market vary greatly depending on the type of agreement. The spread can be as low as 3 to 4 basis points for a two- or three-year generic swap, while spreads for nonstandard, custom-tailored swaps tend to be much higher.

The generic swap

As an illustration of the mechanics of a simple interest rate swap, consider the example of a generic swap. Fixed interest payments on a generic swap typically are based on a 30/360 day-count convention, meaning that they are calculated assuming each month has 30 days and the quoted interest rate is based on a 360-day year. Given an All-In-Cost of the swap, the semiannual fixed-rate payment would be

$$(N)(AIC)(180/360),$$

where N denotes the notional principal amount of the agreement.

Floating-rate payments are based on an actual/360-day count, meaning that interest payments are calculated using the actual number of days elapsed since the previous payment date, based on a 360-day year. Let d_t denote the number of days since the last settlement date. Then, the floating-rate payment is determined by the formula

$$(N)(LIBOR)(d_t/360).$$

To illustrate, suppose a dealer quotes an All-In-Cost for a generic swap at 10 percent against six-month LIBOR flat. If the notional principal amount of the swap is $1 million, then the semiannual fixed payment would be

$$\$50,000 = (\$1,000,000)(0.10)(180/360).$$

Suppose that the six-month period from the effective date of the swap to the first payment date (sometimes also termed a settlement date) comprises 181 days and that the corresponding LIBOR was 8 percent on the swap's effective date. Then, the first floating-rate payment would be

$$\$40,222.22 = (\$1,000,000)(0.08)(181/360).$$

Often a swap agreement will call for only the net amount of the promised payments to be exchanged. In this example, the fixed-rate payer would pay the floating-rate payer a net amount of

$$\$9,777.78 = \$50,000.00 - \$40,222.22.$$

A payment frequency "mismatch" occurs when the floating-rate payment frequency does not match the scheduled frequency of the fixed-rate payment. Mismatches typically arise in the case of swaps that base floating-rate payments on maturities shorter than the six-month payment frequency common for fixed-rate payments. Macfarlane, Ross, and Showers (1990) discuss swap mismatches in some detail.

Day-count conventions

A wide variety of day-count conventions are used in the swap market. Fixed payments can be quoted either on an actual/365 (bond equivalent) basis or on an actual/360 basis. Floating-rate payments indexed to private-sector interest rates typically follow an actual/360 day-count convention commonly used in the money market. Floating-rate payments tied to Treasury bill rates are calculated on an actual/365 basis, however.

Nongeneric swaps

An interest rate swap that specifies an exchange of payments based on the difference between two different variable rates is known as a 'basis swap." For example, a basis swap might specify the exchange of payments based on the difference between LIBOR and the prime rate. Other interest rate swaps include the forward swap, in which the effective date of the swap is deferred; the swaption, which is an option on an interest rate swap; and puttable and callable swaps, in which one party has the right to cancel the swap at certain times. This list is far from exhaustive – many other types of interest rate swaps are currently traded, and the number grows with each year. Abken (1991b) describes a variety of different swap agreements.

Swap valuation

Interest rate swaps can be viewed as implicit mutual lending arrangements. A party to an interest rate swap implicitly holds a long position in one type of interest-bearing security and a short position in another. Swap valuation techniques utilize this fact to reduce the problem of pricing an interest rate swap to a straightforward problem of pricing two underlying hypothetical securities having a redemption or face value equal to the notional principal amount of the swap. The method used to value a fixed/floating swap is outlined below.

Partitioning a swap
A fixed/floating swap can be partitioned into (1) a bond paying a fixed coupon and (2) a variable-rate note with payments tied to the variable-rate index. Let $S(0,T)$ denote the value of a T-period swap on its initial settlement date (date 0), $B(0,T)$ the value of a hypothetical T-period fixed-rate bond paying a coupon equal to the fixed-rate payments specified by the agreement, and $V(0,T)$ the value of a variable-rate note maturing at date T. Assuming that the face or redemption value of both hypothetical securities is equal to the notional principal amount of the swap, the value of the swap to a fixed-rate payer can be expressed as

$$S(0,T) = V(0,T) - B(0,T).$$

Pricing the variable-rate note
A variable-rate note whose payments are indexed to market interest rates is valued at par upon issuance and just after each interest payment is made. Thus, assuming that payment dates coincide with interest rate reset dates, the value of the hypothetical variable-rate note $V(0,T)$ will just equal the notional principal amount of the swap on every reset date. On any other date the value of a variable-rate note – exclusive of accrued interest – is just the present value of the next known interest payment plus the present value of the face value of the note, the latter amount representing the value of all remaining payments on the note as of the next settlement date.

Pricing the fixed-rate note
The hypothetical fixed-rate note $B(0, T)$ can be priced using standard bond valuation techniques. The convention in swap markets is to quote the AIC as a semiannual bond-equivalent rate. The formula for valuing a bond paying semiannual fixed coupon payments is

$$B(0,T) = \sum_{t=0}^{2T} [(C/2)/(1 + y/2)^t] + [N/(1 + y)^T],$$

where C is the annual coupon payment, T the number of years to maturity, N the principal or face value, and y the yield-to-maturity of the bond.

By definition, the All-In-Cost of a fixed/floating swap is the yield to maturity that just makes the value of the hypothetical fixed-rate bond equal to the notional principal amount of the swap. The annual coupon payment for this hypothetical bond is determined by the AIC and the notional principal amount of the agreement:

$$C = (AIC/100)(N),$$

where AIC is expressed as a percentage rate. It is easy to see that the value of the hypothetical bond implicit in this fixed/floating swap will be par (the notional principal amount of the swap) when

$$y = AIC/100.$$

Nonpar swaps

In most cases swaps are priced so that the initial value of the agreement is zero to both counterparties; that is, so that the value of both hypothetical component securities is just equal to the notional principal amount of the swap. Occasionally, however, a swap may be priced such that one party owes money to the other at initial settlement, resulting in a 'nonpar" swap. Nonpar swaps are used to offset existing positions in swaps entered into in previous periods where interest rates have changed since the original swap was negotiated, or in cases where a given cash flow needs to be matched exactly (Dattatreya 1992). Valuation methods for nonpar swaps are somewhat more involved than the simple case discussed above. Interested readers can find more comprehensive discussions of swap valuation in Beckstrom (1990), Iben (1990), and Macfarlane, Ross, and Showers (1990).

The effect of changes in market interest rates on swap values

A change in market interest rates affects the value of a fixed/floating swap in much the same way that it affects the value of a corporate bond with a comparable maturity. To see why, note that a change in market interest rates will have no effect on the value of the hypothetical variable-rate note implicit in a fixed/floating swap on interest rate reset dates. Therefore, on reset dates a change in market interest rates will affect the value of the swap only through its effect on the value of the hypothetical fixed-rate bond. Since an increase in interest rates lowers the value of the bond, it increases the value of the swap position for a fixed-rate payer to the same degree it would increase the value of a short position in a fixed-rate bond.

Between interest rate reset dates the amount of the next payment due on the variable-rate note is predetermined. Thus, a change in market interest rates affects the values of both the hypothetical variable-rate note and the hypothetical fixed-rate bond. The change in the value of the variable-rate note partially offsets the change in the value of the fixed-rate note in this case. As a general rule the price behavior of a fixed/floating interest rate swap will approximate the price behavior of a fixed-rate note with a maturity equal to the term of the swap less the maturity of the variable interest rate. For example, a two-year generic swap indexed to six-month LIBOR will approximate the behavior of a fixed-rate bond with a term to maturity of between 18 and 24 months, depending on the amount of time since the last interest rate reset date (Burghardt et al. 1991, p. 86).

The value of a fixed/floating swap generally changes over time when the term structure of interest rates is upward-sloping. Only when the term structure is flat and market interest rates remain unchanged will the value of an interest rate swap remain unchanged over the life of the agreement (Smith, Smithson, and Wakeman 1988).

3. Interest Rate Caps

The buyer of an interest rate cap pays the seller a premium in return for the right to receive the difference in the interest cost on some notional principal amount any time a specified index of market interest rates rises above a stipulated "cap rate."

Figure 3   U.S. dollar caps, collars, and floors

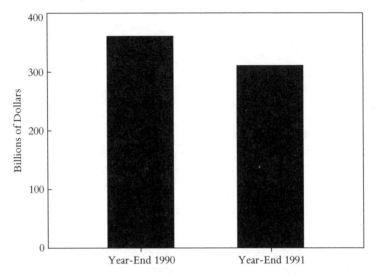

Source: *Market Survey Highlights, Year End 1991*, International Swap Dealers Association, Inc.

The buyer bears no obligation or liability if interest rates fall below the cap rate, however. Thus, a cap resembles an option in that it represents a right rather than an obligation to the buyer.

Caps evolved from interest rate guarantees that fixed a maximum level of interest payable on floating-rate loans. The advent of trading in over-the-counter interest rate caps dates back to 1985, when banks began to strip such guarantees from floating-rate notes to sell to the market (Kahle 1992). The leveraged buyout boom of the 1980s spurred the evolution of the market for interest rate caps. Firms engaged in leveraged buyouts typically took on large quantities of short-term debt, which made them vulnerable to financial distress in the event of a rise in interest rates. As a result, lenders began requiring such borrowers to buy interest rate caps to reduce the risk of financial distress (Burghardt et al. 1991). More recently, trading activity in interest rate caps has declined as the number of new leveraged buyouts has fallen. Figure 3 shows that the total notional principal amount of caps, floors, and collars outstanding at the end of 1991 actually fell to $311 billion from $360 billion at the end of 1990 (floors and collars are discussed below).

Market conventions

An interest rate cap is characterized by:

 - a notional principal amount upon which interest payments are based;
 - an interest rate index, typically some specified maturity of LIBOR;
 - a cap rate, which is equivalent to a strike or exercise price on an option; and
 - the period of the agreement, including payment dates and interest rate reset dates.

Figure 4   The payoff to buying a one-period interest rate cap

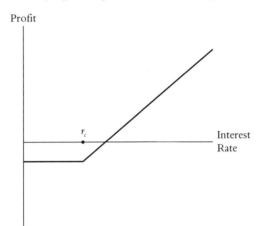

Payment schedules for interest rate caps follow conventions in the interest rate swap market. Payment amounts are determined by the value of the index rate on a series of interest rate reset dates. Intervals between interest rate reset dates and scheduled payment dates typically coincide with the term of the interest rate index. Thus, interest rate reset dates for a cap indexed to six-month LIBOR would occur every six months with payments due six months later. Cap buyers typically schedule interest rate reset and payment intervals to coincide with interest payments on outstanding variable-rate debt. Interest rate caps cover periods ranging from one to ten years with interest rate reset and payment dates most commonly set either three or six months apart.

If the specified market index is above the cap rate, the seller pays the buyer the difference in interest cost on the next payment date. The amount of the payment is determined by the formula

$$(N) \max (0, r - r_c)(d_t/360),$$

where N is the notional principal amount of the agreement, r_c is the cap rate (expressed as a decimal), and d_t is the number of days from the interest rate reset date to the payment date. Interest rates quoted in cap agreements follow money market day-count conventions, so that payment calculations assume a 360-day year.

Figure 4 depicts the payoff to the buyer of a one-period interest rate cap. If the index rate is above the cap rate, the buyer receives a payment of $(N)(r - r_c)(d_t/360)$, which is equivalent to the payoff from buying an FRA.[2] Otherwise, the buyer receives no payment and loses the premium paid for the cap. Thus, a cap effectively gives its buyer the right, but not the obligation, to buy an FRA with a forward rate equal to the cap rate. Such an agreement is known as a call option. A one-period cap can be viewed as a European call option on an FRA with a strike price equal to the cap rate r_c.[3] More generally, multi-period caps, which specify a series of future interest rate reset and payment dates, can be viewed as a bundle of European call options on a sequence of FRAs.

Example of an interest rate cap

Consider the example of a one-year interest rate cap that specifies a notional principal amount of $1 million and a six-month LIBOR cap rate of 5 percent. Assume the agreement covers a period starting January 15 through the following January 15 with the interest rate to be reset on July 15. The first period of a cap agreement typically is excluded from the agreement, so the cap buyer in this example will be entitled to a payment only if the six-month LIBOR exceeds 5 percent on the July 15 interest rate reset date. Suppose that six-month LIBOR is 5.5 percent on July 15. Then, on the following January 15 (184 days after the July 15 reset date) the seller will owe the buyer

$$\$2{,}555.56 = (\$1{,}000{,}000)(0.055 - 0.050)(184/360).$$

Comparison of caps and futures options

A one-period cap can be compared to a put option on a Eurodollar futures contract. To see why, note that the payoff at expiration to a put option on Eurodollar futures is

$$(N) \max (0, K - F)(90/360),$$

where N is the notional principal amount of the agreement ($1 million for a Eurodollar futures option), K is the strike price and F is the price of the underlying futures contract. The price index used for Eurodollar futures can be written as $F = 100 - r$, where r is the three-month LIBOR implied by the futures price. Now, write $K = 100 - r_k$, where r_k is the futures interest rate implied by the strike price K. Then, the payoff at expiration to a Eurodollar futures option can be expressed as

$$(N) \max [0, 100 - r_k - (100 - r)](90/360) = (N) \max (0, r - r_k)(90/360).$$

The right-hand side of this expression is just the payoff to a one-period interest rate cap indexed to three-month LIBOR with a cap of r_k.

Despite the similarities between the caps and Eurodollar futures options, the two instruments differ in a number of noteworthy respects. First, futures options are standardized, exchange-traded instruments, whereas caps are over-the-counter instruments whose payments can be tailored to match the payment schedule of any variable-rate loan. Eurodollar futures options are based on three-month LIBOR, whereas caps can be bought over the counter to match virtually any maturity interest rate up to one year. Second, futures options are American-style options that can be exercised at any time before the expiration date. In contrast, caps resemble a strip of European options – a cap can be "exercised" only if the specified index rate is above the cap rate on a given reset date. Third, Eurodollar futures options are cash settled on the option expiration date, while a cap is settled in arrears – that is, the payment period falls some time after the interest rate reset date.

Figure 5   The effect of buying a cap on interest expense

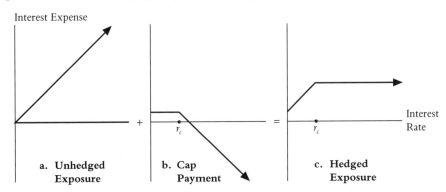

a. **Unhedged**
   Exposure

b. **Cap**
   Payment

c. **Hedged**
   Exposure

Hedging uses of caps

Figure 5 illustrates the effect that buying a cap has on the interest expense associated with a floating-rate loan. The first panel depicts the unhedged or inherent exposure of a firm with a loan tied to six-month LIBOR. The firm is exposed to the risk that market interest rates will rise before the next interest rate reset date on the loan and drive up its interest costs. The second panel illustrates the effect that buying a cap has on interest expense. If interest rates rise above the 5 percent cap rate, the payment received from the cap seller offsets the firm's increased interest expense. The hedged position, illustrated in the third panel, shows how buying a cap limits the firm's interest expense to a maximum amount determined by the cost of servicing the debt at the cap rate plus the premium paid for the instrument.

4. Interest Rate Floors

The buyer of an interest rate floor pays the seller a premium in return for the right to receive the difference in interest payable on a notional principal amount when a specified index interest rate falls below a stipulated minimum, or "floor rate." Buyers use floors to fix a minimum interest rate on an asset paying a variable interest rate indexed to some maturity of LIBOR. Like an interest rate cap, a floor is an option-like agreement in that it represents a right rather than an obligation to the buyer. The buyer of an interest rate floor incurs no obligation if the index interest rate rises above the floor rate, so the most a buyer can lose is the premium paid to the seller at the outset of the agreement.

The payment received by the buyer of an interest rate floor is determined by the formula

$$(N) \max (0, \ r_f - r)(d_t/360),$$

where N is the notional principal amount of the agreement, r_f is the floor rate or strike price, and d_t is the number of days from the last interest rate reset date to the payment date. Figure 6 depicts the payoff to a one-period floor as a function of the

Figure 6   The payoff to buying a one-period interest rate floor

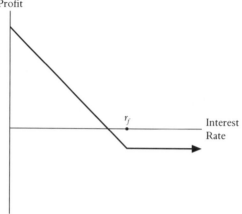

value of the underlying index rate. If the index rate is below the floor rate on the interest rate reset date the buyer receives a payment of $(N)(r_f - r)(d_t/360)$, which is equivalent to the payoff from selling an FRA at a forward rate of r_f. On the other hand, if the index rate is above the floor rate the buyer receives no payment and loses the premium paid to the seller. Thus, a floor effectively gives the buyer the right, but not the obligation, to sell an FRA, which makes it equivalent to a European put option on an FRA. More generally, a multi-period floor can be viewed as a bundle of European-style put options on a sequence of FRAs maturing on a succession of future maturity dates.

Comparison of floors and futures options

Purchasing a one-period interest rate floor yields a payoff closely resembling that of a long Eurodollar futures call option. The payoff to a call option on a Eurodollar futures contract is

$$(N) \max (0, F - K)(90/360),$$

were $F = 100 - r$ is the index price of the underlying futures contract and K is the strike price. As before, write $K = 100 - r_k$. Then, the payoff to a Eurodollar futures call option can be expressed in terms of the underlying interest rate as

$$(N) \max (0, r_k - r)(90/360),$$

which is the same as the payoff to a one-period interest rate floor indexed to 90-day LIBOR with a floor rate equal to r_k. The one noteworthy difference between the two instruments is that a Eurodollar futures option can be exercised at any time, while a floor resembles a European option that can only be exercised on its expiration date. Like caps, interest rate floors settle in arrears, whereas a futures option settles on its expiration date.

Figure 7   The payoff to buying a one-period, zero-cost collar

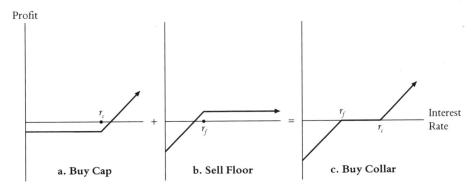

5. Interest Rate Collars

The buyer of an interest rate collar purchases an interest rate cap while selling a floor indexed to the same interest rate. Borrowers with variable-rate loans buy collars to limit effective borrowing rates to a range of interest rates between some maximum, determined by the cap rate, and a minimum, which is fixed by the floor strike price; hence, the term "collar." Although buying a collar limits a borrower's ability to benefit from a significant decline in market interest rates, it has the advantage of being less expensive than buying a cap alone because the borrower earns premium income from the sale of the floor that offsets the cost of the cap. A zero-cost collar results when the premium earned by selling a floor exactly offsets the cap premium.

The amount of the payment due to or owed by a buyer of an interest rate collar is determined by the expression

$$(N)[\max (0, r - r_c) - \max (0, r_f - r)](d_t/360),$$

where, as before, N is the notional principal amount of the agreement, r_c is the cap rate, r_f is the floor rate, and d_t is the term of the index in days. Figure 7 illustrate the payoff to buying a one-period zero-cost interest rate collar. If the index interest rate r is less than the floor rate r_f on the interest rate reset date, the floor is in-the-money and the collar buyer (who has sold a floor) must pay the collar counterparty an amount equal to $(N)(r_f - r)(d_t/360)$. When r is greater than r_f but less than the cap rate r_c, both the floor and the cap are out-of-the-money and no payments are exchanged. Finally, when the index is above the cap rate the cap is in-the-money and the buyer receives $(N)(r - r_c)(d_t/360)$.

Figure 8 illustrates a special case of a zero-cost collar that results from the simultaneous purchase of a one-period cap and sale of a one-period floor when the cap and floor rates are equal. In this case the combined transaction replicates the payoff of an FRA with a forward interest rate equal to the cap/floor rate. This result is a consequence of a property of option prices known as put-call parity.

More generally, the purchase of a cap and sale of a floor with the same notional principle, index rate, strike price, and reset dates produces the same payout stream

Figure 8 Put-call parity

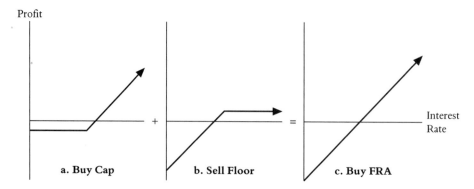

a. Buy Cap + b. Sell Floor = c. Buy FRA

Figure 9 The effect of buying an interest rate collar on interest expense

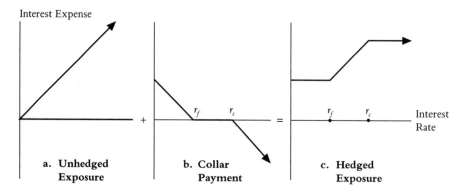

a. Unhedged Exposure + b. Collar Payment = c. Hedged Exposure

as an interest rate swap with an All-In-Cost equal to the cap or floor rate. Since caps and floors can be viewed as a sequence of European call and put options on FRAs, buying a cap and selling a floor with the same strike price and interest rate reset and payment dates effectively creates a sequence of FRAs, all with the same forward rate. But note that an interest rate swap can be viewed as a sequence of FRAs, each with a forward rate equal to the All-In-Cost of the swap. Therefore, put-call parity implies that buying a cap and selling a floor with the same contract specifications results in the same payment stream that would be obtained by buying an interest rate swap.

In recent years dealers in the OTC derivatives market have shown a great deal of ingenuity in devising new hybrid instruments yielding an almost endless variety of payout patterns. Interested readers can find descriptions of other types of derivatives in Abken (1989), Burghardt et al. (1991), Smith and Smithson (1990), and Smith, Smithson, and Wilford (1989).

Hedging uses of interest rate collars

Figure 9 illustrates the effect that buying a one-period, zero-cost collar has on the exposure to changes in market interest rates faced by a firm with outstanding variable-rate debt. The first panel depicts the firm's inherent or unhedged interest exposure, while the second panel illustrates the effect that buying a collar has on interest expense. Finally, the third panel combines the borrower's inherent exposure with the payoff to buying a collar to display the effect of a change in market interest rates on a hedged borrower's interest expense. Note that changes in market interest rates can only affect the hedged borrower's interest expense when the index rate varies between the floor and cap rates. Outside this range, the borrower's interest expense is completely hedged.

6. Risk and Regulation in the Over-the-counter Derivatives Market

Regulatory concerns

The OTC derivatives market is often characterized as unregulated because no federal regulatory agency oversees trading activity in this market, as the Commodity Futures Trading Commission (CFTC) does with futures markets or the Securities and Exchange Commission (SEC) does with securities markets.[4] Yet it would be misleading to characterize the OTC derivatives market as completely unregulated. Many of the largest derivatives dealers are affiliates of commercial banks, which rank among the most heavily regulated of all firms. Bank regulatory agencies routinely conduct on-site examinations to review procedures in place for controlling risks at the institutions they supervise. Additionally, regulations imposed by the federal banking agencies include minimum capital requirements designed to take account of credit risk exposure arising in connection with derivative instruments.[5] While not subject to the comprehensive regulatory oversight applied to commercial banks, investment banks dealing in OTC derivatives are subject to SEC scrutiny. And the International Swap Dealers Association (ISDA) – an industry association organized by the major OTC derivatives dealers – sets standards for market practices and addresses the legal and public policy issues affecting the market.

Nonetheless, the rapid growth and sheer size of the OTC derivatives market has sparked debate over the risks posed by the growth of trading in derivative instruments and the appropriate scope of market regulation.[6] When all types of derivative agreements are taken into account, including currency swaps, caps, floors, collars, and swaptions, the total notional principal amount of outstanding agreements exceeded $4 trillion at the end of 1991, with derivatives dealers acting as middlemen to most transactions. Much of the trading activity in this market takes place between a relatively small number of large dealers, resulting in an interdependent web of obligations among those dealers.[7] Unlike exchange-traded derivatives such as futures contracts and futures options, where the exchange clearinghouses guarantee contract performance through a system of margin requirements, daily settlement of gains and losses, and the backing of the capital of clearing member firms, OTC derivative instruments are bilateral arrangements that carry no independent third-party guarantee. As a result, counterparties to OTC instruments face the risk of default, known as counterparty credit risk. Moreover, the absence of contract standardization means that OTC derivatives tend to be less liquid than exchange-traded derivatives, which can make it difficult to execute transactions in periods of extreme price volatility or when a counterparty's credit standing is questioned.

A recent joint study by the three federal banking agencies examined the risks posed by the growth of trading in OTC derivatives (Board of Governors of the Federal Reserve System, Federal Deposit Insurance Corporation, and Office of the Comptroller of the Currency 1993). The study found that risks associated with OTC derivatives differed little from the risks traditionally borne by financial intermediaries. Although it did identify a number of concerns, the study concluded that trading in derivative instruments has not contributed to the overall fragility of the financial system and does not pose undue risks for organizations active in this market. To the contrary, it cited at least one instance – namely, the period of exchange rate turbulence in European currencies in September of 1992 – where it concluded that foreign currency markets were not likely to have performed as well as they did during the crisis without the existence of foreign currency derivatives that enabled financial institutions to manage their currency positions.

The joint study identified six different types of risks in connection with derivative instruments: credit risk, market risk, liquidity risk, settlement risk, operating risk, and aggregation risk. As noted earlier, much of the concern over the growth of the market has centered around the issue of counterparty credit risk because of the sheer size of the market and the size of credit exposures borne by dealers. Because derivative instruments tie together so many different markets around the world, regulators have expressed concerns that aggregation, or interconnection risk, might make it difficult to contain a financial crisis to keep it from spreading to other markets. The remainder of this article discusses some of the risks associated with OTC derivatives and the legal, regulatory, and market arrangements that have developed to deal with such risks.

Counterparty credit risk

Measuring the credit risk exposure of an FRA
The credit risk exposure associated with an FRA, or any other derivative instrument for that matter, differs from that of a debt instrument because an FRA is not a funding transaction and therefore involves no exchange of principal. At its inception the value of an FRA is zero to both parties, so there is no initial credit risk. Potential credit risk is bilateral: a party to an FRA is exposed to credit risk when the value of the agreement becomes positive to him or her, and the value of an FRA can change so as to gain value to either party. Unlike a loan agreement, where financial distress on the part of a borrower always exposes the lender to default risk, financial distress on the part of an FRA counterparty does not necessarily expose the other counterparty to the risk of default. A financially distressed firm has no incentive to default on an agreement that has positive value to it – and even if such a counterparty were to default, the nondefaulting party would suffer no loss.

Since an FRA involves no exchange of principal, potential credit risk exposure is a small fraction of the notional principal amount of the agreement. Credit risk exposure is determined by the value of the FRA, which corresponds to the cost of replacing the FRA. To illustrate, recall the earlier example of a 1 × 4 FRA with a notional principal of $1 million and a forward rate of 5 percent. If market interest rates rise by 50 basis points immediately after the agreement is negotiated, the value of the FRA to the buyer is just the current present value of $1,250 (50 basis points × $25 per basis point), or

$$\$1,229.51 = \$1,250/[1 + 0.050(120/360)].$$

This calculation determines the value of the agreement exactly 30 days before its scheduled settlement, or maturity date. The credit risk exposure borne by the FRA buyer in this example is just over 1/10 of 1 percent of the notional principal amount of the agreement.

Measuring the credit risk exposure of an interest rate swap
A swap counterparty's credit risk exposure is determined by the cost of replacing the agreement in the event of a default. The cost of obtaining a replacement swap is determined by the difference between the All-In-Cost of the old swap and the AIC on a replacement swap. As an illustration, consider the case of a fixed-rate payer in a swap with one year left to maturity and a 7 percent AIC. If the floating-rate payer defaults when the prevailing market rate on a one-year replacement swap is 8 percent, the nondefaulting party will be required to pay an extra 1 percent per year on the notional principal to replace the swap. The replacement value of the swap is just the net present value of the difference in interest payments.

In discussing swap valuation methods it was useful to view a swap as an implicit mutual lending arrangement in which the counterparties exchanged loans indexed to two different interest rates. In looking at credit risk exposure, however, it can be useful to view a swap as a bundle of FRAs, all with forward rates equal to the All-In-Cost of the swap. Thus, the swap in the above example can be viewed as a combination of a 0 × 6 FRA and a 6 × 12 FRA, each with a forward rate of 7 percent. The replacement cost of the swap is just equal to the value of the two component FRAs when the underlying index rate is 8 percent.

As with FRAs, the potential credit risk exposure of an interest rate swap typically is a small fraction of the notional principal amount of the agreement. By one estimate, the expected lifetime credit exposure associated with an interest rate swap varies from 0.002 percent of the notional principal for a swap with a one-year maturity to 4.5 percent for a swap with a ten-year maturity (Simons 1989).

Credit risk exposure of caps, floors, and collars
Sellers of caps and floors face no credit risk, since neither type of agreement requires the buyer to make any payments other than the initial premium. But cap and floor buyers face the risk of nonperformance on the part of the seller any time a cap or floor goes "in-the-money" – that is, any time the seller is required to make payments to the buyer. Since a collar involves a short position in a floor and a long position in a cap, it can expose both the buyer and seller to counterparty credit risk.

The credit risk exposure faced by the buyer of an interest rate cap can be compared to the risk exposure of a fixed-rate payer in an interest rate swap. In both cases, the buyers face the risk that the seller will default when interest rates rise. Similarly, the buyer of an interest rate floor faces a credit risk exposure analogous to that of a floating-rate payer, or seller, of an interest rate swap. The total credit risk exposure in each case is determined by the cost of buying a replacement cap or floor.

Netting arrangements

When dealers first began acting as intermediaries in swap agreements the risk associated with each swap was accounted for separately. As the market grew, swap dealers found themselves parties to multiple agreements with the same counterparty. Concern over their growing aggregate exposure led many dealers to adopt "master" agreements that treated all their transactions with a given counterparty as supplements to a single consolidated agreement. These master agreements gave swap counterparties the right to terminate all supplemental swap agreements in the event of default on any one of the swaps. The advent of the master agreement represented an attempt by swap dealers to limit the credit risk exposure with any single counterparty to the net value of all swaps with that counterparty. Today virtually all OTC derivatives utilize a standardized master agreement designed by the International Swap Dealers Association (Gooch and Pergam 1990).

The status of OTC derivatives under bankruptcy law
Before the enactment of recent amendments to the Bankruptcy Code, there was some question as to whether master swap agreement netting provisions would be legally enforceable in the event of bankruptcy. The U.S. Bankruptcy Code grants a firm in bankruptcy proceedings an 'automatic stay" from the claims of its creditors. The automatic stay allows a bankrupt firm to postpone scheduled debt payments and overrides most other contractual obligations pending the resolution of all claims against the firm. Thus, although virtually all lending agreements give creditors the right to demand accelerated repayment of a loan in the event of a default on a scheduled payment, default inevitably delays repayment in practice. Often, creditors of the bankrupt firm receive only a fraction of the amounts owed them even if the firm ultimately emerges from bankruptcy proceedings as a reorganized entity. Swap market participants faced the risk that the Bankruptcy Courts might enforce the automatic stay against swap agreements, making the netting provisions of the ISDA master swap agreement unenforceable. Nondefaulting counterparties would then face the risk that a bankruptcy trustee might selectively default only on swaps having a negative value to a bankrupt counterparty, a practice known as "cherry picking."

Public Law 101–311, enacted on June 25, 1990, amended the Bankruptcy Code to exempt swap agreements executed under a single master agreement such as the ISDA master agreement from the automatic stay normally applicable to creditors of a bankrupt firm. The amendments were enacted to make the netting provisions of the ISDA master swap agreement enforceable in the event of bankruptcy. The Bankruptcy Code amendments also authorize nondefaulting swap counterparties to utilize any collateral posted in connection with a swap agreement to offset the net amount owed by a bankrupt counterparty (Rogers 1990). In this respect, the law treats OTC derivatives analogously to exchange-traded futures contracts.[8] These provisions greatly mitigate the potential loss faced by swap counterparties when the parties involved have multiple agreements with one another.

The status of swap agreements under banking law
Commercial banks and thrift institutions are not subject to the provisions of the Bankruptcy Code. Instead, bank failure resolution is governed by federal and state

banking laws, which gives the Federal Deposit Insurance Corporation (FDIC) and the Resolution Trust Corporation (RTC) (in the case of certain savings and loan institutions) considerable discretion in dealing with failing federally insured depository institutions. The FDIC and RTC may act in the capacity of either a conservator or a receiver. An institution placed in conservatorship is not declared legally insolvent. It continues its normal business operations under the close scrutiny of federal regulators pending resolution of its financial difficulties. Institutions in conservatorship are either returned to private sector control, through a sale or merger, or they are eventually declared insolvent. When a federally insured depository institution is declared legally insolvent either the FDIC or RTC becomes the receiver for the institution. Regulators may resolve bank failures either through a "purchase and assumption" transaction in which the failed institution is taken over by another bank or thrift or, less often, through liquidation.[9]

The Financial Institutions Reform, Recovery, and Enforcement Act of 1989 (FIRREA) contains provisions similar to the netting provisions of the Bankruptcy Code requiring the receiver of a failed bank or conservator of a failing bank to treat all supplemental swap agreements executed under a single master agreement as a single contract. In the event of a default or liquidation of a bank or thrift, the institution's counterparties maintain the right to accelerate repayment of all swap agreements made under a single master agreement. Counterparties do not have an automatic right to terminate existing swap agreements when an institution is placed into conservatorship, however, because an institution in conservatorship has not legally failed (although they do retain the right to demand accelerated repayment in the event of a default or breach of another covenant). FIRREA gives bank regulators the express right to transfer all derivative instruments covered by a single master agreement, along with other bank assets, to another institution, either when the institution is in conservatorship or in the case of a purchase and assumption transaction. But in this latter case the master agreement and all its supplements must be treated as a single agreement and transferred together with all applicable collateral. Thus, the law discourages federal regulators from cherry picking among individual OTC agreements that are part of a larger master agreement.[10] Nondefaulting counterparties still face the risk that their agreements might be assigned to a counterparty with a relatively weak credit standing, however.

Although recent legislation has reduced the legal risks faced by domestic counterparties, derivatives dealers with exposures to counterparties outside of the United States still face risks arising from the uncertain legal status of netting arrangements under foreign laws. At present, ISDA is working with authorities in other countries to enact bankruptcy legislation resembling the recent Bankruptcy Code amendments enacted in the United States. Until such legislation is enacted, however, internationally active OTC derivatives dealers face considerable legal risk.

Aggregation or interconnection risk

Aggregation or interconnection risk refers to the risk that a disruption in one market, caused by the default of a major institution or some other event, might cause widespread difficulties throughout the OTC derivatives market or even spread to other financial markets. Market liquidity risk is one source of interconnection risk. OTC derivatives dealers operate in many different markets at once. They must often execute complex, multi-legged transactions to create custom-tailored instruments for their customers while attempting to hedge the resulting exposure to market risk. The successful execution of such operations depends on the ability to complete a number of transactions in different markets almost simultaneously. But experience shows that market liquidity can evaporate quickly, especially in times of financial stress when market participants have reason to question the creditworthiness of potential counterparties. Reduced liquidity can make it difficult for a dealer to hedge its exposure to market price risk or, in the event of a default by a counterparty, make obtaining a replacement swap a costly proposition.

Counterparty credit risk can also be a source of aggregation risk because such a large fraction of trading in OTC derivatives takes place between the dealers themselves. The default of a single major dealer could have a significant effect on the outstanding positions of other major dealers. In addition to potential losses from credit risk exposures, a default by a major derivatives dealer would leave other dealers exposed to considerable price risk. Dealers use derivatives both to hedge their outstanding commitments to other OTC counterparties as well as other asset holdings. These dealers would need to rebalance their portfolios, either by buying or selling new derivative instruments or by quickly selling existing asset holdings. The resulting flurry of activity might conceivably disrupt not only the OTC derivatives market, but other markets as well.

To date, losses incurred by counterparties to OTC derivatives have yet to even approach the magnitude of losses incurred in the course of more traditional lending and investment activities. Worth noting in this regard is that financial markets have survived at least one default by a major derivatives dealer – that of Drexel Burnham Lambert in 1990 – without serious disruption, although it has certainly provided headaches for Drexel's former counterparties. Recent legislation recognizing netting arrangements was designed to help contain the consequences of a default by a major derivatives dealer in the United States, although, as noted earlier, other countries have been slow to enact such legislation.

Market arrangements for controlling risks

Managing the credit risk associated with a position in an instrument such as an interest rate swap requires credit evaluation skills of the type commonly associated with bank lending. Thus, as the swaps market evolved into a dealer market where financial intermediaries assumed the role of counterparty to the end users of swap agreements, commercial banks, which have traditionally specialized in credit risk evaluation and have the capital reserves necessary to support credit risk management, came to dominate the market for swaps and other OTC derivatives. Only in cases where a counterparty is deemed a poor credit risk are performance bonds, such as margin requirements of the type employed by futures exchanges, used to substitute for credit evaluation. When performance bonds are used, the agreement often provides for the periodic settlement of changes in the value of a derivative instrument using a process resembling the daily marking-to-market of futures contracts, although settlement generally takes place at less frequent intervals with OTC derivatives (Smith, Smithson, and Wakeman 1986).

The widely publicized financial difficulties of many firms and banks in recent years has made market participants sensitive to the issue of counterparty credit risk.

As a result, dealers with less than AA credit ratings have found it increasingly difficult to trade in OTC derivatives. The heavy loan losses and resulting financial difficulty experienced by many commercial banks in recent years has hampered the ability of such institutions to compete in this market. At the same time, a number of investment banks have formed separately capitalized subsidiaries so as to enhance their credit standing and remain competitive in the derivative market.[11] Thus, market discipline has had the salutary effect of restricting the activities of less creditworthy counterparties.

7. Concluding Comments

The evolution of the over-the-counter derivatives market has revolutionized the nature of financial intermediation in money markets in a span covering a little more than a decade. Along with the benefits derivatives offer firms in managing cash flows, however, the rapid growth of the market has raised new concerns for regulators and policymakers. Industry spokesmen argue that existing market arrangements are adequate to address such concerns, a view increasingly shared by regulators and policymakers.[12] The development of the ISDA master agreement in recent years, along with recent changes in banking laws and in the U.S. Bankruptcy Code, has gone far to minimize the potential for widespread market disruption that could result from a default on the part of a major dealer in the swaps market. And concerns about counterparty credit risk have led market participants themselves to limit the activities of dealers with less than outstanding credit ratings.

Notes

The author benefited from conversations with the following individuals: Keith Amburgey of the International Swap Dealers Association, Inc., Albert Bashawaty of Morgan Guarantee Trust Company, Richard Cohen of Chase Manhattan Bank, N. A., Steen Parsholt of Citibank, N. A., David E. Schwartz and Robert J. Schwartz of Mitsubishi Capital Market Services, Inc., and Robert M. Spielman of Chase Manhattan Bank. Timothy Cook, Bob LaRoche, John Walter, and John Weinberg read earlier drafts of this article and made many helpful editorial suggestions. Any remaining errors or omissions are the sole responsibility of the author. Opinions expressed herein are those of the author and do not necessarily reflect those of the Federal Reserve Bank of Richmond or the Federal Reserve System.

1. See Wall and Pringle (1988) for a more comprehensive survey of market participants.
2. One difference between the payoff to an FRA and the payoff to an in-the-money cap is that an FRA pays the present value of the change in interest payable on the notional principal at settlement (which corresponds to the reset date of a cap), while payments on caps are deferred. The value of the payment has the same present value in both cases, however, so that the comparison between the payoff to a cap and a call option on an FRA remains accurate.
3. A European option can be exercised only on its expiration date. Similarly, a cap buyer can only "exercise" his option if the index rate is above the cap rate on the interest rate reset date, so that the interest rate reset date corresponds to the expiration date on a European-style option.
4. See Abken (1991a, reprinted as chapter 4 of this volume) for a description of these other markets.

5. Rogers (1990) discusses capital requirements for OTC derivatives.
6. For example, see Corrigan (1992), Bank for International Settlements (1992), and Hansell and Muehring (1992).
7. Data in ISDA's *Market Survey Highlights*, Second Half 1991, indicates that 47 percent of all new interest rate swaps arranged in 1991 were between ISDA member organizations.
8. Williams (1986) stresses the importance of the exemption of futures margin requirements from the automatic stay as a prime reason for the existence of futures markets.
9. Dotsey and Kuprianov (1990) describe bank failure resolution policies in more detail.
10. See Gooch and Pergam (1990) and Rogers (1990) for more details on banking law and netting arrangements.
11. Federal regulators have yet to grant commercial banks approval to form separately capitalized subsidiaries of the type investment banks have begun to use. See Chew (1992, 1993) and Peltz (1993) for a more detailed discussion of this trend.
12. For example, see Hansell and Muehring (1992), Phillips (1992), and Shale (1993).

References

Abken, Peter A. "Globalization of Stock, Futures, and Options Markets," Federal Reserve Bank of Atlanta *Economic Review*, vol. 76 (July/August 1991), pp. 1–22.

——. "Beyond Plain Vanilla: A Taxonomy of Swaps," Federal Reserve Bank of Atlanta *Economic Review*, vol. 76 (March/April 1991), pp. 12–29.

——. "Interest-Rate Caps. Collars, and Floors," Federal Reserve Bank of Atlanta *Economic Review*, vol. 74 (November/December 1989), pp. 2–24.

Bank for International Settlements. *Recent Developments in International Interbank Relations*. Basle, Switzerland: Bank for International Settlements, 1992.

Beckstrom, Rod A. "Fundamental Models for Pricing Swaps," in Robert J. Schwartz and Clifford W. Smith, Jr., eds., *The Handbook of Currency and Interest Rate Risk Management*. New York: New York Institute of Finance, 1990.

Board of Governors of the Federal Reserve System, Federal Deposit Insurance Corporation, and Office of Comptroller of the Currency. "Derivative Product Activities of Commercial Banks," Joint study conducted in response to questions posed by Senator Riegle on derivative products. January 27, 1993.

Brown, Keith C., and Donald J. Smith. "Plain Vanilla Swaps: Market Structures, Applications, and Credit Risk," in Carl R. Beidleman, ed., *Interest Rate Swaps*. Homewood, Ill.: Business One Irwin, 1990.

Burghardt, Galen, Belton, Lane, Luce, and McVey. *Eurodollar Futures and Options*. Chicago: Probus Publishing Company, 1991.

Chew, Lillian. "Judgement of Salomon," *Risk*, vol. 6 (March 1993), pp. 8–9.

——. "Kings of the Road," *Risk*, vol. 5 (September 1992), p. 94–98.

Corrigan, E. Gerald. "Painful Period Has Set Stage for Banking Rebound," *American Banker*, February 3, 1992, pp. 12–13.

Dattatreya, Ravi E. 'Interest Rate Swaps," *The 1992 Dictionary of Derivatives*, pp. 31–35. Supplement to the June 1992 issue of *Euromoney*. London: Euromoney Publications PLC, 1992.

Dotsey, Michael, and Anatoli Kuprianov. "Reforming Deposit Insurance: Lessons from the Savings and Loan Crisis," Federal Reserve Bank of Richmond *Economic Review*, vol. 76 (March/April 1990), pp. 3–28.

Gooch, Anthony C., and Albert S. Pergam. 'United States and New York Law," in Robert J. Schwartz and Clifford W. Smith, Jr., eds., *The Handbook of Currency and Interest Rate Risk Management*. New York: New York Institute of Finance, 1990.

Grabbe, J. Orlin, *International Financial Markets*, 2d ed. New York: Elsevier, 1991.

Hansell, Saul, and Kevin Muehring. "Why Derivatives Rattle the Regulators," *Institutional Investor*, September 1992, pp. 49–62.

Iben, Benjamin. "Interest Rate Swap Valuation," in Carl R. Beidleman, ed., *Interest Rate Swaps*. Homewood, Ill.: Business One Irwin, 1990.

Kahle, Jeff. "Caps and Floors," *The 1992 Dictionary of Derivatives*, pp. 6–8. Supplement to the June 1992 issue of *Euromoney*. London: Euromoney Publications PLC, 1992.

Macfarlane, John, Daniel R. Ross, and Janet Showers. 'The Interest Rate Swap Market: Yield Mathematics, Terminology, and Conventions," in Carl R. Beidleman, ed., *Interest Rate Swaps*. Homewood, Ill.: Business One Irwin, 1990.

Norfield, Anthony. "Forward Rate Agreements," *The 1992 Dictionary of Derivatives*, pp. 25–27. Supplement to the June 1992 issue of *Euromoney*. London: Euromoney Publications PLC, 1992.

Peltz, Michael. "Wall Street's Triple-A for Effort," *Institutional Investor*, vol. 27 (May 1993), pp. 89–92.

Phillips, Susan M. "Challenges Posed by OTC Derivative." Remarks of Susan M. Phillips, Member, Board of Governors of the Federal Reserve System, at the Tenth Annual Meeting of the National Futures and Options Society, December 3, 1992.

Rogers, William P., Jr. "Regulation of Swaps in the United States," in Robert J. Schwartz and Clifford W. Smith, Jr., eds., *The Handbook of Currency and Interest Rate Risk Management*. New York: New York Institute of Finance, 1990.

Shale, Tony. "How ISDA Got the Message," *Risk*, vol. 6 (April 1993), pp. 7–8.

Simons, Katerina. "Measuring Credit Risk in Interest Rate Swaps," Federal Reserve Bank of Boston *New England Economic Review*, November/December 1989, pp. 29–38.

Smith, Clifford W., Jr., and Charles W. Smithson. "Financial Engineering: An Overview," in Clifford W. Smith Jr. and Charles W. Smithson, eds., *The Handbook of Financial Engineering*. New York: Harper Business, 1990.

——, and Lee Macdonald Wakeman. "The Market for Interest Rate Swaps," *Financial Management*, vol. 17 (1988), pp. 34–44.

——. "The Evolving Market for Swaps," *Midland Corporate Finance Journal*, vol. 3 (Winter 1986), pp. 20–32.

Smith, Clifford W., Jr., Charles W. Smithson, and D. Sykes Wilford. "Managing Financial Risk," *Journal of Applied Corporate Finance*, vol. 1 (1989), pp. 27–48.

Wall, Larry D., and John J. Pringle. "Interest Rate Swaps: A Review of the Issues," Federal Reserve Bank of Atlanta *Economic Review*, vol. 73 (November/December 1988), pp. 22–37.

Williams, Jeffrey. *The Economic Function of Futures Markets*. Cambridge, England: Cambridge University Press, 1986.

SECTION D

Exotics

7

Path-dependent Options

William C. Hunter
and David W. Stowe

A relatively new class of options – the so-called path-dependent options – has become increasingly popular in recent years. Like other options, these contracts give their owners the right – but not the obligation – to buy or sell a specific quantity of an underlying asset (stock, bond, futures contract, commodity, and so forth) at a specified price, called the strike or exercise price, during a specific time period.

Since 1982 the use of path-dependent options has grown dramatically. A path-dependent option has a payout directly related to movements in the price of the underlying asset during the option's life. In principle, these options take many forms and can be contingent on virtually any statistic of the underlying asset's price path – for example, the high price, the low price, or the average price over some time period. Today path-dependent options are available on a host of assets including common stock, interest rate products, precious metals, commodities, foreign currencies, and stock indexes; they are often used with convertible securities issues and in merger transactions and have recently begun trading on two major exchanges.[1]

In many cases these options allow investors to limit their potential losses (and gains) and thus have a type of built-in insurance feature. They also allow investors with specialized knowledge about asset price volatility to exploit this information better in their investing and hedging activities. While factors such as cost or risk mean that path-dependent options will not satisfy every investor's needs, these options have generated interest by filling several voids or niches in derivative securities markets.

The sections that follow introduce the notion of path dependency, review the modern origins of path-dependent options, and give several examples of reasons that investors and institutions find these options attractive. The discussion also describes some essential features of three types of path-dependent options – the lookback option, the barrier option, and the average-rate or Asian option. A forthcoming article in this *Economic Review* will describe in detail the valuation and pricing of these options, illustrate how they are used by individual investors and firms, and discuss their advantages and disadvantages (risks) as investment vehicles.

The American Put Option

A call option conveys to its owner the right to buy the underlying asset while a put conveys the right to sell the underlying asset. An option that allows its owner to buy or sell the underlying asset (exercise the option) at any time during the life of the option is called an American option. An option allowing the owner to exercise his or her right only at the option's expiration or maturity date is called a European option.

The payoff on a European call or put option written on a share of common stock that pays no dividends depends only on the market price of the underlying common stock at maturity. That is, if T is the maturity date of the option, t is the current date, X is the exercise price, and S is the market price of the underlying common stock at time $T > t$, then the payoff or intrinsic value at T is equal to the larger of the quantities $(S - X)$ and zero for the call option and $(X - S)$ and zero for the put option. Using standard options notation, the payoff on the European call at time T is written as $max(S - X, 0)$ while the payoff on the European put at time T is equal to $max(X - S, 0)$. Payoff at time T, $(T > t)$, on the European call or put option on a stock that pays no dividends is independent of the particular path taken by the stock price during the period between the times t and T. Such standard European call and put options on a nondividend paying stock are the simplest examples of what are called path-independent options.

In contrast, an American put option written on a share of common stock has a path-dependent payoff structure. (This happens to be the case irrespective of whether the stock pays a dividend or not.) For example, looking forward from the perspective of date t, the payoff at time $T > t$ on the American put option depends not only on the price of the underlying stock at time T but also on the particular time path followed by the stock between times t and T.

An illustration will demonstrate the straightforward intuition behind the statement that the American put is an example of a path-dependent option. Assume that the underlying stock pays no dividend and that the put option is in the money – that is, the market price of the stock is less than the exercise price. The investor holding the put could exercise the option and receive an amount of cash equal to the exercise price minus the current price of the stock that he has just sold, $X - S$. In turn, this cash can be invested at the risk-free rate of interest to earn money during the remaining life of the option. At expiration the investor receives the amount $X - S$, his original investment, plus the interest earned over the remaining life of the option. An investor choosing not to exercise the put and waiting until expiration would receive only the amount $X - S$. It should be obvious that if the stock price is close enough to zero at the date the investor chooses to exercise early, he or she will be better off; the principal and interest received from investing the proceeds will exceed the difference between the exercise price and the stock price at the option's maturity date. In addition, the cases in which early exercise is optimal occur when the put is selling for $X - S$ so that selling it would be less profitable than exercising it and investing the proceeds. The key condition making early exercise preferable is that the stock price follows a path that drops close enough to zero over the life of the option to make the principal and interest earned by exercising the option greater than the exercise price minus the stock price at maturity. Thus, the payoff to the investor is seen as path dependent.

The Modern Origins of Path-dependent Options: The Lookback Option

For both standard options and securities, specific examples having characteristics similar to path-dependent options can probably be traced back at least to the early

1800s. However, the modern treatment of these securities – the rigorous valuation or pricing of these claims on the basis of dynamic hedging principles – is a more recent phenomenon, set in motion in 1979 with publication of an article by M. Barry Goldman, Howard Sosin, and Mary Ann Gatto. The authors had derived an explicit valuation formula for a hypothetical option epitomizing the age-old finance dictum of buy low (cheap) and sell high (dear) – the so-called lookback option. To allow buying low and selling high, the exercise price on the lookback option is set at the expiration of the contract instead of at contract origination (as it is for standard options). That is, at expiration the owner could "look back over the life of the option" and choose as the exercise price the most favorable price that had occurred.

If a lookback call option were exercised, the owner would be able to buy the underlying asset at the lowest price that occurred during the life of the option. Similarly, the owner of a lookback put would be able to sell the underlying asset at its highest price realized over the life of the option. It is clear that the payoff on a lookback option depends not only on the underlying asset's price on the expiration date of the option but also on the particular path followed by the price of the asset over the life of the option, hence the path dependency.

Countering the argument that their research was a purely hypothetical exercise in contingent claims valuation, Goldman, Sosin, and Gatto (1979) argued that lookback options could be of value to investors as speculative and hedging instruments and could survive as traded securities. In less than two-and-a-half years the authors were proven correct. On March 16, 1982, Macotta Metals Corporation of New York introduced and began trading lookback options on gold, silver, and platinum. The lookback call gave an investor the right to buy gold, silver, or platinum at its ex post realized low price, and the lookback put allowed the investor to sell the precious metal at its ex post realized high price.

Uses of Path-dependent Options

The choice of the particular price-path statistic on which a path-dependent option is based depends on the motivation of the option writer, ranging from wanting to control some particular risk to filling some niche in the market. Some specific examples illustrate this point.

On April 22, 1982, Manufacturers Hanover Corporation sold a $100 million note offering. The sale required holders to convert the securities at maturity in 1992 into shares of the company's common stock. The conversion price would be the lower of $55.55 and the average closing price of the common stock for the thirty-day period immediately preceding the notes' maturity. By making the conversion price dependent on the average price of the common stock, the company alleviated suspicions among investors that management would fraudulently manipulate the stock price upward just before the conversion date.[2]

The "capped" stock-index option is an example of an exchange-traded path-dependent option developed to fill a special niche or appeal to specific investors in the market. Capped stock-index options, fairly new examples of path-dependent options, are so named because they place ceilings on profitability. Because of these ceilings, capped options are cheaper than traditional stock-index options. Capped options were launched during the fall of 1991 on both the Chicago Board Options Exchange and the American Stock Exchange. Like other index options, they can be used to protect the values of stock portfolios by providing a cheaper way to obtain portfolio insurance.

Capped options trade off the Standard and Poor's (S&P) 100 and 500 Indexes on the CBOE and the Major Market and Institutional Indexes on the Amex. Like the standard call option, the value of a capped call option increases if its underlying index goes up, and a capped put option's value increases if the index declines. If the underlying index fails to attain the level specified by the option contract, known as the strike price, the options expire worthless and the sellers keep all of the premiums they collected. On the other hand, if the indexes reach the strike price, sellers must pay the optionholders the difference between the index level and the strike price but no more than a fixed cap value.

Each of these options has a cap price. For the options currently trading on the CBOE the cap price is set thirty points above the strike price for a call and thirty points below the strike price for a put, giving the options a cap value of $3,000 (thirty points times $100 per point). For those trading on the Amex the cap price is set at twenty points above and below the strike price, yielding a cap value of $2,000 (20 points times $100 per point). The purpose of the cap price is to force automatic exercise of the options. If the underlying index closes at or above the cap price for a call option or at or below the cap price for the put option, the options are automatically exercised and the cap buyers are paid the cap value two days after exercise.

The following scenario illustrates the mechanics of the capped option. An investor believes that the stock market will rally modestly from its closing value of 378 for the S&P 500 index on, say, January 12, 1992, and the third Friday in March 1992, the expiration date for the cap. The strike or exercise price on capped calls is 390, making the cap price 420 (390 plus the thirty points for the S&P 500 index). If the index closes at or above 420 between January 12 and the third Friday in March 1992, the capped call purchaser will be paid $3,000 (the net profit would be less by the amount of the premium). If the index closes at a figure less than 420 but greater than the strike price of 390 – for example, 400 – the purchaser will be paid an amount equal to the value of the index minus the strike price, in this case ten points times $100 per point or $1,000. On the other hand, if the index fails to reach the strike price of 390, the option expires worthless and the seller keeps the entire premium collected.

As is true for other exchange-traded options, the owners of capped options can sell them in the open market before maturity. Clearly, the payoff on the capped option depends on the particular path the underlying index follows over the life of the option; the option is path dependent. One appealing characteristic of the capped put or call option is that the seller's or writer's risk is limited to the cap amount or value while theoretically there is no limit to the risk faced by the writer or seller of a standard stock-index or -equity option. This feature of capped options, which is essentially a kind of built-in insurance, should make investors more willing to write options on the indexes offering them.

Other Popular Path-dependent Options

The average-rate option and the barrier option are two other frequently used path-dependent options that are growing in popularity. Both are currently used most extensively in the foreign exchange markets. However, their structure is such that their use will most likely increase in domestic markets in the future. The capped option discussed above exhibits some of the essential features of a barrier option.

Barrier options

Simply stated, a barrier option is a path-dependent option that is either canceled, activated, or exercised if the underlying instrument (the stock index in the case of a capped index option) reaches a certain level, regardless of the point at which the underlying asset is trading at maturity. Barrier options, also known as knock-out, knock-in, or trigger options, are typically straight European options until or from the time the underlying instrument reaches the barrier price.

There are four popular types of barrier options: up-and-out, up-and-in, down-and-out, and down-and-in. With the up-and-out barrier, the option is canceled should the underlying instrument rise above a certain level. The up-and-in option, on the other hand, is worthless unless the underlying instrument rises above a certain level or price, at which point it becomes a normal put option. Down-and-out options are canceled if the underlying instrument falls below a certain price. Down-and-ins are activated only when the underlying instrument's price falls to a certain level.

Because of these extinguishing or activating features, barrier options are cheaper than ordinary European options and are thus attractive to investors who are averse to paying large premiums. In addition, as illustrated in the case of the capped option, the sellers or writers of barrier options may be able to limit their downside risk.

Average-rate options

Average-rate or Asian options are path-dependent options, European in structure, for which the strike price is based on the average (geometric or arithmetic) price of the underlying instrument over a specified period of time, so the actual strike price is not determined until the exercise date on the contract. For foreign exchange average-rate options, the actual practice is for the average to be taken from the option's start date to a preagreed setting date. For example, suppose that a U.S. exporter buys an average-rate floating-strike call option to purchase a foreign currency for U.S. dollars at the average exchange rate over some given period, with the option expiring at the end of the period. If the average exchange rate over the period is less than the spot exchange rate at the time payment is due to the foreign importer, the exporter would profit more from exercising the option than transacting at the spot exchange rate. On the other hand, if the period's average exchange rate exceeds the spot rate, the exporter is better off converting dollars at the current spot exchange rate, in which case the option expires worthless. This example also shows that it is possible to use average rate options to hedge or limit the uncertainty associated with regular foreign cash inflows and outflows as a result of volatile exchange rates.

Many multinational corporations use average-rate put options on foreign currencies to hedge their estimated monthly foreign exchange income in an effort to achieve some budgeted average exchange rate for the year. Hence, the design of this particular option is of great value to these corporations that are in the market on a regular basis. Current accounting principles provide for foreign currency transactions to be translated at either the spot rate at the time of the transaction or the spot rate for the date of the firm's balance sheet. Any variations can be flowed through into the firm's income. For a path-dependent put, the option can be exercised if the balance-sheet rate is less than the strike (average) rate, resulting in the appearance of additional income. This additional income is calculated by multiplying the nominal amount by the difference between the strike rate and the spot rate and subtracting from this figure the amount of premium paid.

Large multinational commercial banks offer average-rate currency options to their multinational customers because these companies' usual spot dealings leave them with an average exchange rate on their books. By selling path-dependent average-rate currency options, the banks offset the average-rate foreign exchange risk exposure on their books. The premiums banks receive enhance yield by reducing their funding costs or by lowering their average exchange rate. In addition, these banks stand to earn management fees and commissions in other areas as a result of these activities, so it is worth the risk they take. Because average-rate options have lower volatility than standard European options, they are cheaper to purchase.

Valuation of Path-dependent Options

This section attempts to offer some insights into the valuation of two path-dependent options – the lookback and the average-rate option.

Valuing the lookback option

As is the case for most options, the key condition required to price the lookback option in the modern tradition is that it must be possible to hedge its risk. That is, it must be shown that the cashflow obligation(s) of the writer of a lookback call option can be exactly met by the payoff from another portfolio (a hedge portfolio). Indeed, Goldman, Sosin, and Gatto (1979) showed that such a hedge portfolio could be constructed so that the lookback option can be valued without regard to the risk premium in the underlying asset's expected return. These authors showed that when the risk-free interest rate was equal to exactly one-half the underlying asset's variance, the lookback call option is identical to the purchase of a straddle (a portfolio of puts and calls on the same assets at the same strike price) on the asset. Therefore, the writers of lookback calls can simply hedge their obligation by purchasing a straddle on the same underlying asset. Because the lookback option can be hedged, it can be valued using the risk-neutral pricing technology associated with the Black-Scholes (1973) paradigm.

Valuing an average-rate (Asian) option

There are two types of average-rate or Asian options: the fixed-strike and floating-strike options. The payoff on a floating-strike Asian call option at expiration is equal to the greater of either zero or the difference between the underlying asset's terminal spot price and the average value of the asset over the life of the option – that is, $max(S - Avg_s, 0)$. It is comparable to a lookback call option for which the strike price is the average value of the underlying asset as opposed to its minimum value. Because mathematical complexities have prevented development of a closed-form analytic model (such as the Black-Scholes equation) to price such an instrument, these options must be valued with a numerical approximation technique such as Monte Carlo analysis.[3]

The value of an Asian option can never be greater than the value of a regular lookback call option, for which the strike price is the achieved minimum of the asset. Thus, the price of a regular lookback option sets an upper boundary on the average-rate option's value (because the minimum value is an extreme and the average is never equal to an extreme value unless all of the values are equal).

For fixed-strike options, the second type of average-rate option, the terminal payoff is the maximum of either zero or the difference between the average value of the underlying asset and a fixed strike price – $max(Avg_s - X, 0)$. The average can be computed using either the geometric average or the arithmetic average. Again, because of mathematical complexities no closed-form equation has been developed for pricing the average-rate option written on the arithmetic average.

Under the standard risk-neutral (Black-Scholes) pricing approach, it is assumed that the natural logarithm of stock price returns are normally distributed. In valuing an Asian option written on the geometric average of an asset's value over time, this standard assumption still holds because the product of the logarithm of stock price returns is normally distributed, and this option can be valued in closed form using the Black-Scholes approach. However, the assumption breaks down for an Asian option written on the arithmetic average because the sum of the logarithm of the stock price returns over time is no longer normally distributed. As a result, it is necessary to employ other valuation techniques for an average-rate option written on the arithmetic average of the underlying asset's price.[4]

Conclusion

It should be clear from this overview of path-dependent options that risk management is not a static field. New products and financial instruments are continuously being developed to meet new needs. While many risks can be managed with traditional hedging instruments such as standard options, futures contracts, and swaps, the rapid development of exotic options like the path-dependent options suggests that the market for innovative risk-management products is in no way saturated. The demand for these new instruments is likely to continue growing as long as risk-management techniques using traditional hedging vehicles require close monitoring, involve fairly high commissions or management costs, and fail to reduce risks in the way desired.

The development of path-dependent options is, however, only one response to the demand for innovative risk-management instruments. In addition, because these instruments build on existing standardized derivative products, they may not serve the needs of every investor or institution. Their future development is likely to tend toward greater customizing for specific situations.

It is well known that a portfolio of existing standard products can replicate the payoffs on most of the new derivative products such as those discussed here. Indeed, this very fact allows creation of risk-free hedge portfolios for these contracts and also makes it possible to price them using the familiar risk-neutral pricing technology. However, the management and effort required for existing products to duplicate the payoff from the newer contracts tend to be too expensive an alternative for individual investors. Thus, the financial services firms that produce these new contracts add value to the market. These products have made a place for themselves because they are tailored to meet specific risk-management and investment needs.

Notes

1. The Chicago Board Options Exchange (CBOE) and the American Stock Exchange (AMEX) both trade path-dependent options know as "capped options." These options are described in detail below.
2. Such suspicions on the part of investors were not totally unwarranted. In a separate case, two Merrill Lynch vice presidents were fired for allegedly artificially driving up the price of options on a portfolio under their management on Christmas eve of 1981 in an attempt to maximize their bonus, which was tied to the portfolio's December 24, 1981, closing value (*Wall Street Journal*, January 21, 1982, 4). This example also points out the advantage of making this type of path-dependent option contingent on the average price of the underlying asset over some extended period rather than the closing price on some particular day, as the chances for artificial manipulation are greatly reduced. The growing popularity of tying conversion prices or ratios to time averages of prices in mergers seems to reflect similar concerns.
3. Monte Carlo simulating is a numerical approximation technique that can be used to compute option values by simulating the path taken by the price of the asset underlying the option over time. By simulating numerous such price paths, the technique allows one to compute the expected value or price of the option with increasing precision as the number of iterations or runs of the simulation are increased. This technique is described in detail in the forthcoming *Review* article examining the valuation of path-dependent options.
4. A more thorough discussion of the valuation or pricing of the lookback and the average-rate options, including a brief tutorial on the basic tenets of option pricing using the modern risk-neutral pricing technology pioneered by Black and Scholes (1973), will appear in the forthcoming *Review* article referred to above. The article explains how Monte Carlo analysis can be used to price Asian options written on the arithmetic average as well as how these options can be used to hedge foreign exchange risks from the viewpoint of individual investors and multinational corporations. The reader interested in the basics of option pricing is referred to Hull (1990) and Kolb (1991).

References

Black, Fischer, and Myron Scholes. "The Pricing of Options and Corporate Liabilities." *Journal of Political Economy* 81 (May/June 1973): 637–59.

Goldman, M. Barry, Howard Sosin, and Mary Ann Gatto. "Path-Dependent Options: Buy at the Low, Sell at the High." *Journal of Finance* 34 (December 1979): 1111–27.

Hull, John. *Options, Futures, and Other Derivative Securities.* Englewood Cliffs, N.J.: Prentice-Hall, Inc., 1989.

Hunter, William C., and David W. Stowe. "Path-Dependent Options: Valuation and Applications." Federal Reserve Bank of Atlanta *Economic Review* (forthcoming 1992).

Kolb, Robert W. *Options: An Introduction.* Miami: Kolb Publishing Company, 1991.

8

Path-dependent Options: Valuation and Applications

William C. Hunter
and David W. Stowe

Path-dependent options, unlike most claims whose value depends on the behavior of some other assets, are contracts entitling their holders to a cash flow that depends on the price path taken by the asset (stock, bond, commodity, and the like) underlying the contract. A relatively new class of options, their popularity has grown dramatically over the last decade, since they were first traded in 1982. That year, the trading of lookback options – so-named because at expiration the owner can "look back" over the life of the option and choose to buy or sell the underlying asset at the most favorable price that had occurred – demonstrated the value for investors of such path-dependent options as speculative and hedging instruments and proved their viability as traded securities.[1]

Standard European call and put options (giving the right to buy or sell, respectively, an underlying asset only on a particular expiration date) written on shares of common stock that pay no dividends have what are termed path-independent payoff structures. That is, their payoff is not influenced by the changes in market price of the underlying common stock between the date the option is written and its maturity date. In contrast, the payoff structures of path-dependent options are directly related to the price path followed by the option's underlying asset over the life of the option. For example, a standard American put option (one that allows its owner to sell the underlying asset [exercise the option] at any time during the life of the option) written on a common stock has a path-dependent payoff structure.

Such path-dependent options have generated interest by filling several niches in derivative securities markets. Investors find them attractive because their design matches that of some financial contracts, giving them a kind of built-in insurance feature that makes it possible to limit potential losses and gains, and because they allow investors to better use their knowledge of asset price volatility in investing and hedging. Although path-dependent options do offer certain benefits, factors such as design mismatches and cost or risk mean that they will not satisfy the needs of every investor. The discussion of their pricing that follows will consider in greater depth both the advantages and risks of using these instruments.

This article focuses on two popular kinds of path-dependent options – the lookback option described above and the average-rate or Asian option – and their valuation using hedge portfolio and risk-neutral pricing techniques. Used most extensively in the foreign exchange markets, the average-rate option is European in structure and has a strike price based on the geometric or arithmetic average of the price of its underlying instrument over a specific period. The essential characteristics of these two types of path-dependent options along with the history of their development and uses as investment vehicles are described in a complementary article in the March/April 1992 issue of this *Review*. In addition to describing some basic features of the pricing models used to value these options, the sections that follow illustrate how these pricing models are implemented in practice.

The discussion also includes a brief presentation of the basic tenets of option pricing using the modern risk-neutral pricing technology developed by John Cox and Stephen Ross (1976). In addition, it explains how Monte Carlo analysis can be used to price Asian options written on the arithmetic average as well as how these options can be used to hedge foreign exchange risks from the viewpoint of individual investors and multinational corporations.

Valuation of Path-dependent Options

Path-dependent options, like most contingent claims (that is, those whose value is tied to some other asset's behavior), can be priced using the hedge portfolio valuation methodology developed by Black and Scholes (1973) mentioned above. In simple terms, this approach implies that the cash flow obligation(s) involved in, for example, a lookback call option can be exactly met by the payoff from another portfolio – a hedge or replicating portfolio. More technically, if stocks and bonds can be used to construct a portfolio investment strategy that would provide the same cash flows as the contingent claim at the same points in time, then at any point throughout the lifetime of the contingent claim the claim's price must equal the value of the stock-bond portfolio at that time. This stock-bond portfolio hedge strategy forms the basis of the risk-neutral valuation methodology. The fundamentals of this methodology are presented in Box 1. More thorough discussions of option pricing fundamentals can be found in John Hull (1989) and Robert W. Kolb (1991). (Readers might also find helpful the standard options pricing notation collected in Box 2.)

The following discussion examines the valuation or pricing of lookback and average-rate or Asian options.

Valuing a lookback call option

The lookback option is often referred to as a "minimize regret" option because it gives the purchaser the right to buy an asset at its lowest price or sell it at its highest price attained over the option's life. On a more sophisticated level, because its value is determined by the high or low price of the underlying asset over the life of the contract, the lookback option has the advantage of allowing investors to better use their knowledge about an underlying asset's price volatility. As noted earlier, the key to pricing this instrument in the Black-Scholes framework is that the lookback option must be hedgeable.

In their 1979 article, M. Barry Goldman, Howard B. Sosin, and Mary Ann Gatto developed a model to value the lookback option using the Black-Scholes option pricing methodology and showed that a hedge portfolio could be constructed, allowing the lookback option to be valued without regard to the risk premium in

Box 1

Valuing standard European call options

Like many analytical models in finance, the basic model for pricing a standard European call option written on a share of common stock – the Black-Scholes option pricing model (named after its developers, Fischer Black and Myron Scholes 1973) – is based on a set of assumptions which, though abstract, work to simplify the valuation process. That is, it is assumed that

- there are no transactions costs, taxes, or riskless arbitrage opportunities;
- the asset underlying the option does not pay dividends;
- stock prices follow a continuous time stochastic process;
- short selling with full use of proceeds is permitted; and
- the risk-free interest rate, r, is constant and the same for all maturities.

At the time a call option on a stock expires, its worth is the greater of either the difference between the stock price at that time and the option's exercise price or zero, represented as $max(S^* - X, 0)$. Without this condition a riskless arbitrage opportunity would arise. To price the option today when there is time remaining before expiration, $T - t > 0$, the option's terminal price has to be approximated and the present value of this price computed using an appropriate discount rate.

The movements of stock prices over time can be modeled as following a random or stochastic process called geometric Brownian motion, which means that the stock price returns, which are defined as the natural logarithm of the ratio of successive stock prices, $ln(S/S_{t-1})$, are lognormally distributed. This model of stock price movement can be generalized to a continuous-time Markov process known as an Ito process. In simple terms, a Markov process is a stochastic process in which the observed value of the stock price (state variable) tomorrow depends only on its observed value today. The Ito process is characterized by a smooth predictable

component – for example, the expected rate of return on the stock – and a highly erratic component that adds uncertainty or noise to the stock price movement. (See Box 3 for further discussion.)

Given the properties of a log-normal distribution, the expected stock value at the option's expiration date, S^*, can be determined using the following equation:

$$E(S^*) = Se^{(\mu-\sigma^2/2)(T-t)}. \qquad (B1)$$

That is, the stock price is expected to rise continuously from today, t, until time period T, by its instantaneous continuously compounded expected rate of return μ, less one-half the stock's variance. The term σ represents the standard deviation of expected returns, and the term $(\mu - \sigma^2/2)$ is called the drift rate of the stock price process.

A key aspect of the Black-Scholes model, however, is that one does not have to be concerned with the risk-adjusted expected return on a stock, μ. It has been shown that if an investor held a portfolio containing a long position in a proportionate share of a stock, ΔS, and a short position in one call option on the stock, $-C$, then the investor would be perfectly hedged, with the portfolio generating a riskless rate of return. Perfectly hedged, the portfolio is equivalent to investing in a risk-free bond, B. This portfolio is given by

$$B = \Delta S - C. \qquad (B2)$$

As is true for a risk-free bond, arbitrage will force the hedge portfolio to earn the riskless rate of return (Cox and Ross 1976). Therefore, an option's value will not be affected by a particular stock's expected rate of return, μ, since it can be replaced with the riskless interest rate, r, using the Cox-Ross risk-neutral valuation framework.

If a call option at the time of expiration has a payoff of $max(S^* - X, 0)$, the call option's value today is the present value of this expected payoff at expiration. That is,

$$c = e^{-r(T-t)}E[max(S* - X, 0)], \qquad (B3)$$

where the term $e^{-r(T-t)}$ represents continuous discounting of the terminal payoff. The call value can also be derived using equation (B2) since the payoff from investing in a call option can be replicated by purchasing a proportionate share of stock, ΔS, and borrowing at the risk-free rate, that is, short selling a Treasury security. Thus,

$$c = \Delta S - B. \qquad (B4)$$

Black and Scholes derived an equation that essentially consolidates all of the steps required to compute the discounted value of a call option's expected payoff at expiration. This equation can be written as follows (see Robert Jarrow and Andrew Rudd 1983):

$$c = e^{-r(T-t)}E(S* \mid S* > X) \qquad (B5)$$
$$prob(S* > X)e^{-r(T-t)}Xprob(S* > X).$$

The first term in equation (B5), $e^{-r(T-t)}E(S* \mid S* > X)$, represents the present value of the expected stock price at the time of the option's expiration, given that $S*$ is greater than the exercise price. The second term, $prob(S* > X)$, represents the probability that the stock price will be greater than the exercise price at expiration. The third term, $e^{-r(T-t)}Xprob(S* > X)$, is the present value of the exercise price times the probability that the stock price will be greater than the exercise price at expiration. In short, the call option is worth the value of receiving the stock at expiration, conditional on the stock price being higher than the exercise price, minus the present value of paying the exercise price, conditional on exercising the option.

The general Black-Scholes model for computing an option's value over a longer period of time can be written in the following, more convenient closed form:

$$c = SN(d_1) - e^{-r(T-t)}XN(d_2), \qquad (B6)$$

where

$$d_1 = [ln(S/X) + (r + \sigma^2/2)$$
$$(T - t)/\sigma\sqrt{(T - t)}, \qquad (B7)$$

$$d_2 = d_1 - \sigma\sqrt{(T - t)}. \qquad (B8)$$

In short, this model gives the discounted expected value of a call option at expiration. In this model, $N(d_1)$ is the cumulative standard normal distribution function giving the probability that a random variable would be less than or equal to the value d_1. It reflects the uncertainty regarding the stock's value on the option's expiration date. Given a calculation of d_1, the value of $N(d_1)$ can be found in the tables in the back of most statistics textbooks or approximated numerically. Compared to equation (B5), the term $SN(d_1)$ in equation (B6) represents ΔS, or the proportionate share of stock, and the term $e^{-r(T-t)}XN(d_2)$ represents the remainder, $c - \Delta S$, or B.

The Black-Scholes formula shows that, to value a European call option, one needs to know only the current stock price, the exercise price, the time to expiration, the volatility of the stock's returns, and the risk-free interest rate. With the exception of the volatility parameter, all of these variables can be directly observed. The volatility parameter can be estimated from historical data.

Although the Black-Scholes model employs some restrictive and likely unrealistic assumptions, it has nevertheless been shown to be quite robust when the underlying assumptions are modified.

the underlying asset's expected return. As the example in Box 1 illustrates, the domestic risk-free interest rate, r, can be used in estimating the expected terminal stock price as well as to discount the option's terminal value to the present. Goldman, Sosin, and Gatto showed that when the risk-free interest rate is equal to exactly one-half the asset's volatility (as measured by variance), the lookback call option is identical to the purchase of a straddle (a portfolio of puts and calls on the same asset with the same strike price) on the asset. In this case, the writers of lookback

Box 2 ───

Guide to options pricing notation

S^*	Terminal price of underlying asset at the time the option expires, T.	σ	The volatility of a stock's return per annum – standard deviation. It is assumed to be known and constant.
S	Spot price today. For foreign currency options, S is the spot exchange rate, which is the price in U.S. dollars to buy one unit of a foreign currency today.	T	Expiration date of the option.
		t	Today.
		$T{-}t$	Time remaining until option expires expressed relative to 365 days.
L	For lookback options only, it is the achieved minimum of the underlying asset's price from the date of the option's inception until t.	e	The natural number 2.78.
		μ	The instantaneous expected return on the stock.
C	Call value at time of expiration.	ε	A random drawing from a standardized normal distribution with mean 0 and standard deviation of 1.
c	Call value today.		
r	Risk-free interest rate – for example, the three-month U.S. Treasury-bill yield. Assumed to be known and constant.	$E(S^*)$	Expected value of stock price at time of option's expiration in a risk-neutral world.
r_f	Foreign "risk-free" interest rate.	Δ	Delta; the change in the value of the call option given a \$1 change in the value of the stock.
δ	$r{-}r_f$, the interest rate differential.		
λ	$2\delta/\sigma^2$. For the strike bonus option (lookback option model), it is the "speed" parameter.	$N(\cdot)$	The cumulative standard normal distribution.

calls can simply hedge their obligation by purchasing a straddle on the same underlying asset.

The examples that follow employ a more general model developed by Mark B. Garman (1989) to illustrate the lookback option's essential features. The Garman model, while based on the work of Goldman, Sosin, and Gatto (1979), is simpler and offers additional insight into the option's valuation by separating it into two underlying options. Moreover, unlike the earlier model, it can be used to value a European option on a "dividendpaying" asset such as a foreign currency option.

The Garman (1989) model for valuing a European lookback call option on a foreign currency, presented in equation (3) below, is a combination of two separate model: a European call option (see Garman and Steven W. Kohlhagen 1983), given by equation (1), and what Garman refers to as a strike-bonus option, shown in equation (2).

$$c = Se^{-r_f(T-t)}N(d_1) - Xe^{-r(T-t)}N(d_2); \tag{1}$$

$$d_1 = \frac{ln\left(\dfrac{S}{X}\right) + \left(r - r_f + \dfrac{\sigma^2}{2}\right)(T - t)}{\sigma\sqrt{T - t}};$$

$$d_2 = d_1 - \sigma\sqrt{T - t}.$$

$$V_{sb} = \frac{S}{\lambda}\left[e^{-r(T-t)}\left(\frac{S}{L}\right)^{-\lambda} N(d_1) - \frac{1}{\lambda}e^{-r_f(T-t)}N(d_2) \right];$$ (2)

$$d_1 = \frac{-ln\left(\dfrac{S}{L}\right) - \left(\delta + \dfrac{\sigma^2}{2}\right)(T - t)}{\sigma\sqrt{(T - t)}} + 2\delta\frac{\sqrt{(T - t)}}{\sigma};$$

$$d_2 = d_1 - 2\delta\frac{\sqrt{(T - t)}}{\sigma}.$$

$$Lookback_{call} = c + V_{sb}.$$ (3)

Equation (1) is a simple Black-Scholes valuation model for a foreign currency. The intuition behind this component of the model is explained in Box 1, with the difference that the foreign risk-free interest rate, r_f, has been introduced to represent the continuous "dividend" or interest on the foreign currency. Equation (2) is similar to equation (1) except that the strike price is replaced by the underlying asset's achieved minimum value, L, from the time the option originated, along with other modifications. In the basic Black-Scholes model for a nondividend-paying stock, the valuation is carried out in a risk-neutral setting so that a stock's expected rate of return is equal to the risk-free interest rate, r. With a foreign currency, however, the return provided by the foreign interest rate, which does involve risk, must also be taken into account. The expected proportional growth rate of the spot exchange rate, S_t, must be reduced by r_f to allow for the fact that the foreign currency can be invested to earn the foreign interest rate.

Equation (1) can be thought of as the value of an option to buy the asset at its minimum value achieved to date, from time t_0 to t. The strike-bonus option represented by equation (2) captures and prices or values the right to buy the underlying asset (the foreign currency) at the new minimum value likely to be achieved over the remaining life of the option, from time t until the expiration date T – that is, $(T - t)$.

In general, the lookback call option is similar to a basic call option. For example, as it is for the basic call option, the value of the lookback call is positively correlated with the spot price of the underlying asset, the domestic risk-free interest rate, the time remaining until the option expires, and, most importantly, the volatility of the underlying asset. In addition, in both cases the option is negatively correlated with the contract's exercise price and the foreign risk-free interest rate.

Charts 1 and 2 illustrate the price behavior of a basic European call option and a strike-bonus option, respectively, over various initial strike prices ranging from $0.80 to $1.00. In these charts the initial strike price used for the basic call and the strike-bonus option is the minimum value, L, achieved by the underlying asset since the option's origination. Chart 3 gives the value of the lookback call option (the sum of the value of the European call option and the strike-bonus option) over the same range of initial strike prices.

Although Charts 1 and 3 appear similar, the values of the basic call and lookback options (on the y-axis) differ as L is increased. The two options have approximately

Chart 1 The price behavior of a basic European call option

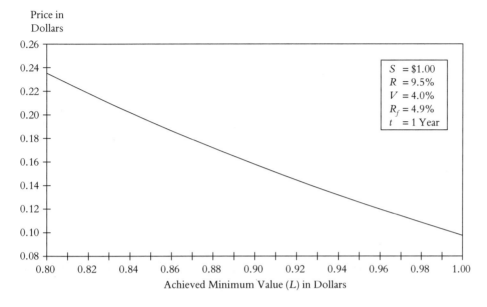

Chart 2 The price behavior of a strike-bonus option

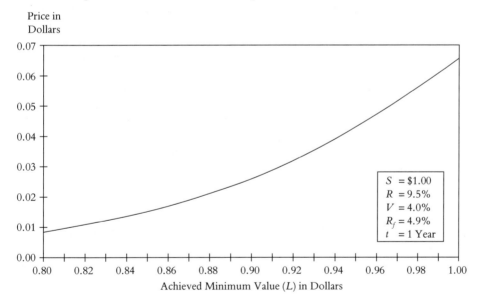

the same value when L is very low relative to the spot price, S. At this point, the call option is "deep in-the-money" – the price of the underlying asset exceeds the strike or exercise price, and the lookback's value is derived primarily from the basic call option's value. The strike-bonus option is relatively worthless. However, the value of the basic call option declines further than that of the lookback call option as its strike price, L, is increased to $1.00 (and is said to be "at-the-money"). Hence,

Chart 3   The price behavior of a lookback call option

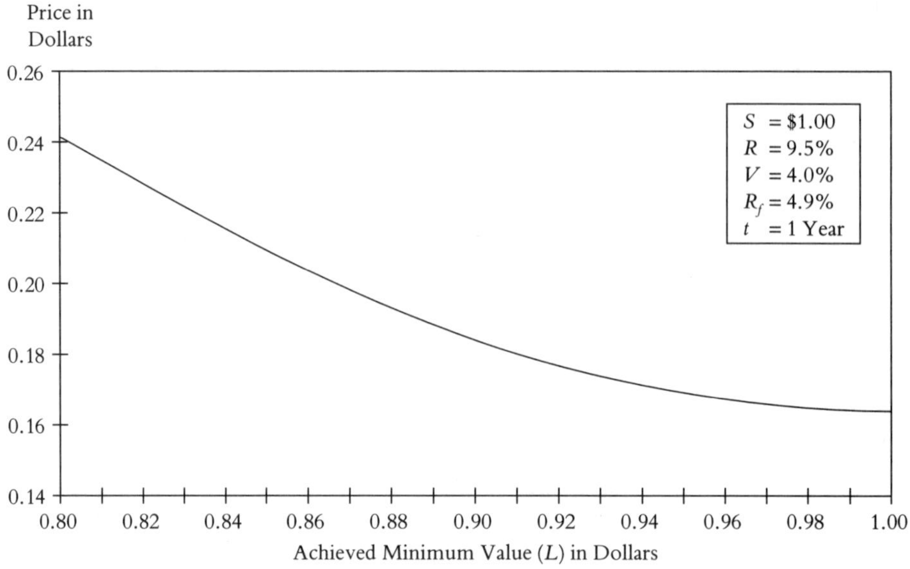

Price in
Dollars

$S = \$1.00$
$R = 9.5\%$
$V = 4.0\%$
$R_f = 4.9\%$
$t = 1$ Year

Achieved Minimum Value (L) in Dollars

the closer the achieved minimum asset price is to the spot price, the higher the value
of the strike-bonus option. As the call option moves closer to being at-the-money,
the value of the strike-bonus option pushes the lookback's price above the price of
the basic call.

Thus, while the relationship between the lookback call option's value and the
initial strike price, L, is similar to that of the basic call option, the relationship
between the value of the lookback's strike-bonus component and the strike price is
opposite that of the basic call option. That is, other things being equal, the value
of the strike-bonus option is positively correlated with the initial strike price.

As stated earlier, the strike-bonus option gives the holder the right to buy the
asset at a new minimum value anticipated from the perspective of time t. Given a
very low initial minimum value, L, relative to the spot price, the probability is low
that the asset's price will fall to a new minimum value and then rise again before
the option expires, so the strike-bonus option has little value. On the other hand,
if the option were at-the-money – the achieved minimum equals the spot price –
the asset very likely would establish a new minimum price and subsequently rise
before expiration. The strike-bonus option derives its value from the probability
that the asset's price will achieve such a new minimum value. Therefore, for options
having initial at-the-money prices, the lookback call option's value can be substantially higher than that of a comparable basic call option.

Besides the relationship between the exercise or strike price and the value of the
underlying asset – the moneyness of the option – another factor influencing the
value of both the basic call and the lookback call option is the underlying asset's
volatility. While either option's value is positively correlated with volatility, for a
lookback call option this factor is more significant because it affects the probability
that the price of the underlying asset will achieve a new minimum prior to the
expiration date. For instance, holding other factors constant, the value of the basic

at-the-money call option priced above increased by 1.5 percent given an increase from 2.0 percent to 2.1 percent in the estimated variance of the underlying asset. In this same situation, however, the value of the strike-bonus option increased by 2.34 percent.

Valuing an average-rate (Asian) option

There are two types of average-rate or Asian options: the fixed-strike and the floating-strike. The fixed-strike average-rate option is one for which the terminal payoff is the maximum of either the difference between the average value of the underlying asset and a fixed strike price or zero: $max(Avg_s - X, 0)$. The floating-strike Asian call option is similar to the lookback option given that its payoff at expiration is equal to the greater of the difference between the underlying asset's terminal spot price and its average value over the life of the option or zero – that is, $max(S - Avg_s, 0)$.

The floating-strike average-rate option is comparable to a lookback call option for which the strike price is the average value of the underlying asset, as opposed to its minimum value. The value of this option can never be greater than the value of a regular lookback call option, whose strike price is the achieved minimum of the asset, because the average is never equal to an extreme value such as the minimum unless all of the values are equal. Thus, the price of a regular lookback option sets an upper bound on the value of the floating-strike average-rate option.

The fixed-strike average-rate option is more commonly used in practice than the floating-strike option and will be the focus of this discussion. For both the floating- and fixed-strike average-rate options, the average can be computed as either the geometric or the arithmetic average. Although in practice the arithmetic average is typically used, no closed-form equation has been developed for pricing the average-rate option written on the arithmetic average because of mathematical complexities. Thus, a numerical approximation technique must be used to value an option written on the arithmetic average of the underlying asset's price (see A. G. Z. Kemna and A. C. F. Vorst 1990).[2] In the study presented here Monte Carlo simulation was the numerical approximation valuation methodology chosen. (See Box 3.)

Limiting bounds on the value of an arithmetic average-rate option Theoretically the value of an option written on an asset's arithmetic average should lie between the values of a comparable European call option and an average-rate option written on the geometric average of the asset's price. The primary difference between the fixed-strike average rate option and a comparable basic call option is the volatility of the underlying spot price. Because the variance used to compute the value of the basic European call option exceeds the variance used to compute the value of the call option written on the average price of the same underlying asset, the value of the call option on the asset's average value will never be greater than the value of a standard European call option on the asset. Furthermore, because the arithmetic average is always greater than the corresponding geometric average, the value of an option written on the geometric average of an asset's price provides a lower bound for the value of an option written on the arithmetic average of the price of the same asset.

Chart 4 shows the bounds imposed on an Asian option's value written on the arithmetic average. The value of a basic European call option forms the upper

Box 3

Monte Carlo simulation: a tutorial

Monte Carlo simulation is a numerical procedure used to approximate the expected value of a random variable or vector. The procedure approximates the expected value by generating random variables or vectors with a given probability density or joint probability density and, using the law of large numbers, takes the average of these values as an estimate of the expected value.

The Monte Carlo method is used to compute the expected value of a European-style call option. The value is computed by simulating the path taken by the price of the asset underlying the option over time. By simulating numerous such price paths, the technique allows computing the expected value or price of the option with increasing precision as the number of iterations or runs of the simulation are increased. The example that follows illustrates the technique.

In this exercise the objective is to compute the expected payoff of a European-style call option as of its expiration date, $E[max(S* - X, 0)]$ and then to compute the present value of this quantity – that is, $e^{-r(T-t)} E[max(S* - X,0)]$. Given a model for stock price movements over time, the Monte Carlo simulation technique will allow computation of the price expected at expiration.

Each iteration or sample run of the Monte Carlo simulation gives a stock price at time T. Increasing the number of runs of the simulation increases the reliability of the estimate for $S*$. (For example, 100,000 iteration would be reasonable.) The expected value of $S*$ is an average of the values obtained over the number of iterations.

The stock's price path can be modeled using the following equation:

$$S_{t+1} = S_t e^{r - \sigma^2/2\Delta t + S\sigma\varepsilon\sqrt{\Delta t}}. \qquad (M1)$$

In equation (M1), S_t is the value of the stock price today, r is the risk-free interest rate, σ is the standard deviation of stock returns, Δ_t represents a very small change in time (a day, for example), and $\varepsilon\sqrt{\Delta t}$ is

a discrete approximation to an increment in a Wiener process, in which ε represents a random drawing from a standardized normal distribution (a normal distribution with mean 0 and variance 1).

Suppose, for example, that the stock price today, S_t, is $50.00, Δt is 1/365 years, and the annual risk-free interest rate and standard deviation of the stock's expected return are 8 percent and 20 percent, respectively. Then, using the model in equation (M1), the stock's price one day hence can be approximated by

$$S_{t+1} = 50 \, e^{(.08-.02)(.0027)+(.20)(\sqrt{.0027})\varepsilon}.$$

To complete the approximation of S_{t+1}, a value of ε needs to be randomly selected from a standardized normal distribution. (This task can typically be accomplished with an internal function available in many computer program languages.) If, for example, the random selection for ε is 2.1, the stock's price one day hence would be expected to be $51.11. Another random sampling for ε would yield a different stock price for S_{t+1}.

In practice, these steps would be repeated numerous times to get a stock price path from S_t to S_{t+n}, where S_{t+n} would be the stock price as of n days from now – that is, $S*$ at expiration. The option's terminal value would then be computed and this amount would be discounted back to today using the formula

$$Call = e^{-r(T-t)}max(S* - K, 0). \qquad (M2)$$

These steps would complete one sample iteration of this Monte Carlo simulation.

After performing the appropriate number of runs, the expected call option value, *Call*, is computed as the average of the estimates of the call option's value obtained over the iterations. Next, the standard deviation of the estimates of *Call* is computed. Finally, given an expected value of *Call* and the standard deviation of the expected value, a confidence interval – a range within which there is some level of assurance that the actual value will fall – can be constructed for the value of the option. For normally distributed variables there is a 95 percent probability that the actual value of the variable will lie within a range of ±2 standard deviations from its sample mean.

Suppose, for example, that a European-style call option on a stock has eighty-seven days until expiration and an exercise price of $35.00. Today's stock price is $40.00, its annual volatility is 20 percent, and the yield on a Treasury bill with just over eighty-seven days until maturity is 2.96 percent. The Monte Carlo simulation consists of 10,000 iterations, giving 10,000 approximations for the present value of the call option. The mean value of the call is $5.361, and the standard deviation of the estimate was $0.0335. A 95 percent confidence interval for the value of the call can be constructed as follows:

$5.361 ± 2(.0335) = [$5.29, $5.43].

That is, there is a 95 percent probability that the actual value of this call option is within the computed range. This confidence interval can be tightened – thus obtaining a more reliable estimate – by increasing the number of iterations in the simulation or by employing a variance reduction technique (see note 4). The desired level of accuracy depends on a particular application.

In short, the Monte Carlo method simulates the random movement of stock prices and provides a probabilistic solution to the option pricing problem. Thus, by the technique's very nature, the final value derived using the Monte Carlo simulation will not be exact, no matter how accurate the equations in the model.

The advantage of using this simulation technique is that it can accommodate complex payoffs such as those that depend on the history of the underlying asset's price over time – for example, lookback and average-rate options. However, the technique has the disadvantage of being time-consuming, depending on the number of iterations required to obtain a reasonably accurate approximation, and it may therefore be infeasible for some practical applications.

Chart 4   Average-rate option value boundaries (*Arithmetic Average*)

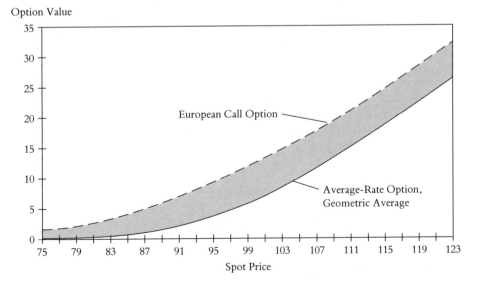

bound, and the value of a call option written on the geometric average delineates the lower bound, both having the same underlying parameters (S, X, r, σ, and t). The price of the arithmetic Asian option for a given spot price, computed using the Monte Carlo method, lies within the shaded area. The following relationships hold:[3]

$$Call_{European} \geq Asian\ Call_{arithmetic} > Asian\ Call_{geometric}.$$

The sections that follow illustrate the application of the valuation models discussed above to investment and hedging decisions in the foreign exchange markets. A Monte Carlo analysis like that used in Box 3 is employed to value the Asian option written on the arithmetic average with the exception that in the example the terminal price of the underlying asset is taken to be the arithmetic average of the n daily stock prices, where n is the number of days from time t until expiration.[4]

Numerical examples   Suppose that a U.S. investor firmly believes that the Japanese economy will improve dramatically relative to other industrialized countries' economies during the upcoming year. To act on this expectation, the investor purchases a one-year call option on the Japanese yen with a strike price of $0.0073. In this context the investor is speculating or predicting that the cost of the yen in U.S. dollar terms will rise by the time the option expires – that is, the yen will appreciate against the U.S. dollar. Assume that as of the current date it costs the investor $0.0073 to buy one unit of Japanese yen (1/$0.0073 translates to a current exchange rate of 136.9 yen per one U.S. dollar) and that this cost rises to $0.0079 (126.6 yen/$) over the one-year period. At the end of the year it costs more U.S. dollars ($0.0079–$0.0073) to purchase one unit of Japanese yen (the dollar depreciated). Because the option is very valuable at expiration, the investor's decision to purchase the one-year call option with a $0.0073 strike price turns out to have been a profitable one.

The example illustrates how an investor can use a basic currency call option in speculating on foreign currency movements. On the other hand, if the investor knew that dollars would have to be exchanged for yen at the end of the year – as might be the case for a business that imported goods from Japan with a commitment to make payment in yen – the purchase of the yen call option would constitute a foreign exchange risk hedging transaction.[5]

The following discussion illustrates more extensively how the path-dependent call option valuation models presented in this article are implemented using actual foreign exchange data on the Japanese yen and the German deutsche mark. The performance of these options is compared with that of a basic European call option written on the same currencies, and some of the risks inherent in using these instruments are pointed out.

The data and assumptions   Consider that on January 8, 1991, an investor is aware that one year from this date it will be necessary to purchase one million units of each of two foreign currencies: Japanese yen and deutsche marks. The investor's objective is to eliminate the upside exchange rate risk in this purchase requirement. That is, he or she wishes to avoid being adversely affected by a rise in the foreign currencies' value over the next year.

Table 1 A hedging/investment application[a]

	Yen	*Mark*
Estimated volatility	14.14%	13.06%
Foreign interest rate	7.64%	9.13%
U.S. interest rate	6.91%	6.91%
Strike price (set equal to spot price of 01/08/91)	$0.0073	$0.6536
Average exchange rate over option's life	$0.0075	$0.6047
Minimum exchange rate achieved over option's life	$0.0070	$0.5435
Spot (terminal) exchange rate (01/10/92)	$0.0079	$0.6329
The U.S. dollar's net change	Depreciated	Appreciated
Estimated Initial Cost of Call Option Contract **(at the money)[b]**		
Asian (floating-strike)	$208	$14,930
Asian (fixed-strike)	$209	$15,032
Lookback call	$710	$54,000
Basic European call	$359	$25,200
Option Value at Expiration **(01/10/92)**		
Asian (floating-strike) max (Spot[T] – Average, 0)	$400	$28,200
Asian (fixed-strike) max (Average – Strike, 0)	$123	$0
Lookback call max (Spot[T] – Minimum, 0)	$823	$89,433
Basic European call max (Spot[T] – Strike, 0)	$542	$0
Profit/(Loss) on Option[c]		
Asian (floating-strike)	$192	$13,270
Asian (fixed-strike)	($86)	($15,032)
Lookback call	$113	$35,433
Basic European call	$183	($25,200)

[a] Option contract size is one million units of foreign currency. Time remaining until expiration (01/08/91–01/10/92) is 367 days.
[b] Premium times one million units of currency.
[c] Terminal values minus initial costs.

The investor is assumed to have four alternative options on the foreign currencies from which to choose: a basic call option, a lookback call option, a fixed-strike Asian option, and a floating-strike Asian option.[6] All four options are European style, and the size of each option contract is for the purchase of one million units of the underlying foreign currency. To simplify matters, all options will be initially at-the-money. In other words, on the date they were purchased (time t_0), the spot foreign exchange rates were equal to the options' strike prices.

As will be discussed further, the choice of instruments can be difficult. In terms of the cost or premium required to purchase these options, the average-rate options are inexpensive relative to the lookback option. However, depending on the behavior of the exchange rates, the investor's hedging needs, and his or her knowledge of exchange rate volatility, the more expensive lookback could be preferred.

Table 1 provides a hypothetical example of a buy-and-hold strategy on each of the four types of call options available to this investor. Each option's performance

Chart 5   Daily exchange rates, U.S. dollar versus Japanese yen[a] (*January 8, 1991, to January 10, 1992*)

[a] Exchange rates shown are actual exchange rates multiplied by 1,000.

as a hedging or investment vehicle is analyzed using the Japanese yen and the deutsche mark, given the net changes in each currency's exchange rate over the one-year period.

Option transactions are initiated on January 8, 1991, to expire January 10, 1992 (367 calendar days). The basic data for this analysis are given in the first panel. So that all options will be priced at-the-money, the strike price is set equal to the initial spot exchange rate for the yen – $0.0073 per one unit of yen (the inverse of 133.3 yen per one U.S. dollar) and $0.6536 per one deutsche mark. The table also includes the domestic and foreign risk-free interest rates and estimates of asset price volatility for this time period.

The estimated initial cost of each option is shown in the second panel. The calculated premium for each option was multiplied by one million units of each currency to obtain the cost of the option contract. For both the fixed- and floating-strike average rate or Asian options, the Monte Carlo method was used in estimating value. Equations (3) and (1) were used to value the lookback and basic call options. Note the high cost of the at-the-money lookback call option relative to the basic call, as would be expected in light of the earlier discussion of the value of the strike-bonus option component of the lookback option.

The third panel shows the values of the four options at expiration. At this time the options are worth the greater of their intrinsic values, $S - X$, or zero since no time premium remains. The profit/loss on each position reported in the fourth panel represents the options' terminal values minus their initial costs.

Summary of the results   As can be seen in the fourth panel, for the yen options all but the fixed-strike Asian call ended the period profitable. The fixed-strike Asian

Chart 6   Daily exchange rates, U.S. dollar versus German mark[a] (*January 8, 1991, to January 10, 1992*)

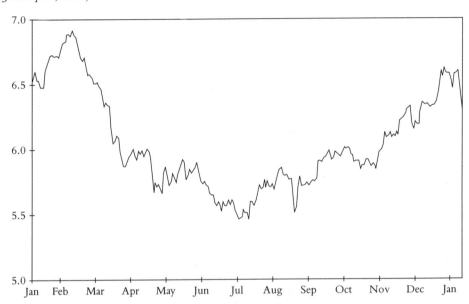

[a] Exchange rates shown are actual exchange rates multiplied by 10.

option cost $86.00 more than its value at expiration (computed as the difference between the average of the daily exchange rates over 367 days and the strike price). Over the period analyzed the yen appreciated, net, from $0.0073 to $0.0079. Thus it cost more in U.S. dollar terms to purchase one yen at the maturity date than at origination. As can be seen, the basic call option struck initially at-the-money expired in-the-money, generating a profit of $183.00. The lookback call option was also profitable even though its initial cost was nearly twice that of the basic call. This value reflects the path taken by the yen over the period. As illustrated in Chart 5, the yen initially declined through June 1991 and then began to trend upward thereafter.

In the case of the deutsche mark, it is interesting that only the lookback options were profitable at expiration. The lookback call and the floating-strike average rate option generated profits of $35,433.00 and $13,270.00, respectively. The basic call option position resulted in a loss of $25,200.00 and the fixed-rate Asian option produced a loss of $15,032.00. As Chart 6 shows, over this one-year period the mark depreciated, net, against the U.S. dollar. If the dollar/mark exchange rate had followed a downward path over the period, all of the option positions would have expired worthless. However, the mark depreciated significantly in the first half of the year and then appreciated thereafter, ending just below its beginning rate.

As in the case with the Japanese yen, the profit associated with the lookback option can be attributed to the range achieved by the exchange rate during the period. In initially pricing the lookback call on the mark an annualized volatility estimate of 13.06 percent was used. The actual volatility over this period was a much higher 17.4 percent, and the unexpected increase in volatility positively affected the lookback option's value.

An investor who accurately forecasts the range of the dollar/mark exchange rate over the assumed investment or hedging horizon given in this example would have found the lookback call or floating Asian options attractive investment vehicles. It should be emphasized, however, that investors must understand the risks inherent in these instruments to use them effectively (as is the case with most derivative products). This point takes on added importance given that these contracts are used mostly in foreign exchange transactions. For a variety of reasons it is extremely difficult to forecast exchange rates, even when using large-scale structural econometric models. It is likely that such forecasting difficulties will also be encountered when attempting to forecast parameters of the price processes that determine the value of path-dependent foreign exchange options. In any number of cases other, more traditional derivative instruments such as futures and forwards or various types of swap products may represent a more cost-effective way for investors or hedgers to achieve their stated objectives. Thus, while many may find contracts including path-dependent options attractive, they will not satisfy the needs of every investor or hedger.

Conclusion

This article describes the way in which two popular path-dependent options – the lookback option and the average-rate or Asian option – are priced using modern options pricing techniques. The hedge portfolio and risk-neutral pricing approaches associated with the modern options pricing paradigm are used to price the lookback option, and Monte Carlo simulation is used in pricing the floating-strike and the fixed-strike average-rate or Asian options. A simple numerical example involving these options demonstrates the possible benefits, costs, and risks associated with their use.

Since their formal introduction in 1979, these options have experienced rapid growth. In one form or another they are now traded on exchanges, are used extensively in foreign exchange markets to hedge foreign exchange risks, and have found use in corporate mergers and acquisitions. While these options are likely to continue to find new applications and uses as hedging and/or investment vehicles, investors are advised to develop a full understanding of the risks inherent in these instruments before adding them to their investment or hedging portfolios.

Notes

The authors thank Hugh Cohen, Peter Abken, and Michael Chriszt for invaluable technical advice and assistance.
1. Research published in 1979 by Goldman, Sosin, and Gatto paved the way for the modern treatment of path-dependent options. The authors had derived an explicit valuation formula for a hypothetical option with an exercise price to be set at the contract's expiration rather than at origination, as it is for standard options. Payoff on such "lookback" options would depend on the price path followed by the contract's underlying asset over the life of the option as well as on the option's expiration date. Goldman, Sosin, and Gatto suggested that such options could be of value to investors, and they were proven correct when Macotta Metals Corporation of New York began trading lookback options on gold, silver, and platinum on March 16, 1982 (Hunter and Stowe 1992).

2. The Black-Scholes environment assumes that the natural logarithms of stock price returns, $ln(S_t/S_{t-1})$, are normally distributed. In valuing an option written on the geometric average of an underlying asset's value over time, this crucial assumption still holds because the product of the logarithms of stock price returns is normally distributed. However, this assumption fails to hold in the case of an Asian option written on the arithmetic average because the sum of the logarithms of the stock price returns over time is no longer normally distributed. Therefore, there is no closed-form analytical pricing equation for the average-rate option written on the arithmetic average (Ritchken, Sankarnsubramanian, and Vijh 1990).

3. The closed-form equation for pricing the Asian option written on the geometric average is derived in Ritchken, Sankarnsubramanian, and Vijh (1990).

4. In valuing the arithmetic average-rate option, knowledge of the valuation principles for the geometric average-rate option can be used to lower the standard error of the estimated value and therefore reduce the number of iterations required in the simulation. This procedure is known as the variance reduction technique and is described in Hull (1989) and Kemna and Vorst (1990).

5. Although the discussion to this point has focused only on the lookback call option, in the case of foreign currency options a call on one currency can be thought of as a put on another currency. That is, a call option to buy yen for U.S. dollars can be thought of as a put to sell U.S. dollars for yen. Thus, the same methodology discussed for valuing a lookback call option on a foreign currency can be used to value a lookback put option on a foreign currency.

6. Although this example considers only the use of the lookback call, average-rate, and basic European call option, in practice other hedging vehicles would also be considered or evaluated by the investor, depending on the investor's objective.

References

Black, Fischer, and Myron Scholes. "The Pricing of Options and Corporate Liabilities." *Journal of Political Economy* 81 (May/June 1973): 637–59.

Cox, John, and Stephen Ross. "The Valuation of Options for Alternative Stochastic Processes." *Journal of Financial Economics* 3 (1976): 145–66.

Garman, Mark B. "Recollection in Tranquillity." *Risk* 2 (March 1989): 16–18.

——, and Steven W. Kohlhagen. "Foreign Currency Option Values." *Journal of International Money and Finance* 2 (December 1983): 231–37.

Goldman, M. Barry, Howard B. Sosin, and Mary Ann Gatto. "Path-Dependent Options: 'Buy at the Low, Sell at the High.'" *Journal of Finance* 34 (December 1979): 1111–27.

Hull, John. *Options, Futures, and Other Derivative Securities.* Englewood Cliffs, N.J.: Prentice-Hall, Inc., 1989.

Hunter, William C., and David W. Stowe. "Path-Dependent Options." Federal Reserve Bank of Atlanta *Economic Review* 77 (March/April 1992): 29–34.

Jarrow, Robert, and Andrew Rudd. *Options Pricing.* Homewood, Ill.: Richard D. Irwin, 1983.

Kemna, A. G. Z., and A. C. F. Vorst. "A Pricing Method for Options Based on Average Asset Values." *Journal of Banking and Finance* 14 (March 1990): 113–29.

Kolb, Robert W. *Options: An Introduction.* Miami: Kolb Publishing Company, 1991.

Ritchken, Peter, L. Sankarnsubramanian, and Anand M. Vijh. "The Economic Analysis of Path-Dependent Contracts on the Average." Case Western University, Department of Operations Research, Working Paper, 1990.

9

An Introduction to Special-purpose Derivatives: Path-dependent Options

——————————————————————— Gary Gastineau

Gary Gastineau, An Introduction to Special-purpose Derivatives; this copyright material is reprinted with permission from the *Journal of Derivatives*, a publication of Institutional Investor, Inc., 488 Madison Avenue, New York, NY 10022.

This is the second in a series of articles on special-purpose derivatives, sometimes known as "exotic" options. Each article in the series focuses on a certain class or type of derivative instrument and discusses several varieties currently being traded. We describe the defining elements of each instrument and show how the payout is determined. Important applications and primary users are discussed.

This article covers special-purpose derivatives whose payouts depend not only on the final price that is reached on the expiration day, but also on some aspect of the path the price follows prior to expiration:

"In" and "out" options, sometimes known as "barrier" options, either come into existence ("in" options) or expire worthless ("out" options) if the price of the underlying hits a particular level (the "knock-in" or "knock-out" price) prior to expiration.

An "exploding" option has a cap value such that if at any point during its life it goes in the money by at least the cap amount, it immediately matures ("explodes") and pays off the capped value.

For a "reset" or "partial look-back" option, the strike price is set as a function of the path followed by the price of the underlying during the reset period. The strike price on a reset call, for example, is set equal to the lowest price the asset reaches during the reset period.

Finally, the payout on an "average rate" or "average price" option, often known as an "Asian" option, is based not on the final price that is reached at expiration, but on the average price at designated times over the option's life.

Many of the options that investors and liability managers use to meet specialized risk management objectives are path-dependent options. Path-dependence means that an option's value depends not only on the underlying instrument's value at expiration or exercise but also on the price path the underlying takes in getting there.

I. In Option

An in option has a start price or in-strike as well as a start or trade date. If the market price of the underlying drops through the in-strike of a down-and-in call, or rises through the in-strike of an up-and-in put, the payoffs of these instruments will be identical to the payoffs of standard options with otherwise similar terms. If the in-strike is not breached, however, the in option expires worthless, even if the equivalent standard option would have been deep in the money at expiration. The in-strike is also referred to as the in-price or the knock-in price.

Exhibit 1 Payout of a down-and-in call: activated

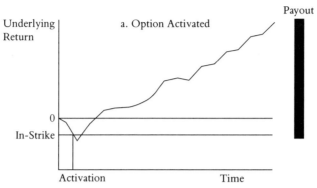

Payout of a down-and-in call: no activation

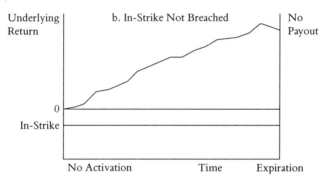

In options, and their mirror image relatives, out options, are often called "barrier" options, because they depend so critically on whether the price of the underlying reaches the barrier of the knock-in or knock-out price before option expiration.

How an in option looks

Exhibit 1 illustrates the payout of a down-and-in call under two possible conditions. In the first case, the in-strike is breached, and the option pays off like a standard call. In the second, the in-strike is not breached during the life of the call, and the option expires valueless on its expiration date.

How it works

Exhibit 2 compares the premiums on down-and-in calls and standard calls at a variety of underlying prices ranging from below the in-strike (for the standard call) to substantially above the in-strike for both options. The closer the underlying is to the in-strike at the time of valuation, the greater the possibility of activation, and the greater the expected value of the in option relative to the standard option.

The fact that the in option is worth a larger fraction of the standard option as the market price of the underlying moves closer to the in-strike may not be precisely

Exhibit 2   Valuation of a down-and-in call

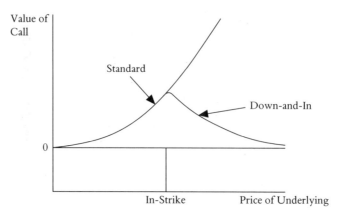

reflected in the in option's market price. The most common reason for a deviation from the predicted price relationship is that the issuer of an in option may face unusual risks in taking a position in the underlying or in another option as a hedge against the liability on the in option.

At other times, possible activation of the in option may create no problem for an issuer. If in options are available at attractive prices, and an investor has a high degree of confidence that the in-strike will be breached and the underlying will subsequently change direction and move significantly into the money, an in option can be a bargain.

The examples illustrated in Exhibits 1 and 2 assume that the in-strike becomes the strike of the standard option created by the breach of the in-strike. In some applications, the strike of the option may be unrelated to the in-strike.

Applications

In options have been more popular in equity and currency markets than in interest rate markets – perhaps because equity and currency market movements often seem more episodic or subject to volatility events. Whether they are asset or liability managers, buyers of in options tend to be either hesitant, price-sensitive option buyers or option buyers who hope to buy participation in a market reversal for a minimum option premium.

Price-sensitive option buyers may focus more on the size of the premium relative to the possible payoff than on the probability of breaching the in-strike. If the in option premium is low enough relative to a standard option premium, and the buyer correctly anticipates a price movement that activates the in option and then reverses to provide a large payoff, the risk/reward ratio can be very favorable.

The viewpoint of the investor who uses an in option to implement market reversal expectations may be complex. This investor might feel that the farther the market moves in one direction, the stronger its reversal will be. A standard option struck at or out of the money does not express these expectations accurately, and it costs too much relative to the payoff the investor expects. The in option provides a potentially larger payoff with the same ultimate move – provided the ultimate move is preceded by a breach of the in-strike.

An in option can be a stand-alone position or a sophisticated portfolio risk management device that acts as a hedge for an existing long or short position in the underlying. For investors expecting a movement in one direction followed by a strong reversal, down-and-in calls and up-and-in puts can be attractive substitutes for standard options.

II. Out Option

An out option is similar to a standard option except that the out option has an expiration price or outstrike as well as an expiration date. If the market price of the underlying does not drop through the outstrike of a down-and-out call, or rise through the outstrike of an up-and-out put, the payoffs of these instruments will be identical to the payoffs of standard options with otherwise similar terms. If the outstrike is breached, however, the out options expire immediately. The outstrike is often referred to as the outprice or the knock-out price.

How it looks

Exhibit 3 illustrates the payout of a down-and-out call under two possible conditions. In the first case, the outstrike has been breached, and the option expires valueless at that point rather than on its expiration date. In the second, the outstrike is not breached during the life of the call, and the option pays off like a standard call option. The price patterns are identical to the patterns in Exhibit 1. A price drop through the in-strike in Exhibit 1 activates the in option. Here, the price drop terminates the out option.

How it works

Exhibit 4 compares the premiums on down-and-out calls and standard calls at a variety of underlying prices ranging from below the outstrike (for the standard call) to substantially in the money for both options. The closer the underlying is to the outstrike at the time of valuation, the greater the possibility of early termination, and the lower the expected value of the option – both absolutely and relative to the standard option.

An out option usually is worth a smaller fraction of the standard option as the market price of the underlying moves closer to the outstrike. The issuer of an out option may face unusual risks in holding a position in the underlying or in another option as a hedge against the liability on the out option. These risks may increase the price of the out option. Nonetheless, if an investor has a high degree of confidence that the outstrike will not be breached during the term of the option, an out option can be an attractive purchase.

Applications

Highly confident option buyers see the chance of breaching the outstrike as quite small. If their view is correct, and the out option premium is significantly lower than a standard option premium, they are buying a "bargain-priced" option.

Exhibit 3   Payout of a down-and-out call

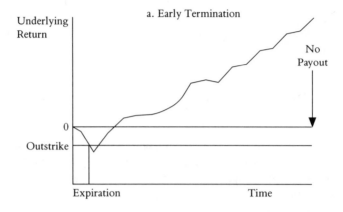

a. Early Termination

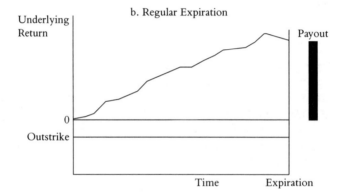

b. Regular Expiration

Exhibit 4   Estimated values of down-and-out and comparable standard calls

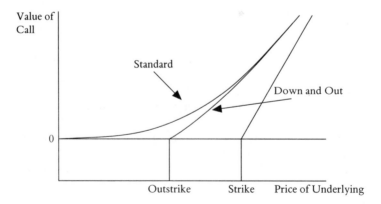

The viewpoint of the investor expecting a volatility event or a period of extreme uncertainty is more complex. Typically, this investor will have a strong – but not unequivocal – view of the direction of movement in the underlying. In the event that this investor's expectations are incorrect – a nagging uncertainty – the outcome could be *very* different, and any remaining value in a standard call would be small if the underlying hit the outstrike. In the minds of investors with this kind of market view, down-and-out calls and up-and-out puts are potential substitutes for standard options.

An up-and-out put can provide low-cost insurance for an equity, fixed-income, or currency position if an investor is comfortable that a movement through the outstrike means that the insurance feature of the option is unlikely to be needed in the subsequent market environment.

Valuation of in and out options

Closed-form valuation equations exist for the standard in and out options described here, as well as for more elaborate structures. Hull [1993] and Rubinstein [1991] provide the appropriate equations. Unfortunately, neither source gives closed-form equations for the deltas of these options.

III. Exploding Option

An exploding option is a single contract put spread or call spread – standing alone or embedded in a structured product, such as a medium-term note – that has a special expiration price as well as an expiration date. The primary difference between an exploding option and any other capped call or floored put is that the options expire at parity when the underlying trades at or through a trigger price, typically (but not always) the cap or floor strike.

CAPS, traded by the CBOE on the S&P 100 and S&P 500 indexes, are probably the most familiar exploding option. The CBOE refers to the path-dependent exercise terms for its CAPS contracts as "capped European-style exercise."

How it looks

Exhibit 5 illustrates the payoff patterns at expiration of an exploding call and an exploding put option spread. The early exercise trigger range – all prices for the underlying above the trigger price of the call spread and below the trigger price of the put spread – illustrates the price range in which the option "explodes" (i.e., matures when the price of the underlying touches or enters this range).

How it works

The exploding option – actually an exploding spread – differs from a traditional call or put spread in which the short cap or floor option will still have value if the underlying moves above the cap strike or below the floor strike. With the traditional call or put spread, the net long position does not settle at its maximum value even after the cap or floor strike has been breached unless the underlying is beyond the cap or floor strike at expiration.

As Exhibit 6 illustrates, the value of an exploding call option will fall between the value of an uncapped call and the corresponding traditional call spread. The relative values of these positions will depend on strikes, volatilities, and the precise terms on which the exploding feature is implemented.

Exhibit 5   Payoff patterns of exploding put and call spreads

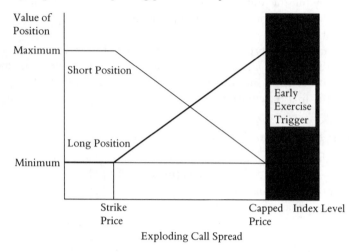

Exploding Call Spread

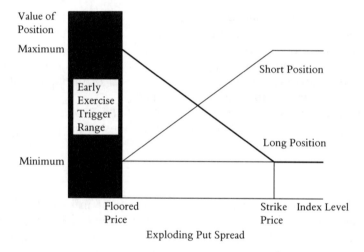

Exploding Put Spread

Exhibit 6   Comparison of value patterns of a standard call, exploding call option, and call spread

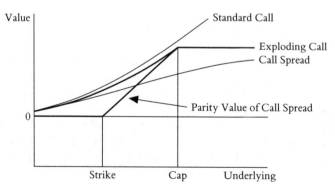

The examples illustrated in Exhibits 5 and 6 are exploding options terminated by a very brief contact with an underlying trigger price equal to the cap or floor strike. If the closing price for a day or a week is the only price that counts in breaching the trigger, or if some other condition is imposed on the trigger, the valuation of the exploding option will be more complex. (Generally, the cost of an exploding option will be more than the similar standard spread with a cap strike equal to the exploding strike.)

Applications

An exploding option can be more attractive to an investor than a long position in a standard option or a traditional option spread if the exploding option terms conform more closely to the investor's expectations for the underlying. For example, expectation of a sharp market move sometime before the expiration date that will trip the exploding option's trigger might lead an investor to prefer the exploding option to other structures even at a somewhat higher option premium. The exploding option will be particularly attractive if the investor feels the move beyond the cap or floor might not be sustainable until expiration of the options in a traditional spread.

IV. Reset or Partial Look-back Option

A reset option is a put or call option whose strike may be reset – to a lower strike in the case of a call or a higher strike in the case of a put – if the option is out of the money on the reset date or during the reset period. There may be a limit to the magnitude of the strike adjustment, and the reset may be triggered by a specific price on the underlying, set on a specific reset date, or set during a limited reset period.

Reset options come in many variations and are called by many names (including anti-crash warrants, election warrants, partial look-back options, step-down warrants, and strike reset options). A full look-back option – with the reset period equal to the life of the option – is an important special case.

How it looks

The reset call option illustrated in Exhibit 7 lets the holder reset the strike to the lowest market price the underlying reaches during the reset or partial look-back period. If the underlying instrument sells below the initial strike during the reset period, the value of a reset call option that is in the money at expiration will be greater than that of a standard option with a strike equal to the underlying market price at the time of option purchase. Once the reset or partial look-back period is over, the reset option is equivalent to a standard call option with a strike fixed at the lower level determined during the reset period.

How it works

The bar graphs at the right side of Exhibit 7 illustrate that the payoff of a reset option will always be at least as great as the payoff of a standard option with

Exhibit 7   Reset effect of a reset or partial look-back call option

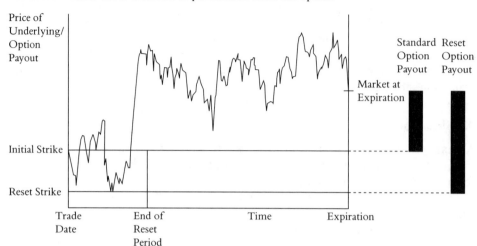

otherwise similar terms. Correspondingly, the reset option will command a higher initial premium than a comparable standard option. The valuation modification consists of an adjustment for the fact that the strike can be reset to a more favorable level during some part of the life of the option.

An investor would have to pay a substantially increased premium for a full look-back option. (A full look-back option would extend the reset period to the full term of the option, and the option would pay off on the strike set at the lowest underlying price reached during the life of the call in Exhibit 7 or the highest underlying price reached during the life of a full look-back put.)

If an investor wants the ability to modify a position in response to events and the passage of time, it is possible to create roughly similar payoff patterns with separate put and call contracts, switchback options, or other option structures that require preset strike adjustment levels or a decision by the option holder during the life of the contract. To many investors, an important attraction of reset options is that they do not require an active decision from the holder to time the reset. Often, the need to make a second market judgment holds less attraction for an investor than buying a reset option.

Applications

The principal interest in limited-period reset options stems from the opportunity to pay an additional premium for the right to a more attractive strike set during a short reset period. Buyers of reset options ordinarily anticipate that a near-term development might cause a setback to their longer-term expectations, but that the impact will be only temporary.

Election- or other event-oriented instruments are a common variety of reset options. Other applications include options whose lives span possible currency realignments, central bank interest rate policy shifts, or any other natural or policy-dictated phenomenon that can bring on a period of substantial short-term volatility or a significant temporary adverse price change. The most common applications of reset options are in the equity markets, although a possible currency realignment or a monetary policy change could create an interest in reset options in currencies or debt instruments. Election warrants and anti-crash warrants, whose early lives span elections and periods of economic or financial uncertainty, have been publicly offered in Europe.

The premium of a reset option will be higher than the premium on a standard option – usually by the expected value of the reset benefit.

Valuation of reset options

Several authors discuss (full) look-back options and provide valuation formulas, including Hull [1993], Rubinstein [1991], and Garman [1992], who also gives an equation for the delta. The original work on this subject is by Goldman, Sosin, and Gatto [1979].

V. Average Rate or Price Options (Asian Options)

An average rate or price option (hereafter referred to and described as an average rate option) is a put or call option contract whose payout at maturity is based on the difference between the option's strike rate and the *average* market rate on the underlying instrument at designated times over the life of the option. The buyer and seller of an average rate option agree on the strike rate, the start date, the number and timing of rate observations over the life of the option (called the frequency), which will be used to calculate the average market rate, the expiration date of the option, and, of course, the option premium.

The average rate observation process can begin at any time before expiration (even before the start date in rare instances), and specific contributing dates can be chosen. If the rates observed on designated dates are given different weights, the option is called a weighted average rate option. Average rate options are also called Asian options.

How it looks

Exhibit 8 shows the observations used to calculate the value of an average rate call option with a frequency of twelve monthly, observation dates and an average rate of 11.

How it works

With a strike rate of 10, the payoff on the average rate option is 11 minus 10, or one times the number of units underlying the option contract.

(Average Rate – Strike Rate) × Underlying Units = Call Option Payoff
(11 – 10) × Underlying Units = Call Option Payoff

Exhibit 8   Monthly observations for an average rate option

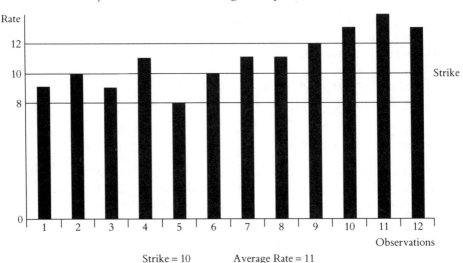

Strike = 10   Average Rate = 11

The final observation in this series is 13. A standard option expiring on the date of the last observation would have been worth three times as much as the average rate option if the standard option had been held to expiration.

(Final Rate – Strike Rate) × Underlying Units = Call Option Payoff
(13 – 10) × Underlying Units = Call Option Payoff

Apart from the fact that in this specific case the final rate was higher than the average rate, an investor should expect the average rate option's payoff to be lower than the payoff of an otherwise similar standard option. For several reasons, the average rate option is usually less valuable at purchase than a standard option or a strip of standard options because two key components of option value – volatility and forward pricing – have a relatively smaller impact on average rate option value.

1. Volatility has a smaller impact on average rate options because extreme observations often cancel each other's effect on value. Observations taken when the market rate or price is below the strike are averaged with observations taken when the market is above the strike. In valuing a standard option or a strip of options, observations below the strike do not drag the aggregate payout down. In most option structures, an observation far out of the money has the same effect on the option's final value as an observation at the strike. In contrast, a deep out-of-the-money observation can sharply reduce the value of an average rate option. In the example illustrated in Exhibit 8, a few additional observations well below the strike rate of 10 could have eliminated the option payoff completely.

2. In a rising forward rate or price environment, the *average forward value* is below the *end point forward value*. Under the most common market circumstances, early observations will be made at lower expected (forward) prices. These early observations usually reduce the expected value of the average rate option. In

Exhibit 9 Typical premium comparisons: standard option, strip of standard options, average rate option – 90 strike Swiss franc call on Japanese yen with spot at 90 (all figures in millions of Swiss francs or Japanese yen)

Term	Standard call		Strip of calls		Average rate call	
	Face (SF)	Premium (JY)	Face (SF)	Premium (JY)	Face (SF)	Premium (JY)
12	120.0	428.4	10.0	35.8	120.0	264.0
11			10.0	34.4		
10			10.0	33.5		
9			10.0	31.9		
8			10.0	30.4		
7			10.0	28.6		
6			10.0	26.7		
5			10.0	24.9		
4			10.0	22.5		
3			10.0	19.7		
2			10.0	16.2		
1			10.0	11.7		
Total	120.0	428.4	120.0	316.3	120.0	264.0

the less common case – where a forward rate in a currency or an interest rate term structure is *below* the spot rate – an average rate call might sell for as much as or more than a standard European-style option.

In general, both the averaging process and the shorter average maturity of the average rate option reduce the value and the cost of the option. Exhibit 9 illustrates the "typical" relationships among an average rate call option, a standard call option, and a strip of standard call options with expirations on each monthly "observation day." The widely varying forward rate relationships limit the validity of generalizations from this example.

The rough generalization (illustrated in Exhibit 9) that the average rate option will usually be worth less than a single-strike standard option or a strip of standard options has an offsetting benefit in many applications: it reduces the premium the buyer pays for average rate options. If the average rate option meets a risk management need at a lower cost than a standard option, the lower value/cost of the specialized contract is an advantage.

Exhibit 10 takes the comparison of average rate options with other option structures one step farther. Using the rates at each observation date in Exhibit 8, we compare the value of an average rate option with the payoff of a strip of options and a standard call – all with identical strikes. If the market price at the last observation had been 10 or less, the payoff per period of the average rate and strip options would have declined slightly, and the standard option would have had no payoff at all.

Exhibit 10   Comparison of impact of market prices on option payoffs

Observation date	Market price	Average rate	Payoff impact Strip	standard
1	9	−1	0	
2	10	0	0	
3	9	−1	0	
4	11	1	1	
5	8	−2	0	
6	10	0	0	
7	11	1	1	
8	11	1	1	
9	12	2	2	
10	13	3	3	
11	14	4	4	
12	13	3	3	3
Net Payoff/Period		1	1.25	3

Applications

The leading use of average rate and weighted average rate options is in the management of foreign currency exposures arising from cross-border, cross-currency transactions. The classic application is in a business that is subject to costs in one currency and revenues in another. Typically, the average rate call option assures translation of the business's foreign currency receipts into the *base currency* in which it incurs costs at a minimum relationship of average exchange rates over the life of the option. The currency translation can be reversed with an average rate put (a call on the other currency) if the business uses the currency it receives as its base currency.

The weighted average rate option adjusts the weight of each rate observation to anticipated seasonal weightings of the business's receipts or incorporates special transactions.

If currency relationships stay within a narrow rate range, the company needs little currency protection, and the average rate option, correspondingly, has little value. If the foreign currency fluctuates widely or moves to an unfavorable exchange rate relative to the base currency and stays there, the average rate option will provide the necessary protection – limiting the average currency exposure to the strike rate plus the option premium. Because average rate option premiums tend to be modest, the option buyer will not have to pay a high premium for unneeded exchange rate protection.

Average interest rate options can be used to convert a floating-rate asset or liability into a term rate position or a term rate into a floating-rate. Correspondingly, an average price option can assure an investor of the opportunity to buy or sell a common stock or stock index at its average price during a specified period. This opportunity may be important to a portfolio manager who pays or receives periodic cash flows more frequently than a portfolio is rebalanced.

Valuation of Asian options

An Asian option presents almost an easy valuation problem. A simple closed-form solution exists for an option whose payoff depends on the *geometric* average price (or rate) over an interval. Unfortunately, actual Asian derivative contracts are almost all based on an *arithmetic* average, which does not produce a closed-form equation.

Several approximation procedures are discussed by Levy and Turnbull [1992] and Carverhill and Clewlow [1992], as well as Hull [1993] and Rubinstein [1991]. Kemna and Vorst [1990] describe a Monte Carlo procedure, using the "control variate" technique, in which efficiency is greatly enhanced by modeling not the value of the arithmetic average option per se, but its *deviation* from the value of the otherwise equivalent geometric average option.

One useful fact is that option deltas tend to be much less sensitive than theoretical values to small changes in assumptions, so the delta for an arithmetic average option should normally be very close to the delta of the geometric average option with the same terms.

References

Carverhill, Andrew, and Lew Clewlow. "Flexible Convolution." Reprinted in *From Black-Scholes to Black Holes: New Frontiers in Options. Risk Magazine*, 1992.

Garman, Mark. "Recollection in Tranquility." Reprinted in *From Black-Scholes to Black Holes: New Frontiers in Options. Risk Magazine*, 1992.

Goldman, M. Barry, Howard B. Sosin, and Mary Ann Gatto. "Path-Dependent Options: 'Buy at the Low, Sell at the High'." *Journal of Finance*, 34 (December 1979), pp. 1111–1127.

Hull, John C. *Options, Futures, and Other Derivative Securities*, 2nd ed. Englewood Cliffs, NJ: Prentice-Hall, 1993.

Kemna, A. G. Z., and A. C. F. Vorst. "A Pricing Method for Options Based on Average Asset Values." *Journal of Banking and Finance*, 14 (1990), pp. 113–130.

Levy, Edmund, and Stuart Turnbull. "Average Intelligence." Reprinted in *From Black-Scholes to Black Holes: New Frontiers in Options. Risk Magazine*, 1992.

Rubinstein, Mark. "Exotic Options." University of California, Walter A. Haas School of Business Research Program in Finance Working Paper No. 220, 1991.

PART II

Risk Management Applications

Introduction

Overview

In their article, "Managing Financial Risk," Clifford W. Smith, Jr., Charles W. Smithson, and D. Sykes Wilford, address three related issues: measuring the risk of a firm to exchange rates, interest rates, and inflation, determining what financial tools are available for managing risk, and using the financial tools to manage the risk. In the process of exploring these issues, Smith, Smithson, and Wilford show that the process can be simplified considerably by viewing particular financial derivatives as building blocks, each with a particular payoff signature. By combining these simple building blocks, the risk manager can devise a strategy for managing a complex risk that may be quite specific to the firm.

Debt Markets

Many historically popular hedging strategies do not fully consider the interest rate sensitivity of the instrument that is to be hedged. Robert W. Kolb and Raymond Chiang try to account for the interest rate sensitivity of the instrument to be hedged in their article, "Improving Hedging Performance Using Interest Rate Futures." Kolb and Chiang argue that the duration (a measure of how a bond's price will change for a change in yields) of the underlying instrument must be considered in deriving the appropriate hedging strategy.

A bond protfolio is considered to be immunized if its value is insensitive to changes in interest rates. For example, if a zero net worth balance sheet has assets and liabilities with equal durations, a rise in interest rates will cause asset and liability values to fall by the same amounts. In "Immunizing Bond Portfolios with Interest Rate Futures," Gerald D. Gay and Robert W. Kolb show how a given portfolio can be immunized by trading interest rate futures against the portfolio. Because futures markets exhibit great liquidity and low trading costs, it is often more efficient to implement immunization strategies with futures. Also, if the immunization is to be conducted with futures, the cash portfolio can be left undisturbed.

A strip is a package of futures with expirations on successive dates. For example, a position of 3 Eurodollar futures, with one contract expiring in each of three expiration months (e.g., March, June, and September), would be a Eurodollar strip. In his article, "Interest Rate Swaps versus Eurodollar Strips," Ira G. Kawaller shows that a Eurodollar strip is essentially similar to a certain kind of interest rate swap. In many applications, Kawaller shows, the choice between the swap and the strip will depend on the pricing.

Equity Markets

Derivatives have proven to be powerful tools for managing the risk of stock portfolios. The key technique for managing this risk is *portfolio insurance*. Portfolio insurance consists of a set of techniques in which traders use financial derivatives to protect the value of a stock portfolio. In essence, traders take an existing portfolio and trade derivatives (usually stock index futures or options) against the portfolio to insure that the entire value of the stock/derivatives portfolio will not fall below a specified level. This insurance, of course, has a cost in the form of reducing the upside potential for the portfolio.

The actual implementation of portfolio insurance strategies can be complicated. Thomas O'Brien clarifies the implementation of portfolio insurance in his article, "The Mechanics of Portfolio Insurance." As O'Brien explains, the dynamic hedging approach of insuring a portfolio by trading futures requires careful monitoring of the position to achieve the desired results.

In the strictest sense, a portfolio insurance strategy guarantees that the value of a portfolio will not fall below a specified level over a given time horizon. When strategies are implemented via dynamic hedging, there exists a possibility that the dynamic strategy may not achieve the idealized goal of maintaining the specified portfolio value with certainty. Mark Rubinstein explores the issues involved in implementing portfolio insurance in his paper, "Alternative Paths to Portfolio Insurance."

On October 19, 1987, the stock market sustained its greatest single-day loss of the twentieth century, losing about 22 percent of its value. This contrasted with a 12 percent drop that signaled the beginning of the Great Depression. Naturally, an event of this magnitude has called forth an analysis of trading unprecedented in the history of financial markets. Many observers believe that active markets in equity derivatives were responsible for the severity of the crash.

G. J. Santoni analyzes some of the claims that have been advanced about the Crash of 1987 in his article, "The October Crash: Some Evidence on the Cascade Theory." According to the "cascade theory," trading strategies popular in the futures market (stock index arbitrage and portfolio trading) generated sell orders in response to the initial large drop in stock prices. The selling of futures generated a further drop in the stock market, due to the normal linkages between cash and futures prices. This subsequent stock market drop triggered yet more sales of stock index futures and options, leading in turn to a greater drop in the stock market. This cycle repeated itself throughout the day on October 19, 1987, causing prices to cascade downward. Santoni weighs the evidence on the cascade theory and finds it lacking. Nonetheless, many observers continue to believe the cascade theory and these beliefs have probably led to changes in trading rules in the stock and stock derivatives markets.

Mark Rubinstein considers the connection between the Crash of 1987 and one popular stock index derivates trading strategy in his paper, "Portfolio Insurance and the Market Crash." Rubinstein finds that portfolio insurance strategies were probably not important in fueling the crash. He then goes on to consider the performance of portfolio insurance strategies during the crash and finds them lacking. As a consequence, Rubinstein suggests that portfolio insurance will probably move away from dynamic trading strategies and begin to seek implementation through the direct trading of options.

Over-the-counter Markets

Over-the-counter financial derivatives, notably swaps, are proving to be extremely popular and powerful instruments for managing risk in many corporate finance contexts. Anatoli Kuprianov focuses on the corporate applications of swaps in his second article in this volume, "The Role of Interest Rate Swaps in Corporate Finance." Kuprianov discusses typical corporate applications of swaps and analyzes the phenomenal growth of the swaps market.

"A Tale of Two Bond Swaps," by Andrew Kalotay and Bruce Tuckman, is essentially a set of two case studies. Kalotay and Tuckman examine two swaps initiated by subsidiaries of U.S. West that were both used to swap one debt obligation for another. Kalotay and Tuckman show that both swaps conferred substantial benefits on U.S. West by reducing the net present value of their outstanding liabilities. This reduction was made possible largely through tax savings.

Financial derivatives include futures, forwards, options, futures option, and custom-tailored instruments. These custom-tailored instruments are traded in an over-the-counter market, in contrast to futures and options that generally trade on exchanges. Peter A. Abken investigates the riskiness of these off-exchange instruments in his article, "Over-the-counter Financial Derivatives: Risky Business?" While some observers have campaigned for more stringent regulation of the over-the-counter market for derivatives, Abken stresses the importance of strong corporate oversight and control to manage the risk of improperly using derivatives.

SECTION A

Overview

10

Managing Financial Risk

Clifford W. Smith, Jr.,
Charles W. Smithson,
and D. Sykes Wilford

There is no doubt that the financial environment is a lot more risky today than it was in the 1950s and 1960s. With changes in some macroeconomic institutional structures – notably, the breakdown of the Bretton Woods agreement in 1972 – have come dramatic increases in the volatility of interest rates, foreign exchange rates, and commodity prices.

Such increased volatility will not come as "news" to most corporate executives. Since the 1970s, many CEOs and CFOs have watched the profitability of their firms swing widely in response to large movements in exchange rates, interest rates, and commodity prices. What may be news, however, are the techniques and tools now available for measuring and managing such financial risks.

Recognition of the increased volatility of exchange rates, interest rates, and commodity prices should lead managers of the firm to ask three questions:

1. To what extent is my firm exposed to interest rates, foreign exchange rates, or commodity prices?
2. What financial tools are available for managing these exposures?
3. If my firm is significantly exposed, how do I use the financial tools to manage the exposure?

It is with these three questions that the following discussion deals.

Identifying and Measuring Financial Risk

The risk profile

U.S. savings and loans (S&Ls) are a widely cited example of firms subject to interest rate risk. Because S&Ls typically fund long-lived assets (e.g., 30-year fixed-rate mortgages) with liabilities that reprice frequently (passbook deposits), their value is negatively related to interest rates. When interest rates rise, the value of S&Ls' assets declines significantly, but the value of their liabilities changes little. So, the value of shareholders' equity falls.

The resulting relation between interest rates and the value of S&Ls is portrayed graphically in a *risk profile* in Figure 1.

The negative slope reflects the inverse relation between the financial price – i.e., interest rates – and the value of the S&L. The precise measure of the exposure is

Figure 1   The risk profile for a U.S. S&L

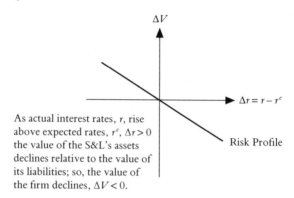

As actual interest rates, r, rise above expected rates, r^e, $\Delta r > 0$ the value of the S&L's assets declines relative to the value of its liabilities; so, the value of the firm declines, $\Delta V < 0$.

reflected by the slope of the line; and it is a measure of the slope that the techniques described below will provide.

But before considering the size of the exposure, the first question is: How do we go about identifying such exposures? In the case of S&Ls, the exposure to interest rates is apparent from the firm's balance sheet; the mismatch of maturities between assets and liabilities is obvious. Many companies, however, have economic or "operating" exposures that are not reflected on their balance sheets. Take, for example, the vulnerability of building products firms to increases in interest rates. Increases in interest rates decrease the demand for building products. As sales and thus cash inflows decline – and to the extent that its costs and liabilities are fixed – the value of a building products firm declines.

We can make a similar observation about foreign exchange risk. In some instances, exposures are apparent. For example, a U.S. importer orders product from Germany and is expected to pay in Deutsche Marks (DM) for the products when they are delivered in 90 days. If, during those 90 days, the price of a DM rises – that is, the value of the dollar declines – the U.S. importer will have to pay more for the product. In this case, an increase in the price of the foreign currency leads to a decrease in the value of the importer.

Since 1972, firms have become adept at dealing with such transaction exposures.[1] However, a firm's exposure to foreign exchange rate risk can be more subtle; even firms that have no foreign receipts or payments may still be exposed to foreign exchange risk. If the dollar is strong, the dollar price of foreign products to U.S. consumers becomes cheaper and foreign firms make inroads into the U.S. market, thereby decreasing net cash flows to the U.S. producers and thus reducing their value. The reverse is true when the value of the dollar falls. Obvious for firms like automakers, this economic or competitive (or "strategic") risk is receiving more attention by the managers of other U.S. firms as well.[2]

Not surprisingly, the same relations appear with respect to commodity price risk. The exposures can be apparent: For example, as the price of oil rises, the costs for an airline rise; so rising oil prices are linked to falling firm values. Or, the exposures can be subtle. For example, a primary input in aluminum production is electric energy. Aluminum manufacturers in Iceland use electricity generated by that country's abundant geothermal energy. As the price of oil rises, the costs of competitors rise while the costs of Icelandic producers remain unchanged, thus improving the competitive position and increasing the value of Icelandic firms. It is when oil prices fall and competitors' costs decline that Icelandic producers worry.[3]

Financial price risk, then – whether caused by changes in interest rates, foreign exchange, or commodity prices – consists of more subtle economic exposures as well as the obvious balance sheet mismatches and transactional exposures. And the *risk profile* mentioned earlier, in order to provide a useful measure of a firm's overall economic exposure, must reflect the total effect of both kinds of price risk.

The question that naturally arises, then, is: How do you determine the slope of the risk profile? That is, how do you estimate the change in firm value expected to accompany a given change in a financial price ($\Delta V/\Delta P$)?

Quantifying financial risk: a special case

Financial institutions, particularly banks, were the first to devote significant attention to quantifying financial exposures. Our S&L example is admittedly an extreme case of interest rate exposure, even for a financial institution. Nevertheless, because some mismatch between the maturities of assets and liabilities almost inevitably occurs in the normal course of their business, all financial institutions generally face some degree of interest rate risk. To measure this exposure to interest rates, financial institutions rely on two techniques: gap and duration.

Gap   The method most financial corporations use to measure their exposure to interest rate changes is called the "maturity gap" approach.[4] The approach gets its name from a procedure designed to quantify the "gap" between the market values of rate-sensitive assets (RSA) and rate-sensitive liabilities (RSL) – that is, GAP = RSA – RSL.[5] The financial institution determines the "gapping period" – the period over which it wants to measure its interest rate sensitivity – say, 6 months, one year, five years, and so forth. Then, for each of these periods, it measures its gap as defined above. In the context of a gap model, changes in interest rates affect a financial institution's market value by changing the institution's Net Interest Income (NII). Hence, once the GAP is known, the impact on the firm of changes in the interest rate can be calculated as follows:

$$\Delta NII = (GAP) \times (\Delta r)$$

Duration   Some financial institutions use an alternative to the GAP approach called "duration analysis" to measure their interest rate exposure.[6] In essence, the duration of a financial instrument provides a measure of when on average the present value of the instrument is received.

For example, let's look at the duration of a business loan with a maturity of 2.5 years and a sinking fund. Because part of the value is received prior to maturity, the duration of the instrument is clearly less than 2.5 years. To find out how much less, we need to ask the question "When on average is the present value received?"

Table 1 provides an illustration. Columns 1–4 provide the present value of the bond. To determine *when* the present value will be received, on average, we need to calculate the weighted average time of receipt. Column 5 provides the weights.

Table 1   Calculation of the value & duration of the business loan

(1) Time to receipt (Years)	(2) Cash flow	(3) Discount rate	(4) PV	(5) Weight	(6) Weight × Time
0.5	90	7.75%	86.70	0.22	0.11
1.0	90	8.00%	83.33	0.21	0.21
1.5	90	8.25%	79.91	0.20	0.30
2.0	90	8.35%	76.66	0.19	0.38
2.5	90	8.50%	73.40	0.18	0.45
			400.00 Present Value		1.45 Duration

Multiplying these weights (column 5) by the times the cash flows are received (column 1) and summing gives the duration of this business loan – 1.45 years.

The use of duration effectively converts a security into its zero-coupon equivalent. In addition, duration relates changes in interest rates to changes in the value of the security.[7] Specifically, duration permits us to express the percentage change in the value of the security in terms of the percentage change in the discount rate $(1 + r)$ and the duration of the security, as follows:[8]

$$\frac{\Delta V}{V} = \frac{\Delta(1+r)}{(1+r)} \times D$$

For example, if the duration of a security is 1.45 years, and the discount rate increases by 1 percent (that is, if $\Delta (1 + r)/(1 + r) = 0.01$), the market value of the 2.5 year business loan will decrease by 1.45 percent. The concept of duration, moreover, can be extended to provide a measure of the interest rate exposure of an entire bank or S&L.

Quantifying financial price risk: the general case

While gap and duration work well for financial institutions, these techniques offer little guidance in evaluating the interest rate sensitivity of a nonfinancial institution; and, neither gap nor duration is useful in examining a firm's sensitivity to movements in foreign exchange rates or commodity prices. What is needed is a more general method for quantifying financial price risk – a method that can handle firms other than financial institutions and financial exposures other than interest rates.

To get a measure of the responsiveness of the value of the firm to changes in the financial prices, we must first define a measure of the value of the firm. As with interest rate risk for financial institutions, this value measure could be a "flow" measure (gap analysis uses net interest income) or a "stock" measure (duration uses the market value of the portfolio).

Flow measures   Within a specific firm, estimation of the sensitivity of income flows is an analysis that can be performed as part of the planning and budgeting process.

The trade press suggests that some firms have begun using simulation models to examine the responsiveness of their pre-tax income to changes in interest rates, exchange rates, and commodity prices.[9] Beginning with base case assumptions about the financial prices, the firm obtains a forecast for revenues, costs, and the resulting pre-tax income. Then, it considers alternative values for an interest rate or an exchange rate or a commodity price and obtains a new forecast for revenues, costs, and pre-tax income. By observing how the firm's projected sales, costs and income move in response to changes in these financial prices, management is able to trace out a risk profile similar to that in Figure 1.

In making such an estimation, two inherent problems confront the analyst: (1) this approach requires substantial data and (2) it relies on the ability of the researcher to make explicit, accurate forecasts of sales and costs under alternative scenarios for the financial prices. For both these reasons, such an approach is generally feasible only for analysts within a specific firm.

Stock measures   Given the data requirements noted above, analysts outside the firm generally rely on market valuations, the most widely used of which is the current market value of the equity. Using a technique much like the one used to estimate a firm's "beta," an outside observer could measure the historical sensitivity of the company's equity value to changes in interest rates, foreign exchange rates, and commodity prices.

For example, suppose we wished to determine the sensitivity of a company's value to the following financial prices:

- the one-year T-bill interest rate;
- the Deutsche Mark / Dollar exchange rate;
- the Pound Sterling / Dollar exchange rate;
- the Yen / Dollar exchange rate; and
- the price of oil.

We could estimate this relation by performing a simple linear regression as follows:[10]

$$R_t = a + b_1 \left(\frac{\Delta P_{TB}}{P_{TB}} \right)_t + b_2 \left(\frac{\Delta P_{DM}}{P_{DM}} \right)_t + b_3 \left(\frac{\Delta P_{\pounds}}{P_{\pounds}} \right)_t + b_4 \left(\frac{\Delta P_y}{P_y} \right)_t + b_5 \left(\frac{\Delta P_{OIL}}{P_{OIL}} \right)_t$$

where R is the rate of return on the firm's equity; $\Delta P_{TB}/P_{TB}$ is the percentage change in the price of a one-year T-bill; $\Delta P_{DM}/P_{DM}$, $\Delta P_{\pounds}/P_{\pounds}$, and $\Delta P_y/P_y$ are the percentage changes in the dollar prices of the three foreign currencies; and $\Delta P_{OIL}/P_{OIL}$ is the percentage change in the price of crude oil. The estimate of b_1 provides a measure of the sensitivity of the value of the firm to changes in the one-year T-bill rate; b_2, b_3, and b_4 estimate its sensitivity to the exchange rates; and b_5 estimates its sensitivity to the oil price.[11]

To illustrate the kind of results this technique would yield, we present three examples: a bank, Chase Manhattan, an industrial, Caterpillar, and an oil company, Exxon. For the period January 6, 1984 to December 2, 1988 we calculated weekly (Friday close to Friday close) share returns and the corresponding weekly percentage changes in the price of a one-year T-bill rate, the dollar prices of a Deutsche Mark, a Pound Sterling, and a Yen, and the price of West Texas Intermediate

Table 2   Measurements of exposures to interest rate, foreign exchange rates, and oil prices

	Chase Manhattan		Caterpillar		Exxon	
Percentage change in	*Parameter estimate*	*T value*	*Parameter estimate*	*T value*	*Parameter estimate*	*T value*
Price of 1-Year T-Bill	2.598*	1.56	−3.221**	1.76	1.354	1.24
Price of DM	−0.276	0.95	0.344	1.07	−0.066	0.35
Price of Sterling	0.281	1.16	−0.010	0.38	0.237*	1.50
Price of Yen	−0.241	0.96	0.045	0.16	−0.278**	1.69
Price of WTI Crude	0.065	1.21	−0.045	0.77	0.082***	2.33

*   Significant at 90% single tailed
**   Significant at 90%
***   Significant at 95%

Table 2.A

Bank	Estimated sensitivity	T-value
Bank of America	3.2	1.5
Bankers Trust	2.2	1.4
Chase	2.6	1.6
First Chicago	3.0	1.6
Manufacturers Hanover	3.2	1.9

crude. Using these data, we estimated our regression equation. The results of these estimations are displayed in Table 2.

Given the tendency of banks to accept short-dated deposits to fund longer-dated assets (loans), it is not surprising that our estimates for Chase Manhattan indicate an inverse exposure to interest rates. Although only marginally significant, the positive coefficient indicates that an increase in the one-year T-bill rate (or a decrease in the price of the T-bill) is expected to lead to a decrease in the bank's value.

Additional information can be obtained by comparing the coefficient estimates among firms in the same industry. For example, we can compare the estimated sensitivity of Chase's value to the one-year T-bill rate to the sensitivities of other banks as shown in Table 2.A.

In contrast to the bank's inverse exposure, Caterpillar appears to have a positive exposure to the one-year T-bill rate. That is, the negative regression coefficient indicates that increases in the one-year T-bill rate (or decreases in the price of the T-bill) lead to increases in the value of the firm.

Even more surprising, though, given much that has been written about Caterpillar's exposure to foreign currency changes, is the lack of any significant exposure to the yen. This result is more understandable if we break up this 5-year span into shorter intervals and look at Caterpillar's sensitivity to the price of the yen on a

Table 2.B

	1984	1985	1986	1987	1988
Parameter estimate for percentage change in price of yen	1.72	0.15	0.33	−1.08	−0.85
T-value	1.59	0.31	0.65	1.08	1.53

Table 2.C

	1984	1985	1986	1987	1988
Parameter estimate for percentage change in price of oil	0.80	0.15	0.09	0.05	−0.01
T-value	3.94	0.85	2.79	0.37	0.17

year-by-year basis. (See Table 2.B.) The data reflect the fact that, as Caterpillar has moved its production facilities, the firm has changed from being positively exposed to the yen (such that an increase in the value of the dollar would harm Caterpillar) to being negatively exposed to the yen (an increase in the value of the dollar now helps Caterpillar).

Unlike the other two firms, the estimate for Exxon's exposure to interest rates is not statistically significant (not, at least, to the one-year T-bill rate). Exxon does exhibit the expected positive exposure to the price of oil. But our estimates also reflect the now common view, reported in the financial press and elsewhere, that Exxon's exposure to the price of oil has been declining over time – both in size and consistency (as measured by statistical significance). (See Table 2.C.) Given its international production and distribution, as well as its international portfolio of assets, Exxon also exhibits marginally significant exposures to foreign exchange rates. Our estimates suggest Exxon benefits from an increase in the value of the pound but is harmed by an increase in the value of the yen.

Measuring corporate exposure: summing up

The purpose of this first section, then, has been to outline a statistical technique (similar to that used to calculate a firm's "beta") that can be used to provide management with an estimate of the sensitivity of firm value to changes in a variety of financial variables. Such measures can be further refined by using information from other sources. For example, the same regression technique can be used, only substituting changes in the firm's periodic earnings and cash flows for the changes in stock prices in our model. There are, however, two principal advantages of our procedure over the use of such accounting numbers: (1) market reactions are likely to capture the entire capitalized value of changes in firm value in response to financial price changes; and (2) regression analysis using stock prices, besides being much faster and cheaper, can be done using publicly available information.

The Tools for Managing Financial Risk: A Building Block Approach[12]

If it turns out that a firm is subject to significant financial price risk, management may choose to hedge that risk.[13] One way of doing so is by using an "on-balance-sheet" transaction. For example, a company could manage a foreign exchange exposure resulting from overseas competition by borrowing in the competitor's currency or by moving production abroad. But such on-balance sheet methods can be costly and, as firms like Caterpillar have discovered, inflexible.[14]

Alternatively, financial risks can be managed with the use of off-balance-sheet instruments. The four fundamental off-balance-sheet instruments are forwards, futures, swaps, and options.

When we first began to attempt to understand these financial instruments, we were confronted by what seemed an insurmountable barrier to entry. The participants in the various markets all seemed to possess a highly specialized expertise that was applicable in only one market to the exclusion of all others (and the associated trade publications served only to tighten the veil of mystery that "experts" have always used to deny entry to novices). Options were discussed as if they were completely unrelated to forwards or futures, which in turn seemed to have nothing to do with the latest innovation, swaps. Adding to the complexities of the individual markets was the welter of jargon that seems to have grown up around each, thus further obscuring any common ground that might exist. (Words such as "ticks," "collars," "strike prices," and "straddles" suddenly had acquired a remarkable currency.) In short, we seemed to find ourselves looking up into a Wall Street Tower of Babel, with each group of market specialists speaking in different languages.

But, after now having observed these instruments over the past several years, we have been struck by how little one has to dig before superficial differences give way to fundamental unity. And, in marked contrast to the specialized view of most Wall Street practitioners, we take a more "generalist" approach – one that treats forwards, futures, swaps, and options not as four unique instruments and markets, but rather as four interrelated instruments for dealing with a single problem: managing financial risk. In fact, we have come up with a little analogy that captures the spirit of our conclusion, one which goes as follows: The four basic off-balance-sheet instruments – forwards, futures, swaps, and options – are much like those plastic building blocks children snap together. You can either build the instruments from one another, or you can combine the instruments into larger creations that appear (but appearances deceive) altogether "new."

Forward contracts

Of the four instruments, the forward contract is the oldest and, perhaps for this reason, the most straightforward. A forward contract obligates its owner to buy a specified asset on a specified date at a price (known as the "exercise price") specified at the origination of the contract. If, at maturity, the actual price is higher than the exercise price, the contract owner makes a profit equal to the difference; if the price is lower, he suffers a loss.

Figure 2   Payoff profile for forward contract

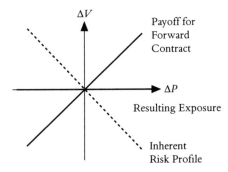

In Figure 2, the payoff from buying a forward contract is illustrated with a hypothetical risk profile. If the actual price at contract maturity is higher than the expected price, the inherent risk results in a decline in the value of the firm; but this decline is offset by the profit on the forward contract, Hence, for the risk profile illustrated, the forward contract provides an effective hedge. (If the risk profile were positively instead of negatively sloped, the risk would be managed by selling instead of buying a forward contract.)

Besides its payoff profile, a forward contract has two other features that should be noted. First, the default (or credit) risk of the contract is two-sided. The contract owner either receives or makes a payment, depending on the price movement of the underlying asset. Second, the value of the forward contract is conveyed only at the contract's maturity; no payment is made either at origination or during the term of the contract.

Futures contracts

The basic form of the futures contract is identical to that of the forward contract; a futures contract also obligates its owner to purchase a specified asset at a specified exercise price on the contract maturity date. Thus, the payoff profile for the purchaser of a forward contract as presented in Figure 2 could also serve to illustrate the payoff to the holder of a futures contract.

But, unlike the case of forwards, credit or default risk can be virtually eliminated in a futures market. Futures markets use two devices to manage default risk. First, instead of conveying the value of a contract through a single payment at maturity, any change in the value of a futures contract is conveyed at the end of the day in which it is realized. Look again at Figure 2. Suppose that, on the day after origination, the financial price rises and, consequently, the financial instrument has a positive value. In the case of a forward contract, this value change would not be received until contract maturity. With a futures contract, this change in value is received at the end of the day. In the language of the futures markets, the futures contract is "marked-to-market" and "cash settled" daily.

Because the performance period of a futures contract is reduced by marking to market, the risk of default declines accordingly. Indeed, because the value of the futures contract is paid or received at the end of each day, Fischer Black likened a futures contract to "a series of forward contracts [in which] each day, yesterday's contract is settled and today's contract is written."[15] That is, a futures contract is like a sequence of forwards in which the "forward" contract written on day 0 is settled on day 1 and is replaced, in effect, with a new "forward" contract reflecting the new day 1 expectations. This new contract is then itself settled on day 2 and replaced, and so on until the day the contract ends.

The second feature of futures contracts which reduces default risk is the requirement that all market participants – sellers and buyers alike – post a performance bond called the "margin."[16] If my futures contract increases in value during the trading day, this gain is added to my margin account at the day's end. Conversely, if my contract has lost value, this loss is deducted from my margin account. And, if my margin account balance falls below some agreed-upon minimum, I am required to post additional bond; that is, my margin account must be replenished or my position will be closed out.[17] Because the position will be closed before the margin account is depleted, performance risk is eliminated.[18]

Note that the exchange itself has not been proposed as a device to reduce default risk. Daily settlement and the requirement of a bond reduce default risk, but the existence of an exchange (or clearing-house) merely serves to transform risk. More specifically, the exchange deals with the two-sided risk inherent in forwards and futures by serving as the counterparty to all transactions. If I wish to buy or sell a futures contract, I buy from or sell to the exchange. Hence, I need only evaluate the credit risk of the exchange, not of some specific counterparty.

The primary economic function of the exchange is to reduce the costs of transacting in futures contracts. The anonymous trades made possible by the exchange, together with the homogeneous nature of the futures contracts – standardized assets, exercise dates (four per year), and contract sizes – enables the futures markets to become relatively liquid. However, as was made clear by recent experience of the London Metal Exchange, the existence of the exchange does not in and of itself eliminate the possibility of default.[19]

In sum, a futures contract is much like a portfolio of forward contracts. At the close of business of each day, in effect, the existing forward-like contract is settled and a new one is written.[20] This daily settlement feature combined with the margin requirement allows futures contracts to eliminate the credit risk inherent in forwards.

Swap contracts[21]

A swap contract is in essence nothing more complicated than a series of forward contracts strung together. As implied by its name, a swap contract obligates two parties to exchange, or "swap," some specified cash flows at specified intervals. The most common form is the interest rate swap, in which the cash flows are determined by two different interest rates.

Panel A of Figure 3 illustrates an interest rate swap from the perspective of a party who is paying out a series of cash flows determined by a fixed interest rate ($\bar{R}$) in return for a series of cash flows determined by a floating interest rate ($\tilde{R}$).[22]

Panel B of Figure 3 serves to illustrate that this swap contract can be decomposed into a portfolio of forward contracts. At each settlement date, the party to this swap contract has an implicit forward contract on interest rates: the party illustrated is

Figure 3

Panel A: An Interest Rate Swap

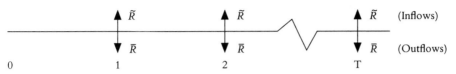

Panel B: An Interest Rate Swap As a Portfolio of Forward Contracts

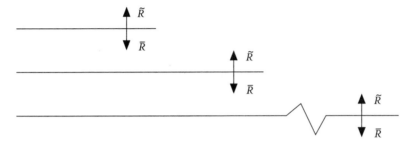

obligated to sell a fixed-rate cash flow for an amount specified at the origination of the contract. In this sense, a swap contract is also like a portfolio of forward contracts.

In terms of our earlier discussion, this means that the solid line in Figure 2 could also represent the payoff from a swap contract. Specifically, the solid line in Figure 3 would be consistent with a swap contract in which the party illustrated receives cash flows determined by one price (say, the U.S. Treasury bond rate) and makes payments determined by another price (say, LIBOR). Thus, in terms of their ability to manage risk, forwards, futures, and swaps all function in the same way.

But identical payoff *patterns* notwithstanding, the instruments all differ with respect to default risk. As we saw, the performance period of a forward is equal to its maturity; and because no performance bond is required, a forward contract is a pure credit instrument. Futures both reduce the performance period (to one day) and require a bond, thereby eliminating credit risk. Swap contracts use only one of these mechanisms to reduce credit risk; they reduce the performance period.[23] This point becomes evident in Figure 3. Although the maturity of the contract is T periods, the performance period is generally not T periods long but is instead a single period. Thus, given a swap and a forward contract of roughly the same maturity, the swap is likely to impose far less credit risk on the counterparties to the contract than the forward.

At each settlement date throughout a swap contract, the changes in value are transferred between the counterparties. To illustrate this in terms of Figure 3, suppose that interest rates rise on the day after origination. The value of the swap contract illustrated has risen. This value change will be conveyed to the contract owner not at maturity (as would be the case with a forward contract) nor at the end of that day (as would be the case with a futures contract). Instead, at the first settlement date, part of the value change is conveyed in the form of the "difference check" paid by one party to the other. To repeat, then, the performance period is

Figure 4   Payoff profiles of puts and calls

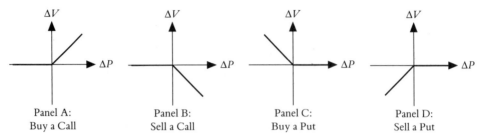

| Panel A: | Panel B: | Panel C: | Panel D: |
| Buy a Call | Sell a Call | Buy a Put | Sell a Put |

less than that of a forward, but not as short as that of a futures contract.[24] (Keep in mind that we are comparing instruments with the same maturities.)

Let us reinforce the two major points made thus far. First, a swap contract, like a futures contract, is like a portfolio of forward contracts. Therefore, the payoff profiles for each of these three instruments are identical. Second, the primary difference among forwards, futures, and swaps is the amount of default risk they impose on counterparties to the contract. Forwards and futures represent the extremes, and swaps are the intermediate case.

Option contracts

As we have seen, the owner of a forward, futures, or swap contract has an *obligation* to perform. In contrast, an option gives its owner a *right*, not an obligation. An option giving its owner the right to buy an asset at a pre-determined price – a call option – is provided in Panel A of Figure 4. The owner of the contract has the right to purchase the asset at a specified future date at a price agreed-upon today. Thus, if the price rises, the value of the option also goes up. But because the option contract owner is not obligated to purchase the asset if the price moves against him, the value of the option remains unchanged (at zero) if the price declines.[25]

The payoff profile for the party who sold the call option (also known as the call "writer") is shown in Panel B. In contrast to the buyer of the option, the seller of the call option has the *obligation* to perform. For example, if the owner of the option elects to exercise his option to buy the asset, the seller of the option is obligated to sell the asset.

Besides the option to buy an asset, there is also the option to sell an asset at a specified price, known as a "put" option. The payoff to the buyer of a put is illustrated in Panel C of Figure 4, and the payoff to the seller of the put is shown in Panel D.

Pricing options   Up to this point, we have considered only the payoffs to the option contracts. We have side-stepped the thorniest issue – the valuation of option contracts.

The breakthrough in option pricing theory came with the work of Fischer Black and Myron Scholes in 1973.[26] Conveniently for our purposes, Black and Scholes took what might be described as a "building block" approach to the valuation of options. Look again at the call option illustrated in Figure 4. For increases in the financial price, the payoff profile for the option is that of a forward contract. For

Figure 5

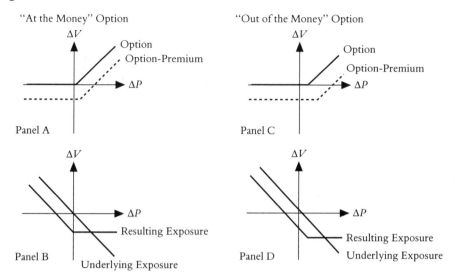

decreases in the price, the value of the option is constant – like that of a "riskless" security such as a Treasury bill.

The work of Black and Scholes demonstrated that a call option could be replicated by a continuously adjusting ("dynamic") portfolio of two securities: (1) forward contracts on the underlying asset and (2) riskless securities. As the financial price rises, the "call option equivalent" portfolio contains an increasing proportion of forward contracts on the asset. Conversely, the replicating portfolio contains a decreasing proportion of forwards as the price of the asset falls.

Because this replicating portfolio is effectively a synthetic call option, arbitrage activity should ensure that its value closely approximates the market price of exchange-traded call options. In this sense, the value of a call option, and thus the premium that would be charged its buyer, is determined by the value of its option equivalent portfolio.

Panel A of Figures 5 illustrates the payoff profile for a call option which includes the premium. This figure (and all of the option figures thus far) illustrates an "at-the-money" option – that is, an option for which the exercise price is the prevailing expected price. As Panels A and B of Figure 5 illustrate, an at-the-money option is paid for by sacrificing a significant amount of the firm's potential gains. However, the price of a call option falls as the exercise price increases relative to the prevailing price of the asset. This means that if an option buyer is willing to accept larger potential losses in return for paying a lower option premium, he would then consider using an "out-of-the-money" option.

An out-of-the-money call option is illustrated in Panel C of Figure 5. As shown in Panel D, the out-of-the-money option provides less downside protection, but the option premium is significantly less. The lesson to be learned here is that the option buyer can alter his payoff profile simply by changing the exercise price.

For our purposes, however, the most important feature of options is that they are not as different from other financial instruments as they might first seem. Options

Figure 6

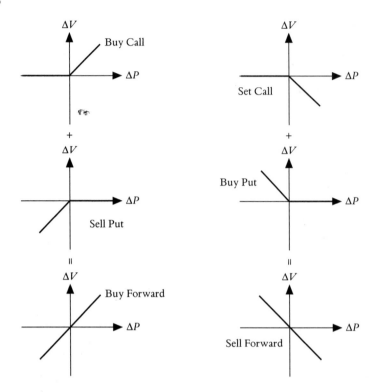

do have a payoff profile that differs significantly from that of forward contracts (or futures or swaps). But, option payoff profiles can be duplicated by a combination of forwards and risk-free securities. Thus, we find that options have more in common with the other instruments than was first apparent. Futures and swaps, as we saw earlier, are in essence nothing more than portfolios of forward contracts; and options, as we have just seen, are very much akin to portfolios of forward contracts and risk-free securities.

This point is reinforced if we consider ways that options can be combined. Consider a portfolio constructed by buying a call and selling a put with the same exercise price. As the left side of Figure 6 illustrates, the resulting portfolio (long a call, short a put) has a payoff profile equivalent to that of buying a forward contract on the asset. Similarly, the right side of Figure 6 illustrates that a portfolio made up of selling a call and buying a put (short a call, long a put) is equivalent to selling a forward contract.

The relationship illustrated in Figure 6 is known more formally as "put-call parity." The special import of this relationship, at least in this context, is the "building block construction" it makes possible: two options can be "snapped together" to yield the payoff profile for a forward contract, which is identical to the payoff profile for futures and swaps.

At the beginning of this section, then, it seemed that options would be very different from forwards, futures, and swaps – and in some ways they are. But we discovered two building block relations between options and the other three

Figure 7

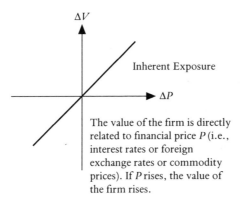

ΔV

Inherent Exposure

ΔP

The value of the firm is directly
related to financial price P (i.e.,
interest rates or foreign
exchange rates or commodity
prices). If P rises, the value of
the firm rises.

instruments: (1) options can be replicated by "snapping together" a forward, futures, or swap contract together with a position in risk-free securities; and (2) calls and puts can be combined to become forwards.

The financial building blocks

Forwards, futures, swaps, and options – they all look so different from one another. And if you read the trade publications or talk to the specialists that transact in the four markets, the apparent differences among the instruments are likely to seem even more pronounced.

But it turns out that forwards, futures, swaps, and options are not each unique constructions, but rather more like those plastic building blocks that children combine to make complex structures. To understand the off-balance-sheet instruments, you don't need a lot of market-specific knowledge. All you need to know is how the instruments can be linked to one another. As we have seen, (1) futures can be built by "snapping together" a package of forwards; (2) swaps can also be built by putting together a package of forwards; (3) synthetic options can be constructed by combining a forward with a riskless security; and (4) options can be combined to produce forward contracts – or, conversely, forwards can be pulled apart to replicate a package of options.

Having shown you all the building blocks and how they fit together in simple constructions, we now want to demonstrate how they can be used to create more complicated, customized financial instruments that in turn can be used to manage financial risks.

Assembling the Building Blocks

Using the building blocks to manage an exposure

Consider a company whose market value is directly related to unexpected changes in some financial price, P. The risk profile of this company is illustrated in Figure 7. How could we use the financial building blocks to modify this inherent exposure?

Figure 8

Use a forward or futures or swap . . .

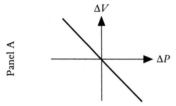

Panel A

to neutralize the risk

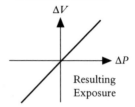

Resulting
Exposure

Or, use an at-the-money option . . .

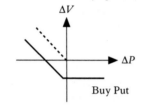

Buy Put

Panel B

to minimize adverse outcomes

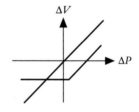

Or, use an out-of-the-money option . . .

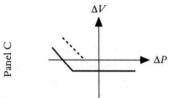

Panel C

to get lower cost insurance

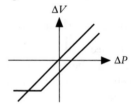

Or, buy and sell options . . .

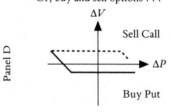

Sell Call

Buy Put

Panel D

to eliminate out-of-pocket costs

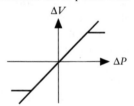

Or, use a forward/futures/swap with options . . . to provide customized solutions

Panel E

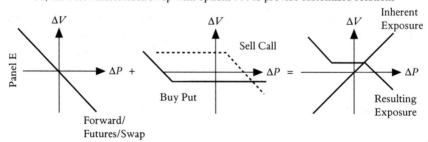

Forward/
Futures/Swap

Buy Put

Sell Call

Inherent
Exposure

Resulting
Exposure

The simplest solution is to use a forward, a futures, or a swap to neutralize this exposure. This is shown in Panel A of Figure 8.

But, the use of a forward, a futures, or a swap eliminates possible losses by giving up the possibility of profiting from favorable outcomes. The company might want to minimize the effect of unfavorable outcomes while still allowing the possibility of gaining from favorable ones. This can be accomplished using options. The payoff profile of an at-the-money option (including the premium paid to buy the option) is shown on the left side of Panel B. Snapping this building block onto the inherent exposure profile gives the resulting exposure illustrated on the right side of panel B.

A common complaint about options – especially at-the-money options – is that they are "too expensive." To reduce the option premium, you can think about using an out-of-the-money option. As Panel C of Figure 8 illustrates, the firm has thereby given up some protection from adverse outcomes in return for paying a lower premium.

But, with an out-of-the-money option, some premium expense remains. Panel D illustrates how the out-of-pocket expense can be *eliminated*. The firm can sell a call option with an exercise price chosen so as to generate premium income equal to the premium due on the put option it wishes to purchase. In building block parlance, we snap the "buy-a-put" option onto the inherent risk profile to reduce downside outcomes; and we snap on the "sell-a-call" option to fund this insurance by giving up some of the favorable outcomes.

Panel E reminds us that forwards, futures, and swaps can be used in combination with options. Suppose the treasurer of the company we have been considering comes to you with the following request:

> *I think that this financial price, P, is going to fall dramatically. And, while I know enough about financial markets to know that P could actually rise a little, I am sure it will not rise by much. I want some kind of financial solution that will let me benefit when my predictions come to pass. But I don't want to pay any out-of-pocket premiums. Instead, I want this financial engineering product to pay me a premium.*

If you look at the firm's inherent risk profile in Figure 7, this seems like a big request. The firm's inherent position is such that it would lose rather than gain from big decreases in P.

The resulting exposure profile shown on the right side of Panel E is the one the firm wants: it benefits from large decreases in P, is protected against small increases in P (though not against large increases) and receives a premium for the instrument.

How was this new profile achieved? As illustrated on the left side of Panel E. we first snapped a forward/futures/swap position onto the original risk profile to neutralize the firm's inherent exposure. We then sold a call option and bought a put option with exercise prices set such that the income from selling the call exceeded the premium required to buy the put.

No high level math was required. Indeed, we did this bit of financial engineering simply by looking through the box of financial building blocks until we found those that snapped together to give us the profile we wanted.

Figure 9   Pay Fixed, Receive Floating for Period 1 through T

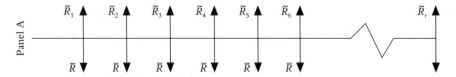

PLUS Pay Floating, Receive Fixed for Periods 1 through 4

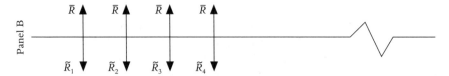

EQUALS A four-period forward contract on a Pay Fixed, Receive Floating Swap

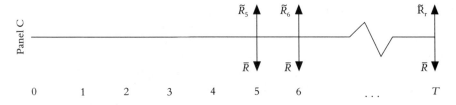

Using the building blocks to redesign financial instruments

Now that you understand how forwards, futures, swaps, and options are all fundamentally related, it is a relatively short step to thinking about how the instruments can be combined with each other to give one financial instrument the characteristics of another. Rather than talk about this in the abstract, let's look at some examples of how this has been done in the marketplace.

Combining forwards with swaps   Suppose a firm's value is currently unaffected by interest rate movements. But, at a known date in the future, it expects to become exposed to interest rates: if rates rise, the value of the firm will decrease.[27] To manage this exposure, the firm could use a forward, futures, or swap commencing at that future date. Such a product is known as a *forward* or *delayed start* swap. The payoff from a forward swap is illustrated in Panel C of Figure 9, where the party illustrated pays a fixed rate and receives floating starting in period 5.

   Although this instrument is in effect a forward contract on a swap, it also, not surprisingly, can be constructed as a package of swaps. As Figure 9 illustrates, a forward swap is equivalent to a package of two swaps:

Swap 1 – From period 1 to period T, the party pays fixed and receives floating.
Swap 2 – From period 1 to period 4, the party pays floating and receives fixed.

Figure 10

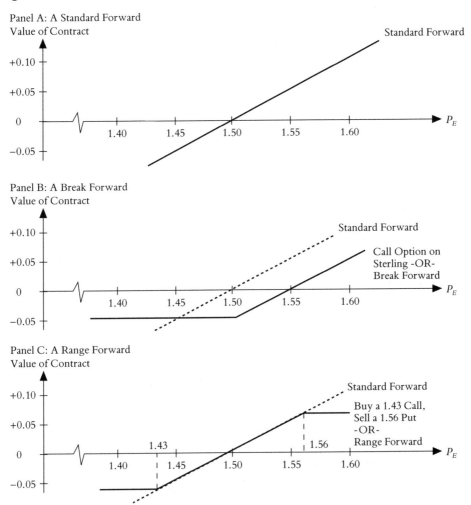

Panel A: A Standard Forward

Panel B: A Break Forward

Panel C: A Range Forward

Forwards with option-like characteristics   The addition of option-like characteristics to forward contracts first appeared in the foreign exchange markets. To see how this was done, let's trace the evolution of these contracts.

Begin with a standard forward contract on foreign exchange. Panel A of Figure 10 illustrates a conventional forward contract on sterling with the forward sterling exchange rate (the "contract rate") set at $1.50 per pound sterling. If, at maturity, the spot price of sterling exceeds $1.50, the owner of this contract makes a profit (equal to the spot rate minus $1.50). Conversely, if at maturity the spot price of sterling is less than $1.50, the owner of this contract suffers a loss. The owner of the forward contract, however, might instead want a contract that allows him to profit if the price of sterling rises, but limits his losses if the price of sterling falls.[28] Such a contract would be a call option on sterling. Illustrated in Panel B of Figure 10 is a call option on sterling with an exercise price of $1.50. In this illustration we have assumed an option premium of 5 cents (per pound sterling).

The payoff profile illustrated in Panel B of Figure 10 could also be achieved by altering the terms of the standard forward contract as follows:

1. Change the contract price so that the exercise price of the forward contract is no longer $1.50 but is instead $1.55. The owner of the forward contract agrees to purchase sterling at contract maturity at a price of $1.55 per unit; and
2. Permit the owner of the contract to break (i.e. "unwind") the agreement at a sterling price of $1.50.

This altered forward contract is referred to as a *break forward* contract.[29] In this break forward construction, the premium is effectively being paid by the owner of the break forward contract in the form of the above market contract exchange rate.

From our discussion of options, we also know that a call can be paid for with the proceeds from selling a put. The payoff profile for such a situation is illustrated in Panel C of Figure 10. In this illustration, we have assumed that the proceeds of a put option on sterling with an exercise price of $1.56 would carry the same premium as a call option on sterling with an exercise price of $1.43.[30]

A payoff profile identical to this option payoff profile could also be generated, however, simply by changing the terms of a standard forward contract to the following:

*   at maturity, the buyer of the forward contract agrees to purchase sterling at a price of $1.50 per pound sterling;
*   the buyer of the forward contract has the right to break the contract at a price of $1.43 per pound sterling; and
*   the seller of the forward contract has the right to break the contract at a price of $1.56 per pound sterling.
    Such a forward contract is referred to as a *range forward.*[31]

Swaps with option-like characteristics   Given that swaps can be viewed as packages of forward contracts, it should not be surprising that swaps can also be constructed to have option-like characteristics like those illustrated for forwards. For example, suppose that a firm with a floating-rate liability wanted to limit its outflows should interest rates rise substantially; at the same time, it was willing to give up some potential gains should there instead be a dramatic decline in short-term rates. To achieve this end, the firm could modify the interest rate swap contract as follows:

> *As long as the interest rate neither rises by more than 200 basis points nor falls more than 100 basis points, the firm pays a floating rate and receives a fixed rate. But, if the interest is more than 200 basis points above or 100 basis points below the current rate, the firm receives and pays a fixed rate.*

The resulting payoff profile for this floating floor-ceiling swap is illustrated in Panel A of Figure 11.

Conversely, the interest rate swap contract could have been modified as follows:

> *As long as the interest rate is within 200 basis points of the current rate, the firm neither makes nor receives a payment; but if the interest rate rises or falls by more than 200 basis points, the firm pays a floating rate and receives a fixed rate.*

Figure 11 Pay-off profile for floor-ceiling swaps

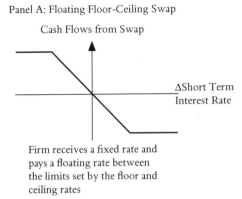

Panel A: Floating Floor-Ceiling Swap

Cash Flows from Swap

ΔShort Term Interest Rate

Firm receives a fixed rate and pays a floating rate between the limits set by the floor and ceiling rates

Panel B: Fixed Floor-Ceiling Swap

Cash Flows from Swap

Firm receives a fixed rate and pays a floating rate outside the limits set by the floor and ceiling rates.

Figure 12

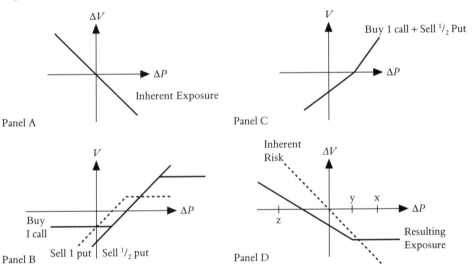

Panel A

Inherent Exposure

Panel C

Buy 1 call + Sell $^1/_2$ Put

Panel B

Buy I call

Sell 1 put | Sell $^1/_2$ put

Panel D

Inherent Risk

Resulting Exposure

The payoff profile for the resulting fixed floor-ceiling swap is illustrated in Panel B of Figure 11.

Redesigned options To "redesign" an option, what is normally done is to put two or more options together to change the payoff profile. Examples abound in the world of the option trader. Some of the more colorfully-named combinations are *straddles, strangles,* and *butterflies.*[32]

To see how and why these kinds of creations evolve, let's look at a hypothetical situation. Suppose a firm was confronted with the inherent exposure illustrated in Panel A of Figure 12. Suppose further that the firm wanted to establish a floor on losses caused by changes in a financial price.

As you already know, this could be done by purchasing an out-of-the-money call option on the financial price. A potential problem with this solution, as we have seen, is the premium the firm has to pay. Is there a way the premium can be eliminated?

We have already seen that buying an out-of-the-money call can be financed by selling an out-of-the-money put. However, suppose that this out-of-the-money call is financed by selling a put with precisely the same exercise price – in which case, the put would be in-the-money. As illustrated in Panel B of Figure 12, the proceeds from selling the in-the-money put would exceed the cost of the out-of-the-money call. Therefore, to finance one out-of-the-money call, one would need sell only a fraction of one in-the-money put.

In Panel B, we have assumed that the put value is twice the call value; so, to finance one call, you need sell only 1/2 put. Panel C simply combines the payoff profiles for selling 1/2 put and buying one call with an exercise price of X. Finally, Panel D of Figure 12 combines the option combination in Panel C with the inherent risk profile in Panel A.

Note what has happened. The firm has obtained the floor it wanted, but there is no up-front premium. At the price at which the option is exercised, the value of the firm with the floor is the same as it would have been without the floor. The floor is paid for not with a fixed premium, but with a share of the firm's gains above the floor. If the financial price rises by X, the value of the firm falls to the floor and no premium is paid. If, however, the financial price rises by less, say Y, the value of the firm is higher and the firm pays a positive premium for the floor. And, if the financial price falls, say, by Z, the price it pays for the floor rises.

What we have here is a situation where the provider of the floor is paid with a share of potential gains, thereby leading to the name of this option combination – a *participation*. This construction has been most widely used in the foreign exchange market where they are referred to as *participating forwards*.[33]

Options on other financial instruments

Options on futures contracts on bonds have been actively traded on the Chicago Board of Trade since 1982. The valuation of an option on a futures is a relatively straightforward extension of the traditional option pricing models.[34] Despite the close relation between futures and forwards and futures and swaps, the options on forwards (*options on forward rate agreements*) and options on swaps (*swaptions*) are much more recent.

More complicated analytically is the valuation of an option on an option, also known as a *compound option*.[35] Despite their complexity and resistance to valuation formulae, some options on options have begun to be traded. These include options on foreign exchange options and, most notably, options on interest rate options (caps), referred to in the trade as *captions*.

Using the building blocks to design "new" products

It's rare that a day goes by in the financial markets without hearing of at least one "new" or "hybrid" product. But, as you should have come to expect from us by now, our position with respect to "financial engineering" is that there is little new under the sun. The "new" products typically involve nothing more than putting the building blocks together in a new way.

Reverse floaters   One example of a hybrid security is provided in Figure 13. If we combine the issuance of a conventional fixed rate loan and an interest rate swap

Figure 13   Using a swap to create a reverse floating rate loan

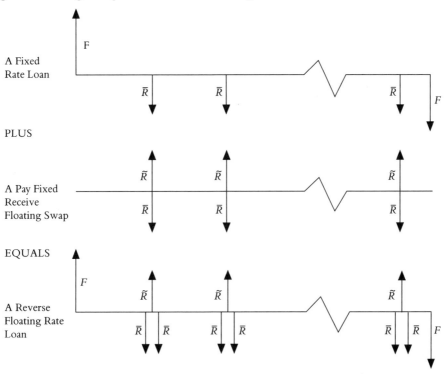

where the issuing party pays fixed and receives floating, the result is a reverse floating-rate loan. The net coupon payments on the hybrid loan are equal to twice the fixed rate ($\bar{r}$) minus the floating rate ($\tilde{r}$) times the principal (P), or

$$\text{Net Coupon} = (2\bar{r} - \tilde{r})P = 2\bar{R} - \tilde{R}$$

If the floating rate ($\tilde{r}$) rises, the net coupon payment falls.

Bonds with embedded options   Another form of hybrid securities has evolved from bonds with warrants. Bonds with warrants on the issuer's shares have become common. Bond issues have also recently appeared that feature warrants that can be exercised into foreign exchange and gold.

And, in 1986, Standard Oil issued a bond with an oil warrant. These notes stipulated that the principal payment at maturity would be a function of oil prices at maturity. As specified in the Prospectus, the holders of the 1990 notes will receive, in addition to a guaranteed minimum principal amount, "the excess . . . of the Crude Oil Price . . . over $25 multiplied by 170 barrels of Light Sweet Crude Oil." What this means is that the note has an embedded four-year option on 170 barrels of crude oil. If, at maturity, the value of Light Sweet Oklahoma Crude Oil exceeds $25, the holder of the note will receive (Oil Price – $25) × 170 plus the guaranteed minimum principal amount. If the value of Light Sweet Oklahoma Crude is less than $25 at maturity, the option expires worthless.[36]

Figure 14

An Off-Market-
Rate Bond

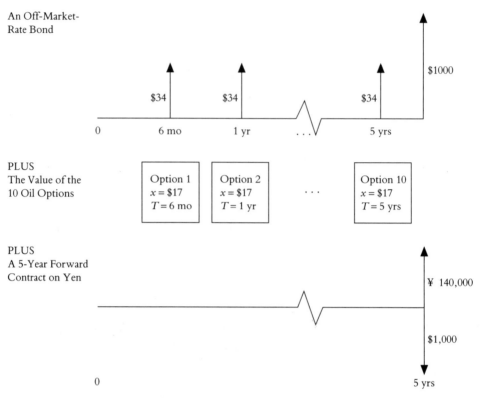

PLUS
The Value of the
10 Oil Options

PLUS
A 5-Year Forward
Contract on Yen

The building block process has also been extended to changes in the timing of the options embedded in the bond. For a traditional bond with an attached warrant, there is only one option exerciseable at one point in time. More recent bonds have involved packages of options which can be exercised at different points in time.

The first time we saw this extension was in Forest Oil Corporation's proposed *Natural Gas Interest Indexed Debentures.* As set forth in the issue's red herring prospectus of July 1988, Forest Oil proposed to pay a stipulated base rate plus four basis points for each $0.01 by which the average gas spot price exceeds $1.76 per MMBTU (million British Thermal Units). In effect, then, this proposed 12-year "hybrid" debenture is a package consisting of one standard bond plus 24 options on the price of natural gas with maturities ranging from 6 months to 12 years.[37]

And, if we want to get a little fancier, we can consider the possibility of an *Oil Interest-Indexed, Dual-Currency Bond.*[38] Assume that the maturity of this issue is 5 years, with the semi-annual coupon payments indexed to the price of crude oil and the final principal repayment indexed to the value of yen. More specifically, assume that, for each $1000 of principal, the bondholder receives the following: (1) the greater of $34 or the value of two barrels of Sweet Light Crude Oil at each coupon date; and (2) 140,000 yen at maturity.

How would we value such a complicated package? The answer, again, is by breaking it down into the building blocks. As shown in Figure 14, this oil-indexed, dual currency bond consists of three basic components: (1) a straight bond paying

$34 semi-annually; (2) 10 call options on the price of oil with an exercise price of $17 per barrel ($34/2) maturing sequentially every six months over a five-year period; and (3) a five-year forward contract on yen with an exercise price of 140 yen/dollar. As it turns out, then, this complicated-looking bond is nothing more than a combination of a standard bond, a series of options, and a forward contract.

Concluding Remarks

The world is more volatile today than it was two decades ago. Today's corporate risk manager must deal with the potential impact on the firm of significant month-to-month (and sometimes day-to-day) changes in exchange rates, interest rates, and commodity prices. Volatility alone could put a well-run firm out of business, so financial price risk deserves careful attention. As this summary has demonstrated, there now exist techniques and tools for accomplishing this task.

This article makes three major points:

First, there are simple techniques that allow management (and outsiders as well) to identify and measure a firm's exposures. Besides managing "one-off" exposures (such as interest rate exposures from floating-rate borrowings or foreign exchange transaction and translation exposures), many firms are now recognizing their economic exposures. To measure such economic exposures, we have introduced the concept of the *risk profile*. Using this concept, we have proposed simple methods for quantifying the extent of an individual firm's exposures to interest rates, foreign exchange rates, and commodity prices. In the case of a financial firm's exposure to interest rate risk, the techniques of "gap" and "duration" analysis can be applied directly. For the more general case, we demonstrate how simple regression analysis (the same technique used in calculating a firm's "beta") can be used to measure a variety of exposures.

Second, the tools for managing financial risk are more simple than they appear. These financial instruments can be viewed as building blocks. The basic component is a forward contract. Both futures and swaps are like bundles of forward contracts; forwards, in fact, can be combined to yield futures and swaps. The primary differences between these two instruments are the way they deal with default risk and the degree of customization available.

Even options, moreover, can be related to forward contracts. An option on a given asset can be created by combining a position in a forward contract on the same asset with a riskless security; in short, forwards and T-bills can be combined to produce options.[39] Finally, options can be combined to create forward positions; for example, buying a call and shorting a put produces the same position as buying a forward contract.

Third, once you understand the four basic building blocks, it is a straightforward step to designing a customized strategy for managing your firm's exposure. Once the exposure is identified, it can be managed in a number of ways:

- by using one of the financial instruments – for example, by using an interest rate swap to hedge a building products firm's exposure to rising interest rates;
- by using combinations of the financial instruments – for example, buying a call and selling a put to minimize the out-of-pocket costs of the hedge; or

- by combining financial instruments with a debt instrument to create a hybrid security – for example, issuing an oil-indexed bond to hedge a firm's exposure to oil prices.

Our final point in all of this is very simple. Managing financial price risk with "financial engineering" sounds like something you need a degree from Caltech or M.I.T. to do. Designing effective solutions with the financial building blocks is easy.

Notes ──

This article is an abbreviated version of Chapters 2, 3, and 19 of *Managing Financial Risk*, forthcoming Ballinger/*Institutional Investor Series*. This material is used with the permission of the publisher.

1. A transaction exposure occurs when the firm has a payment or receipt in a currency other than its home currency. A translation exposure results when the value of foreign assets and liabilities must be converted into home currency values.
2. A case in point is Kodak, which has begun to manage "overall corporate performance in the long run." See Paul Dickens. "Daring to Hedge the Unhedgeable," *Euromoney Corporate Finance*. August 1988.
3. For this useful story about Icelandic aluminum producers, we are indebted to J. Nicholas Robinson of Chase Manhattan Bank.
4. For a discussion of the maturity gap model, see Alden L. Toevs, "Measuring and Managing Interest Rate Risk: A Guide to Asset/Liability Models Used in Banks and Thrifts," Morgan Stanley Fixed Income Analytical Research Paper, October 1984. (An earlier version of this paper appeared in *Economic Review*, The Federal Reserve Bank of San Francisco, Spring, 1983.)
5. The assets and liabilities that are "rate sensitive" are those that will reprice during the gapping period.
6. For a discussion of duration, see George G. Kaufman, "Measuring and Managing Interest Rate Risk: A Primer," *Economic Perspectives*, Federal Reserve Bank of Chicago. See also Stephen Schaefer, "Immunisation and Duration: A Review of the Theory, Performance, and Applications," *Midland Corporate Finance Journal*, Vol. 2 No. 3, Fall 1984.
7. Note the contrast with the gap approach, which relates changes in the interest rate to changes in net interest income.
8. The calculations in Table 1 are based on the use of MacCauley's duration. If we continue to apply MacCauley's duration (D), this equation is only an approximation. To be exact, modified duration should be used. For a development of this relation, see George G. Kaufman, G. O. Bierwag, and Alden Toevs, eds. *Innovations in Bond Portfolio Management: Duration Analysis and Immunization* (Greenwich, Conn.: JAI Press, 1983).
9. See for instance, Paul Dickens, cited in note 2.
10. In effect, this equation represents a variance decomposition. While it is a multifactor model, it is not related in any important way to the APT approach suggested by Ross and Roll. Instead, it is probably more accurate to view the approach we suggest as an extension of the market model. In its more complete form, as described in Chapter 2 of our book, *Managing Financial Risk*, the regression equation would include the rate of return to the market ("beta") as well as the percentage changes in the financial prices, and would thus look as follows:

$$R_t = a + \beta R_{m,t} + b_1 PC(P_{TB}) + b_2 PC(P_{DM}) + b_3 PC(P_{\pounds}) + b_4 PC(P_y) + b_5 PC(P_{OIL})$$

This more complete model is based on a number of earlier studies: French/Ruback/ Schwert (1983) ("Effects of Nominal Contracting on Stock Returns," _Journal of Political Economy_, Vol. 91 No. 1) on the impact of unexpected inflation on share returns, Flannery/ James (1984) ("The Effect of Interest Rate Changes on Common Stock Returns of Financial Institutions," _Journal of Finance_ Vol. 39 No. 4) and Scott/Peterson (1986) ("Interest Rate Risk and Equity Values of Hedged and Unhedged Financial Inter- mediaries," _Journal of Financing Research_ Vol. 9 No. 6) on the impact of interest rate changes on share prices for financial firms, and Sweeney/Warga (1986) ("The Pricing of Interest Rate Risk: Evidence from the Stock Market," _Journal of Finance_ Vol. 41 No. 2) on the impact of interest rate risk on share prices for nonfinancial firms. This model does exhibit the problems of measuring the reaction of firm value to changes in exchange rates, which are described by Donald Lessard in "Finance and Global Com- petition: Exploiting Financial Scope and Coping with Volatile Exchange Rates," _Mid- land Corporate Finance Journal_ (Fall 1986).

For expositional purposes, we use in this paper the shorter form of the equation. This abbreviated model is acceptable empirically given the small correlations which exist between the percentage changes in the financial prices and the market return.

11.   These coefficients actually measure elasticities. Further, had we used the percentage change in the quantity, (1 + one-year T-bill rate), instead of the percentage change in the price of the one-year T-bill, the coefficient b_1 could be interpreted as a "duration" measure.

12.   This section of the article is adapted from Charles W. Smithson, "A LEGO Approach to Financial Engineering: An Introduction to Forwards, Futures, Swaps, and Options," _Midland Corporate Finance Journal_ 4 (Winter 1987).

13.   In this paper we do not address the question of why public corporations hedge. For a discussion of the corporate decision whether or not to hedge financial price exposures, see Alan Shapiro and Sheridan Titman, "An Integrated Approach to Corporate Risk Management," _Midland Corporate Finance Journal_ 3 (Summer 1985). For other useful theoretical discussions of the corporate hedging decision, see David Mayers and Clifford Smith, "On the Corporate Demand for Insurance," _Journal of Business_ 55 (April 1982) (a less technical version of which was published as "The Corporate Insurance Deci- sion," _Chase Financial Quarterly_ (Vol. 1 No. 3) Spring 1982); Rene Stulz, "Optimal Hedging Policies," _Journal of Financial and Quantitative Analysis_ 19 (June 1984); Clifford Smith and Rene Stulz, "The Determinants of Firms' Hedging Policies," _Journal of Financial_ and _Quantitative Analysis_ 20 (December 1985).

For some empirical tests of the above theoretical work, see David Mayers and Clifford Smith, "On the Corporate Demand for Insurance: Some Empirical Evidence," work- ing paper, 1988; and Deana Nance, Clifford Smith, and Charles Smithson, "The De- terminants of Off-Balance-Sheet Hedging: An Empirical Analysis," working paper 1988.

14.   See "Caterpillar's Triple Whammy," _Fortune_, October 27, 1986.

15.   See Fischer Black "The Pricing to Commodity Contracts," _Journal of Financial Econom- ics_ 3 (1976), 167–179.

16.   Keep in mind that if you buy a futures contract, you are taking a long position in the underlying asset. Conversely, selling a futures contract is equivalent to taking a short position.

17.   When the contract is originated on the U.S. exchanges, an "initial margin" is required. Subsequently, the margin account balance must remain above the "maintenance mar- gin." If the margin account balance falls below the maintenance level, the balance must be restored to the initial level.

18. Note that this discussion has ignored daily limits. If there are daily limits on the movement of futures prices, large changes in expectations about the underlying asset can effectively close the market. (The market opens, immediately moves the limit, and then is effectively closed until the next day.) Hence, there could exist an instance in which the broker desires to close out a customer's position but is not able to immediately because the market is experiencing limit moves. In such a case, the statement that performance risk is "eliminated" is too strong.

19. In November of 1985, the "tin cartel" defaulted on contracts for tin delivery on the London Metal Exchange, thereby making the exchange liable for the loss. A description of this situation is contained in "Tin Crisis in London Roils Metal Exchange," *The Wall Street Journal*, November 13, 1985.

    From the point of view of the market, the exchange does not reduce default risk. The expected default rate is not affected by the existence of the exchange. However, the existence of the exchange can alter the default risk faced by an individual market participant. If I buy a futures contract for a specific individual, the default risk I face is determined by the default rate of that specific counterparty. If I instead buy the same futures contract through an exchange, my default risk depends on the default rate of not just my counterparty, but on the default rate of the entire market. Moreover, to the extent that the exchange is capitalized by equity from its members, the default risk I perceive is further reduced because I have a claim not against some specific counterparty, but rather against the exchange. Therefore, when I trade through the exchange, I am in a sense purchasing an insurance policy from the exchange.

20. A futures contract is like a portfolio of forward contracts; however, a futures contract and a portfolio of forward contracts become identical only if interest rates are "deterministic" – that is, known with certainty in advance. See Robert A. Jarrow and George S. Oldfield, "Forward Contracts and Futures Contracts," *Journal of Financial Economics* 9 (1981), 373–382; and John A. Cox, Jonathan E. Ingersoll, and Stephen A. Ross, "The Relation between Forward Prices and Futures Prices," *Journal of Financial Economics* 9 (1981), 321–346.

21. This section is based on Clifford W. Smith, Charles W. Smithson, and Lee M. Wakeman, "The Evolving Market for Swaps," *Midland Corporate Finance Journal* Winter (1986), 20–32.

22. Specifically, the interest rate swap cash flows are determined as follows: The two parties agree to some notional principal, P. (The principal is notional in the sense that it is only used to determine the magnitude of cash flows; is is not paid or received by either party.) At each settlement date, 1, 2, ... T the party illustrated makes a payment $\bar{R} = \bar{r}P$, where $\bar{r}$ is the T-period fixed rate which existed at origination. At each settlement, the party illustrated receives $\tilde{R} = \tilde{r}P$, where $\tilde{r}$ is the floating rate for that period (e.g., at settlement date 2, the interest rate used is the one-period rate in effect at period 1).

23. There are instances in a which bond has been posted in the form of collateral. As should be evident, in this case the swap becomes very like a futures contract.

24. Unlike futures, for which all of any change in contract value is paid/received at the daily settlements, swap contracts convey only part of the total value change at the periodic settlements.

25. For continuity, we continue to use the ΔV ΔP convention in figures. To compare these figures with those found in most texts, treat ΔV as deviations from zero $(\Delta V = V - 0)$ and remember that ΔP measures deviations from expected price $(\Delta P = P - P_e)$.

26. See Fischer Black and Myron Scholes, "The Pricing of Options and Corporate Liabilities," *Journal of Political Economy* 1973. For a less technical discussion of the model, see

"The Black-Scholes Option Pricing Model for Alternative Underlying Instruments," *Financial Analysts Journal*, November–December, 1984, 23–30.

27. For example, the firm may know that, in one year, it will require funds which will be borrowed at a floating rate, thereby giving the firm the inverse exposure to interest rates. Or, the firm may be adding a new product line, the demand for which is extremely sensitive to interest rate movements – as rates rise, the demand for the product decreases and cash flows to the firm decrease.

28. This discussion is adapted from Warren Edwardes and Edmond Levy, "Break Forwards: A Synthetic Option Hedging Instrument," *Midland Corporate Finance Journal* 5 (Summer 1987) 59–67.

29. According to Sam Srinivasulu in "Second-Generation Forwards: A Comparative Analysis," Business International Money Report. September 21, 1987, break forward is the name given to this construction by Midland Bank. It goes under other names: Boston Option (Bank of Boston), FOX – Forward with Optional Exit (Hambros Bank), and Cancelable Forward (Goldman Sachs).

30. These numbers are only for purposes of illustration. To determine the exercise prices at which the values of the puts and calls are equal, one would have to use an option pricing model.

31. As Srinivasulu, cited note 29, pointed out, this construction also appears under a number of names: range forward (Salomon Brothers), collar (Midland Montagu), flexible forward (Manufacturers Hanover), cylinder option (Citicorp), option fence (Bank of America) and mini-max (Goldman Sachs).

32. For a discussion of traditional option strategies like straddles, strangles, and butterflies, see for instance chapter 7 of Richard M. Bookstaber, *Option Pricing and Strategies in Investing* (Addison-Wesley, 1981).

33. For more on this construction, see Srinivasulu cited in note 29 and 31.

34. Options on futures were originally discussed by Fischer Black in "The Pricing of Commodity Options," *Journal of Financial Economics* 3 (January–March 1976). A concise discussion of the modifications required in the Black-Scholes formula is contained in James F. Meisner and John W. Labuszewski, "Modifying the Black-Scholes Option Pricing Model for Alternative Underlying Instruments," *Financial Analysts Journal* November/December 1984.

35. For a discussion of the problem of valuing compound options, see John C. Cox and Mark Rubinstein, *Options Markets* (Prentice-Hall, 1985) 412–415.

36. Note that this issue did have a cap on the crude oil price at $40. Hence, the bondholder actually holds two options positions: long a call option at $25 per barrel and short a call option at $40 per barrel.

37. As reported in the *Wall Street Journal* on September 21, 1988, Forest Oil withdrew its Natural Gas Indexed Bond in favor of a straight issue. However, in November of 1988, Magma Copper did issue senior subordinated notes on which the coupon payments were linked to the price of copper in much the same way as Forest's coupons would have been linked to the price of natural gas.

38. Unlike the other structures discussed, this one has not yet been issued.

39. This is most often referred to as a synthetic option or as dynamic option replication.

SECTION B

Debt Markets

11

Improving Hedging Performance Using Interest Rate Futures

Robert W. Kolb
and Raymond Chiang

Effective hedging of interest rate risk depends on four key factors:

1. The maturity of the hedged and hedging instrument;
2. The coupon structure of the hedged and hedging instruments;
3. The varying risk structure of interest rates; and
4. The changes in the term structure of interest rates.

Many practical guides to hedging interest rate risk use examples in which equal face value amounts of the hedged and hedging instrument are employed [1, 5, 6, 10, 13]. For a hedger seeking to minimize interest rate risk, this is almost always incorrect. The only time it is correct is when all four factors mentioned above are perfectly matched.[1] Under any other circumstances a better hedge can be devised.[2]

In the past, when interest rates have fluctuated relatively little, naive approaches to hedging interest rate risk have served relatively well. Today, with extremely volatile interest rates affecting bankers, investors, corporations, and underwriters to a much greater extent than ever before, the development of more efficient hedging techniques has become crucial. Furthermore, the recent development of interest rate futures markets with standardized contracts has enriched the hedging opportunities of all market participants and lowered the cost of hedging. This paper formulates more efficient hedging rules and illustrates their application and usefulness.

More Efficient Hedging Techniques

Upon entering the futures market to hedge some interest rate risk, the hedger knows the maturity and coupon structure of the hedged and hedging instruments. He does not know the changes in the risk and term structure of interest rates that will occur while the hedge is in effect. (If he could know the future course of interest rates, the prospective hedger would not hedge anyway. He would simply alter his portfolio to profit from the rate changes that were about to occur.)

Because these two elements are unknown when the hedge is initiated, it is impossible to guarantee in advance that the hedge will be perfect. (A perfect hedge is one that leaves the hedger's wealth unchanged.) If changes in the term and risk structure are assumed known, it is possible to derive a hedge ratio that protects against interest rate risk caused by a mismatch of maturity and coupon between the hedged and hedging instrument.

All hedging strategies make some implicit assumption about the kinds of interest rate changes that will occur, and any hedging rule implies beliefs about the future course of interest rates. In the derivation of our hedge ratio, we explicitly assume that the yield curve remains flat for the life of the hedge. (Throughout the paper we ignore the difference between the yield to maturity and the expected return, which is tantamount to assuming that both instruments have zero default risk.) We make this assumption for several reasons. First, it helps to make the mathematics tractable. Second, a flat yield curve is a convenient approximation to the more realistic case of a yield curve that has "shape," but that maintains the same shape, changing only its level.

The basic strategy revolves around choosing some number of units (N) of futures contract j to hedge one unit of asset i with the goal that, over the life of the hedge:

$$\Delta P_i + \Delta P_j (N) = 0, \tag{1}$$

where P_i and P_j are, respectively, the values of the bond to be hedged and the futures contract. Clearly, for any given interest rate shock the size of ΔP_i and ΔP_j depends on the sensitivity of i and j to a change in interest rates. Our problem, then, is to choose the number of futures contracts to trade (N) to balance out the different interest rate sensitivities of i and j, and thereby to preserve the truth of Equation (1). (Note that the technique hedges against a single interest rate shock.) As the equation implies, the perfect hedge we wish to find is the hedge that makes wealth invariant to a change in interest rates.

One important and useful measure of a financial asset's sensitivity to interest rates is its duration (D), which we may define as:

$$D_k = \frac{\displaystyle\sum_{t=1}^{K} \frac{t C_{kt}}{(R_k)^t}}{\displaystyle\sum_{t=1}^{K} \frac{C_{tk}}{(R_k)^t}} \tag{2}$$

where
C_{kt} = the tth period cash flow from asset k;
$R_k = 1 + r_k$;
r_k = yield to maturity on k; and
K = term to maturity.

This is the duration measure as developed by Macaulay. (For an exposition of the concept, see [14]; [9] gives an account of duration's development.)

In Equation (2) the denominator is simply the price of asset k. The numerator is the present value of a single cash flow (C_{kt}) multiplied by (t), the number of periods until the payment is received. The result, duration, is the negative of the asset's price elasticity with respect to a change in the discount factor (R_k).

We show in the appendix that to hedge one unit of asset i with financial futures contract j one should trade N units of j, where N is given by:

$$N = \frac{-\overline{R}_j P_i D_i}{\overline{R}_i FP_j D_j} \tag{3}$$

where
$\ \ \ \ R_F = 1 +$ the risk-free rate;
$\ \ \ \ \overline{R}_j = 1 +$ the rate expected to obtain on the asset *underlying* futures contract j;
$\ \ \ \ \overline{R}_i = 1 +$ the expected yield to maturity on asset i;
$\ \ \ \ FP_j =$ the price agreed upon in the futures contract for title to the asset *underlying* j;
$\ \ \ \ P_i =$ the price of asset i expected to prevail on the planned termination date of the hedge;
$\ \ \ \ D_i =$ the duration of asset i expected to prevail on the planned termination date of the hedge; and
$\ \ \ \ D_j =$ the duration of the asset *underlying* futures contract j expected to prevail on the planned termination date of the hedge.

The Treasury bill futures contract

Treasury bill futures contracts call for the delivery of $1,000,000 face value of 90-day Treasury bills upon maturity of the futures contract. Consequently, for every Treasury bill hedge $D_j = \frac{1}{4}$ year. Prices of Treasury bill futures are quoted according to the IMM Index, which is simply $100 -$ bank discount rate. (See [10] for an exposition of the IMM Index.) This is not a true yield, and it requires conversion to $\overline{R}_j$. For example, if the IMM Index is 87.47, the bank discount rate is 12.53% which is equivalent to a true yield of 13.576%, or an $\overline{R}_j = 1.13576$. This means that:

$$FP_j = \frac{\$1,000,000}{(\overline{R}_j)^{0.25}}. \tag{4}$$

For a hedge with a Treasury bill futures contract, N is given by the simpler expression:[3]

$$N = \frac{-4(\overline{R}_j)^{1.25} P_i D_i}{\overline{R}_i(\$1,000,000)}. \tag{5}$$

The values needed to calculate N in Equation (5) are easily determined from the *Wall Street Journal*.

The Treasury bond futures contract

The Treasury bond futures hedge is slightly more complicated because of the fact that Treasury bonds have coupons. Treasury bond futures contracts call for the delivery of $100,000 face value of 8% coupon Treasury bonds having a maturity of at least 15 years, or at least 15 years to their first call date. Bonds with a coupon other than 8% may be delivered to fulfill the futures contract subject to an adjustment. Long maturity bonds having an 8% coupon may be delivered against the futures contract with no adjustment. Generally, it is cheapest to deliver the longest maturity lowest coupon Treasury bond against the future contract.

From discussions with representatives of the Chicago Board of Trade, it appears that the market is well aware of this fact. For the most recent month on record, the bonds delivered were all of maturity in excess of 21 years. The *Wall Street Journal* reports implicit yields assuming a 20-year 8% coupon bond. The futures market, however, must price the actual bond that is to be delivered if it is efficient. Currently, the longest-maturity lowest-coupon bonds mature between 2005 and 2010 and have a coupon of 10%. To be consistent with the values reported in the *Wall Street Journal*, we assume an 8% 20-year bond for delivery against the futures contract.

In the *Wall Street Journal*, Treasury bond futures prices are quoted in "points and 32^{nd}s of par." A futures price of 71–24 means that the price is 71 24/32% of par. As for the whole contract par = $100,000, a futures price quoted as 71 24/32 would correspond to an FP_j = $71,750 (71 24/32% × $100,000 = $ 71,750). Because Treasury bonds have coupons, D_j varies with $\overline{R}_j$. The exhibit provides a table of D_j and $\overline{R}_j$ for selected bonds with prices between 60–00 and 100–00 assuming a 20-year maturity and an 8% coupon. The values in the exhibit make it easy to calculate N for the Treasury bond futures hedge with Equation (3).

How to Apply the Hedging Rules

To illustrate the hedging rules developed, consider a portfolio manager who learns on March 1 that he or she will receive $5 million to invest on June 1 in AAA corporate bonds with a coupon rate of 5% and a maturity of 10 years. The manager finds current AAA yields attractive, and he or she wishes to lock in that rate for June 1 investment by trading in the futures market now. There are two possibilities. In the first case, rates on the hedged and hedging instruments change by the same amount, while in the second, they change by different amounts. For the two alternatives we can examine the hedging actions and outcomes for the naive strategy (face value dollar for face value dollar) and the method developed earlier, which we call the price-sensitivity (PS) strategy.

Case 1

Assume the following rates obtain:[4]

	Treasury Bill Futures	Treasury Bond Futures	AAA
March 1	8.00	8.50	9.50
June 1	7.58	8.08	9.08

As of March 1, when the hedge is initiated, the price expected to hold June 1 for the AAA bond must be $717.45 ($P_i$), given the current rate of 9.5%. Its duration (D_i) on June 1 will be 7.709 years. We can now calculate the hedge ratio (N) for hedging with Treasury bill futures from Equation (5):

$$N = \frac{-4(1.08)^{1.25}(-\$717.45)(7.709)}{(1.095)(\$1,000,000)} = 0.022244. \tag{6}$$

This means that 0.022244 Treasury bill futures contracts should be traded for each bond. As the manager knows he or she will have $5 million to invest, expecting the price of the bond to be $717.45 on June 1, he or she is planning to buy 6,969.1268 bonds ($5,000,000/$717.45). Consequently, he or she should buy 155.0213 Treasury bill futures contracts (6,969.1268 × 0.022244).[5]

Given the interest rate changes shown above, the price of the bond on June 1 is $739.08, not the expected $717.45. For the manager buying the bonds on June 1, this represents an opportunity loss of $21.63 on each bond, and $150,742.21 on the entire position. Let us now compare the hedging effectiveness of the two strategies: the naive vs. the PS.

According to the naive strategy, one will trade one dollar of face value in the futures market per dollar of bonds. The naive hedge is to buy five Treasury bill futures contracts, whereas the PS strategy recommends 155.0213 contracts. When the rates drop from 8.00 to 7.58%, this generates a gain on a futures contract of $956.02:

$$\frac{\$1,000,000}{(1.0758)^{0.25}} - \frac{\$1,000,000}{(1.08)^{0.25}} = \$956.02.$$

For the naive strategy the total gain in the futures market is $4,780.10, while for the PS strategy it is $148,203.46. The following table depicts the results:

Bond Market	Treasury Bill Futures Market	
Opportunity Loss	Naive Strategy	PS Strategy
−$150,742.21	+$4,780.10	+$148,203.46
ERROR	−$145,962.11	−$2,538.75

The PS strategy is not perfect, losing $2,539 because of the fact that the change in rates was discrete. The error from the naive strategy, though, is 57.5 times the error from the PS strategy.

Part of the explanation for this difference in the performance of the two strategies stems from the short maturity and absence of coupons of Treasury bills. The naive strategy should be closer in dollar amount to the performance of the PS strategy using Treasury bond futures, for Treasury bonds more closely match the maturity and coupon structure of the bond being hedged. To hedge with Treasury bond futures, the correct hedge ratio is given by Equation (3):

Exhibit   Prices, yield, and durations for 20-year 8% treasury bonds

60– 0	1.1449	7.746	72–16	1.1189	8.718	85– 0	1.0995	9.512
60– 8	1.1443	7.768	72–24	1.1184	8.735	85– 8	1.0991	9.527
60–16	1.1437	7.789	73– 0	1.1180	8.753	85–16	1.0988	9.542
60–24	1.1431	7.810	73– 8	1.1175	8.770	85–24	1.0985	9.556
61– 0	1.1425	7.831	73–16	1.1171	8.787	86– 0	1.0981	9.570
61– 8	1.1419	7.853	73–24	1.1167	8.804	86– 8	1.0978	9.584
61–16	1.1413	7.874	74– 0	1.1163	8.821	86–16	1.0975	9.598
61–24	1.1407	7.894	74– 8	1.1158	8.839	86–24	1.0972	9.612
62– 0	1.1401	7.916	74–16	1.1154	8.856	87– 0	1.0968	9.627
62– 8	1.1395	7.937	74–24	1.1150	8.873	87– 8	1.0965	9.640
62–16	1.1390	7.957	75– 0	1.1145	8.890	87–16	1.0962	9.655
62–24	1.1384	7.977	75– 8	1.1141	8.906	87–24	1.0959	9.668
63– 0	1.1378	7.998	75–16	1.1137	8.923	88– 0	1.0955	9.682
63– 8	1.1373	8.018	75–24	1.1133	8.939	88– 8	1.0952	9.696
63–16	1.1367	8.039	76– 0	1.1129	8.956	88–16	1.0949	9.709
63–24	1.1361	8.060	76– 8	1.1125	8.972	88–24	1.0946	9.723
64– 0	1.1356	8.079	76–16	1.1121	8.989	89– 0	1.0942	9.737
64– 8	1.1351	8.099	76–24	1.1117	9.006	89– 8	1.0939	9.751
64–16	1.1345	8.120	77– 0	1.1113	9.022	89–16	1.0936	9.764
64–24	1.1340	8.139	77– 8	1.1109	9.038	89–24	1.0933	9.778
65– 0	1.1334	8.159	77–16	1.1105	9.054	90– 0	1.0930	9.791
65– 8	1.1329	8.179	77–24	1.1101	9.070	90– 8	1.0927	9.804
65–16	1.1324	8.199	78– 0	1.1097	9.087	90–16	1.0924	9.818
65–24	1.1318	8.219	78– 8	1.1093	9.102	90–24	1.0921	9.832
66– 0	1.1313	8.238	78–16	1.1089	9.119	91– 0	1.0918	9.844
66– 8	1.1306	8.256	78–24	1.1085	9.134	91– 8	1.0915	9.858
66–16	1.1303	8.277	79– 0	1.1082	9.150	91–16	1.0912	9.871
66–24	1.1298	8.296	79– 8	1.1078	9.166	91–24	1.0909	9.884
67– 0	1.1293	8.315	79–16	1.1074	9.181	92– 0	1.0906	9.897
67– 8	1.1288	8.334	79–24	1.1070	9.187	92– 8	1.0903	9.910
67–16	1.1283	8.353	80– 0	1.1066	9.213	92–16	1.0900	9.923
67–24	1.1278	8.372	80– 8	1.1063	9.228	92–24	1.0897	9.936
68– 0	1.1273	8.391	80–16	1.1059	9.244	93– 0	1.0894	9.949
68– 8	1.1268	8.410	80–24	1.1055	9.259	93– 8	1.0891	9.962
68–16	1.1263	8.428	81– 0	1.1051	9.275	93–16	1.0888	9.975
68–24	1.1258	8.447	81– 8	1.1048	9.290	93–24	1.0885	9.987
69– 0	1.1253	8.466	81–16	1.1044	9.305	94– 0	1.0882	10.000
69– 8	1.1248	8.484	81–24	1.1041	9.320	94– 8	1.0879	10.013
69–16	1.1244	8.502	82– 0	1.1037	9.335	94–16	1.0876	10.026
69–24	1.1239	8.521	82– 8	1.1033	9.350	94–24	1.0873	10.038
70– 0	1.1234	8.539	82–16	1.1030	9.365	95– 0	1.0871	10.051
70– 8	1.1229	8.558	82–24	1.1026	9.380	95– 8	1.0868	10.063
70–16	1.1225	8.576	83– 0	1.1023	9.395	95–16	1.0865	10.075
70–24	1.1220	8.594	83– 8	1.1019	9.410	95–24	1.0862	10.088
71– 0	1.1216	8.611	83–16	1.1016	9.425	96– 0	1.0859	10.100
71– 8	1.1211	8.629	83–24	1.1012	9.439	96– 8	1.0856	10.113
71–16	1.1207	8.647	84– 0	1.1009	9.454	96–16	1.0854	10.125
71–24	1.1202	8.665	84– 8	1.1005	9.469	96–24	1.0851	10.137
72– 0	1.1197	8.683	84–16	1.1002	9.484	97– 0	1.0848	10.149
72– 8	1.1193	8.700	84–24	1.0998	9.498	97– 8	1.0845	10.162

Exhibit (Cont'd)

97–16	1.0843	10.174	98–24	1.0829	10.234	100– 0	1.0816	10.292
97–24	1.0840	10.186	99– 0	1.0826	10.246	100– 8	1.0813	10.304
98– 0	1.0837	10.198	99– 8	1.0824	10.257	100–16	1.0811	10.316
98– 8	1.0835	10.210	99–16	1.0821	10.269	100–24	1.0808	10.327
98–16	1.0832	10.222						

The exhibit presents prices, discount rates, and durations for a wide variety of Treasury bonds assuming 20 years to maturity and an 8% coupon paid semi-annually. These values of $\bar{R}_j$ and D_j may be used in Equation (3) for the calculation of the proper hedge ratio N. Prices are presented in "points and $32^{nd}s$ of par" to correspond to the *Wall Street Journal* listings. To calculate N the prices in the exhibit must be converted to FP_j. For bonds with prices not in the table, one may simply interpolate.

$$N = \frac{-(1.085)(-\$717.45)(7.709)}{(1.095)(\$96,875)(10.143)} = 0.005577.$$

To implement the hedge with Treasury bond futures, we will trade 38.8667 ($0.005577 \times 6,969.1268$) contracts according to the PS strategy, and 50 contracts according to the naive strategy (the Treasury bond future contract is for $100,000 face value of bonds).

From the exhibit one observes that a drop in rates from 8.5 to 8.08% causes the futures price to rise from $96,875 to $100.750, for a gain of $3,875 per contract. For the two strategies this gives the following hedging results:

	Treasury Bond Futures Market	
Opportunity Loss	*Naive Strategy*	*PS Strategy*
–$150,742.21	+$193,750.00	+$150,608.46
ERROR	+$43,007.79	–$133.75

In this case, the error of the naive strategy is 321.6 times that of the PS strategy, but the dollar difference between the two is smaller, as the price sensitivity of Treasury bonds is closer to that of the bond being hedged than is the case with Treasury bills. The PS strategy is almost perfect, hedging 99.91% of the $150,742.21 opportunity loss in the bond market.

Case 2

This case allows the rates to change by different amounts from the same original starting point. Assume now that the following rates obtain:

	Treasury Bill Futures	Treasury Bond Futures	AAA
March 1	8.00	8.50	9.50
June 1	7.58	8.08	9.25

As long as the starting rates are all the same, the hedge ratios will all be the same as above. For the futures, the rates conform to the previous sample, but the yield change for the bonds has been decreased. With a rate of 9.25% the price of the bond will be $730.24 on June 1. For the bond position the total opportunity loss is $89,135.13 (6,969.9268 × $12.79). For the Treasury bill hedge the new results are:

Bond Market Opportunity Loss	Treasury Bill Futures Market	
	Naive Strategy	PS Strategy
−$89,135.13	+$4,780.10	+$148,203.46
ERROR	−$84,335.03	+$59,068.33

For the Treasury bond hedge the result would be:

Bond Market Opportunity Loss	Treasury Bill Futures Market	
	Naive Strategy	PS Strategy
−$89,135.13	+$193,750.00	+$150,608.46
ERROR	+$104,614.87	+$61,473.33

In both cases, the PS strategy gives a smaller error. If rates change by different amounts on the hedged and hedging instruments, it is possible for the naive strategy to outperform the PS strategy, but that would occur only by infrequent coincidence. This possibility notwithstanding, the naive hedger subjects himself or herself to considerable risk that the hedger following the PS strategy can avoid.

Some Final Hints

The PS strategy presented here provides a rational procedure for hedging interest rate risk by trading in the Treasury bill and Treasury bond futures market. The method takes account of differences between the maturity and coupon structures of the hedged and hedging instruments. With a flat yield curve and an infinitesimal change in interest rates, the PS strategy results in a perfect hedge. In the real world one cannot expect the PS strategy to provide a perfect hedge, for rates change constantly by discrete amounts, and the term structure is not flat. Yet the method we develop can be expected to improve hedging performance in actual trading.

To apply the PS strategy, it is better to use a futures instrument with a maturity and coupon structure matching that of the bond to be hedged. (That is why the error was smaller with the Treasury bond hedge.) The method can also be applied to bond portfolios by simply using portfolio values, durations, and interest rates. Finally, as rates vary over time, the hedging performance can be improved by periodic rebalancing of the hedge. The PS strategy is designed to hedge against a single interest rate shock. Hedging performance can be improved by periodic recalculation of N and by adjusting the hedge accordingly. The frequency of rebalancing depends upon the size of the position, transactions costs of changing the hedge, and the anticipated volatility of interest rates.

Notes

The authors would like to thank the Center for Econometrics and Decision Sciences at the University of Florida for its financial support.
1. When the four factors match perfectly, the hedged and hedging instruments will respond in the same way to interest rate changes (factors 1 and 2), and they will experience the same changes in their risk and term structures (factors 3 and 4). The conceptual background is common to the bond immunization literature. See [2].
2. See [5] and [14] for another approach to developing more efficient hedging strategies. The "portfolio approach" attempts to minimize the variance of the value of the entire hedge over its life; [14] also develops an approach similar in spirit to ours.
3. Note that N is calculated to hedge the position as of some one moment – the planned termination date of the hedge. $\bar{R}_i$ and $\bar{R}_j$ are the rates expected at that time, and the P_i and D_i are the price and duration expected to prevail at that time, given $\bar{R}_i$.
4. Numerically these Treasury bond yields are the same as those used in an example of a perfect hedge in [7], page 8. We assume, however, that the rates are the true rates, corresponding to the $\bar{R}_j$ and the $\bar{R}_i$. Compare our results with that of the CBT example.
5. The cost of a Treasury bill futures contract is negligible. It takes $60 in transactions costs and a margin of $1,000 for daily resettlement for one contract ($1 million in denomination). In our example, we assume interest rates change at the end of the hedge period. With interest rates changing frequently in the real world, the manager will need a small amount of cash for daily resettlement, and rebalancing will be necessary.

References

1. P. Bacon and R. Williams, "Interest Rate Futures: New Tool for the Financial Manager," *Financial Management* (Spring 1976), pp. 32–38, reprinted in G. Gay and R. Kolb, eds., *Interest Rate Futures: Concepts and Issues*, Richmond, Robert F. Dame, Inc., 1981.
2. G. Bierwag, G. Kaufman, and C. Khang, "Duration and Bond Portfolio Analysis: An Overview," *Journal of Financial and Quantitative Analysis* (November 1978), pp. 671–682.
3. J. Cox, J. Ingersoll, and S. Ross, "A Re-Examination of Traditional Hypotheses about the Term Structure of Interest Rates," University of Chicago Working Paper (November 1980).
4. J. Cox, J. Ingersoll, and S. Ross, "A Theory of the Term Structure of Interest Rates," University of Chicago Working Paper (August 1978).
5. L. Ederington, "The Hedging Performance of the New Futures Market," *Journal of Finance* (March 1979), pp. 157–170, reprinted in G. Gay and R. Kolb, eds., *Interest Rate Futures: Concepts and Issues*, Richmond, Robert F. Dame, Inc., 1981.
6. W. Feller, *An Introduction to Probability Theory and Its Applications*, Volume II, New York, John Wiley & Sons, 1971.
7. "Hedging Interest Rate Risks," Chicago, Chicago Board of Trade, 1977.
8. J. Ingersoll, J. Skelton, and R. Weil, "Duration Forty Years Later," *Journal of Financial and Quantitative Analysis* (November 1978), pp. 627–650.
9. "An Introduction to the Interest Rate Futures Market," Chicago, Chicago Board of Trade, 1978.

10. E. Kane, "Market Incompleteness and Divergences between Forward and Futures Interest Rates," *Journal of Finance* (May 1980), pp. 221–234, reprinted in G. Gay and R. Kolb, eds., *Interest Rate Futures: Concepts and Issues*, Richmond, Robert F. Dame, Inc., 1981.

11. R. Kolb and R. Chiang, "Duration, Immunization, and Hedging with Interest Rate Futures," *Journal of Financial Research* (forthcoming), reprinted in G. Gay and R. Kolb, eds., *Interest Rate Futures: Concepts and Issues*, Richmond, Robert F. Dame, Inc., 1981.

12. A. Loosigian, *Interest Rate Futures*, Princeton, N.J., Dow Jones Books, 1980.

13. R. McEnally, "Duration as a Practical Tool for Bond Management," *Journal of Portfolio Management* (Summer 1977), pp. 53–57.

14. R. McEnally and M. Rice, "Hedging Possibilities in the Flotation of Debt Securities," *Financial Management* (Winter 1979), pp. 12–18, reprinted in G. Gay and R. Kolb, eds., *Interest Rate Futures: Concepts and Issues*, Richmond, Robert F. Dame, Inc., 1981.

15. "Treasury Bill Futures," Chicago, International Monetary Market, 1977.

Appendix. Derivation of Hedge Ratios

Assume:

1. That the yield curves are flat for each instrument, so that all future payments associated with an instrument are appropriately discounted at a single rate – the instruments' yield to maturity; and

2. That cash flows occur on a futures contract immediately upon a change in its value, which corresponds to the current institutional arrangement of daily resettlement.

Notation

Instrument i is to be hedged by financial futures contract j, where:

P_i, P_j = the value of instruments i and j, respectively;

C_{it}, C_{jt} = the tth period cash flows for instrument i and for the financial asset underlying financial futures contract j, respectively;

FP_j = the price specified for the delivery of the instrument in futures contract j;

D_i, D_j = Macaulay's duration measure for instrument i and the asset underlying financial futures contract j, respectively;

R_F = 1 + the risk-free rate;

$\tilde{R}_i$, $\overline{R}_i$ = 1 + the yield to maturity on i and the expected value of $\tilde{R}_i$, respectively;

$\tilde{R}_j$, $\overline{R}_j$ = 1 + the yield to maturity on the asset underlying financial futures contract j expected to obtain at the planned termination date of the hedge, and the expected value of $\tilde{R}_j$, respectively;

R_j^* = the yield to maturity implied by FP_j for the instrument underlying financial futures contract j;

N = the hedge ratio to be derived – the number of futures contracts j to trade to hedge a one-unit position in asset i; and

I, J = the term to maturity of asset i and the term to maturity of the financial asset underlying futures contract j.

The goal of the hedge is to insure, insofar as possible, that as of the planned termination date of the hedge:

$$\Delta P_i + (\Delta P_j) N = 0. \tag{A-1}$$

To find N we must solve the equation:

$$\frac{dP_i}{dR_F} + \frac{dP_j}{dR_F} N = 0. \tag{A-2}$$

As i is a bond, its price is given at any time by:

$$P_i = \sum_{t=1}^{I} \frac{C_{it}}{(R_i^*)^t}. \tag{A-3}$$

At any time the value of the futures contract is given by (ignoring the problem of Jensen's Inequality):

$$P_j = \sum_{t=1}^{J} \frac{C_{jt}}{(\overline{R}_j)^t} - \sum_{t=1}^{J} \frac{C_{jt}}{(R_j^*)^t}. \tag{A-4}$$

Equation (A-4) has an important economic interpretation. When one purchases a futures contract, one agrees to pay the futures price, FP_j, at the maturity of the futures contract, in exchange for the series of flows C_{jt}. Consequently, it must be the case that:

$$FP_j = \sum_{t=1}^{J} \frac{C_{jt}}{(R_j^*)^t}. \tag{A-5}$$

It is reasonable to agree to pay FP_j only if one believes, at the time of entering the futures contract, that $\overline{R}_j = R_j^*$. Otherwise one of the parties to the futures contract expects a loss. Consequently, at the time of entering the futures contract, $P_j = 0$ for Equation (A-4). Later, during the life of the futures contract, it may be that $\overline{R}_j \neq R_j^*$, and then $P_j \neq 0$.

Substituting (A-3) and (A-4) into (A-2) gives:

$$\frac{d\sum_{t=1}^{I} \frac{C_{it}}{(\overline{R}_i)^t}}{d\overline{R}_i} \frac{d\overline{R}_i}{dR_F} + \frac{d\left[\sum_{t=1}^{J} \frac{C_{jt}}{(\overline{R}_j)^t} - \sum_{t=1}^{J} \frac{C_{jt}}{(R_j^*)^t}\right]}{d\overline{R}_j} \frac{d\overline{R}_j}{dR_F} N = 0, \tag{A-6}$$

from which we derive:

$$\frac{1}{\overline{R}_i} \sum_{t=1}^{I} \frac{-tC_{it}}{(\overline{R}_i)^t} \frac{d\overline{R}_i}{dR_F} + \frac{N}{\overline{R}_j} \sum_{t=1}^{J} \frac{-tC_{jt}}{(\overline{R}_j)^t} \frac{d\overline{R}_j}{dR_F} = 0. \tag{A-7}$$

Solving for N, we find

$$N = -\frac{\overline{R}_j}{\overline{R}_i} \frac{\sum\limits_{t=1}^{I} \frac{tC_{it}}{(\overline{R}_i)^t} \frac{d\overline{R}_i}{dR_F}}{\sum\limits_{t=1}^{J} \frac{tC_{jt}}{(\overline{R}_j)^t} \frac{d\overline{R}_j}{dR_F}}.$$ (A-8)

Equation (A-8) is a general expression for N applying to any bond i and any futures contract j. Recall Macaulay's duration measure, D, is:

$$D_i = \frac{\sum\limits_{t=1}^{I} \frac{tC_{it}}{(\overline{R}_i)^t}}{\sum\limits_{t=1}^{I} \frac{C_{it}}{(\overline{R}_i)^t}}.$$ (A-9)

Substituting (A-3) and (A-9) into (A-8) gives:

$$N = \frac{-R_j P_i D_i}{\overline{R}_i FP_j D_j} \frac{\frac{d\overline{R}_i}{dR_F}}{\frac{d\overline{R}_j}{dR_F}}.$$ (A-10)

Note that, in Equation (A-10), P_i, D_i, FP_j, and D_j are all evaluated as of the planned termination date of the hedge. Because we have assumed that the yield curve is flat, they are the prices and durations that will obtain at current rates.

Assuming $d\overline{R}_i/dR_F$ and $d\overline{R}_F$ can be estimated, those estimates should be included in the computation of N for improved hedging performance. For illustrative purposes, we assume $d\overline{R}_i/dR_F = d\overline{R}_j/dR_F$, so Equation (A-10) becomes:

$$N = \frac{-\overline{R}_j P_i D_i}{\overline{R}_i FP_j D_j},$$ (A-11)

and Equation (A-11) is used for the computation of N throughout the paper.

12

Immunizing Bond Portfolios with Interest Rate Futures

Robert W. Kolb
and Gerald D. Gay

The concept of duration has attained a significant place in the finance literature since its introduction by Macaulay more than forty years ago.[1] During the same time, duration has attained unparalleled acceptance as a practical technique for the management of bond portfolio risk.[2] Because of the important role of duration in bond portfolio management, it is crucial that duration oriented strategies be implemented as effectively and efficiently as possible.

To that end this paper explains the important role that interest rate futures can play in bond portfolio management. Basically, the strategy advanced here maintains that, by trading interest rate futures in conjunction with the holding of a bond portfolio, one can effectively adjust the duration of the bond portfolio. Further, if the duration of the portfolio is adjusted by using interest rate futures, the holdings of the bond portfolio itself need not be altered. This means that the portfolio manager may maintain the bond portfolio itself without disturbing favored maturities or issues. Since the bonds in the portfolio are not traded, one avoids the problem of a lack of marketability of the bonds. Also, the transaction costs associated with adjusting the duration are much lower if one uses interest rate futures, and the task can be accomplished with little or no capital, since one must make only a margin deposit to trade the futures contract. Finally, the technique of using interest rate futures for duration adjustment is compatible with all of the more sophisticated duration techniques that have been developed recently.

Duration and Immunization

Macaulay introduced the concept of duration (D) which he defined as:

$$D_i = \sum_{t=1}^{m} \left[\frac{\dfrac{tC_{it}}{(1 + K_i)^t}}{P_i} \right] \qquad (1)$$

where
C_{it} = cash flow from the ith financial instrument at time t,
K_i = the instrument's yield to maturity,

t = an element of a time vector ranging over the time to maturity,
P_i = the instrument's price.

It can be proven that D_i is the negative of the instrument's price elasticity with respect to a change in the discount factor $(1 + K_i)$. From this it follows that, for infinitesimal changes in $(1 + K_i)$:

$$\Delta P_i = -D_i \frac{\Delta(1 + K_i)}{(1 + K_i)} P_i \tag{2}$$

For discrete changes in the discount factor, (2) holds as a close approximation. Although (1) strictly applies to a single instrument, the duration of a portfolio (D_p) with N assets each having weight W_i in the portfolio is given by:

$$D_p = \sum_{i=1}^{N} W_i D_i \tag{3}$$

So defined, the concept of duration has two distinct uses. The first case, which can be called the "Bank Immunization Case," assumes that one agent holds both an asset and liability portfolio of equal value. Then, as Equation (2) suggests, by setting the duration of the asset and liability portfolios equal, any change in K affects both portfolios equally.[3] Consequently, the portfolio holder incurs no wealth change due to a shift in interest rates. In an important sense, he can be said to be "immunized" against interest rate changes.[4] The second use of duration, for the "Planning Period Case," is directed toward a portfolio holder who has some planning period in mind, after which he plans to liquidate the portfolio. By setting the duration of the portfolio equal to the time remaining until the end of the planning period, the investor can guarantee a certain minimal rate of return.[5] If interest rates fluctuate, the return may be higher over the life of the planning period, but it cannot be less. If rates rise over the planning period, this generates a capital loss, but it also creates an offsetting benefit because the reinvestment rate, at which the cash throw-off from the portfolio can be reinvested, is higher. Exactly the opposite trade-off occurs if rates fall.[6]

As has been well recognized, Equations (1) and (2) rely on some unrealistic assumptions. Strictly speaking, Equation (1) is correct only if the term structure is flat, since it implicitly discounts all future cash flows at the uniform rate K. In itself, this difficulty is surmountable by simply re-defining D_i as D_i^* to take account of term structures with shape:

$$D_i^* = \sum_{t=1}^{M} \left[\frac{\dfrac{tC_{it}}{\displaystyle\prod_{j=1}^{t}(1 + K_j)}}{\displaystyle\sum_{t=1}^{M} \dfrac{C_{it}}{\displaystyle\prod_{j=1}^{t}(1 + K_j)}} \right] \tag{4}$$

where
K_j = the appropriate one-period rate for the jth period.

D_i^* allows for each flow to be discounted at a unique rate commensurate with its true discount rate as given by the term structure.

A second deeper difficulty emerges from Equation (2), which also implicitly assumes that when rates change, all rates change by the same amount. Even if D_i^* is allowed to accommodate term structure shape, Equation (2) assumes that all rate changes preserve the same shaped yield curve. The parallel, or additive, shifts of the yield curve presupposed by (2) are, of course, the rare exception, not the rule. Instead, non-shape preserving term structure changes, or twisting yield curves, are more normal. Even so, the situation is perhaps not desperate. It can be shown that an appropriate duration hedging formulation exists for any given yield curve twist. However, the impending twist must be correctly anticipated, and the duration strategy adjusted accordingly, if the immunization is to be perfect.[7] This fact offers small comfort for two reasons. First, no one knows what yield curve twist is about to occur. Second, if one did know he would simply trade on this knowledge and would not be concerned with immunization.

In the final analysis, then, one cannot use the duration techniques to guarantee perfect immunization. This is clear from a consideration of the Bank Immunization Case. Assume some difference in coupon and maturity structure of the asset and liability portfolios. (If no differences exist, one has a net zero position and no discussion of immunization need be undertaken. The portfolio is of necessity perfectly immunized.) Also assume any desired duration measure and that the durations of the asset and liability portfolios are matched. Then some yield curve twist is possible that will generate a wealth change.

In spite of the fact that perfect immunization cannot be guaranteed, the practical consequence is small. Elaborate simulation of different yield curve twists leads to the conclusion that the use of Macaulay's duration (D_i of Equation (1)) is very effective in achieving nearly perfect immunization.[8] Also, the immunization is made more nearly perfect by matching the maturities of the asset and liability portfolios in the Bank Immunization Case, and by matching the maturity of the portfolio to the planning period in the Planning Period Case.[9]

No matter which measure of duration is used, the immunization holds only for a single instantaneous change in rates that occurs when either the asset portfolio duration equals that of the liability portfolio (the Bank Immunization Case), or when the duration of the portfolio equals the planning period (the Planning Period Case). But, durations of instruments change due to (1) the mere passage of time or (2) a shift in yields. These two factors mean that the originally initiated immunization condition cannot be preserved, without re-adjusting the portfolio. Maintaining the immunization condition at all times necessitates continuous adjustment. But this is costly, so for practical purposes, portfolios are only re-adjusted periodically. In the light of this need for re-adjustment, the cost and practicality of the adjustment process requires attention.

Duration and Interest Rate Futures

In the strictest sense, futures contracts do not have a price, which means that they have no duration either, since the duration Equation (1) involves division by the price. The fact that future contracts have no price *per se* can be seen from the fact that one need not pay anything to enter a futures contract. Rather the "futures prices" that are quoted are better thought of as expected future prices for their respective underlying instruments at the time of delivery. For an interest rate futures contract (j), this expected future price (FP_j) depends upon the promised yield to maturity that is expected to prevail on the underlying instrument at the delivery date (K^*) and the cash flows (C_{jt}) associated with that underlying instrument. Thus, for any interest rate futures contract:

$$FP_j = \sum_{t=0}^{M} \frac{C_{jt}}{(1 + K^*)^t} \qquad (5)$$

Note here that the index for the summation runs over the period from the delivery date ($t = 0$) to the maturity of the underlying instrument. Equation (5) treats futures contracts as though they are forward contracts, in spite of significant institutional differences between the two contracts. Further, recent research [14, 24] has shown that futures and forward prices need not be equal even in perfect markets, if interest rates are stochastic. Recent evidence [12] has shown that these differences are very small, even insignificant, for the foreign currency market. Consequently, we ignore the difference between futures and forward contracts.[10]

The question can then be raised: What is the relationship between the forward or futures price and the expected future spot price to prevail at the maturity of the forward or futures contract? Under certain conditions, the forward or futures price equals the expected future spot price. Fischer Black [6, p. 167] analyzes forward and futures price behavior in a CAPM setting and shows that: "If changes in the futures price are independent of the return on the market, the futures price is the expected spot price." This must be the case if there is no systematic risk, since only the bearing of systematic risk is compensated in an efficient market. With no systematic risk (and ignoring transaction costs), the holding of a forward or futures contract is a pure zero sum game. As Black shows [6] such a situation requires that the equilibrium forward or futures price must equal the expected future spot price.

The key issue then becomes whether futures contracts exhibit systematic risk. While the question has not been fully resolved, the best available evidence concludes that the systematic risk of futures contracts is zero [15]. In accordance with this evidence, this analysis assumes that the futures and forward contracts are essentially similar in their institutional features and that they exhibit no systematic risk. Consequently, forward and futures prices may be interpreted as the market's best estimate of the futures spot price to prevail upon delivery.

From Equation (5) for infinitesimal changes in K^*:

$$\Delta FP_j = -D_j \frac{\Delta(1 + K^*)}{(1 + K^*)} FP_j \qquad (6)$$

Note here, however, that D_j is the duration of the underlying financial instrument that is expected to prevail at the delivery date. This means that D_j is based on K^*, the yield on the underlying instrument expected to prevail on the delivery date of the futures contract:

$$D_j = \sum_{t=1}^{M} \left[\frac{\dfrac{tC_{jt}}{(1 + K^*)^t}}{\displaystyle\sum_{t=1}^{M} \dfrac{C_{jt}}{(1 + K^*)^t}} \right] \tag{7}$$

So while the futures contract itself does not have a duration, its price sensitivity depends upon the duration and yield of the underlying instrument that is expected to prevail on the delivery date.

Earlier changes in the duration of a financial instrument were said to be a function of changes in yields and the passage of time. When one considers the duration of the instrument underlying a futures contract, two related points are evident. First, D_j of Equation (7) clearly depends upon changes in K^*. Second, D_j does not change with the passage of time over the life of the futures contract. This differentiates Equations (2) and (6). D_j cannot change over the life of the futures contract, barring changes in K^*, because the maturity of the deliverable instrument is fixed by the terms of the futures contract. This fact helps to make futures contracts particularly useful for the implementation of immunization strategies.

The similarity of duration measures for bonds (1) and futures contracts (7) makes clear the susceptibility of futures contracts to all analyses that have been applied to a "bonds only" approach. In the context of portfolio immunization, futures contracts also suffer basis risk [13], can be applied to immunizing for multiple planning periods [4], and can be used in active and passive management strategies [3].

Available Futures Contracts

Futures contracts are currently available on T-bills, -notes, and -bonds, GNMAs (certificate delivery and collateralized depository receipts), certificates of deposit, Eurodollars and commercial paper (30 and 90 day maturities). Most immunization strategies concern portfolios of non-mortgage related instruments, so GNMA futures will not be considered. Currently, markets for commercial paper and T-note futures contracts are extremely thin.[11] Since T-bill and T-bond contracts enjoy very robust futures markets, and since they lie at the two ends of the duration spectrum, they appear to be the most applicable for the implementation of immunization strategies.

A T-bill futures contract calls for delivery of $1,000,000 face value of T-bills having 90 days remaining until maturity. Since T-bills are pure discount instruments, their duration, as given by Equation (7), will always be equal to M, which is 90 days or .25 years. This will be the same for every T-bill, no matter what its yield. For T-bonds the situation is more complex. To fulfill a T-bond futures contract, one may deliver any T-bond not maturing and not callable within 15 years from the time of delivery. This means that several different bonds are deliverable. For example, in February 1982, 18 different T-bonds were deliverable, with call or maturity dates ranging from 16 to 24 years and coupons ranging from 2½ to 15¾%. Clearly the prices and durations of these deliverable instruments vary widely. The rules of the Chicago Board of Trade (CBT), the largest T-bond futures market, specify price differentials based on which bond is actually delivered.[12] However,

Exhibit 1   Instruments used in the analysis

	Coupon	Maturity	Yield	Price	Duration
Bond A:	8%	4 yrs.	12%	885.59	3.475
Bond B:	10%	10 yrs.	12%	903.47	6.265
Bond C:	4%	15 yrs.	12%	463.05	9.285
T-Bond Futures:*	8%	20 yrs.	12%	718.75	8.674
T-Bill Futures:*	—	¼ yr.	12%	972.07	.25

* For purposes of comparability, we assume face values of $1000 for these instruments.

usually one bond is cheapest to deliver and the futures market tends to trade to that bond [9]. Consequently, the duration of the underlying T-bond must be computed from Equation (7). For greatest accuracy, it should be computed for the T-bond that is cheapest to deliver.[13]

How to Immunize with Interest Rate Futures

Here two examples are presented, one for the Planning Period Case and one for the Bank Immunization Case. In Exhibit 1, three bonds are considered, along with the T-bill and T-bond futures contracts. The Exhibit reflects the assumption of a flat yield curve and instruments of the same risk level.[14] Since the yield curve is flat, duration is appropriately calculated by Equation (1) or (7). Only parallel shifts in the yield curve are considered in these examples, and all market imperfections are ignored.

The planning period case

Assume a $100 million bond portfolio of Bond C with a duration of 9.285 years. Assume now that the portfolio duration is to be shortened to 6 years to match the planning period. The shortening could be accomplished by selling Bond C and buying Bond A until the following conditions are met:

$$W_A D_A + W_C D_C = 6 \text{ years}$$
$$W_A + W_C = 1$$

where:
W_I = percent of portfolio funds committed to asset I.

This means that 56.54% of the $100 million must be put in Bond A, the funds coming from the sale of Bond C. Call this Portfolio 1.

Alternatively, one could adjust the portfolio's duration to match the 6 year planning period by trading interest rate futures. For Portfolio 2, the problem is to continue to hold $100,000,000 in Bond C, yet to achieve the same price action as Portfolio 1. If Portfolio 2 is to be comprised of Bond C and T-bill futures, the T-bill futures position must be chosen to satisfy the condition:

$$\Delta P_P = \Delta P_C N_C + \Delta FP_{\text{TBILL}} N_{\text{TBILL}}$$

where:

$$P_P = \text{value of the portfolio,}$$
$$P_C = \text{price of bond C,}$$
$$FP_{\text{TBILL}} = \text{T-bill futures price,}$$
$$N_C = \text{number of C bonds,}$$
$$N_{\text{TBILL}} = \text{number of T-bills.}$$

Applying the same price change formula (2) to the portfolio value, Bond C, and the T-bill futures:

$$-D_P \frac{\Delta(1+r)}{(1+r)} P_P = \left[-D_C \frac{\Delta(1+r)}{(1+r)} P_C \right] N_C + \left[-D_{\text{TBILL}} \frac{\Delta(1+r)}{1+r} FP_{\text{TBILL}} \right] N_{\text{TBILL}}$$

which reduces to:

$$D_P P_P = D_C P_C N_C + D_{\text{TBILL}} FP_{\text{TBILL}} N_{\text{TBILL}}$$

Since the goal is to mimic Portfolio 1, which has a total value of \$100,000,000 and a duration of 6 years, it must be that:

$$P_P = \$100,000,000$$
$$D_P = 6$$
$$D_C = 9.285$$
$$P_C = \$463.05$$
$$N_C = 215,959$$
$$D_{\text{TBILL}} = .25$$
$$FP_{\text{TBILL}} = 972.07$$

Solving for $N_{\text{TBILL}} = -1,351,747$ indicates that this many T-bills (assuming \$1,000 par value) must be sold short in the futures market. Since T-bill futures are denominated in \$1,000,000 face value, this technique requires that 1,352 contracts be sold.

The same technique used to created Portfolio 2 can be applied using a T-bond futures contract, which gives rise to Portfolio 3. Solving:

$$D_P P_P = D_C P_C N_C + D_{\text{TBOND}} FP_{\text{TBOND}} N_{\text{TBOND}}$$

For N_{TBOND} gives $N_{\text{TBOND}} = -52,691$. Since T-bond futures contracts have a face value denomination of \$100,000,527 T-bond futures contracts must be sold.
For each of the three portfolios, Exhibit 2 summarizes the relevant data.

Now we assume an instantaneous drop in rates for all maturities from 12% to 11%. Assume also that all coupon receipts during the six-year planning period can be re-invested at 11% until the end of the planning period.[15] With the shift in interest rates the new prices become:

$$P_A = 913.57$$
$$P_C = 504.33$$
$$FP_{\text{TBILL}} = 974.25$$
$$FP_{\text{TBOND}} = 778.13$$

Exhibit 2   Portfolio characteristics for the planning period case

		Portfolio 1 (Bonds only)	Portfolio 2 (Short T-bill futures)	Portfolio 3 (Short T-bond futures)
Portfolio	W_A	56.54%	—	—
Weights	W_C	43.46%	100%	100%
	W_{CASH}	0	0	0
Number	N_A	63,844	0	—
of	N_C	93,856	215,959	215,959
Instruments	N_{TBILL}	—	(1,351,747)	—
	N_{TBOND}	—	—	(52,691)
Value	$N_A P_A$	56,539,608	—	—
of each	$N_C P_A$	43,460,021	99,999,815	99,999,815
Instrument	$N_{TBILL}\ FP_{TBILL}$	—	1,313,992,706	—
	$N_{TBOND}\ FP_{TBOND}$	—	—	37,871,656
	Cash	371	185	185
	Portfolio Value $(N_A P_A + N_C P_C + \text{cash})$	100,000,000	100,000,000	100,000,000

Exhibit 3   Effect of a 1% drop in yields on realized portfolio returns

	Portfolio 1	Portfolio 2	Portfolio 3
Original Portfolio Value	100,000,000	100,000,000	100,000,000
New Portfolio Value	105,660,731	108,914,787	108,914,787
Gain/Loss on Futures	-0-	(2,946,808)	(3,128,792)
Total Wealth Change	5,660,731	5,967,979	5,785,995
Terminal Value of All Funds at $t = 6$	197,629,369	198,204,050	197,863,664
Annualized Holding Period Return Over 6 Years	1.120234	1.120776	1.120455

Exhibit 3 presents the effect of the interest rate shift on portfolio values, terminal wealth at the horizon (year 6), and on the total wealth position of the portfolio holder.

As Exhibit 3 reveals, each portfolio has the same response to the shift in yields. The slight differences that can be observed are attributable to either (1) rounding errors or (2) the fact that the duration price change formula holds exactly only for infinitesimal changes in yields. The largest difference (between terminal values for Portfolios 1 and 2) is only .29%, which reveals the effectiveness of the alternative strategies.

The bank immunization case

Assume that a bank holds a $100,000,000 liability portfolio in Bond B, the composition of which is fixed. Bonds A and C are available for its asset portfolio, and the bank wishes to hold an asset portfolio that will protect the wealth position of the bank from any change as a result of a change in yields.

Five different portfolio combinations illustrate different means to achieve the desired result:

Portfolio 1: Hold Bond A and Bond C (the traditional approach)
Portfolio 2: Hold Bond C, SELL T-bill futures short
Portfolio 3: Hold Bond A, BUY T-bond futures
Portfolio 4: Hold Bond A, BUY T-bill futures
Portfolio 5: Hold Bond C, SELL T-bond futures short

For each portfolio, the full $100,000,000 is put in a bond portfolio (and is balanced out by cash). Portfolio 1 exemplifies the traditional approach of immunizing by holding an all bond portfolio with no futures contracts added. Portfolios 2 and 5 are comprised of the highly volatile Bond C, and that volatility is offset by selling interest rate futures. By contrast, the low volatility Bond A is held in Portfolios 3 and 4. In conjunction with Bond A, the overall interest rate sensitivity is increased by buying interest rate futures. The composition of these five portfolios is presented in Exhibit 4.

Now assume an instantaneous drop in rates from 12 to 11%, affecting all maturities. Exhibit 5 presents the effect on each of the portfolios. As the rows reporting wealth changes reveal, all five methods are comparable in their performance. The small differences that exist are due to rounding errors and the discrete change in interest rates.

Transaction Costs

One important concern in the implementation of immunization strategies is the transaction costs involved. As one wishes to re-adjust the immunized position over time, the commission charges, marketability, and liquidity of the instruments involved become increasingly important. These considerations highlight the practical usefulness of interest rate futures in bond portfolio management.

Consider as an example the transaction costs associated with the different immunization portfolios for the Planning Period Case. Starting from the initial position of $100,000,000 in Bond C, and wishing to shorten the duration to 6 years. Exhibit 6 shows the trades necessary and the estimated costs involved. To implement the "bonds only" traditional approach of Portfolio 1, one must sell 122,103 bonds of type C and buy 63,844 bonds of type A. Assuming a low commission charge of $2 per bond, this results in a total cost of $371,894. By contrast one could sell 1,352 T-bill futures contracts to immunize Portfolio 2, or sell 527 T-bond futures contracts for Porfolio 3, at total costs of $20,280 and $7,905, respectively. (Additionally one would have to deposit approximately $2,000,000 margin for the T-bill strategy or $800,000 for the T-bond strategy. But this margin deposit can be in the form of interest earning assets.)

Clearly, there is a tremendous difference in transaction costs between trading the cash and futures instruments. In an extreme example of this type, the transaction cost for the "bonds only" case is prohibitive, amounting to almost .4% of the total portfolio value.[16] But also it is practically impossible for another reason.

Exhibit 4 Liability portfolio and five alternative immunizing asset portfolios

		Liability portfolio	Portfolio 1 (bonds only)	Portfolio 2 (short T-bill futures)	Portfolio 3 (long T-bond futures)	Portfolio 4 (long T-bill futures)	Portfolio 5 (short T-bond futures)
Portfolio Weights	W_A	0	51.98%	0	100%	100%	0
	W_B	100%	0	0	0	0	0
	W_C	0	48.02%	100%	0	0	100%
	W_{CASH}	0	0	0	0	0	0
Number of Instruments	N_A	0	58,695	0	112,919	112,919	0
	N_B	110,684	0	0	0	0	0
	N_C	0	103,704	215,959	0	0	215,959
	N_{TBILL}	0	0	(1,242,710)	0	1,148,058	0
	N_{TBOND}	0	0	0	44,751	0	(48,441)
	$N_A P_A$	0	51,979,705	0	99,999,937	99,999,937	0
	$N_B P_B$	99,999,673	0	0	0	0	0
	$N_C P_C$	0	48,020,137	99,999,815	0	0	99,999,815
	Cash	327	158	185	63	63	185
	$N_{TBILL} P_{TBILL}$	0	0	(1,208,001,110)	0	1,115,992,740	0
	$N_{TBOND} P_{TBOND}$	0	0	0	32,164,781	0	(34,816,969)
	Portfolio Value	100,000,000	100,000,000	100,000,000	100,000,000	100,000,000	100,000,000

Exhibit 5 Effect of a 1% drop in yields on total wealth

	Liability	Portfolio 1	Portfolio 2	Portfolio 3	Portfolio 4	Portfolio 5
Original Portfolio Value	100,000,000	100,000,000	100,000,000	100,000,000	100,000,000	100,000,000
New Portfolio Value	105,910,526	105,923,188	108,914,788	103,159,474	103,159,474	108,914,788
Profit/(Loss) on Futures	0	—	(2,709,108)	2,657,314	2,502,766	(2,876,427)
Total Wealth Change (On Portfolio Plus Futures)	5,910,527	5,923,188	6,205,680	5,816,788	5,662,240	6,038,361
Total Wealth Change (Asset-Liability Portfolio)	—	12,622	295,154	(93,738)	(248,286)	127,835
% Wealth Change	—	.00013	.00295	(.00094)	(.00248)	.00128

Exhibit 6   Transaction costs for the planning period case

	Portfolio 1	Portfolio 2	Portfolio 3
Number of Instruments Traded			
Bond A	63,844	—	—
Bond C	(122,103)	—	—
T-Bill Futures Contracts	—	1,352	—
T-Bond Futures Contracts	—	—	527
One Way Transaction Cost			
Bond A @ $2	127,688	—	—
Bond C @ $2	244,206	—	—
T-Bill Futures @ $15	—	20,280	—
T-Bond Futures @ $15	—	—	7,905
Total Cost of Becoming Immunized	$371,894	$20,280	$7,905

The volume of bonds to be traded is enormous, exceeding any reasonable volume for bonds of even the largest issue. The superior marketability and liquidity of the futures market is clearly evident. The 1,352 T-bill futures contracts are about 10% of the daily volume or .5% of the current open interest. Likewise, the 527 T-bond futures constitute only 1% of daily volume and .2% of the current open interest. The evident ability of the futures market to absorb the kind of activity involved in this example demonstrates the practical usefulness of interest rate futures in managing bond portfolios.

Summary

To date, immunization strategies for bond portfolios have focused on all bond portfolios. This paper has shown that interest rate futures can be used in conjunction with bond portfolios to provide the same kind of immunization. The method advocated here works equally well for both types of immunization: the Planning Period Case and the Bank Immunization Case.

Note that all of the examples assumed parallel shifting yield curves. If the change in interest rates brings about non-parallel shifts in the yield curve, then the "bonds only" and "bonds-with-futures" approaches will give different results. Which method turns out to be superior would depend upon the particular pattern of interest rate change that actually occurred.

Notes

The authors gratefully acknowledge the support of the Chicago Board of Trade Foundation in the conduct of this research.
  1. For reviews of the history and development of the concept of duration see Weil [34], Ingersoll, Skelton, and Weil [23], and Bierwag, Kaufman, and Khang [2].
  2. McEnally [31] provides a useful introduction to the concept of duration and its applicability to bond portfolio management.
  3. As a practical matter, measuring the duration of a bank's assets and liabilities is at best a difficult process. Demand deposits, for example, represent a case where it is not at all obvious how to measure duration. However, the problems with measuring duration

affect the traditional "bonds only" approach and the "bonds and futures" approach, to be developed here, equally. Here we assume equal values in the asset and liability portfolios. This is only for convenience. The analysis can be extended to the more general case with ease.

4. Grove [21] analyzes this type of portfolio immunization. In a perfect market, the individual investor could trade bonds costlessly, thereby achieving "homemade immunization." Institutional concern with immunization, like firm concern with leverage, stems from market imperfections.

5. Fisher and Weil [17] discuss planning period immunization. This technique was later elaborated by Kaufman [26], in which the nature of the trade-off between capital gains/losses and reinvestment rates is discussed.

6. The immunization guarantees that the return will be at least as large as the promised return. Fisher and Weil [17]. As Bierwag and Khang [5] show, this means that an immunized portfolio stochastically dominates a single bond. Further, a portfolio of coupon bonds, with duration equal to the planning period, stochastically dominates a pure-discount bond with maturity equal to the planning period. This is the case, since the realized yield equals the promised yield for the pure discount bond. For the immunized coupon-bond portfolio one may realize a return greater than the promised yield, but one cannot realize a lower yield. This consideration should give pause to those portfolio managers who welcome the issuance of pure-discount bonds by J. C. Penney, Pepsi, and others.

7. Bierwag and Kaufman [1] derive more sophisticated measures for duration to immunize against non-additive interest rate shocks. Kolb and Chiang [28] treat interest rate futures contracts similarly.

8. The fact that Macaulay's duration measure assumes a flat term structure, contrary to fact, is not of great empirical significance. Gifford Fong Associates [20] presents results from elaborate simulations showing that the Macaulay duration measure performs as well as the complex duration measures for a wide variety of cases.

9. Fong and Vasicek [18] show that immunization is made more nearly perfect when bonds maturing close to the planning horizon are used in the portfolio. In other words, the following strategy is recommended: Minimize the variance of the portfolio payment dates about the portfolio duration subject to the constraint that the duration = planning horizon.

10. Existing studies of interest rate futures market efficiency substantiate the very close relationship between forward yields and futures yields. Since these efficiency studies proceed by comparing returns on futures and forward contracts, and generally find them to be equal [30, 32, 33], forward and futures contracts are very close substitutes and are essentially similar in their institutional respects. For further justification of this position, see Kolb [27], Chapter IV.

11. Recently both commercial paper contracts showed zero open interest on the CBT. The open interest on 2-year 8% Treasury notes was 630 contracts on the COMEX.

12. For these rules see CBT [11]. The calculation of the invoice price requires conversion factors from Financial Publishing Co. [16].

13. For sample durations based on a 20 year 8% T-bond, see [29], Appendix.

14. The constant yields of Exhibit 1 are consistent with this assumption of homogeneous risk. One may think of the bond portfolio as consisting of U.S. Treasury issues. However, the argument of the paper does not require the assumption of uniform yields, but only parallel shifting yield curves.

15. In reality the re-investment rate is not certain. No matter what re-investment rates prevail, the "bonds only" and "bonds with futures" immunization give the same terminal wealth. Consequently, the assumption of an 11% re-investment rate merely simplifies the example without any loss in generality.

16. Gushee [22] recommends two "bonds only" strategies which involve high transaction costs.

References

1. G. Bierwag and G. Kaufman, "Coping with the Risk of Interest Rate Fluctuations: A Note," *Journal of Business* (July 1977), pp. 364–370.
2. G. Bierwag, G. Kaufman, and C. Khang, "Duration and Bond Portfolio Analysis: An Overview," *Journal of Financial and Quantitative Analysis* (November 1978), pp. 671–682.
3. G. Bierwag, G. Kaufman, R. Schweitzer, and A. Toevs, "The Art of Risk Management in Bond Portfolio Management," *Journal of Portfolio Management* (Spring 1981), pp. 27–36.
4. G. Bierwag, G. Kaufman, and A. Toevs, "Immunization for Multiple Planning Periods," unpublished, 1979.
5. G. Bierwag and C. Khang, "An Immunization Strategy Is a Minimax Strategy," *Journal of Finance* (May 1979), pp. 389–399.
6. F. Black, "The Pricing of Commodity Contracts," *Journal of Financial Economics* (January/March 1976), pp. 167–179.
7. Z. Bodie and V. Rosansky, "Risk and Return in Commodity Futures," *Financial Analysts Journal* (May/June 1980), pp. 27–39.
8. Chicago Board of Trade, "An Introduction to the Interest Rate Futures Market," Chicago 1978.
9. Chicago Board of Trade, "An Introduction to Financial Futures," Chicago, 1980.
10. Chicago Board of Trade, "Financial Instruments Markets: Cash Futures Relationships," Chicago, 1980.
11. Chicago Board of Trade, "Understanding the Delivery Process in Financial Futures," Chicago, 1980.
12. B. Cornell and M. Reinganum, "Forward and Futures Prices: Evidence from the Foreign Exchange Markets," *Journal of Finance* (December 1981), pp. 1035–1045.
13. J. Cox, J. Ingersoll, and S. Ross, "Duration and the Measurement of Basis Risk," *Journal of Business* (January 1979), pp. 51–61.
14. J. Cox, J. Ingersoll, and S. Ross, "The Relation Between Forward Prices and Futures Prices," *Journal of Financial Economics* (December 1981), pp. 321–346.
15. K. Dusak, "Futures Trading and Investor Returns: An Investigation of Commodity Market Risk Premiums," *Journal of Political Economy* (November 1973), pp. 1387–1406.
16. Financial Publishing Company, "Treasury Bond and Note Futures Conversion Tables," Publication No. 765, Boston, 1980.
17. L. Fisher and R. Weil, "Coping with the Risk of Interest Rate Fluctuations: Returns to Bondholders from Naive and Optimal Strategies," *Journal of Business* (October 1971), pp. 408–431.
18. G. Fong and O. Vasicek, "A Risk Minimizing Strategy for Multiple Liability Immunization," unpublished, 1980.
19. G. Gay and R. Kolb (eds.) 1982. *Interest Rate Futures: Concepts and Issues*. Robert F. Dame, Inc., Richmond, Virginia.
20. Gifford Fong Associates, "Immunization: Definition and Simulation Study," unpublished, 1979.
21. M. A. Grove, "On Duration and the Optimal Maturity Structure of the Balance Sheet," *The Bell Journal of Economics and Management Science* (Autumn 1974), pp. 696–709.
22. C. Gushee, "How to Hedge a Bond Investment," *Financial Analyst Journal* (March/April 1981), pp. 44–51.
23. J. Ingersoll, J. Skelton, and R. Weil, "Duration Forty Years Later," *Journal of Financial and Quantitative Analysis* (November 1978), pp. 627–650.
24. R. Jarrow and G. Oldfield, "Forward Contracts and Futures Contracts," *Journal of Financial Economics* (December 1981), pp. 373–382.

25. E. Kane, "Market Incompleteness and Divergences Between Forward and Futures Interest Rates," *Journal of Finance* (May 1980), pp. 221–234.

26. G. Kaufman, "Measuring Risk and Return for Bonds: A New Approach," *Journal of Bank Research* (Summer 1978), pp. 82–90.

27. R. Kolb, 1982. *Interest Rate Futures: A Comprehensive Introduction*, Robert F. Dame, Inc., Richmond, Virginia.

28. R. Kolb and R. Chiang, "Duration, Immunization, and Hedging with Interest Rate Futures," forthcoming, *Journal of Financial Research* (1982).

29. R. Kolb and R. Chiang, "Improving Hedging Performance Using Interest Rate Futures," *Financial Management* (Autumn 1981), pp. 72–79.

30. R. Kolb, G. Gay, and J. Jordan, "Are There Arbitrage Opportunities in the Treasury-Bond Futures Market?" forthcoming, *The Journal of Futures Markets* (Fall 1982).

31. R. McEnally, "Duration as a Practical Tool for Bond Management," *The Journal of Portfolio Management* (Summer 1977), pp. 53–57.

32. R. Rendleman and C. Carabini, "The Efficiency of the Treasury Bill Futures Market," *Journal of Finance* (September 1979), pp. 895–914.

33. A. Vignola and C. Dale, "The Efficiency of the Treasury Bill Futures Market: An Analysis of Alternative Specifications," *Journal of Financial Research* (Fall 1980), pp. 169–188.

34. R. Weil, "Macaulay's Duration: An Appreciation," *Journal of Business* (October 1973), pp. 589–592.

13

Interest Rate Swaps versus Eurodollar Strips

Ira G. Kawaller

An interest rate swap is essentially a contract between two parties, A and B. A calculates his interest obligation on the basis of a floating rate benchmark such as LIBOR. B calculates his obligation based on a known fixed rate. A periodic adjustment is made between the two parties, commensurate with the difference between the two obligations. A swap allows A to convert from a floating rate sensitivity to a fixed rate, and it does the opposite for B. In practice, such swaps are often designed to offset, or "hedge," existing rate exposures.

The Eurodollar futures contract sets rates on Eurodollar time deposits, beginning on a specific forthcoming date. As interest rates rise, futures prices will fall, and vice versa. The futures market participant can maintain either a long position (in which case he will benefit if yields fall) or a short position (which would benefit from rising yields). The participant will have to mark the contract to market on a daily basis and make daily cash settlements for changes in value.

Strips of Eurodollar futures are simply the coordinated purchase or sale of a series of contracts with successive expiration dates, the objective being to "lock in" a rate of return for a given term. The construction of the strip will depend on the prices of the contracts, the amount of principal plus interest received in each quarter and the number of days in each quarter. Actual return from a correctly constructed hedge should come very close to the expected return.

Both interest rate swaps and strips of Eurodollar futures contracts allow a manager to decrease (or increase) exposure to interest rate changes by converting a floating rate exposure to a fixed rate (or vice versa). With swaps, however, the precise fixed rate is readily identifiable. The ultimate outcome with interest rate strips is somewhat uncertain. This article provides a framework for making direct comparisons between Eurodollar strips and interest rate swaps. This will considerably ease the task of identifying the more attractively priced instrument.

Swaps

Figure A summarizes the standard, "plain vanilla" swap agreement. Here two counterparties enter into a contract whereby A calculates an interest rate expense obligation based on a floating interest rate benchmark and B calculates an obligation based on a known, fixed rate.

The amount of the interest expense for which A is responsible will clearly rise in a rising rate environment and fall with declining rates. In contrast, B's obligation

Figure A   Plain vanilla swap

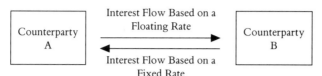

is constant, based on the stated, notional amount specified by the swap agreement and the contractually determined fixed interest rate. The swap requires periodic interest payments whereby the difference between the two interest obligations (the net) is passed from the party with the greater obligation to the party with the lesser obligation.

Consider the case where A agrees to pay B based on the London Interbank Offered Rate (LIBOR) on three-month Eurodollar deposits, and B agrees to pay A based on a fixed, money market rate of 10 percent.[1] Assume a notional amount of $100 million for the swap and quarterly interest payments. With each fixing of LIBOR, A establishes his forthcoming interest obligation.

If LIBOR were equal to 10 percent at the first rate setting, for example, no cash adjustment would be made by either party. If LIBOR were 11 percent, counterparty A would pay B $250,000 (i.e., $100 million × 0.11 × ¼ – $100 million × 0.10 × ¼). If LIBOR were 9 percent, counterparty B would pay A $250,000 (i.e., $100 million × 0.09 × ¼ – $100 million × 0.10 × ¼). This process would continue for the term of the contract, following each reset of LIBOR.

If both A and B had no exposure to interest rates prior to executing the swap contract, the swap would expose A to the risk of higher short-term rates and the opportunity of lower rates; B's exposure would be the opposite. Often, however, counterparties will use swaps to offset existing exposures. In the first case, the swap is being used as a trading vehicle; in the second, it is being used as a hedge.

Eurodollar Strips

The Eurodollar futures contract sets rates on Eurodollar time deposits, commencing on a specific forthcoming date – the third Wednesday of March, June, September, or December, depending on the contract expiration month. Operationally, futures prices are derived by subtracting an interest rate (in percentage points, carried to two decimal places) from 100. As interest rates rise, futures prices will fall, and vice versa.

The face amount of the Eurodollar futures contract is one million dollars, and its maturity is three months. Every basis-point move in the futures price (yield) translates to a value of $25 (= $1,000,000 × 0.0001 × 90/360). In general, movements in the Eurodollar futures market are closely correlated with yield movements in the underlying Eurodollar time deposit market, although changes are not precisely equal over any given period.

The futures market participant can maintain either a long position (hoping the market will rise in price and decline in yield) or a short position (hoping the market will decline in price and rise in yield). In either case, the participant will be obligated to mark the contract to market on a daily basis and make daily cash settlements for any change in value. This obligation can be terminated at any time by simply "trading out" of the position (i.e., making the opposite transaction to the initial trade). Upon expiration of the contract, any participant still maintaining contracts will make a final mark-to-market adjustment, with the final settlement price based on an average derived from a survey of London bankers who report their perceptions of the cash market three-month LIBOR to the Chicago Mercantile Exchange at the time of the survey.

Strips of Eurodollar futures are simply the coordinated purchase or sale of a series of futures contracts with successive expiration dates. The objective is to "lock in" a rate of return for a term equal to the length of the strip. For example, a strip consisting of contracts with four successive expirations would lock up a one-year term rate, eight successive contracts would lock up a two-year rate, and so on. As is the case with swaps, futures strips may be used to take on additional interest rate risk in the hope of making trading profits, or as an offset or hedge to an existing exposure.

Calculating Strip Yields

What is the term rate that can be expected to result from employing a strip of Eurodollar futures? And how should the hedge be constructed to achieve this rate?

The answers depend on the objectives of the strip creator with respect to the accruing interest. That is, creation of a synthetic zero-coupon fixed income security would require one particular hedge construction, while creation of a synthetic coupon-bearing security would require another.

The Zero-coupon Strip

Consider the problem of creating a one-year, zero-coupon strip with four successive contract expirations. Assume the prices for these contracts are 92.79, 92.51, 92.27, and 92.05, respectively. Under these conditions, the hedger would have four hedgeable events designed to lock up rates of 7.21 percent (100 − 92.79) in the first quarter, 7.49 percent (100 − 92.51) in the second quarter, 7.73 percent (100 − 92.27) in the third quarter, and 7.95 percent (100 − 92.05) in the fourth quarter.

To arrive at the number of contracts required for the hedge, the hedger would first determine the amount of principal plus interest at the end of each quarter. Assume the number of days in each of the quarters are 91, 91, 91 and 92, respectively. At the end of the first quarter, the principal plus interest would be calculated as the starting principal plus that principal multiplied by the first futures' interest rate (7.21 percent) multiplied by 91/360.[2] This end-of-quarter value would serve as the amount to be hedged in the second quarter. Table 1 illustrates the process over the four quarters, assuming an initial value of $100 million.

The number of contracts required is found by dividing the value per basis point of each quarter's amount to be hedged (the prior quarter's principal plus interest) by $25, which is the value of the basis point per futures contract. The actual hedge

Table 1 Strip hedge objectives

Quarter	Amount to be hedged (millions)	Quarterly futures interest rate (%)	Days per quarter	Principal plus interest (end of quarter)
1	$100.00	7.21	91	$101.82
2	101.82	7.49	91	103.75
3	103.75	7.73	91	105.78
4	105.78	7.95	92	107.93

Table 2 Hedge ratio calculations*

Quarter	
1	($100.00 million × (0.0001) × $^{91}/_{360}$)/$25 = 101 contracts
2	($101.82 million × (0.0001) × $^{91}/_{360}$)/$25 = 103 contracts
3	($103.75 million × (0.0001) × $^{91}/_{360}$)/$25 = 105 contracts
4	($105.78 million × (0.0001) × $^{92}/_{360}$)/$25 = 108 contracts

* This hedge construction implicitly assumes that the rate on the Eurodollar strip will move point-for-point with the rate on the exposed instrument. Clearly this assumption may be modified by simply adjusting the hedge ratios by a factor designed to take into account the expected relative rate change.

ratio would have to be rounded to a whole number, of course, as futures cannot be bought or sold in fractional units. Table 2 gives the calculations.

Bond-equivalent Yields

Incorporating the concept of the bond-equivalent yield allows us to generalize from this specific example. The bond-equivalent yield for a strip of virtually any length (up to the maximum number of quarterly expirations available) can be derived from Equation 1.

Equation 1.

$$\left(1 + RF1\frac{DQ1}{360}\right)\left(1 + RF2\frac{DQ2}{360}\right)\ldots\left(1 + RFN\frac{DQN}{360}\right) = (1 + Reff/P)^{(N \times P/4)}.$$

Here $RF1$, $RF2$, and RFN are the respective annual futures rates (100 minus the appropriate futures prices, expressed in decimals). $DQ1$, $DQ2$, and DQN are the days in each three-month period beginning with the third Wednesday of the respective future's expiration months.[3] N is the number of quarters in the strip. $Reff$ is the effective annual bond-equivalent yield for the strip. P is the number of periods per year for which compounding is assumed.

The left-hand side of Equation 1 shows the effect of borrowing (or lending) for each quarter at the interest rate designated by the appropriate futures contract.

Table 3 Interest rates rise to 15 percent

Quarter	Futures results*	End-of-quarter balances
1	101 contracts × (85.00 − 92.79) × \$2500 = −\$1.97 million	100.00 million × $(1 + 0.15 \times {}^{91}/_{360})$ − 1.97 million = \$101.82 million
2	103 contracts × (85.00 − 92.51) × \$2500 = −\$1.93 million	101.82 million × $(1 + 0.15 \times {}^{91}/_{360})$ − 1.93 million = \$103.75 million
3	105 contracts × (85.00 − 92.27) × \$2500 = −\$1.91 million	103.75 million × $(1 + 0.15 \times {}^{91}/_{360})$ − 1.91 million = \$105.78 million
4	108 contracts × (85.00 − 92.05) × \$2500 = −\$1.90 million	105.78 million × $(1 + 0.15 \times {}^{92}/_{360})$ − 1.90 million = \$107.93 million

* As prices are reflective of percentage points, rather than basis points, the multiplier becomes $25 × 100, or $2500.

Table 4 Interest rates decline to 2 percent

Quarter	Futures results	End-of-quarter balances
1	101 contracts × (98.00 − 92.79) × \$2500 = \$1.32 million	100.00 million × $(1 + 0.02 \times {}^{91}/_{360})$ + 1.32 million = \$101.82 million
2	103 contracts × (98.00 − 92.51) × \$2500 = \$1.41 million	101.82 million × $(1 + 0.02 \times {}^{91}/_{360})$ + 1.41 million = \$103.75 million
3	105 contracts × (98.00 − 92.27) × \$2500 = \$1.50 million	103.75 million × $(1 + 0.02 \times {}^{91}/_{360})$ + 1.50 million = \$105.78 million
4	108 contracts × (98.00 − 92.05) × \$2500 = \$1.61 million	105.78 million × $(1 + 0.02 \times {}^{92}/_{360})$ + 1.61 million = \$107.93 million

Table 5 Worst-case scenario

Quarter	Futures results	End-of-quarter balances
1	101 contracts × (84.75 − 92.79) × \$2500 = −\$2.03 million	100.00 million × $(1 + 0.15 \times {}^{91}/_{360})$ − 2.03 million = \$101.76 million
2	103 contracts × (84.75 − 92.51) × \$2500 = −\$2.00 million	101.76 million × $(1 + 0.15 \times {}^{91}/_{360})$ − 2.00 million = \$103.62 million
3	105 contracts × (84.75 − 92.27) × \$2500 = −\$1.97 million	103.62 million × $(1 + 0.15 \times {}^{91}/_{360})$ − 1.97 million = \$105.58 million
4	108 contracts × (84.75 − 92.05) × \$2500 = −\$1.97 million	105.58 million × $(1 + 0.15 \times {}^{92}/_{360})$ − 1.97 million = \$107.65 million

The right-hand side incorporates the effective yield that would be required to generate the same principal plus interest by the end of the term. In all cases, effective yields are approximations, as the periods covered by the futures contracts may either overlap or have gaps.

Despite the fact that futures expire quarterly, one can calculate an effective term rate assuming any compounding frequency. Most likely, the choice of P would reflect the compounding assumptions implicit in the fixed rate quotation of an instrument to which the strip yield may be compared.

If, as in the above example, a one-year strip is arranged with contracts priced at 92.79, 92.51, 92.27, and 92.05, respectively, the target return is 7.93 percent.[4] Tables 3 and 4 illustrate two extreme cases that demonstrate the robustness of this hedge.

For both tables, end-of-quarter balances are found by investing the initial $100 million at the spot LIBOR and adjusting the ending principal plus interest by the gains or losses on that quarter's hedge. This adjusted figure becomes the principal amount to be rolled over and reinvested. Such practice is consistent with the accounting tradition of allocating hedge results to the quarter for which the hedge is designed. (On a cash flow basis, hedge gains and losses for all contracts are generated daily, and variation margin adjustments are called for. Returns calculated from actual cash flows would therefore differ from the calculations shown.)

Table 3 assumes that LIBOR immediately skyrockets to 15 percent following the initiation of the hedge and remains there. Thus all futures are liquidated at 85.00. Table 4 assumes that LIBOR drops to 2 percent and remains there. Thus all futures are liquidated at 98.00. That both cases result in identical ending balances demonstrates the robustness of the hedge.

Real-world Considerations

It should be noted that the analysis above assumes perfect convergence between LIBOR and the Eurodollar futures rate each time a futures contract expires or is liquidated. A nonzero basis at the time of hedge liquidations could alter the results. The size of the alteration would depend on magnitudes and directions of the basis at liquidation.

For the long strip (that is, where the futures contracts are originally purchased), a LIBOR at liquidation higher than the rate implied by the futures contract would be desirable. A LIBOR below the futures rate would be undesirable. For the short strip, the opposite would apply.

It is worthwhile to look at some possible adverse market conditions that might apply when futures contracts are liquidated.[5] Assume, for example, that a long strip is created, as in the examples above. With LIBOR at 15 percent, assume the worst case of futures liquidation at 84.75, or a rate of 15.25 percent for each futures contract. The worst-case projected results differ from the results in Table 3 because of the somewhat greater futures losses in each quarter. The differences equal the number of contracts for that quarter's hedge times 25 basis points times $25 per basis point, as Table 5 shows. Because of the greater futures losses, a return of 7.65 percent results, rather than a bond-equivalent yield of 7.93 percent, as initially targeted.

The above calculation demonstrates that an adverse basis of 25 basis points at each hedge liquidation would lower the perfect convergence target by 28 basis points (7.93 − 7.65) − just about one-for-one. But this represents the results for what has been judged to be a worst-case scenario.

In many cases, the actual shortfall would be substantially smaller. It could be virtually negligible in the case where hedges are scheduled for liquidation at or near futures expiration dates. Furthermore, the basis conditions of hedge liquidation could be favorable, in which case the hedge performance would be better than that indicated by the perfect convergence calculation.

Extensions and Refinements

When considering a strip as an alternative to another fixed income security, the user should try to arrange the strip so that it mirrors the cash flow properties of the competing instrument as closely as possible. For example, if the alternative to the strip is a two-year swap, where the fixed payments are scheduled semiannually, the strip should be formulated to replicate semiannual cash disbursements.

Think about the two-year fixed income obligation as if it were a series of four six-month, zero coupon strips, where the bond-equivalent yield of each six-month strip would be calculated and implemented as explained above. The effective rate for the whole two-year period would reflect compounding of all substrip segments. The appropriate general formula is shown in Equation 2.

Equation 2.
$$(1 + BEY1/P)^t (1 + BEY2/P)^t \ldots (1 + BEYK/P)^t = (1 + R/P)^{Kt},$$

where
$BEYi$ = the bond-equivalent yield of the ith substrip,
P = the assumed number of compounding periods per year,
t = the length of each substrip, in compounding periods and
K = the number of substrips.

Table 6 gives the characteristics relevant to the above synthetic two-year, semi-annual-coupon, fixed income construction. Days per quarter are counted rigorously, from the third Wednesday of the expiration month to that calendar day three months later, and the two-quarter strip yields are calculated using the methodology of Equation (1).[6] Given the bond-equivalent yields from Table 6 and Equation 2, the annualized yield to maturity, r, is 9.18 percent.

As this synthetic construction is designed to mimic a security with semiannual coupons, the amount to be hedged in the first, third, fifth or seventh quarter will be the notional amount of the deal. For a $100 million deal, given the respective days in each of these quarters, the hedge ratios are 100, 100, 102 and 100 contracts, respectively (see Table 7). For the remaining quarters, (two, four, six and eight), the calculation takes the original notional amount plus the interest income from the prior quarter, based on that quarter's futures rate. That is, the hedge ratio for the second quarter depends on the futures rate locked up in the first quarter; the hedge

Table 6   Two-year, semiannual-coupon synthetic

Contract expirations	Futures price	Days per quarter	Bond-equivalent yield (two-quarter strips)
1	91.22	90	
2	91.34	92	8.91
3	91.21	90	
4	91.04	92	9.08
5	90.87	92	
6	90.90	91	9.37
7	90.82	90	
8	90.75	91	9.37

Table 7   Hedge construction for $100 million in semiannual-coupon, two-year-maturity fixed income obligation

Quarter		Hedge ratio
1	$100 million $\times$ 0.0001 $\times$ $\frac{90}{360}$/25 =	100
2	$100 million $\times$ (1 + 0.878 $\times$ $\frac{90}{360}$) $\times$ 0.0001 $\times$ $\frac{92}{360}$/25 =	104
3	$100 million $\times$ 0.0001 $\times$ $\frac{90}{360}$/25 =	100
4	$100 million $\times$ (1 + 0.879 $\times$ $\frac{90}{360}$) $\times$ 0.0001 $\times$ $\frac{92}{360}$/25 =	104
5	$100 million $\times$ 0.0001 $\times$ $\frac{92}{360}$/25 =	102
6	$100 million $\times$ (1 + 0.913 $\times$ $\frac{92}{360}$) $\times$ 0.0001 $\times$ $\frac{91}{360}$/25 =	103
7	$100 million $\times$ 0.0001 $\times$ $\frac{90}{360}$/25 =	100
8	$100 million $\times$ (1 + 0.918 $\times$ $\frac{90}{360}$) $\times$ 0.0001 $\times$ $\frac{91}{360}$/25 =	103

ratio for the fourth quarter depends on the third quarter's future's rate; and so on. These calculations are shown in Table 7.

As was the case with the zero-coupon strip construction, the actual outcomes may differ somewhat from the calculated target because of rounding errors and the prospect of imperfect convergence. Thus appropriate allowance for some deviation from these calculations should be given when determining whether or not to choose a strip as the preferred transaction vehicle. With these considerations in mind, failure to choose the alternative with the more (most) attractive yield necessarily leaves money on the table and thus reflects a suboptimal market decision.

Conclusion

Constructing Eurodollar strip trades requires a certain amount of care. In particular, a strip should match as closely as possible the cash flow provisions of the competing alternative instrument. The payoff for making the correct calculation and implementing it properly is an incrementally superior return. There can be no question that choosing the more attractively priced alternative will necessarily enhance performance.

Notes

This article is reprinted from the September-October 1989 issue of *Financial Analysts Journal*, published by The Financial Analysts Federation, 1633 Broadway, New York, NY 10019.

1.   The terms of the swap will often relate the fixed rate to some benchmark (e.g., 300 basis points above five-year U.S. Treasuries). This allows a general swap agreement to be worked out where the pricing details will reflect market conditions at the time the deal is signed.

2.   The denominator, 360, reflects the convention that LIBOR is quoted as a money market rate, counting the actual number of days during the period in the numerator.

3.   The number of days in the quarter should be measured by counting from the calendar day of the third Wednesday of the expiration month to that same calendar day three months later (e.g., March 17 to June 17, which measures 92 days).

4.   This result follows from an ending principal plus interest of $107.93 million one year after an initial principal of $100 million. It assumes that P equals one.

5.   The existence of gaps or overlaps because of the futures expiration cycle can be considered as a special case contributing to this risk.

6. P in Equation (1) is assumed here to be two, reflecting semiannual compounding.

SECTION C

Equity Markets

14

The Mechanics of Portfolio Insurance

It works . . . at least in theory.

——————————————————————— Thomas J. O'Brien

Although dynamic replication portfolio insurance is not designed to work in anything but an orderly market, it is useful still to understand how the concept should work if the market is orderly. This paper shows in explicit detail how dynamic portfolio insurance should work in theory when the market is orderly. The purpose is to clarify the mysterious "miracle." While the papers referenced below convey the general ideas in applied portfolio insurance, they omit many mechanical details, including the potential drawbacks of insurance even in an orderly market. Some modest progress toward clarifying the mechanics can be found in Sharpe (1985) and Singleton and Grieves (1984), but many practitioners still need considerably more detail on the process. A major objective of this study is to show in more detail just how the principle of dynamic portfolio insurance works, including the use of index futures.

By way of introduction, in 1980 Leland provided a provocative solution to insuring a portfolio against loss below a specified floor: One can insure, in theory and in an orderly market, via a trading strategy based rigidly upon calculated values from option pricing theory. To those who did not quite grasp the relationship of trading, options, and Leland's portfolio insurance, Rubinstein and Leland provided clarification in a 1981 paper. There they explained how a portfolio manager could theoretically act out, or "role play," the Black-Scholes model (1973).

The manager replicates an option through a process of continually revising, in a prescribed manner, the proportions of a portfolio consisting of the underlying asset and the riskless asset. Indeed, Rubinstein and Leland indicate that the replication strategy is helpful in understanding options. The concept implements a version of Pozen's protective put option (1978), extended to an entire portfolio, using a synthetic "portfolio" put option manufactured through "dynamic" trading.

With the introduction of exchange-traded index put options, it seemed theoretically possible for an investor to use these contracts to insure well-diversified portfolios, especially index funds. Nevertheless, investors have not used the option market, for five reasons.

First, adequate contracts, corresponding to the horizons of the institutional managers seeking protection, have not been introduced. Second, the traded options are American, and prices therefore reflect the risk and privilege of early exercise; portfolio insurers with fixed horizon dates do not need to pay this cost. The insurance Leland had in mind is "European," in that it applies to a fixed horizon date corresponding to the expiration time of a European option. The insurance does not apply to times before or after the horizon. Third, there are position limits for exchange-traded puts. Fourth, insurance floors often need to be tailored at a level that is different from the fixed striking prices of traded options.

Fifth, and perhaps most significant, the cost of insuring via the exchange-traded puts is clear, but the dynamic trading approach sometimes is presented in such a way as to give the illusion of producing the insurance out of thin air. See, for example, Wallace's discussion (1982) of the "miracle" of portfolio insurance via dynamic option replication. Nothing in any of the theoretical literature by Leland and Rubinstein, however, suggests any miracles; the nature of the product simply seems to obscure the costs. Yet this literature, including a more recent paper by Ferguson (1986), has managed to convey the seemingly miraculous benefits of the dynamic trading approach without covering the mechanics or costs in sufficient detail.

Attracted to the 'miracle" of portfolio insurance via dynamic trading, practitioners have nevertheless been puzzled by the sophistication of the concept: Besides the complex mathematical nature of the underlying option pricing theory, the strategy calls for buying more stock when the market is going up and selling off some stock as the market goes down. This strategy is contrary to many practitioners' intuition. Moreover, many practitioners believe that the whipsaw potential of buying high and selling low is a drawback in the practical application of the theory.

Practitioners also have been skeptical about the potential amount of trading and thus trading costs that the dynamic approach would entail. To address the trading cost problem, Rubinstein (1985) has argued that index futures could be used as a trading vehicle synthetic to reduce trading costs substantially. Rubinstein's idea also suggests that the insurance can be "obtained" from an advisory that is physically separated from the portfolio to be insured; the insured portfolio itself does not have to be traded, and the portfolio manager can rely upon the advisory's expertise to produce the counter-intuitive "miracles."

Finally, practitioners have been concerned with the possibility of a large gap opening in the market that would prevent the continual trading application at just the time when insurance would be most desirable. Indeed, there has been some concern about the role that insured portfolios themselves would play in exaggerating a market panic. Sellers of portfolio insurance had discounted the possibility of something like a 1929 crash ever happening again, until, of course, October 19, 1987. Unfortunately, a full accounting of what happened to insured portfolios on that day and in the ensuing turbulent weeks had not emerged by the time editorial schedules necessitated completion of this paper.

The device used in my mechanics analysis is a four-date example in the Cox-Ross-Rubinstein (1979) and Rendleman-Bartter (1979) multi-period, two-state option-theoretic intuition of the Black-Scholes theory. This framework permits an extension of the Rubinstein-Leland (1981), Sharpe (1985), and Singleton and Grieves (1984) treatments of portfolio insurance to more periods and more details.

This analysis exposes one aspect of dynamic portfolio insurance that, although not miraculous, is rather remarkable (as long as the market remains orderly): An investor can specify a trading plan that both meets the insurance objective and is entirely "self-financing," regardless of the path taken by random stock prices. This is the insight of Black and Scholes (1973).

Figure 1 Stock price (underlying portfolio value) dynamics

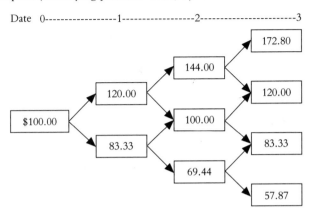

On the other hand, the portfolio insurance cannot be miraculously manufactured at zero cost, even in a theoretical world of zero trading costs. The cost is the forgone returns. This paper gives some details on determining these opportunity costs relative to uninsured equity positions. A more rigorous discussion of the costs relative to optimal asset allocation positions can be found in Rendleman and McEnally (1987).

Stock Price (Underlying Portfolio) Dynamics

The stock price dynamics that underlie the mechanics analysis appear in Figure 1. As the topic is "portfolio" insurance, we may also wish to interpret the dynamics in Figure 1 as characteristic of the *underlying* portfolio in the insurance program. This underlying portfolio with the insurance attached will be referred to as the *insured* portfolio, although sometimes it will be more convenient for me to refer to the underlying portfolio as simply the stock.

The tree diagram in Figure 1 depicts a three-period (or four-date), two-state process, where the movement in an upstate is 1.2 times the current value, and the movement in a downstate is 1/1.2 times the current value. This kind of process is described in Rendleman and Bartter (1979), in their intuitive explanation of the kind of dynamics used in the derivation of the Black-Scholes option model.

Option Valuation and Dynamics

In this framework, options are valued via a "no-arbitrage" argument – start with the expiration-time option price possibilities, and work backward to determine the previous option values. The options in the demonstration are assumed to expire at the end of Period 3. From top to bottom, the potential expiration-time values for a put option with a strike price of $100 would be $0, $0, $16.67, and $42.13.

Figure 2   Put option dynamics if strike price = $100.00

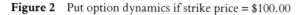

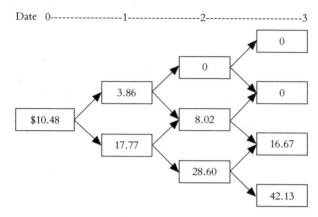

Assuming a risk-free rate of 0.02 per period, these equilibrium "no-arbitrage" put option values are shown in Figure 2.

These option values would correspond to Black-Scholes values if we had a very large number of periods in the tree diagram. The simplified theory of option pricing used here, like that of Black-Scholes, is based on the notion of no-arbitrage, riskless hedging.

Portfolio Insurance via Purchased Options

Before covering dynamic replication insurance, let us first consider insurance via protective puts. If put options for expiration at Time 3 with a strike price of $100.00 are available, a manager who wishes to insure the portfolio (the stock) for $100.00 at Time 0 for the horizon at the end of Period 3 can simply purchase a protective put for $10.48. The tree diagram of the insured portfolio, which appears in Figure 3, is simply the sum of the underlying portfolio value (stock value) and the put value for each of the potential states of nature.

To insure the portfolio at $100.00 via a put in this example, we will need beginning capital of $110.48; $100.00 to put into the underlying portfolio and $10.48 to pay for the put (the insurance premium). In this situation we get one full share of action if share value is above the insurance floor. Later we will see how we can insure at the same level of capital that we start with, or at a higher level, with corresponding costs of forgone upside participation.

Before turning to dynamic replication of the action in Figure 3, we note without proof that the same price dynamics as in Figure 3 apply to a combination of a $100.00 face value riskless asset with a maturity date at the expiration time and a call option with a strike price of $100.00. The Time 0 riskless asset value is $100.00/ $(1.02)^3 = \$94.23$, and the call option value will be $16.25. Again, $110.48 is required to insure at $100.00 via this synthetic approach. Thus, the riskless asset plus call option combination is an alternative, synthetic way to create an insured portfolio. Of course, not all managers can employ this method, as someone must hold the stocks.

Figure 3   Insured portfolio dynamics

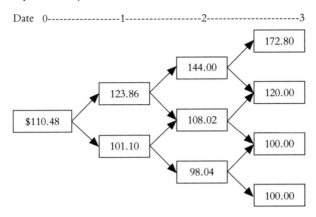

Figure 4   Call option deltas

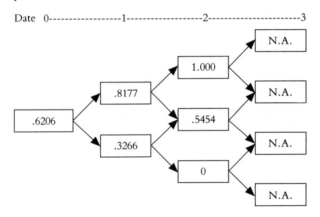

Dynamic Replication

The basic dynamic trading approach involves replicating the insured portfolio's price action with an ever-changing combination of positions in the underlying portfolio and the riskless asset. The underlying portfolio/riskless asset positions are used to create an insured portfolio consisting of a (synthetic) riskless asset plus call option. The proportions allocated to the underlying portfolio and the riskless asset change every period, so that the dynamic insurance strategy requires a significant amount of trading. Later, we will see how the same replication is accomplished (approximately) with either a stock portfolio and short stock futures positions or the riskless asset and long stock futures.

The number of units of the underlying portfolio that must be held long at any given moment will be given by the call option's "delta," the reciprocal of how many calls it takes to hedge a unit of the underlying portfolio. The call deltas in Figure 4 tell us the number of units of the underlying portfolio to hold. The amount of the riskless asset to hold is determined by subtracting the value of the held units of the underlying portfolio from the total value of the insured portfolio.

Figure 5 Dynamic replication of insured portfolio

Node at 100.00

100.00

Buy .6206	shs	62.06
Buy Bills		48.42
Total		110.48

Node at 120.00

120.00 | Insd Port = 123.86

= .6206 shs × 120 + 49.39

Buy .1971 shs at 120
Sell 23.65 Bills

New Portfolio:
.8177 shs at 120 = 98.12
Bills 25.74
Total 123.86

Node at 83.33

83.33 | Insd Port = 101.10

= .6206 shs × 83.33 + 49.39

Sell .2940 shs at 83.33
Buy 24.50 Bills

New Portfolio:
.3266 shs at 83.33 = 27.22
Bills 73.88
Total 101.10

Node at 144.00

144.00 | Insd Port = 144.00

= .8177 shs × 144 + 26.25

Buy .1823 shs at 144
Sell 26.25 Bills

New Portfolio:
1 sh at 144 = 144.00
0 Bills 0
Total 144.00

Node at 100.00

100.00 | Insd Port = 108.02

= Either ① .8177 shs × 100 + 26.25
or ② .3266 shs × 100 + 75.36
if① sell .2722 shs at 100
buy 27.22 Bills
if② buy .2189 shs at 100
sell 21.89 Bills

New Portfolio:
.5455 shs at 100 = 54.55
Bills 53.49
Total 108.02

Node at 69.44

69.44 | Insd Port = 98.04

= .3266 shs × 69.44 + 75.36

Sell .3266 shs at 69.44
Buy 22.68 Bills

New Portfolio:
0 shs 0
Bills 98.04
Total 98.04

Node at 172.80

172.80

Insd Port = 172.80
1 sh at 172.80 = 172.80
0 Bills 0
Total 172.80

Node at 120.00

120.00

Insd Port = 120.00
Either
1 sh at 120 = 120.00
0 Bills 0
Total 120.00
or
.5455 shs at 120 = 65.46
Bills 54.54
Total 120.00

Node at 83.33

83.33

Insd Port = 100.00
Either
.5455 sh at 83.33 = 45.46
Bills 54.54
Total 100.00
or
0 shs 0
Bills 100.00
Total 100.00

Node at 57.87

57.87

Insd Port = 100.00
0 shs 0
Bills 100.00
Total 100.00

For example, at Time 0, the insurance strategy requires 0.6206 units of the underlying portfolio at $100.00 per unit for $62.06, plus $110.48 – 62.06 = $48.42 in the riskless asset. Thus 0.6206 is *not* the proportion of the dynamic hedging portfolio allocated to the underlying portfolio. Insured portfolio proportions can be found in a manner that is similar in principle to the method in Benninga and Blume [1985, Equation (1)].

The detailed, trade-by-trade, mechanics of the dynamic hedging strategy in Figure 5 shed light on the mysteries of portfolio insurance via dynamic trading. Note first that the scheme is self-financing. The purchase of units of the underlying portfolio can always be made with proceeds from the riskless asset sales, and vice versa. For convenience, the price of the underlying stock is given in the upper left-hand corner of each box.

Note also that the units of the underlying portfolio correspond to the call option deltas in Figure 4. Further, note that the stock-plus-put dynamics of Figure 3 can be replicated only with a starting portfolio value of $110.48 – insurance costs $10.48, the Time 0 price of the put. No miracle here, a point also stressed by Singleton and Grieves (1984).

Another way of looking at the cost is the forgone return of the upside. In this example the manager gets only one share of action on the upside in lieu of 1.1048 shares of action that could have been obtained with an uninsured portfolio. The upside value capture ratio is 1/1.1048, or about 91%.

Finally, note especially the middle event at the end of Period 2 in Figure 5, when the value of the underlying portfolio returns to $100.00 from either the previous downstate or the previous upstate. As $100.00 was the Time 0 beginning value of the underlying portfolio, we can compare the value of the insured portfolio, $108.02, with that at Time 0, $110.48. This is the often-discussed "whipsaw," viewed as one of the practical problems of applying the theory in the real world.

In the context of the dynamic allocation strategy, however, this "whipsaw" is part of the plan. It is not so much a problem as it is the natural reduction of the insured portfolio value over time, all else equal, as gradual payment for the insurance. Rather than regarding dynamic portfolio insurance as some kind of miracle with the practical application problem of the whipsaw, it is more appropriate to understand that the whipsaw is the missing cost element of the portfolio insurance "miracle." This point is made as well by Asay and Edelsburg (1986). Of course, the market turbulence after October 19, 1987, might have caused a whipsaw for insured portfolios that was several orders of magnitude greater than the one that theory allows for. In such a case, a more practical perspective has to be taken on the whipsaw issue.

The Use of Futures

Rubinstein (1985) based his insight on the use of index futures to implement dynamic insurance upon the assumption that the portfolio to be insured is well-diversified. Ideally, the insured portfolio would be an index fund. One of the arguments against the use of exchange-traded put options to insure, in fact, is that the underlying portfolio is not necessarily the index; this argument applies also to the use of index futures in dynamic insurance strategies.

Figure 6   Dynamics of a correctly valued futures contract for delivery at time 3

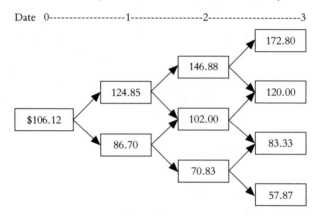

Nevertheless, the low cost and convenience of trading index futures relative to trading the actual portfolio make the basis risk of using the index futures to cross-hedge a fairly well-diversified portfolio a problem that can be lived with. For convenience here, we will assume that the underlying portfolio is the index portfolio.

Portfolio insurance in this case is created dynamically by using the index futures to create a synthetic position in either the riskless security or the underlying portfolio. The dynamics shown in Figure 3 can be replicated by putting 100% of the portfolio into the underlying portfolio and then creating an (adjustable) synthetic riskless asset out of a portion with some short futures positions. Alternatively, we could duplicate the same dynamics by putting 100% of the capital into the riskless asset and then create an (adjustable) synthetic position in the underlying portfolio out of a portion with some long futures positions.

In this section, I demonstrate the use of futures under the ideal assumption that the futures are always priced according to their correct theoretical value in terms of the underlying index. For convenience, I assume a constant interest rate environment, so that the theoretically correct futures price for contract delivery n periods hence will at any time be equal to the spot price of the underlying commodity times $(1 + r)^n$, where n is the number of periods until delivery, and r is the risk-free interest rate per period.

First let us look at the situation where index futures are available with the same delivery date as the horizon date of the insurance program. The theoretically correct futures price dynamics are shown in Figure 6, corresponding to the underlying portfolio dynamics in Figure 1. Note that the end-of-last-period futures prices in Figure 6 are the same as the spot prices, as this is the delivery time of the futures.

In the dynamic replication with combinations of the underlying portfolio and short futures positions, we must determine the number of short index futures contracts to establish by $1/[(1 + r)^{(n-1)}]$ times the quotient of the level of the riskless asset needed and the current price of the underlying stock. For example, at Time 0, we should short $1/[(1.02)^2]$ times $[48.42/100.00]$, which is 0.4654 contracts. The details of the entire replication, similar to Figure 5, are available from the author on request.

In this replication, as the underlying portfolio value rises, some of the short positions are covered, and as the underlying portfolio value falls, additional short positions are taken. These transactions correspond to coming out of the riskless asset and into the underlying portfolio in upswings, and vice versa in downswings.

Typically, futures contracts will not be available for long-horizon insurance programs. If, for example, the insurance program of Figure 3 were envisioned to have a one and one-half year horizon, the investor might have to use a sequence of three six-month index futures contracts. It is still perfectly general to short futures contracts in the amount of $1/[(1 + r)^{(n-1)}]$ times the quotient of the level of the riskless asset needed and the price of the underlying stock. In this example, however, n is always equal to 1, as the futures delivery date is always one period away.

At Time 0, the six-month futures price is $100.00 \times 1.02 = \$102.00$; we will short $1/[1.02^0] (= 1)$ times $48.42/100.00 = 0.4842$ futures. At the end of the first period, if the stock is $120.00 (the upstate), we will have 1.1048 shares at $120.00 minus 0.4842 times ($120.00 − 102.00$), for a total of $123.86; if the stock is $83.33 (the downstate), we will have 1.1048 shares at $83.33 minus 0.4842 times ($83.33 − 102.00$), for a total of $101.10. These Time 1 amounts are exactly in accordance with the insurance plan of Figure 3. The subsequent details of the insurance program using short-term futures are straightforward. We shall now revert to using long-term futures for consistency.

As described so far, the strategy does call for some trading in the underlying portfolio. Units of the underlying portfolio have to be sold to cover futures losses, and futures gains must be reinvested into units of the underlying portfolio. The strategy actually calls for the sale of a small portion of the physical underlying portfolio when values have risen, with a more than offsetting reversing trade in the short futures positions, and vice versa when values of the underlying portfolio have fallen.

In actual practice, we can accomplish the same dynamics as discussed above, without ever trading the original position in the underlying portfolio, by borrowing to cover losses on futures while shorting more futures to hedge the retained excess position in the portfolio in upstates, and by investing futures profits into the riskless asset and shorting fewer futures to compensate for being underinvested in the portfolio in downstates.

For example, if the underlying portfolio value goes to $120.00 at Time 1, then, instead of selling $1.1048 − 1.0322 = 0.0746$ units of the underlying portfolio and shorting 0.2103 futures, we may maintain 1.1048 shares and borrow the $8.72 to cover the futures loss. The new short futures position should be 0.2814 instead of 0.2103. (The entire trading mechanics of this approach are available from the author.) Of course, the borrowing must be repaid at the horizon. The important thing is that the strategy replicates the same insured portfolio's price dynamics as shown in Figure 3.

It is also possible to put on a portfolio insurance program that has the same price dynamics but consists only of long positions in cash and long positions in the index futures. The mechanics of this alternative are easy. We invest fully in cash and then go long futures contracts in an amount determined by dividing the call delta by $(1 + r)^{(n-2)}$. Futures gains and losses are simply paid out of the cash. (The mechanics of this alternative are also available from the author.)

Rubinstein (1985) implied that the flexibility of choosing between the long portfolio/short futures and long cash/long futures approaches allows users to dismiss the problem of futures mispricing, and even to take advantage of it. On the other hand, a manager who has a long stock portfolio to insure may not have the flexibility to sell everything and convert to cash.

Regardless of which approach is chosen at the beginning, all flexibility of capitalizing on futures mispricing is lost. Over time we will have to go long more futures positions in rising markets and short more in falling markets, no matter which approach we had selected in the beginning. If futures are typically overpriced in rising markets when we go to buy, and underpriced in falling markets when we go to sell, then this is a problem. Just how much of a problem this represented on October 19, 1987, has yet to be determined. Perhaps there is more flexibility in this respect when using short-term futures or traded puts and calls.

Using Traded Puts and Calls

While generally it is not possible to buy traded options with an expiration time long enough to coincide with typical insurance program horizons, we can use the traded puts and calls as part of a dynamic trading insurance program. For example, consider a call with a striking price of $95.00 that expires at Time 2. The call's equilibrium Time 0 price is $12.12; the Time 1 contingent prices are $21.87 in the upstate and $2.50 in the downstate. We can solve, using simultaneous equations, for the originating number of shares to go long and the number of calls to write, so that we get $123.86 in the Time 1 upstate and $101.10 in the Time 1 downstate. The answer will be to go long 1.249 shares and sell 1.191 calls. Naturally, the amount of initial capital necessary still turns out to be $110.48. We can then reallocate at Time 1, possibly liquidating all the option positions and rolling forward into other options or futures.

Etzioni (1986), a practicing insurer, indicated in a presentation at an American Stock Exchange Option Colloquium that in reality traded puts are sometimes too overvalued in the market to be useful as a trading vehicle this way. He also said that in actual practice the use of traded calls poses technical problems of another type, an issue beyond the scope of this paper.

Target Insurance Levels and Portfolio Insurance Costs

So far, we have conveniently assumed that the manager has $110.48 and wishes to insure for $100.00. The horizon action above the insurance floor was for that of a full share, representing a "cost" of about 9% of the upside appreciation potential, relative to 100% investment in the underlying portfolio. We may often wish to insure for the starting amount or higher. The target must always be less than the future value of the starting amount (at the risk-free rate), and, the higher the target, the larger the loss of upside participation.

Let us examine the case where we start out with $100.00 and wish to insure at $100.00. In this case, the manager needs to buy m shares and m put options, such that the total expended for the position equals $100.00 and such that the number of puts purchased times their striking price equals the target insurance amount, $100.00.

Table   Analysis of insuring at target level

Strike price (K)	Put price (P)	m (m*K = $100.00)	Total cost (=m*($100.00 + P)1
$100.00	$10.48	1.0000	$110.48
. . .	. . .	. . .	. . .
105.00	12.80	0.9524	107.43
. . .	. . .	. . .	. . .
110.00	16.38	0.9090	105.80
. . .	. . .	. . .	. . .
119.00	19.41	0.8403	100.34
120.00	19.64	0.8333	99.70
. . .	. . .	. . .	. . .

Even though the insurance may be accomplished via dynamic replication, we can look at the problem as if protective puts were being used.

We must know the theoretical put values for various striking prices over a relevant range. The Table supplies some relevant Time 0 put option values, all generated the same way as the one in Figure 2. The table also gives the corresponding m value, such that m times the put's striking price equals the insurance target floor of $100.00. Finally, the table gives the total costs of buying m shares and m puts. The manager must select that "row" of the table for which the total cost figure equals $100.00.

In our example, the objective would be achieved for a put with a striking price between $119.00 and $120.00. For simplicity, let us say the put with the $120.00 striking price is closest. We buy 0.8333 shares at $100.00 per share and 0.8333 puts at $19.64 for an approximate expenditure of $100.00. It should be clear now that, if longer-horizon traded puts with set exercise prices were available, we might still prefer dynamic replication because of the ability to tailor the insurance floor by creating an option with the desired striking price.

The insured portfolio dynamics for the selected strategy are given in Figure 7. These dynamics of course can be replicated. The portfolio is insured against loss below $100.00, but the upside capture has been reduced to 0.8333 of what it would have been if the original $100.00 had been put entirely into the stock. This 0.1667 participation give-up is one way to view the cost of portfolio insurance. The higher the target floor – and it can be above the original stake, guaranteeing a fixed interest rate – the greater will be the participation give-up. The give-up also depends on the stock's volatility and the risk-free interest rate.

Finally, let us see what would happen if we started with $100.00 and used the deltas in Figure 4 to determine the number of shares to hold in the basic stock-bill insurance program. We would start off with bills in the amount of $100.00 minus the stock investment of $62.06, or $37.94. The details of the replication are available on request.

Whichever horizon state occurs, the insured portfolio ends up exactly $11.12 less what it would have been in the insured portfolio cases of Figures 3 and 5. Here is another way to see the insurance cost. The present value of $11.12, discounting at

Figure 7   Insured portfolio dynamics for $100.00 target floor

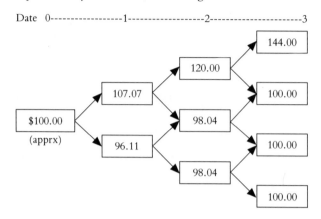

the 2% risk-free rate per period, is $10.48, the Time 0 price that would have been paid for a put with a $100.00 striking price. We can think of this situation as insuring at a $100.00 target and starting with $100.00, but paying a fixed cost for the insurance at the end of the program.

Essentially, the investor is "short" the price of the protection – the price of the put – and this amount must be repaid with interest. Of course, the floor in this example, net of the future value of the insurance cost, is $88.88. As pointed out earlier, if we start with $100.00 and really want a $100.00 horizon insurance floor, we must put on a different program with costs in terms of reduction of upside participation.

Summary and Concluding remarks

This article has presented a line of analysis designed to clarify the mysteries of the basic portfolio insurance concept. A simplified abstraction of reality shows that portfolio insurance works. With an understanding of the mechanics and cost concepts presented here, the analyst may proceed to consider aspects of real-world application.

There are many periods and possible horizon states in actual practice, rather than the four used in the example here. Therefore, the Black-Scholes model is the starting point for calculating deltas and expected insurance costs in the real world. Advanced applications would try to make use of extensions to the Black-Scholes model to factor in the impact of certain real-world issues. Such extensions include work by Merton (1973) to factor in uncertain interest rates, by Leland (1985) to factor in trading costs – and futures mispricing can be viewed as a trading cost (Hill, Jain, and Wood, 1988) – by Johnson and Stulz (1987) to factor in default risk, and by Hull and White (1987) to factor in uncertain volatilities. Clarification of the impact of these real-world issues on horizon outcomes will be welcome.

In the simple, abstract environment assumed here, dynamic portfolio insurance has been shown to work. No guarantee can be made that dynamic replication will be effective against a catastrophe that occurs during a time when the market is closed, or against a "market meltdown" during trading hours, possibly exacerbated by insurance programs. Indeed, the macro-effect of dynamic insurance on the market is still in question. (The words of this concluding paragraph were written prior to October 19, 1987!)

Note

Thomas J. O'Brien gratefully acknowledges that this paper grew from a previous analysis with Richard J. Rendleman, Jr., of the University of North Carolina at Chapel Hill, whose comments on this paper have helped improve the presentation as well. The author is also grateful for the support provided for the earlier project by McMillion/Eubanks, Inc., of Greensboro, NC, and for this project by the Center for Research and Development of Financial Services of the University of Connecticut (Neil B. Murphy, Director).

References

Asay, M., and C. Edelsburg. "Can a Dynamic Strategy Replicate the Returns of an Option?" *Journal of Futures Markets* 6, Spring 1986, pp. 63–70.

Benninga, S., and M. Blume. "On the Optimality of Portfolio Insurance." *Journal of Finance* 40, December 1985, pp. 1341–1352.

Black, F., and M. Scholes. "The Pricing of Options and Corporate Liabilities." *Journal of Political Economy* 81, May–June 1973, pp. 637–654.

Cox, J., S. Ross, and M. Rubinstein. "Option Pricing: A Simplified Approach." *Journal of Financial Economics* 7, September 1979, pp. 229–263.

Etzioni, E. "Rebalance Disciplines for Portfolio Insurance." *Journal of Portfolio Management* 13, Fall 1986, pp. 59–62.

Ferguson, R. "How to Beat the S&P 500 (Without Losing Sleep)." *Financial Analysts Journal* 42, March/April 1986, pp. 37–46.

Gatto, M., R. Geske, R. Litzenberger, and H. Sosin. "Mutual Fund Insurance." *Journal of Financial Economics* 8, September 1980, pp. 283–317.

Hill, J., A. Jain, and R. Wood. "Portfolio Insurance: Volatility Risk and Futures Mispricing," *Journal of Portfolio Management*, Winter 1988, pp. 23–29.

Hull, J., and A. White. "The Pricing of Options with Stochastic Volatilities," *Journal of Finance* 42, June 1987, pp. 281–300.

Johnson, H., and R. Stulz. "The Pricing of Options with Default Risk," *Journal of Finance* 42, June 1987, pp. 267–280.

Leland, H. "Option Pricing and Replication with Transaction Costs." *Journal of Finance* 40, December 1985, pp. 1283–1301.

———. "Who Should Buy Portfolio Insurance?" *Journal of Finance* 35, May 1980, pp. 581–594.

Merton, R. "Theory of Rational Option Pricing," *Bell Journal of Economics and Management Science* 3, Spring 1973, pp. 141–183.

Pozen, R. "The Purchase of Protective Puts by Financial Institutions." *Financial Analysts Journal* 34, July/August 1978, pp. 47–60.

Rendleman, R., and B. Bartter. "Two-State Option Pricing." *Journal of Finance* 34, December 1979, pp. 1093–1110.

Rendleman, R., and R. McEnally. "Assessing the Costs of Portfolio Insurance." *Financial Analysts Journal* 43, May–June 1987, pp. 27–37.

Rubinstein, M. "Alternative Paths to Portfolio Insurance." *Financial Analysts Journal* 41, July/August 1985, pp. 42–52.

Rubinstein, M., and H. Leland. "Replicating Options with Positions in Stock and Cash." *Financial Analysts Journal* 37, July/August 1981, pp. 63–72.

Sharpe, W. "Portfolio Insurance," in *Investments*. Englewood Cliffs, N.J.: Prentice-Hall, Inc., 1985, pp. 509–514.

Singleton, C., and R. Grieves. "Synthetic Puts and Portfolio Insurance Strategies." *Journal of Portfolio Management* 10, Spring 1984, pp. 63–69.

Wallace, A. "Marketing a 'Miracle' Model." *Institutional Investor* 16, September 1982, pp. 101–106.

15

Alternative Paths to Portfolio Insurance

Mark Rubinstein

Portfolio insurance is equivalent to a securities position comprised of an underlying portfolio plus an insurance policy that guarantees the portfolio against loss through a specified policy expiration date. Under true portfolio insurance, the probability of experiencing a loss is zero; the position's return is dependent solely on the ending value of the underlying portfolio, regardless of interim movements in portfolio value; and the expected rate of return is greater than that on any other strategy possessing the first two properties.

European payout-protected puts could be used to provide perfect portfolio insurance. The investor would select a put option on the underlying portfolio such that exercising the put would yield just enough to make up for any decline in portfolio value plus the initial cost of the option. Unfortunately, European options are not available on listed exchanges in the U.S.

In their absence, portfolio insurance may be approximated by using listed options or by a systematic dynamic asset allocation strategy employing either cash and the underlying portfolio or a replicating futures position. Because the longest effective maturities of listed options are two or three months, a portfolio insurance strategy of any reasonable length will be susceptible to interim movements in the underlying portfolio, hence will generally have lower expected returns than true portfolio insurance. Dynamic asset allocation strategies designed to replicate a long-term European protect put come closest to perfect portfolio insurance.

Portfolio insurance, in its purest and simplest form, is equivalent to a securities position comprised of an underlying portfolio plus an insurance policy that guarantees the insured portfolio against loss through a specified policy expiration date. Should the underlying portfolio (including any income earned and reinvested in the portfolio but deducting the cost of buying the insurance) experience a loss by the policy expiration date, the insurance policy can be used to refund the amount of the loss. On the other hand, should the underlying portfolio show a profit, all profit net of the cost of the insurance is retained.

Consider a portfolio with the same composition as the Standard & Poor's 500 and suppose it is covered by an insurance policy that has one year until expiration. The S&P 500 is at 100 at the start of the policy, and the one-year insurance policy costs $3.33. After buying the insurance, an investor with $100 has $96.67, which can buy 0.9667 "shares" of the S&P 500.

Table I shows the pattern of returns this investor will realize at the end of the year. The *minimum* value of the insured portfolio is $100; there will be no loss, even after the cost of the insurance is deducted. On the upside, the value of the insured portfolio depends on the behavior of the full $100 investment in the S&P 500.

Table I   Pattern of Returns from Portfolio Insurance
After One Year

Value of S&P 500 with dividends reinvested	Value of insured S&P 500 portfolio
$ 75	$100
80	100
85	100
90	100
95	100
100	100
105	101.50
110	106.34
115	111.17
120	116
125	120.84
130	125.67

Because the insured portfolio owns 0.9667 shares of the S&P 500, its value on the upside will always be 0.9667 times the value of the S&P 500 with dividends reinvested (e.g., $125 \times 0.9667 = 120.84$). This number is sometimes referred to as the "upside capture."

Properties of Insured Portfolios

The return pattern of the insured portfolio has several important properties:

(A)   The probability of experiencing any losses is zero.
(B)   The return on any profitable position will be a predictable percentage of the rate of return that would have been earned by investing all funds in the S&P 500.
(C)   If the portfolio is restricted to investments in the S&P 500 and cash loans, if the expected rate of return on the S&P 500 exceeds the return on cash, and if the insurance is fairly priced, then among all investment strategies possessing properties (A) and (B), the insured portfolio strategy has the highest expected rate of return.

Stop-loss orders are perhaps the simplest examples of investment strategies that have property A (ignoring jumps through the stop-limit price) but lack property B. To implement a stop-loss order strategy, one invests the entire $100 in the S&P 500 and instructs the broker to sell out completely and convert to cash if the S&P 500 (with dividends reinvested) falls so low that a conversion to cash, given then current interest rates, would result in a value of exactly $100 at the end of the year.

Clearly, this strategy possesses property A. However, the value of the portfolio is not completely determined by the level of the S&P 500. If, midway through the year, the S&P 500 fell low enough to trigger the conversion into cash, then the return on the portfolio from then on would be entirely unrelated to the S&P 500.

It is easy to devise other strategies that have both properties A and B but lack C. Suppose an investor is restricted to "buy and hold" positions using only the S&P 500 and cash and wants to maximize expected rate of return while insuring against a loss. If the interest rate is 10 per cent, he can invest $90.91 in cash and $9.09 in the S&P 500. Now, even if the S&P 500 falls to zero, he would just break even (since $90.91 × 1.1 = $100). If the expected rate of return on the S&P 500 is 16 per cent, the overall expected rate of return from following this strategy would be 10.5 per cent (= (90.91 × 10%) + (9.09 × 16%)).

The proof that portfolio insurance satisfies property C, hence must have a higher expected rate of return than the buy and hold strategy, will not be reproduced here.[1] However, it will be demonstrated by example in the course of the discussion.

Why Purchase Portfolio Insurance?

Clearly, anyone who wants to insure against any losses while maximizing expected return is a candidate for the purchase of portfolio insurance.[2] Equally clearly, for every investor who purchases portfolio insurance there needs to be an investor who sells it.[3] We are thus led to conclude that intelligent buyers of portfolio insurance are typically more sensitive to downside risk than the average investor.

For either the buyer or seller of portfolio insurance, property B still holds: The return from the insured portfolio (S&P 500 plus insurance policy) will be fully determined by the return from the underlying portfolio (S&P 500) at the insurance expiration date. The path taken to reach this level of return will have no effect on the outcome.

Outcomes of "path-dependent" strategies are usually much more difficult to describe and evaluate than those of "path-independent" strategies.[4] That is, predicting returns from path-dependent strategies requires knowledge of many more factors. It is also difficult to see why an investor would want his return to be influenced by intermediate levels of the index, apart from their cumulative effect on the ending level of the index.

The remainder of this article focuses on the purchase of portfolio insurance – specifically, how is it done?

Alternative Paths

We assume that the investor wants to insure against losses in the S&P 500 with dividends reinvested. We further assume the economic environment that gives rise to the Black-Scholes option valuation formula.[5] In particular, the interest rate is known and constant, the dividend yield of the S&P 500 is known and constant, the volatility of the S&P 500 is known and constant, the value of the S&P 500 moves smoothly over time without jumps or gap openings, there are no opportunities for riskless arbitrage profits, and transaction costs are zero.

In the interest of comparability, we will assume that the interest rate is 10 per cent per year, the expected rate of return on the S&P 500 is 16 per cent, the

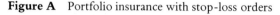

Figure A   Portfolio insurance with stop-loss orders

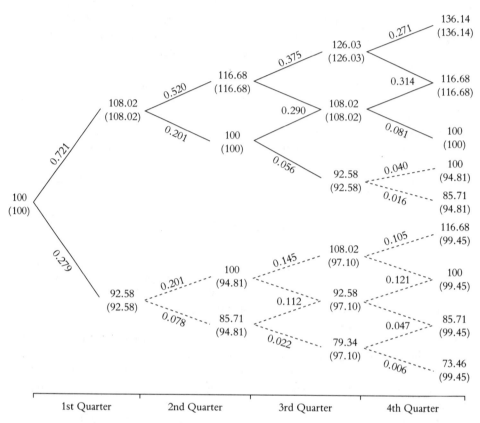

dividend yield on the S&P 500 is 5 per cent, and the (arithmetic) volatility of the S&P 500 is 18 per cent.[6]

Each technique for creating portfolio insurance is designed to be 100 per cent reliable in preventing losses. Our comparison will focus on differences in path-independence and expected rate of return.

Stop-loss Orders

The analysis of stop-loss orders as a method for approximating portfolio insurance is complicated by path-dependence. Suppose, for instance, that the investor executes a stop-loss order at the end of each quarter. To keep things as simple as possible without sacrificing the main elements of the problem, suppose that the S&P 500 (with dividends reinvested) moves either up or down by a fixed percentage over each quarter.

Figure A gives the S&P 500's pattern of movement over the year, given its assumed expected rate of return and volatility.[7] Both the S&P 500 and the value of the stop-loss portfolio (in parentheses) begin at $100. In each quarter, the probability of the index moving up by 8.02 per cent is 0.721, and the probability of the index moving down by 7.42 per cent is 0.279.

As the stop-loss portfolio starts out fully invested in the S&P 500, both the index and the portfolio are at either 108.02 or 92.58 after the first quarter. During the second quarter, however, path-dependence appears. If the index moved up in the first quarter, the portfolio remains fully invested in the S&P 500 during the second quarter; whether the index moves up or down, the portfolio tracks it to either 116.68 or 100.

If, on the other hand, the index moved down during the first quarter, the stop-loss order would be triggered. It is easy to see why. The interest rate must be 2.41 per cent during any quarter if it is to compound out to 10 per cent over the year while remaining at a constant level. If the portfolio is down to 92.58 at the end of the first quarter, it can only reach 99.45 (= 92.58×1.0241^3) by the end of the year, even if it is invested in cash over the remainder of the year. Because this ending level is less than 100, the stop-loss order is executed and the portfolio reverts for the remainder of the year to 100 per cent cash. At the end of the second quarter, the portfolio is thus at 94.81 (= 92.58×1.0241). The dashed lines in Figure A indicate that the portfolio has been stopped out.

When the index is at 100, there is a 0.201 probability (0.721×0.279) that the portfolio will be at 100 and a 0.201 probability (0.279×0.721) that it will be at 94.81. That is, although the index may reach the same level either by moving up and then down or by moving down and then up, the same is not true of the portfolio. The *path* by which the index reaches 100 leads to different values for the stop-loss portfolio.

To evaluate a stop-loss order as a method for creating portfolio insurance, it is necessary to measure its expected rate of return, given its degree of path-dependence. Path-dependence can be measured by the expected absolute deviation of the rate of return conditional on the level of the index; the appendix illustrates the calculation. Perfect portfolio insurance requires that path-dependence be zero; the stop-loss order has a path-dependence of 3.14 per cent. Table II lists the nine distinct possible outcomes from the stop-loss strategy considered above.

European Payout-protected Puts

The stop-loss strategy is path-dependent, but it *is* a step in the right direction. It suggests that there may be a way to transfer systematically between the S&P 500 and cash to generate portfolio insurance. By moving *gradually* into stock from cash as the stock price goes up, and *gradually* out of stock into cash as the stock price falls, it is possible to generate the equivalent of an insured position in stock.[8]

Alternatively, if one-year European payout-protected puts on the S&P 500, were available, these instruments could provide perfect portfolio insurance. An investor would select a put option on the index with striking price K such that K satisfies the following equality:

$$P(K) = K - S.$$

Here, P is the price of the put (shown above as a function of its striking price) and S is the concurrent level of the S&P 500 index.[9] If the index, with dividends

Table II   Possible outcomes of stop-loss strategy

Value of S&P 500 with dividends reinvested	Stop-Loss portfolio return	Probability
$136.14	36.14%	0.270
116.68	16.68%	0.314
116.68	−0.56%	0.105
100.00	0.00%	0.081
100.00	−0.56%	0.121
100.00	−5.19%	0.040
85.71	−0.56%	0.047
85.71	−5.19%	0.016
73.46	−0.56%	0.006

reinvested, were to fall below its initial level by the end of the year, it could be sold by exercising the put at price K; this would be just enough to make up for the index decline and the initial cost P of the put.

This strategy is 100 per cent reliable in preventing losses. In addition, because the payoff of such a put would be solely dependent on the year-end level of the S&P 500 (with dividends reinvested), the protective put position would be completely path-independent. Assuming, as before, that the S&P 500 has an arithmetic expected rate of return and a volatility of 16 and 18 per cent, respectively, the striking price of the put would need to be 103.45 to provide insurance against losses. The expected rate of return on the insured portfolio (S&P 500 plus put) is 14.30 per cent.[10] The payoff pattern given in Table I is from just this strategy.

Of course, the investor must pay for the index put out of his initial $100. The ratio of the initial S&P 500 level to the striking price of the put is 0.9667 (100/103.45). The investor thus ends up with 0.9667 shares of the S&P 500 and 0.9667 puts, each at a striking price of 103.45. He must invest $3.33 ($3.45 × 0.9667) in puts and $96.67 in the S&P 500.

Several other types of instruments can be used to effect the same pattern of returns. From the European put-call parity relation, we know that a protective put is equivalent to a *fiduciary call* (purchased call plus cash), where the call has the same time to expiration and striking price as the put.[11] Moreover, with known rates of interest, a European put (or call) on the S&P 500 is equivalent to a European put (or call) on S&P 500 futures contracts, provided the expiration date of the option coincides with the delivery date of the underlying futures contracts.[12] Perfect portfolio insurance could be provided by either a *protective index futures put or a fiduciary index futures call.*

If a one-year European payout-protected option were available on each stock in the S&P 500, these instruments could be used to insure the S&P 500 by insuring each stock in the portfolio against loss for the year. However, use of conventional options on individual stocks leads to path-dependent outcomes with lower expected rates of return than index option strategies.[13]

Unfortunately, currently listed index options do not have the terms we have assumed. First, all listed options are *American*. American options can be exercised at any time before expiration, whereas European options can be exercised only at expiration. Because American options have every advantage of European options (they can be turned into European options by holding them to expiration) as well as the increased flexibility of early exercise, American options should be more expensive than otherwise identical European options. Second, listed options are not protected against dividends. As a result, they can be used to insure the capital appreciation component of stock returns, but not the dividend component. Third, all listed options have maturities of less than nine months. Because almost all trading volume is concentrated in the nearest maturities, the longest effective maturities are about three months for index futures options and two months for index spot options.[14] Finally, listed options have highly standardized striking prices that do not typically match the striking prices needed for portfolio insurance. This, combined with the advisability of early exercise of some American options, means that no American options of particular striking prices may survive in the market, even though European options of the same striking price would.

Sequential Short-term Index Options

Although the listed markets do not offer options with the proper terms, there may still be some way of using these options to approximate portfolio insurance. In order to focus on the most significant feature of listed index options, we will assume that payout-protected European options are available in maturities of less than a year.

If six-month payout-protected European options were available, an investor could approximate portfolio insurance by rolling over a position in index puts every six months. He might start with a protective put that would insure the portfolio against loss over the first six months. If, at mid-year, the S&P 500 has declined so that it pays to exercise the put, the investor will buy another protective put to insure the portfolio over the next six months. At worst, by the end of the year, he should break even.

But suppose the S&P 500 rises over the first six months, so that the put is not exercised. In this case, the investor would buy a put that will insure the portfolio's mid-year value with a deductible equal to the profit earned over the first six months.

Figure B illustrates this strategy when the year is divided into four (binomial) intervals. Using the Black-Scholes formula, the striking price of the purchased six-month put at the beginning of the year is $103.86 (in brackets). After two quarters, the S&P 500 index is at 85.71, 100 or 116.68. In each case, the striking price of the six-month put purchased next is different.

When the index is at 85.71 or 100, the portfolio has just broken even over the first six months; the investor can't afford to lose money over the next six months. He must purchase a put with the same striking price relative to the stock price as the put he purchased at the beginning of the year.[15] When the index is at 116.68, however, such conservatism is not needed. Now, the investor can afford to lose $12.34 during the next six months and still break even at the end of the year. He can purchase a put with a striking price considerably below the current value of the portfolio.

This strategy is 100 per cent reliable in preventing losses, but it does suffer from path-dependence. Its expected rate of return, moreover, will usually fall short of the

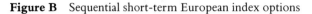

Figure B   Sequential short-term European index options

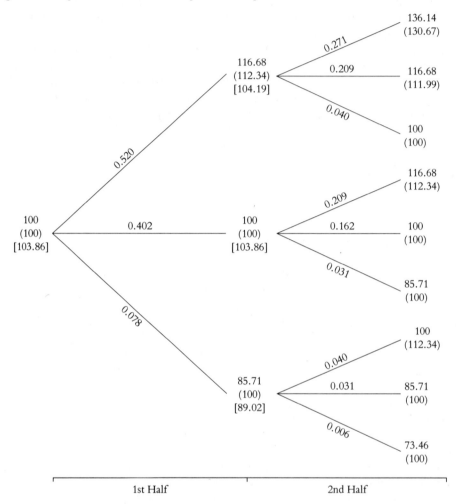

1st Half	2nd Half

expected rate of return that could be achieved with a one-year protective European put, if one were available or could be created from a dynamic asset allocation strategy. Table III (which assumes the year is divided into 144 binomial intervals) provides estimates of the magnitudes of path-dependence and rate of return for different roll-over periods. As the roll-over becomes more frequent, the path-dependence increases and the expected rate of return decreases.

The limited availability and liquidity of listed striking prices that are distant from the money, and the five-point intervals at which they are listed, force the investor to be more conservative in practice than he might want to be.[16] Suppose that striking prices are only available in three-point intervals and the deepest out-of-the-money put available is at most eight points out-of-the-money (relative to an S&P 500 level of 100). The numbers in parentheses in Table III show the degree to which this constraint increases path-dependence and reduces expected rate of return.

Table III Path-dependence and expected rates of return for roll-over of short-term protective European puts*

Roll-over period	Path-dependence	Expected rate of return
one year	0.00%	14.30%
six months	1.50 (1.67%)	14.04 (13.74%)
four months	2.12 (2.39)	13.96 (13.63)
three months	2.56 (2.90)	13.90 (13.53)
two months	2.97 (3.45)	13.86 (13.44)
stop-loss orders	3.73	14.70

* These results are particularly sensitive to the assumptions that volatility is known in advance and that there are no jump movements in the S&P 500 index.

Real-world Considerations

The discussion so far has ignored complications created by American options, uncertain interest rates, uncertain volatility, jumps in security price movements, apparently mispriced securities, and transaction costs.

American Options

As building blocks for portfolio insurance, even long-term American index puts pose an unfortunate dilemma: It is either impossible to provide path-independence and 100 per cent reliability in preventing losses, or the insurance must be purchased at an excessive price!

As noted, if it is to insure a portfolio against loss, the index put must have a striking price K such that $P(K) = K - S$. Because of the possibility of early exercise; however, this is the lowest price an American option can have. Furthermore, if the option is priced properly, it would pay to exercise it immediately.

If the put were worth less than $K - S$, an investor could earn a riskless arbitrage profit by buying the put and the underlying stock and then immediately exercising the put to receive $K > P + S$. If the put were worth exactly $K - S$, the investor who exercised the option immediately would get the full benefit of the put and also be able to start earning interest on the net receipt of $K - S$. By pricing the put at its exercisable value, the market implies that the interest that can be received through early exercise of the put outweighs its time value.

Using American puts to generate portfolio insurance thus presents an awkward choice. On the one hand, buying a put priced higher than $K - S$ can lead to a portfolio loss equal to the premium over parity $(P - (K - S))$ if the index falls. On the other hand, a put priced such that $P = K - S$ will be overpriced, inasmuch as the insurance purchaser doesn't plan to exercise it immediately. The investor must steer between Scylla and Charybdis; as he avoids one difficulty, he approaches the other. In brief, the American put purchaser pays for something he doesn't want – the right to exercise the option early.

Uncertain Interest Rates

In all the strategies we have considered, except the use of long-term European payout-protected index options, uncertain interest rates increase the difficulty of predicting upside returns. The strategies' ability to protect against loss is unaffected, however, if care is taken to measure changes in interest rates and to factor these changes into the ongoing strategy.

In the case of the stop-loss strategies, for example, declining interest rates during the year translate into a shorter time to the stopout point. For the sequential option strategies (since option prices are partly determined by interest rates) uncertainty regarding interest rates increases the uncertainty regarding the prices that must be paid for options at future dates; nevertheless, changes in the option prices offset interest rate changes, preserving full loss protection.

Within the context of Black-Scholes assumptions, there is no reason to distinguish between options and their replicating dynamic asset allocation strategies; both produce identical results. With uncertain interest rates, however, dynamic strategies no longer have the power to replicate long-term European options exactly. Nonetheless, dynamic strategies that transfer holdings between stock and cash can hedge changes in interest rates over the year. Proper implementation using one-year Treasury bills as the hedging instrument (cash) should make conventional dynamic strategies less susceptible to shifts in shorter-term rates than either the stop-loss or sequential option strategies.

Dynamic option replication strategies can be implemented by using index futures. A purchased index futures contract, if held to the delivery date, implicitly embodies a long position in the index coupled with an equal amount of borrowing at a risk-free rate over the life of the contract. Instead of selling stock and lending the proceeds (as in conventional dynamic asset allocation), the investor can sell futures to accomplish similar ends by much simpler means. If the futures delivery date is less than a year, however, it will be necessary to roll over the futures hedge during the year. The strategy is thus more susceptible to uncertainty surrounding upside returns than conventional dynamic asset allocation utilizing one-year Treasury bills.

Uncertain Volatility

In practice, the source of the greatest difference between options and dynamic strategies is uncertain volatility. Not only does predicted volatility have an important effect on option prices but, of all their determinants, it is the most difficult to measure. Purchasing an index option amounts to insuring against fluctuations in the volatility of the index through the expiration date of the option. Proper implementation of the replicating dynamic asset allocation strategy retains full loss protection, but the upside capture now depends on the realized volatility over the year. The greater the volatility, the less the upside capture. This introduces a form of path-dependence into the outcome.

Sequential option strategies are exposed to a similar form of path-dependence. The prices of options to be purchased at future dates are dependent on the market's future predictions of volatility.

Security Price Jumps

As noted, stop-loss strategies may be threatened by jumps in security prices. For this reason, as contingent immunization (a form of stop-loss order applied to bond portfolio management) is practiced, the position remains 100 per cent invested in the actively managed bond portfolio as long as the stopout point is sufficiently distant. However, when the stopout point comes into view, the active portfolio is gradually transferred into the immunized portfolio.

In the case of dynamic asset allocation, this gradual transition to cash is an automatic and continuous feature. Because the portfolio will tend to be invested mostly in cash just before a jump that could create a loss, jumps will be less of a problem. The additional conservatism required of stop-loss orders to prevent losses from jumps will tend to equalize the expected rates of return from the stop-loss and dynamic asset allocation strategies.

Mispriced Securities

The investor who believes he can identify mispriced index futures, index options or even conventional options on common stocks may want to consider different approaches to portfolio insurance at different times. For example, when index calls are underpriced relative to index puts, he should give preference to fiduciary calls in place of protective puts as a means of creating portfolio insurance. If he thinks he can identify relatively underpriced calls on individual stocks, he may want to use a portfolio of fiduciary calls on individual stocks, despite the disadvantages of this strategy. If index futures appear to be underpriced, the preferred method may be to buy futures against a position in cash, rather than selling futures against a long position in the index.

Transaction Costs

By far the most liquid spot index option contracts are the S&P 100 options traded on the CBOE, which now comprise in total about 33 per cent of all CBOE options volume – typically representing trades to more than 20 million shares of the index per day (about $3 billion). The S&P 500 index futures traded on the CME are also highly liquid, representing trades to over 25 million shares per day (about $3.750 billion).

Currently, almost all trading volume for both index futures and options is concentrated in the nearest maturing contracts. As a result, it is necessary in the case of large trades to turn over options hedges about once every two months and futures hedges about once every four months to obtain sufficient liquidity. For options, we assume a 2 per cent one-way commission and a 1 per cent one-way spread give-up for a total one-way transaction cost of 3 per cent – about 12 cents on a $4 option, or about 0.08 per cent of the spot index. Additional costs from terminating index options at their expiration are ignored, because of their cash resettlement feature. For futures, we estimate a round-trip commission of $30 per contract and a $25 spread give-up for a total round-trip transaction cost of 0.07 per cent of the spot index price.

With a turnover of six times per year for a sequential options strategy, the total annual options transaction cost is 0.48 per cent of the spot index price. For dynamic asset allocation using index futures, turnover comes from two sources – from rolling the futures over three times per year (each time on an average of half the index portfolio) and from the requirements of dynamic asset allocation (which, based on simulation, is roughly 50 per cent per year). In total, futures would need to be bought or sold on 2.5 times the value of the index portfolio, which in turn implies a total annual futures transaction cost of 0.18 per cent of the spot index price.

Conventional dynamic asset allocation, which requires transferring assets between S&P 500 stocks and Treasury bills, is estimated from experience to cost 0.56 per cent of the spot index price.

In summary, conventional dynamic asset allocation is only slightly more expensive than a sequential index options strategy (0.56 per cent versus 0.48 per cent per annum). Dynamic asset allocation implemented with index futures is the cheapest, at about one-third this cost.

Conclusion

Long-term European payout-protected index options provide perfect portfolio insurance, but they do not currently exist in exchange-traded markets. Until they do, it will be necessary to use other instruments to approximate portfolio insurance on broad-based stock market indexes.

Stop-loss order strategies suffer from extreme path-dependence. Sequential index option strategies are also path-dependent and have a lower expected rate of return than perfect portfolio insurance. Of all the methods examined above, dynamic asset allocation, which attempts to replicate a long-term European protective put, seems to come closest to perfect portfolio insurance.

Appendix

Calculating path-dependence

For each ending level of the index, make the best possible estimate of the portfolio rate of return. On average, as Table AI shows, the realized portfolio rate of return may be expected to err by 3.14 per cent. At worst – if the index ends at 116.68 – the error may be expected to be 6.47 per cent.

The overall expected rate of return on the stop-loss strategy is calculated by summing the products of the second and third columns of Table II in the text. This results in 14.57 per cent.

For a very close approximation of the results from continuous S&P 500 movements, divide the year into 50 equally spaced intervals with binomial moves over each interval.[17] In this case, the path-dependence and expected rate of return are 3.73 and 14.70 per cent, respectively. With a continuous process, the stop-loss order could be executed at exactly 100; in that case, the stop-loss strategy would be 100 per cent reliable in preventing losses.

Also of interest for the stop loss strategy are the stopout probability, which is 40 per cent, and the expected time to stopout, which is 0.76 of a year (roughly, the beginning of the fourth quarter).

Table AI Calculation of path-dependence

Value of S&P 500 with dividends reinvested	Conditional portfolio expected value	Expected absolute deviation	Probability
$136.14	$136.14	0.00	0.271
116.68	112.37	6.47	0.418
100.00	98.85	1.35	0.243
85.71	98.28	1.74	0.062
73.46	99.45	0.00	0.006

Path Dependence = $(0.418 \times 6.47) + (0.243 \times 1.35) + (0.062 \times 1.74) = 3.14\%$

Example: When S&P 500 = 116.68:

$$112.37 = \frac{(0.314 \times 116.68) + (0.105 \times 99.45)}{0.314 + 0.105}$$

$$6.47 = \frac{[0.314 \times |116.68 - 112.37|] + [0.105 \times |99.45 - 112.37|]}{0.314 + 0.105}$$

Notes

The author thanks Hayne Leland for his helpful comments.
This article was awarded first prize in the 1984 Institute for Quantitative Research in Finance competition.

1. The proof of this proposition is contained in an unpublished note by Hayne Leland.
2. For a more complete treatment, see Hayne Leland, "Who Should Buy Portfolio Insurance?" *Journal of Finance*, May 1980.
3. It is hypothesized that an investor who sells portfolio insurance wants to maximize the probability of obtaining a specified level of profit (the insurance premium in the case of a no-loss policy). In compensation for this, the investor must absorb all losses in the index.
4. For a proof that rational, risk-averse investors in a complete-markets, random-walk, time-additive utility environment should prefer path-independent to path-dependent strategies, see John C. Cox and Hayne Leland, "A Characterization of Path-Independent Policies." For the special case of investors who maximize the terminal value of their wealth at the end of a specified horizon, the intuition behind their proof is easily grasped. Suppose the only thing an investor cares about is the amount of wealth he will have at his horizon date and he has no reason to be concerned about the implications of past outcomes for future returns (the random walk assumption). Then, if he can achieve path-independent outcomes for the pattern of returns that he desires at his horizon date, he will prefer these to path-dependent outcomes. The additional uncertainty from path-dependence is uncompensated risk. It is as though, in addition to his desired outcome of $120.84, the investor had to flip a coin to determine whether he receives $5 more or $5 less. No risk averter would willingly accept this gamble.
5. See Fischer Black and Myron Scholes, "The Pricing of Options and Corporate Liabilities," *Journal of Political Economy*, May–June 1973.
6. The Black-Scholes option pricing formula uses the logarithmic or continuous volatility (the standard deviation of the *natural logarithm* of one plus the rate of return) as an input, rather than the arithmetic or discrete volatility (the standard deviation of the rate of

return). In our case, the S&P 500 is assumed to have an arithmetic mean and volatility of 16 and 18 per cent, respectively. Assuming lognormality of its rate of return, this translates into a logarithmic volatility of 15.5 per cent.

7. Formulas for transforming the mean and volatility of a lognormal security price process into the sizes and probabilities of the up and down moves of a discrete binomial process are given in John C. Cox, Stephen A. Ross and Mark Rubinstein, "Option Pricing: A Simplified Approach," *Journal of Financial Economics*, September 1979.

8. See M. Rubinstein and H. Leland, "Replicating Options with Positions in Stock and Cash," *Financial Analysts Journal*, July/August 1981.

9. Readers familiar with options may wonder if a striking price K can be chosen satisfying this equation. If the put were American (permitting early exercise), then the striking price would be so high that the put should be immediately exercised. But the put under consideration here is European (it cannot be exercised early), so its price must only satisfy $P > Kr^{-t} - S$, which permits its price to fall such that $P < K - S$ prior to expiration. Here, r is one plus the annual rate of interest and t is the time to expiration. Since a protective European put is always worth $S + P$, it follows that at no time in its life can the value of this position fall below Kr^{-t}. This implies that if, at any time during its life, the put were converted into cash, the investor could realize a minimum $Kr^{-t} \times r^{t} = K$ by the expiration date.

10. This technique for calculating the expected rates of return of European options is developed in Mark Rubinstein, "A Simple Formula for the Expected Rate of Return of an Option over a Finite Holding Period" (Working paper #119, Research Program in Finance, Institute of Business and Economic Research, University of California at Berkeley, March 1984).

11. If S is the stock price, C the call price, P the price of an otherwise similar put, r one plus the annual rate of interest, t the time to expiration of the options, and K their common striking price, according to the put-call parity relationship, at all times during the lives of the options:

$$P + S = C + Kr^{-t}.$$

The left-hand side of this equation is a protective put and the right-hand side is a fiduciary call.

12. Because neither the European spot call nor the European futures call can be exercised early, and because the spot and futures prices must be equal on the expiration date of the options, the cash flows received from either option must be identical.

13. See Mark Rubinstein, "Alternative Paths to Portfolio Insurance: A Detailed Analysis" (Expanded version of this article, May 1984).

14. The most active listed index options, the CBOE S&P 100 options, are not even listed with maturities beyond three months. A casual glance at the *Wall Street Journal* reveals that about 90 per cent of the volume in listed index puts is concentrated in puts with less than 40 days to expiration, with negligible volume in puts with more than 60 days to go.

15. Observe that when the index is at 85.71, the striking price of the next six-month put, relative to the index level is 103.86. (= 89.02/85.71).

16. To preserve reliability at three-point intervals, the investor must buy puts at slightly higher striking prices than optimal. Moreover, when the S&P 500 rises, the eight-point limitation will also force one to buy options at higher than optimal striking prices.

17. With 50 intervals, the minimum number of separate nodes at the end of the tree is 51 and the maximum number is 2^{50} or 123 trillion. In the stop-loss strategy, the number of different ending nodes turns out to be 638.

16

The October Crash: Some Evidence on the Cascade Theory

———————————————————————— G. J. Santoni

"It's the nearest thing to a meltdown that I ever want to see."
John J. Phelan, Jr., Chairman of the New York Stock Exchange

The record one-day decline in stock prices on October 19, 1987, stripped roughly 22 percent from stock values. More disconcerting, however, were the speed of the adjustment, the tumultuous trading activity in financial markets and the uncertainty that prevailed during the week of October 19. These aspects of the crash bore a surprising resemblance to previous financial panics that many thought were historical artifacts outmoded by modern regulatory and surveillance systems as well as by advances in the financial sophistication of market participants. The crash shocked this complacency and reawakened considerable interest in financial panics and their causes.

As with its 1929 predecessor, the list of popular explanations for the panic of 1987 runs the gamut from the purely economic and financial to the frailties inherent in human nature (see following page). Recently, a number of more-or-less official investigating agencies have released reports about the October panic.[1] Generally speaking, these reports do not attempt to identify the reason for the decline in stock prices. Rather, they focus on the factors that characterized it as a panic: the *sharpness* of the decline on October 19 and the *tumultuous* trading activity that occurred on this day and during the following week.

Virtually all of the reports agree that the inability of the New York and other cash market exchanges to process the unprecedented volume of trades quickly contributed importantly to the market turmoil. They disagree widely, however, about the reasons for the sharpness of the decline.

The Brady Commission Report attributes the downward "cascade" in stock prices to programmed trading – more specifically, to the trading strategies known as index arbitrage and portfolio insurance (see above for discussion of these strategies).[2] This conclusion, however, is questioned seriously in reports filed by the Commodity Futures Trading Commission (CFTC) and Chicago Mercantile Exchange (CME).[3] These reports attribute the swift decline in stock prices to a massive revision in investors' perceptions of the fundamental determinants of stock prices.[4] Furthermore, since different rules govern trading in the cash and futures markets, a careful analysis of the effect of these different rules may better explain the evidence advanced by the Brady Commission in support of the cascade theory.[5]

This paper examines minute-by-minute price data gathered from the cash and futures market for stocks from October 15–23 to determine if the data are best explained by the cascade theory or the different trading rules in the two markets.

Some Popular Notions Regarding the Crash of '87

"Wall Street has supplanted Las Vegas, Atlantic City, Monte Carlo and Disneyland as the place where dreams are made, where castles appear in the clouds. It was Pinocchio's Pleasure Island, where children (and the adults whose bodies they inhabited) could do and have whatever they wanted, whenever they wanted it.

But now it's morning and the binge seems to be over. Many have hangovers. Many have worse. The jackasses are clearly identifiable. And the rest of us, who pretended not to notice, are left with the job of cleaning up the mess."

Robert B. Reich, New York Times (October 22, 1987)

'People are beginning to see that the five-year bull market of the Eighties was a new Gatsby age, complete with the materialism and euphoric excesses of all speculative eras. Like the Jazz Age of F. Scott Fitzgerald's . . . , the years combined the romance of wealth and youth with the slightly sinister aura of secret understandings."

William Glaberson, New York Times (December 13, 1987)

"We've been through quite a few years in which we felt we had reached the millennium, which was high rewards and no risk. We are now understanding that that is not the case."

Peter G. Peterson, New York Times (December 13, 1987)

"Ultimately, we will view this period as one in which we made a very important mistake. What we did was divorce our financial system from reality."

Martin Lipton, New York Times (December 13, 1987)

"Investors knew that stocks were overpriced by any traditional valuation measures such as price/earnings ratios and price to book value. They also knew that the combination of program trading and portfolio insurance could send prices plummeting."

Anise C. Wallace, New York Times (November 3, 1987)

"On Monday, October 19, Wall Street's legendary herd instincts, now embedded in digital code and amplified by hundreds of computers, helped turn a sell-off into a panic."

David E. Sanger, New York Times (December 15, 1987)

"Futures and options are like barnacles on a ship. They take their life from the pricing of stocks and bonds. When the barnacles start steering the ship, you get into trouble, as we saw last week."

Marshall Front, Christian Science Monitor (October 30, 1987)

"One trader's gain is another's loss, and the costs of feeding computers and brokers are a social waste."

Louis Lowenstien, New York Times (May 11, 1988).

"We probably would have had only a 100- to 150-point drop if it hadn't been for computers."

Frederick Ruopp, Christian Science Monitor (October 30, 1987)

"This [restrictions on programmed trading] will make it a market where the individual investor can tread without fear of the computers."

Edward A. Greene, New York Times (November 3, 1987).

"In my mind, we should start by banning index option arbitrage and then proceed with other reforms which will restore public confidence in the financial markets. The public has every reason to believe that the present game is rigged. It is. Many would be better off in a casino since there people expect to lose but have a good meal and a good time while they're doing it."

Donald Regan, U.S. Senate Hearing, Committee on Banking, Housing and Urban Affairs (May 24, 1988, pp. 76–77).

The Trading Strategies

Portfolio insurance is an investment strategy that attempts to insure a return for large portfolios above some acceptable minimum. For example, if the acceptable minimum return is 8 percent and the portfolio is currently returning 13 percent, the portfolio's managers may want to decrease the share of the portfolio held in bonds and cash, which are safe but yield relatively low returns, and increase the share of the portfolio held in higher-yielding stock. This increases the expected return of the portfolio but exposes it to more risk. On the other hand, a stock price decline that reduced the return of the portfolio to, say, 10 percent puts the return close to the minimum. In this event, the managers may want to reduce the risk exposure of the portfolio. This can be accomplished by reducing the share of the portfolio held in stock and increasing the shares held in cash and bonds.[1]

This strategy results in stock purchases when stock prices rise significantly and stock sales when stock prices decline significantly.[2] Initially, these portfolio adjustments typically are made by trading in stock index futures, because the transaction cost for large baskets of stock are lower in futures than in the cash market.[3]

Index arbitrage is a trading strategy based on simultaneous trades of stock index futures and the corresponding basket of stocks in the cash market. This trading strategy attempts to profit from typically small and short-lived price discrepancies for the same group of stocks in the cash and futures markets.

Cash and futures prices for the same stock or group of stocks typically differ. The difference – called the basis – results from the "cost of carrying" stocks over the time interval spanned by the futures contract. These costs depend on the relevant interest rate and the dividends the stocks are expected to pay during the interval. On occasion, the observed basis may diverge from the cost of carry. If so, arbitrageurs can expect to profit *if simultaneous trades* can be placed in the two markets – purchasing the relatively low-priced instrument and selling the relatively high-priced instrument. These trades move the basis back to the cost of carry.

Notes

1. See Miller, Hawke, Malkiel and Scholes (1987), p. 12.
2. The purpose of this paper is not to evaluate the wisdom of these trading strategies. Rather, it is to evaluate the proposition that they contributed importantly to the panic.
3. For example, the transaction costs of trading one futures contract based on the Standard and Poor's 500 are about $500 lower than trading the equivalent basket of stocks in the cash market. See Miller, Hawke, Malkiel and Scholes (1987), p. 11, and U.S. General Accounting Office (1988), p. 20.

Resolving this issue is important because of the legislative and regulatory proposals spawned by the October panic. For example, the regulatory proposals advanced by the Brady Commission include:

(1)   One agency to coordinate regulatory issues that have an impact across all financial markets;
(2)   Unified clearing systems across related financial markets;
(3)   Consistent margin requirements in the cash and futures markets;
(4)   Circuit breaker mechanisms (such as price limits and coordinated trading halts); and
(5)   Integrated information systems across related financial markets.[6]

Proposals 3 and 4 clearly reflect the Commission's belief that programmed trading contributed significantly to the panic. Furthermore, the action taken by the New York Stock Exchange (NYSE) to restrict use of its Designated Order Turnaround (DOT) system by program traders suggests that the officials of this exchange also subscribe to the Brady Commission's explanation.[7] This belief was reaffirmed more recently. Beginning February 4, 1988, the NYSE has denied use of the DOT system to program traders whenever the Dow Jones Industrial Average moves up or down by more than 50 points from its previous day's close.

The Cascade Theory

The Brady Commission suggests that the stock market panic is best explained by the "cascade theory." This theory argues that "mechanical, price-insensitive selling" by institutions using portfolio insurance strategies contributed significantly to the break in stock prices.[8] In an effort to liquidate the equity exposure of their portfolios quickly, these institutions sold stock index futures contracts in the Chicago market. Such sales lowered the price of the futures contracts *relative* to the price of the equivalent basket of stocks in the New York cash market. The decline in the futures price relative to the cash price induced index arbitrageurs to purchase futures contracts in the Chicago market (which, in their view, were undervalued) and sell (short) the underlying stocks in the New York market (which, in their view, were overvalued relative to futures). Thus, index arbitrage transmitted the selling pressure from the Chicago futures market to the New York cash market causing cash prices in New York to decline.

The story does not end here. According to the theory, the decline in cash prices triggered a further selling wave in the Chicago market by portfolio insurers that index arbitrageurs, again, transmitted to the New York market. This process was repeated time after time causing a "downward cascade" in stock prices.[9]

The Brady Commission suggests that support for the cascade theory can be found by examining the behavior of the spread (the basis) between the price of stock index futures contracts and the cash prices of the shares underlying the contracts.[10] The basis is normally positive. Stock index futures prices generally exceed cash prices because the net costs of carrying stock forward (interest cost less expected dividends) are typically positive.[11] During the panic, however, the basis turned negative. The Commission suggests that this observation is consistent with the cascade theory.

Chart 1 Cash and December Futures

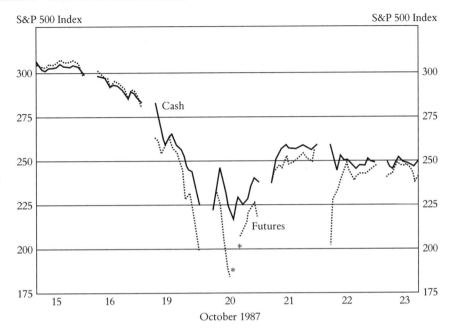

* Futures market closed

Chart 1 plots both the price of the December Standard and Poor's 500 futures contract and the Standard and Poor's index of 500 common stocks. The latter represents the cash price of the stocks underlying the futures contract. The data cover half-hour intervals during October 15–23, 1987. Chart 2 plots the basis – the difference between the two prices shown in chart 1. As one can see, the basis fell below zero in the late afternoon of October 16 and, with a few exceptions, remained negative for the rest of the week. In the Brady Commission's view, this evidence provides important support for the cascade theory.

There is Less to the Cascade Theory than Meets the Eye

The negative basis

As mentioned, proponents of the cascade theory suggest that their theory is supported by the negative basis observed on the afternoon of October 16 and on subsequent trading days during the week of October 19. However, a negative basis does not necessarily support the cascade theory.

Panel A of table 1 calculates the current price of a stock, P_t, assuming that the currently observed dividend, D_t, is $1; the long-term interest rate, r, is 11 percent and the expected growth rate in dividends, g, is 5 percent.[12] Under these assumptions, the current price of the stock is $17.50(= \$1.05/[.11 - .05])$. In addition, panel A calculates the expected price of the stock one year from now, $E_t P_{t+1}$. This expected

Chart 2   Basis = December Futures – Cash

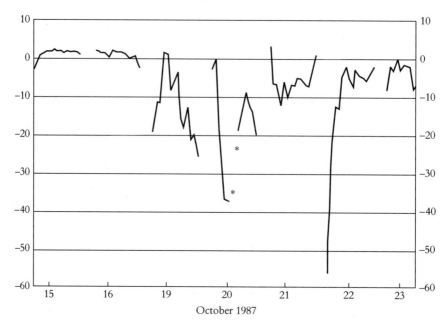

October 1987

* Futures market closed

Table 1   Calculating the Basis

Panel A
Assumptions:
$D_t = \$1.00$
$g = 5.0\%$
$E_t D_{t+1} = D_t(1 + g) = \$1.05$
$r = 11\%$
(1) $P_t = E_t D_{t+1}/(r - g) = \$1.05/0.06 = \$17.50$
(2) $E_t P_{t+1} = P_t(1 + r) - E_t D_{t+1} = \$17.50(1.11) - \$1.05 = \$18.38$
(3) $B = E_t P_{t+1} - P_t = \$18.38 - \$17.50 = \$ .88$

Panel B
Assumptions: Same as A except $g' = 3.0\%$
(1) $P_t' = E_t D_{t+1}'/(r - g') = \$1.03/.08 = \$12.88$
(2) $E_t P_{t+1}' = P_t'(1 + r) - E_t D_{t+1}' = \$12.88(1.11) - \$1.03 = \$13.27$
(3) $B' = E_t P_{t+1}' - P_t' = \$13.27 - \$12.88 = \$ .39$

where:
D_t = the current dividend
$E_t D_{t+1}$ = the expected dividend at year end
P_t = the current share price
g = the expected growth rate in dividends
r = the relevant long-term interest rate

price is the amount to which P_t would grow if invested at r less the dividend expected at the end of the year, $E_t D_{t+1}$.[13] This amount is \$18.38(= \$17.50[1.11] − \$1.05). Assuming that arbitrageurs are rational and that transaction costs are very low, the basis between the price of a futures contract dated to mature in one year and the current cash price of the stock is the difference between the expected price of the stock one year from now and its current price, \$.88(= \$18.38 − \$17.50).

Panel B performs similar calculations assuming that the expected growth rate in dividends, g, falls from 5 percent to 3 percent, while everything else remains constant. Notice that this results in a decline in the current price of the stock from \$17.50 to \$12.88, a reduction of about 30 percent. Furthermore, since the expected price of the stock one year from now falls to \$13.27, the basis falls to \$.39(= \$13.27 − \$12.88). Other things the same, a decline in the expected growth rate of dividends causes a decline in the current price, the futures price and the basis. For reasons discussed later, futures prices typically respond to new information more rapidly than indexes of cash market prices. This was particularly so during the crash. In terms of our example, if the futures price declines immediately to \$13.27 but cash prices adjust less quickly, the *observed* basis may be negative during the adjustment period. In short, there is no need for a special theory, like the cascade theory, to explain the behavior of the basis during the week of October 19.[14]

Irrational price-insensitive traders

Stock prices declined throughout the day of October 19, 1987. The decline was particularly sharp in the afternoon (see chart 1). At about 1:30 p.m. EST, the price of a December S&P 500 futures contract was about 15 points lower than the cash prices of the stocks underlying the contract (that is, the basis was − 15 points, see chart 2). This means that liquidating the basket of stocks underlying the S&P 500 through futures market sales was about \$7,500 more costly (before transaction costs) than liquidating the same basket in the cash market.[15] Yet, according to the cascade theory, portfolio insurers continued to liquidate in the futures market. In the words of the Brady Commission, this apparently anomalous behavior was the result of "mechanical price-insensitive selling." Put more bluntly, the theory attributes the observation to irrationality on the part of portfolio managers who, by most accounts − including those of the Brady Commission − are credited with being highly sophisticated financial experts.

The missing arbs

The cascade theory depends on index arbitrage activity to transmit selling pressure from the futures to the cash market. Yet, by all accounts, index arbitrage virtually ceased about 1:30 p.m. EST on October 19.[16] Cash market prices, however, fell sharply between 1:30 and the market's close. The S&P 500 index lost about 30 points during this time, while the Dow fell by more than 300 points. Furthermore, index arbitrage was severely restricted in subsequent trading days because the NYSE limited use of its DOT system by arbitrageurs. However, this did not prevent a further sharp decline in stock prices on October 26.

Foreign markets and previous panics

The cascade theory fails to explain why stock market panics in foreign markets occurred at the same time as the U.S. panic. Programmed trading is virtually nonexistent in overseas markets. Yet these markets crashed as quickly and by as much as the U.S. market. Between October 16 and 23, for example, the U.K. stock market declined 22 percent, the German and Japanese markets fell 12 percent, the French market fell 10 percent and the U.S. market declined 13 percent. What's more, programmed trading dates back no further than 1982 when stock index futures contracts began trading. U.S. stock market panics have a much longer history. Since the cascade theory does not explain these other panics, there is some reason to be skeptical about its usefulness in explaining the latest U.S. panic.

An Alternative Explanation: Efficient Markets

A long-standing proposition in both economics and finance is that stock prices are formed in efficient markets.[17] This means that all of the relevant information currently known about interest rates, dividends and the future prospects for firms (the fundamentals) is contained in current stock prices. Stock prices change only when new information regarding the fundamentals is obtained by someone. New information, by definition, cannot be predicted ahead of its arrival; because the news is just as likely to be good as it is to be bad, jumps in stock prices cannot be predicted in advance.

If the efficient markets hypothesis is correct, past price changes contain no useful information about future price changes. With some added assumptions, this can be translated into a useful empirical proposition. If transaction costs are low, the expected return to holding stock is constant and the volatility of stock prices does not change during the time period examined, the efficient market hypothesis implies that observed *changes* in stock prices will be uncorrelated. The sequence of price changes are unrelated; they behave as random variables. This is sometimes called "weak form efficiency."

This implication contrasts sharply with a central implication of the cascade theory. The cascade theory suggests that price changes in both the cash and futures markets are positively correlated with their own past. This follows from the theory's circularity which attributes sharp price declines to immediately preceding sharp declines.

The behavior of U.S. stock prices generally conforms to the efficient markets hypothesis in the sense that past changes in stock prices contain no *useful* information about future changes.[18] However, when data on stock price indexes are observed at very high frequency (intra-day but not day-to-day), changes in the level of *cash* market indexes are correlated and appear to lag changes in futures prices.[19] This behavior appears to favor the cascade theory. When differences in the "market-making" techniques employed in the cash and futures markets are taken into account, however, intra-day data from both markets reject the cascade theory, while, on the whole, they are consistent with the efficient markets hypothesis.[20]

Market-making in the cash market

Trading on the NYSE is conducted by members who trade within an action framework at posts manned by specialists.[21] Specialists' activities are concentrated on a

Figure 1   An illustration of limit order supply and demand

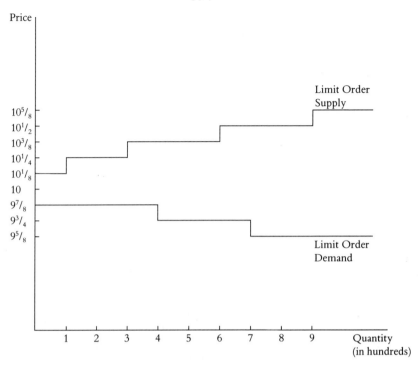

particular group of stocks that are traded at a particular post. One of the main functions of a specialist is to execute limit orders for other members of the Exchange.
A limit order is an order to buy (sell) a specified number of shares of a given stock
when and if the price of the stock falls (rises) to some specified level. The specialist
maintains a book in which these orders are recorded and to which only he has access.
The ability to place a limit order with a specialist frees the broker who places the
order from having to wait at the post for a price movement that may never occur.

For example, suppose the information contained in the specialist's book for shares
of XYZ corporation is summarized in figure 1.[22] The demand curve aggregates the
purchase orders that have been placed with the specialist. These include bids of $9⅞
for 400 shares, $9¾ for 300 shares, etc. The supply curve aggregates the specialist's
sell orders of 100 shares at $10⅛, 200 shares at $10¼, etc. Brokers, standing at the
post, trade XYZ shares with each other and the specialist. At any time, a broker
may request a quote from the specialist who, given the information in figure 1,
would respond "$9⅞ for 400, 100 at $10⅛." This indicates that the specialist has
buy orders for 400 shares at $9⅞ and sell orders for 100 shares at $10⅛. If the buy
and sell orders of the other brokers at the post are in balance at the current price,
trading in XYZ shares will occur within the price range of $9⅞ bid and $10⅛ ask.[23]

Suppose, however, that a broker has a market buy order for 300 shares that he
is unable to cross with a broker with sell orders for 300 shares at the quoted spread
(in this case, at an ask price of $10⅛ or less). Since the specialist's quote indicates
that he will sell 100 shares at $10⅛, the broker will respond "Take it." The broker
has purchased 100 shares from the specialist at $10⅛. Since the broker must buy
another 200 shares, he will ask for a further quote. If nothing further has occurred,

the specialist will quote "$9⅞ for 400, 200 at $10¼." The broker will respond "Take it." The broker has satisfied the market buy order for 300 shares of XYZ. He purchased 100 shares at $10⅛ and 200 shares at $10¼. Of course, the broker could have acquired 300 shares immediately by offering to pay a price of $10¼ but the cost would have been greater. Instead, it pays the broker to try to "walk up" the supply curve by executing a number of trades rather than jumping directly to the price that will get him 300 shares in one trade.[24] Similar reasoning applies to situations in which excess market sell orders exist at the quoted spread.

Notice that this process of "walking up" the supply curve or "walking down" the demand curve can generate a sequence of recorded transaction prices that run in the same direction. The larger the excess of market buy (or sell) orders is relative to the size of the specialist's limit orders at various prices, the longer the sequence of recorded transaction prices that run in the same direction and the greater the likelihood that recorded price changes over the time interval are correlated. This situation is particularly likely to arise during panics when large order imbalances develop at quoted prices.

Specialist rule 104

Specialists are required by rule SR 104 to maintain a "fair and orderly" market. More specifically, the rule states that

[t]he maintenance of a fair and orderly market implies the maintenance of price continuity with reasonable depth, and the minimizing of the effects of temporary disparity between supply and demand.

In connection with the maintenance of a fair and orderly market, it is commonly desirable that a . . . specialist engage to a reasonable degree under existing circumstances in dealings for his own account when lack of price continuity, lack of depth, or disparity between supply and demand exists or is reasonably to be anticipated.[25]

For example, rule SR 104 requires the specialist to buy shares for his own account to assist the maintenance of an orderly market if, in his estimation, sell orders *temporarily* exceed buy orders at the existing market price and conversely. If these imbalances are truly temporary, the trades required by SR 104 will be profitable for the specialist; evidence indicates that specialists typically sell on up ticks in price and buy on down ticks.[26] If large order imbalances develop that threaten the orderliness of the market, the specialist may institute an opening delay or trading halt. The specialist needs the approval of a floor official or governor to do this and to establish a new opening price.[27]

The effect of SR 104 is to smooth what would otherwise be abrupt movements in stock prices, at least over short periods of time (a few minutes). Rather than allowing the price to move directly to some new level, specialist trading temporarily retards the movement. This can generate a sequence of correlated price changes.

Market-making in the futures market

Trading in futures markets is governed by CFTC rules that require all trades of futures contracts to be executed openly and competitively by "open outcry." In particular, the trading arena, or pit, has no single auctioneer through whom all trades are funneled. Rather, the pit is composed of many traders who call out their bids and offers to each other. The traders are not required to stabilize the market. They may at any time take any side of a transaction even though this might add to an imbalance of buy and sell orders at the quoted price, and they may leave the pit (refuse to trade) at any time. At the time of the crash, there was no rule regarding limit moves in the price of the Standard and Poor's futures contract.

These rules contain no requirement to smooth out movements in the price. Traders are free to move the price immediately to a new level. Unlike the cash market, there are no trading rules in futures markets that are likely to result in correlated price changes. Furthermore, since there were no rules that retarded price changes in the futures market, futures prices were free to adjust more quickly than cash prices so changes in futures prices may lead changes in cash prices.

Different instruments

It is important to note that different instruments are traded in the cash and futures markets. Stock index futures contracts are agreements between a seller (short position) and a buyer (long position) to a cash settlement based on the change in a stock index's value between the date the contract is entered by the two parties and some future date.[28] The instrument underlying the futures contract is a large basket of different stocks, that is, the stocks contained in the Major Market Index, the Value Line Index, the S&P 500 Index, etc. No such instrument is traded in the cash market, where purchasing or selling 500 different stocks, for example, requires as many different transactions and can only be executed at significantly higher costs.[29]

The different instruments traded in the cash and futures markets have a further implication for the relationship between observed price changes between the two markets. The cash market prices shown in chart 1, as well as those examined by the Brady Commission, are measured by an index. The index is an average of the prices of all the stocks included in the index. When the index is observed at a very high frequency (say, minute-by-minute), some of the stocks included in the index may not have traded during the interval between observations. If not, the level of cash prices measured by the index includes some prices from previous observations. In other words, the index includes some "stale" prices. The term used to describe this phenomenon is "nonsynchronous trading."

Typically, nonsynchronous trading does not create a serious measurement problem. Under normal conditions, a buy or sell order is executed in about two minutes on the NYSE. On October 16 and during the week of October 19, however, the time required to execute orders rose markedly.[30] On those days, the index contained a considerable number of stale prices.[31] The subsequent piecemeal adjustment of these stale prices for individual stocks could explain correlated changes in the level of the cash market index. This is shown in the table 2 example. The example assumes that the index is a simple average of the prices of three stocks (A, B and C) divided by the average price in period zero and multiplied by 100. The initial prices (in period zero) are equilibrium prices (i.e., they contain all currently available relevant information). Then, new information becomes available in period 1 that eventually will cause a 10 percent decline in all stock prices. If there

Table 2   Stale prices and correlated changes in a price index: a simple example

Period	Share prices			Index[1]	Change in index
	A	B	C		
0	$10	$20	$30	100	
1	9	20	30	98.33	−1.67
2	9	18	30	95.00	−3.33
3	9	18	27	90.00	−5.00

[1] Index $= \dfrac{(A + B + C)/3}{\$20.00} \times 100$

is nonsynchronous trading, the revisions will occur piecemeal for each of the stocks. One example of this is shown in the table: the price of stock A falls in period 1, the price of stock B falls in period 2, etc. If the index is reported in each period, it will display positively correlated changes as shown in the table.

The stale price problem is not relevant for futures market prices; futures prices are actual prices. As a result, changes in futures prices will appear to lead changes in the cash market index if the index contains a substantial number of stale prices.

The Different Implications

The central feature of the cascade theory is that declines in cash and futures prices reinforced each other and led to further declines in both markets. The theory suggests that declines in the price of stock index futures contracts *caused* a decline in the cash prices of the underlying stocks, and this drop *caused* a further decline in the prices of index futures contracts. If the theory is correct, changes in cash prices will be positively correlated with past changes in the price of index futures and conversely. The cascade theory further implies that price changes in each market are positively correlated with their own past changes. This follows from the circularity of the theory which attributes sharp declines in stock prices to immediately preceding sharp declines. Finally, since the cascade theory contends that this specific behavior *caused* the panic, these correlations should be observed during the panic, but not at other times.

The efficient markets hypothesis suggests that market-making in the cash market and nonsynchronous trading could produce intra-day *cash* market price changes that are correlated. Furthermore, the hypothesis suggests that changes in futures prices may lead changes in cash prices. These implications are similar to the implications of the cascade theory. The two differ, however, in three important respects. Unlike the cascade theory, the efficient markets hypothesis suggests that:

(1)   Changes in the price of stock index futures contracts are uncorrelated,
(2)   Changes in cash prices do not lead changes in futures prices, and
(3)   Relationships that exist across the two markets are not unique to the panic.

Testing the Two Theories

These theories are tested using minute-by-minute data on the level of the Standard and Poor's 500 index (S&P 500) and the price of the December 1987 Standard and Poor's 500 index futures contract (S&P 500 Futures). The level of the S&P 500 index represents the cash price of the stocks underlying the S&P 500 futures contract. All tests are conducted using first differences of the natural logs of the levels. This transformation of the data approximates one-minute percentage changes (expressed in decimals) in cash and futures market prices. The data cover the trading days immediately before, during and after the panic: October 16, 19 and 20.[32]

A few comments about the data are important. The NYSE, on which the great bulk of the stocks included in the S&P 500 index are traded, was open from 9:30 a.m. to 4:00 p.m. EST on the above days. The CME, which trades the S&P 500 futures contract, was open from 9:30 a.m. to 4:15 p.m. EST on October 16 and 19; on October 20, however, trading in the S&P 500 futures contract was halted from 12:15 p.m. to 1:05 p.m. EST. All tests reported here *exclude* the period on October 20 when trading in the futures market was halted.

Were changes in stock prices correlated?

Table 3 presents the results of a test (called a Box-Pierce test) based on the estimated autocorrelations of percentage changes in cash market prices. This test is designed to determine whether the data are significantly correlated, that is, whether current changes in cash market prices are related to their own past changes. Both theories discussed in this paper suggest that intra-day, high-frequency cash market price changes will be positively correlated, although the reasons for the positive correlation are considerably different. As a result, these data do not help discriminate between the two theories. If the data prove inconsistent with this implication, however, neither theory performs well in explaining the behavior of cash market prices.

The data in table 3 indicate that minute-to-minute changes in the S&P 500 Index are significantly correlated. Furthermore, the correlations are positive at least over the initial lag.[33]

Table 4 presents the results of the same test for the December S&P 500 futures contract. The efficient markets hypothesis and the absence of specialist traders suggest that these changes are not correlated. Conversely, the cascade theory predicts that percentage changes in the futures price will be positively correlated.

The data presented in table 4 are consistent with the efficient markets hypothesis, not the cascade theory. None of the test statistics for October 16 (panel A), October 20 (panel D) and for the bulk of the trading day on October 19 (panel C) indicate significant correlations at conventional significance levels. These price changes are serially uncorrelated.[34] Data for the first 90 minutes of trading on October 19 (panel B) are an exception. During this period, changes in the futures price were significantly correlated with the change the previous minute. This correlation, however, is negative, not positive as the cascade theory implies.[35] Thus, the evidence presented in table 4 is inconsistent with the cascade theory, while, on the whole, it conforms to the efficient markets hypothesis.

Table 3 Cash market (Autocorrelation coefficients and Box-Pierce statistics for first differences of logs of the minute-by-minute S&P 500 index)

Panel A: October 16, 1987 (9:30 a.m. – 4:00 p.m. EST)

To lag	Autocorrelation coefficient	Box-Pierce statistic[1]
1	.570*	112.09
2	.530*	209.00
3	.385*	260.14
6	.178*	333.81
12	−.148*	352.51
18	−.208	406.39
24	−.072	462.80

Panel B: October 19, 1987 (9:30 a.m. – 4:00 p.m. EST)

To lag	Autocorrelation coefficient	Box-Pierce statistic[1]
1	.342*	37.78
2	.397*	88.69
3	.406*	141.93
6	.264*	237.78
12	.231*	345.66
18	.124	385.52
24	.054	396.34

Panel C: October 20, 1987 (9:30 a.m. – 4:00 p.m. EST)

To lag	Autocorrelation coefficient	Box-Pierce statistic[1]
1	.535*	84.15
2	.561*	176.68
3	.590*	279.02
6	.521*	548.61
12	.311*	845.55
18	.324*	1026.74
24	.250	1155.57

[1] Critical value for 24 lags is 33.20. A Box-Pierce statistic in excess of this indicates significant autocorrelation.
* Exceeds two standard errors

Is the cash market efficient?

The table 3 results indicate that intra-day changes in cash market prices are correlated. Put another way, past price changes contain some information about future changes for the next few minutes. Is this information useful in the sense that it can be profitably exploited by traders? If so, it would suggest that cash market traders do not incorporate information efficiently. This, of course, would provide evidence against the efficient markets hypothesis.

In part, the answer to this question depends on the length of the time period over which the price changes are related. If the time period is short, shorter than the time

Table 4 Futures market (Autocorrelation coefficients and Box-Pierce statistics for first differences of logs of the minute-by-minute price of the December S&P 500 futures contract)

Panel A: October 16, 1987 (9:30 a.m. – 4:15 p.m. EST)

To lag	Autocorrelation coefficient	Box-Pierce statistic[1]
1	.090	2.89
2	.035	3.33
3	−.047	4.12
6	−.020	8.25
12	−.020	16.02
18	.017	19.10
24	−.044	22.29

Panel B: October 19, 1987 (9:30 a.m. – 11:00 a.m. EST)

To lag	Autocorrelation coefficient	Box-Pierce statistic[1]
1	−.309*	8.49
2	.140	10.24
3	.005	10.24
6	−.131	15.41
12	.110	18.95
18	.043	21.69
24	−.020	23.13

Panel C: October 19, 1987 (11:00 a.m. – 4:15 p.m. EST)

To lag	Autocorrelation coefficient	Box-Pierce statistic[1]
1	−.072	1.63
2	.090	4.17
3	−.004	4.18
6	.091	7.21
12	.020	9.60
18	.073	14.95
24	.000	22.37

Panel D: October 20, 1987 (9:30 a.m. – 4:15 p.m. EST)

To lag	Autocorrelation coefficient	Box-Pierce statistic[1]
1	.029	.26
2	.022	.41
3	.042	.95
6	.046	4.22
12	−.071	9.28
18	.033	11.81
24	−.035	17.62

[1] Critical value for 24 lags is 33.20. A Box-Pierce statistic in excess of this value indicates significant autocorrelation.

* Exceeds two standard errors

Table 5   Estimated lag lengths in the cash market

Panel A: October 16, 1987 (9:30 a.m. – 4:00 p.m. EST)

$\Delta LNC_t = -.003 + .401\Delta LNC_{t-1} + .343\Delta LNC_{t-2}$
        (1.19) (7.80)*   (6.51)*
$\overline{R}^2 = .41$
$DW = 2.00$

Panel B: October 19, 1987 (9:30 a.m. – 4:00 p.m. EST)

$\Delta LNC_t = -.016 + .123\Delta LNC_{t-1} + .228\Delta LNC_{t-2} + .242\Delta LNC_{t-3} + .112\Delta LNC_{t-4}$
        (2.46)* (2.20)*   (4.14)*   (4.39)*   (1.99)*
$\overline{R}^2 = .26$
$DW = 2.01$

Panel C: October 20, 1987 (9:30 a.m. – 4:00 p.m. EST)

$\Delta LNC_t = -.001 + .107\Delta LNC_{t-1} + .173\Delta LNC_{t-2} + .258\Delta LNC_{t-3} + .174\Delta LNC_{t-4} + .153\Delta LNC_{t-5}$
        (.132) (1.82)   (2.98)*   (4.52)*   (2.99)*   (2.60)*
$\overline{R}^2 = .48$
$DW = 2.02$

---

* Statistically significant at the 5 percent level

required to execute a transaction, the information contained in past price changes cannot be exploited profitably and the cash market is efficient.

Table 5 helps answer this question. The table 5 data are estimates of the length of the lagged relationship between current and past cash market price changes for October 16, 19 and 20. The estimates were obtained by regressing the contemporaneous minute-to-minute price change on the 15 previous minute-to-minute price changes. Initially, this specification was identified as the unrestricted model. To determine whether the estimated coefficients are sensitive to the lag length and to identify statistically redundant lags, the lag structure was successively shortened by one lag. At each stage, the t-statistic for the coefficient of the most distant lag was examined. If the test indicated the coefficient was statistically insignificant, that lag was dropped and the equation was reestimated with one less lag. This process was repeated until the test rejected the hypothesis that the estimated coefficient of the most distant remaining lag was zero.[36]

The estimates shown in table 5 indicate that the lags ranged from about two minutes on October 16 to five minutes on October 20.[37] It requires about two minutes to execute a trade on the NYSE under normal trading conditions. During the panic, execution times ranged from about 10 to 75 minutes at times.[38] In view of this, the lags estimated in table 5 do not appear to be long enough to reject the efficient markets hypothesis; also, since they varied over the period, it is doubtful that past price changes contained information that could be exploited by traders.

Did stock price changes reinforce each other across markets?

The central features of the cascade theory can be tested by determining whether past price changes in the futures market help explain current price changes in the cash market and conversely. This is done by regressing the change in cash prices

Table 6 Granger tests

Day	Lags	F-statistic Futures → Cash	F-statistic Cash → Futures
October 16	2	17.61*	.76
October 19	4	4.46*	1.57
October 20	5	2.59*	.67

* Statistically significant at the 5 percent level

on past changes in cash prices; then, past changes in futures prices are added to the estimated regression equation to see if they improve the equation's explanatory power. An F-test is conducted to determine whether the addition of the futures market data significantly increases the cash price equation's coefficient of determination (R^2). The test is then reversed, with the change in futures prices as the dependent variable.

The results of this test are presented in table 6 for each of the trading days examined in this paper. The lag length employed on each day is the one identified by the table 5 test.[39] The results for cash market prices show that the addition of past changes in futures prices improve the regression estimates; this suggests that price changes in the futures market preceded those in the cash market. This result is consistent with both the cascade theory and the efficient markets hypothesis. Furthermore, it is not unique to the panic; it has been observed for intra-day price data during other periods as well.[40]

Other table 6 results, however, are inconsistent with the cascade theory. The inclusion of past changes in cash prices in the regressions that estimate the change in futures prices does not significantly improve the estimates. This rejects the notion that past changes in cash prices help explain changes in futures prices. This finding is inconsistent with the central feature of the cascade theory, which suggests the panic was caused by declines in cash and futures prices that became larger as they tumbled over each other on the way down.

Conclusion

This paper has examined the cascade theory, which has been advanced as an explanation of the October 1987 stock market panic. The theory relies on the notion that stock traders behave "mechanically," are "insensitive to price," and execute transactions in markets without regard to transaction costs. These assertions are inconsistent with the behavior of wealth-maximizing individuals. Not only are the theoretical underpinnings of the cascade theory weak, the data do not support the theory. Instead, the observed relationships that do exist between the markets are not unique to the crash and can be explained by a theory that relies on wealth maximizing behavior.

Almost 60 years later, the cause of the "Great Crash" in October 1929 is still being debated. Those with even longer memories know that there is little agreement about what caused the stock market panic in 1907. Although financial reforms followed each of these panics, history indicates that the reforms have done little to reduce the frequency or severity of panics. Without a reliable theoretical guide to the mechanics of a panic, any reform is no more than a "shot in the dark." The evidence presented in this paper suggests that the reforms advanced by proponents of the cascade theory are unlikely to alter this historical pattern.

Notes

Thomas A. Pollmann provided research assistance for this article.

1. See, for example, the *Report of the Presidential Task Force on Market Mechanisms* (1988); U.S. General Accounting Office (1988); U.S. Commodity Futures Trading Commission (1988); and the report of Miller, Hawke, Malkiel and Scholes (1987).
2. See the *Report of the Presidential Task Force on Market Mechanisms* (1988), pp. v, 15, 21, 29, 30 and 34–36.
3. See U.S. Commodity Futures Trading Commission (1988), pp. iv, v, viii and 38–138 (especially p. 137); and Miller, Hawke, Malkiel and Scholes (1987), pp. 6, 8, 10–11, 41–43 and 55–56.
4. See U.S. Commodity Futures Trading Commission (1988), p. ix; and Miller, Hawke, Malkiel and Scholes (1987), p. 6.
5. See Miller, Hawke, Malkiel and Scholes (1987), pp. 21–23, 25, 37 and 49–50.
6. *Report of the Presidential Task Force on Market Mechanisms* (1988), p. vii.
7. The DOT System is a high-speed, order-routing system that program traders use to execute simultaneous trades in the cash and futures markets.
8. *Report of the Presidential Task Force on Market Mechanisms* (1988), p. v.
9. *Ibid.*, pp. 15, 17, 21, 30–36 and 69. It is apparent that our knowledge of stock market panics has advanced considerably in the 58 years since the 1929 crash. "Black Tuesday" was caused by a downward price "spiral." "Bloody Monday" was a "cascade."
10. *Report of the Presidential Task Force on Market Mechanisms* (1988), pp. III.1–III.26, especially III.16–III.22.
11. See Figlewski (1984), pp. 658–60; Burns (1979), pp. 31–57; Cornell and French (1983), pp. 2–4; Modest and Sundaresan (1983), pp. 22–23; Santoni (1987), pp. 23–25; Schwarz, Hill and Schneeweis (1986), pp. 326–46; Working (1977); Kawaller, Koch and Koch (1987), p. 1311.
12. See Brealey (1983), pp. 67–72.
13. The example assumes that the yield curve is flat.
14. See, in addition, Malkiel (1988), pp. 5–6.
15. The value of a S&P 500 futures contract is $500 times the level of the index. Consequently, if the cash market index is about 255 and the futures market index is about 240 as they were at 1:30 p.m. EST on October 19, the value of the basis: $B = \$500(240) - \$500(255) = -\$7,500$.
16. See the *Report of the Presidential Task Force on Market Mechanisms* (1988), pp. vi, 32 and 40; U.S. General Accounting Office (1988), pp. 43 and 45–46; U.S. Commodity Futures Trading Commission (1988), pp. vi and 46.
17. See Brealey and Meyers (1984), pp. 266–81; Malkiel (1981), pp. 171–79; Brealey (1983), pp. 15–18; Leroy (1982) and Fama (1970).
18. Malkiel (1981), Brealey (1983) and Fama (1970).
19. See Perry (1985); Atchison, Butler and Simonds (1987) and Harris (1988).
20. See Grossman and Miller (1988) for a discussion of why trading rules many differ across the markets.
21. Of course, the NYSE is not the only cash market for stocks, but it is a major market. Because of its relative size, the discussion focuses on this market.

22. For purposes of exposition, the figure and discussion ignore the effect of 'stops" and "stop loss orders" on the book.
23. See Stoll (1985), Shultz (1946), pp. 119–44 and *The New York Stock Exchange Market* (1979), pp. 14–21 and pp. 30–31.
24. Under NYSE rules, public orders have precedence over specialists' orders at the same price. See Stoll (1985), p. 7.
25. *Report of the Presidential Task Force on Market Mechanisms* (1988), pp. vi–7. Rule 104 is taken seriously. See pp. vi–9.
26. See Stoll (1985), pp. 35–36.
27. It was the application of SR 104 that resulted in the opening delays and trading halts that occurred during the week of October 19. For stocks included in the S&P 500, these delays and halts averaged 51 minutes on October 19 and 78 minutes on October 20. See U.S. General Accounting Office (1988), p. 56.
28. See Schwarz, Hill and Schneeweis (1986), p. 9.
29. For example, the cost of trading one futures contract based on the Standard and Poor's 500 is about $500 lower than trading the equivalent basket of stocks in the cash market. See Miller, Hawke, Malkiel and Scholes (1987), p. 11, and U.S. General Accounting Office (1988), p. 20.
30. See U.S. General Accounting Office (1988), p. 73.
31. See Harris (1988); *Report of the Presidential Task Force on Market Mechanisms* (1988), p. 30; Miller, Hawke, Malkiel and Scholes (1987), pp. 21–22 and 34–35; U.S. Commodity Futures Trading Commission (1988), pp. v, 15 and B-1 through B-9.
32. Minute-by-minute price data were also examined for October 15 and 21–23. In each case, the qualitative results were the same as those presented here.
33. These correlations are analyzed further below.
34. The same result was obtained when data for October 15 and 21–23 were examined.
35. This puzzling result for the first 90 minutes of trading on October 19 may be due to the fact that many stocks had not yet opened for trading on the NYSE and the rumors at that time that the SEC would call a trading halt. See Miller, Hawke, Malkiel and Scholes (1987), wire report summary.
36. See Anderson (1971), pp. 223 and 275–76. It is possible that this test may reject some lags that are, in fact, significant if taken as a group. To control for this, F-tests were run with the lag length in the unrestricted model set at 15. The number of lags in the restricted model was set at 12 to determine if the three omitted lags were significant. The lags in the restricted model was then reduced to nine and the test repeated, etc.
37. The lag had declined to about three minutes by October 23. The method used in this paper to estimate lag length has the problem that the probability of rejecting the null hypothesis (the estimated coefficient is zero) when it is true rises as the lag length is reduced. Consequently, the true lag lengths may be shorter than those estimated in table 5. See Batten and Thornton (1983), pp. 22–23, and Anderson (1971), pp. 30–43.
38. U.S. Government Accounting Office (1988), p. 73.
39. Hsiao (1981) uses a similar method. These lag lengths apply to the cash market. Analysis of the futures market suggests that the appropriate lag for this market is zero.
40. See Kawaller, Koch and Koch (1987).

References

Anderson, Theodore W. *The Statistical Analysis of Time Series* (John Wiley and Sons, Inc., 1971).

Atchison, Michael D., Kirt C. Butler, and Richard R. Simonds. "Nonsynchronous Security Trading and Market Index Auto-correlation," *Journal of Finance* (March 1987), pp. 111–18.

Batten, Dallas S., and Daniel L. Thornton. "Polynomial Distributed Lags and the Estimation of the St. Louis Equation," Federal Reserve Bank of St. Louis, *Review* (April 1983), pp. 13–25.

Brealey, R. A. *An Introduction to Risk and Return from Common Stocks* (The MIT Press, 1983).

Brealey, Richard, and Stewart Meyers. *Principles of Corporate Finance* (McGraw-Hill, 1984).

Burns, Joseph M. *A Treatise on Markets: Spot, Futures, and Options* (American Enterprise Institute, 1979), pp. 31–55.

Cornell, Bradford, and Kenneth R. French. "The Pricing of Stock Index Futures," *Journal of Futures Markets* (Spring 1983), pp. 1–14.

Fama, Eugene F. "Efficient Capital Markets: A Review of Theory and Empirical Work," *Journal of Finance, Papers and Proceedings* (May 1970), pp. 383–417.

Figlewski, Stephen. "Hedging Performance and Basis Risk in Stock Index Futures," *Journal of Finance* (July 1984), pp. 657–69.

Grossman, Sanford J., and Merton H. Miller. "Liquidity and Market Structure," Princeton University Financial Research Center Memorandum No. 88 (March 1988).

Harris, Lawrence. "Nonsynchronous Trading and the S&P 500 Stock-Futures Basis in October 1987" (University of Southern California Working Paper, processed January 11, 1988).

Hsiao, Cheng. "Autoregressive Modelling and Money-Income Causality Detection," *Journal of Monetary Economics* (January 1981), pp. 85–106.

Kawaller, Ira G., Paul D. Koch, and Timothy W. Koch. "The Temporal Price Relationship Between S&P 500 Futures and the S&P 500 Index," *Journal of Finance* (December 1987), pp. 1309–29.

Leroy, Stephen F. "Expectations Models of Asset Prices: A Survey of Theory," *Journal of Finance* (March 1982), pp. 185–217.

Malkiel, Burton G. "The Brady Commission Report," Princeton University Financial Research Center Memorandum No. 92 (May 1988).

———. *A Random Walk Down Wall Street* (W. W. Norton and Company, 1981).

Miller, Merton H., John D. Hawke, Jr., Burton Malkiel, and Myron Scholes. *Preliminary Report of the Committee of Inquiry Appointed by the Chicago Mercantile Exchange to Examine the Events Surrounding October 19, 1987* (December 22, 1987).

Modest, David M., and Mahadevan Sundaresan. "The Relationship Between Spot and Futures Prices in Stock Index Futures Markets: Some Preliminary Evidence," *Journal of Futures Markets* (Spring 1983), pp. 15–41.

Perry, Philip R. "Portfolio Serial Correlation and Nonsynchronous Trading," *Journal of Financial and Quantitative Analysis* (December 1985), pp. 517–23.

Report of the Presidential Task Force on Market Mechanisms (U.S. Government Printing Office, January 1988).

Santoni, G. J. "Has Programmed Trading Made Stock Prices More Volatile?" Federal Reserve Bank of St. Louis, *Review* (May 1987), pp. 18–29.

Schwarz, Edward W., Joanne M. Hill, and Thomas Schneeweis. *Financial Futures* (Dow Jones-Irwin, 1986).

Shultz, Birl E. *The Securities Market and How It Works* (Harper and Brothers, 1946).

Stoll, Hans R. *The Stock Exchange Specialist System: An Economic Analysis.* Monograph Series in Finance and Economics (Salomon Brothers Center for the Study of Financial Institutions, New York University, 1985).

The New York Stock Exchange Market (New York Stock Exchange, June 1979).

U.S. Commodity Futures Trading Commission. *Final Report on Stock Index Futures and Cash Market Activity During October 1987* (U.S. Commodity Futures Trading Commission, January 1988).

U.S. General Accounting Office. *Financial Markets: Preliminary Observations on the October 1987 Crash* (U.S. General Accounting Office, January 1988).

Working, Holbrook. *Selected Writings of Holbrook Working* (Chicago Board of Trade, 1977).

17

Portfolio Insurance and the Market Crash

The market crash of October 19, 1987, under-mined two preconditions of all portfolio insur-ance programs – (1) low transaction costs and (2) price continuity. As a result, although most portfolio insurance programs did not violate their minimum returns, many did not perform as well as expected. Differential performance across dif-ferent programs probably had more to do with the size of the hedges in place at the time of the crash than with the amount of trading the program undertook. Conservative programs (say, 50 per cent hedged) probably outperformed more aggressive programs.

Did portfolio insurance itself contribute to the crash? Portfolio insurance accounted for perhaps 12 per cent of the dollar change in net sold positions on October 19. Is this substantial? It seems unlikely, given the many other significant events – the twin deficits, the falling dollar, uncertainty over the market system itself – that have been implicated in the press.

In the aftermath of the crash, portfolio insur-ance strategies are likely to be more difficult to implement and riskier in terms of predictability of outcome. We can expect to see fewer dynamic strategies, because of increased transaction costs, and greater use of options markets, which avoid the price discontinuity problem. We might also see a better balance between explicit buyers and sellers of insurance.

The events of the week of October 19, 1987 have raised several questions concern-ing portfolio insurance and securities market regulation:

- How did the market crash affect the performance of portfolio insurance strategies?
- How did portfolio insurance strategies affect the crash?
- What, if anything, should be done to reduce the probability of market crashes in the future?
- How will portfolio insurance strategies be modified in the future?

At present, I have inadequate information to give a definitive answer to any of these questions. Even after all the study and analysis has been completed by regu-latory agencies and academics, we may still not be sure we know the answers. None-theless, based on what I currently know or surmise, I will answer these questions as best I can.

How Did the Crash Affect the Performance of Portfolio Insurance Strategies?

Typical implementation of portfolio insurance has relied on two preconditions – low transaction costs and more or less price-continuous markets.[1] Following an unbroken record of reliability reaching at least as far back as the Great Depression, these preconditions were suddenly and simultaneously violated on October 19, 1987.

Transaction costs

Transaction costs consist of four components – commissions, bid-ask spread, market impact (moving prices through large transactions) and, for investors using index futures markets, differences between futures prices and "fair value." In spot, futures and options markets, bid-ask spreads widened substantially on October 19, and market impact (perhaps on the order of 1 per cent) was significant for investors selling either directly in the spot market or implicitly in futures and options markets. As a general rule, futures should sell above the spot index level. On October 19, however, S&P 500 futures sold (and closed at the end of the day) an average of about 10 per cent below the concurrently reported level of the spot S&P 500 index.

Unfortunately, even under normal market conditions, it is difficult to determine the fair value of an index future because of uncertainty surrounding the concurrent level of the spot index. The individual stocks in the index do not all trade (and thereby register new prices, which may revise the index) at the same time. Indeed, some components of the index commonly trade with lags of several minutes. As a result, the reported index at any time is a combination of prices drawn from different times during the day. My own research suggests that the S&P 500 is typically about five minutes old. To estimate fair value, one would instead like to know what the index would currently be if all the stocks in the index had just traded. During periods when the reported index is moving rapidly up or down, the lag can make it appear that the futures price is significantly different from fair value, when in reality the futures price is just reflecting the level the index would have if all stocks in the index were to trade simultaneously. The common observation that the futures market tends to lead the stock market confirms this view.

On October 19, the measurement problems created by the lag reached unprecedented proportions, primarily because of delayed openings in key S&P 500 stocks, sluggish trading due to order imbalances at intervals throughout the day, and attempts by specialists to absorb massive selling pressure. Compounding these problems was the apparent absence of program traders, who normally serve to transmit price changes between the spot and futures markets.[2] By the end of the day, while the S&P 500 was down 20 per cent compared with the previous day's close, the December S&P 500 futures contract was down 29 per cent.

As was also observed on October 20 and 21, with the relative inactivity of program trading, the futures market was effectively uncoupled from the spot market. Under these circumstances, it was understandable that different individuals observing the reported spot and futures prices would have drawn different conclusions: Some felt the basis (the difference between futures and spot prices) was in fact very large, while others believed that the unadjusted futures price provided the most reliable measure of the concurrent level the index would have if supply and demand imbalances were to be corrected for all stocks in the index.

The differential responses of individual portfolio insurers on October 19 can be traced to this source. If he believed transaction costs were very high, a sensible portfolio insurer would substantially reduce the number of futures contracts sold; if he thought transaction costs were low, large numbers of contracts would be sold.

Ironically, if transaction costs were at just the right level, it would not have mattered what the insurer did. For example, suppose selling futures imposed a transaction cost of 10 per cent and assume that an insurer started out the day with a sold futures position covering 10 per cent of his underlying portfolio. Suppose further that, with no transaction costs, every 1 per cent decline in the S&P 500 index would trigger a 2 per cent increase in sold futures in order to create an insured outcome. With the index falling 20 per cent on October 19, the insurer would then want to increase his sold futures position from 10 to 50 per cent $(0.10 + 2 \times 0.20)$, for an average hedge during the day of 30 per cent $[(0.10 + 0.50)/2]$.

Now compare two extreme responses – an insurer who follows the strategy as if there were no transaction costs and an insurer who, estimating high transaction costs, stays pat and holds his hedge at 10 per cent. The first insurer will lose about 70 per cent $(1 - 0.30)$ of the 20 per cent decline, as well as losing 10 per cent of 40 per cent $(0.50 - 0.10)$ in transaction costs, for a total loss of 18 per cent $[(0.70 \times 0.20) + (0.10 \times 0.40)]$. But the second insurer, who doesn't trade at all, will *also* lose 18 per cent (0.90×0.20). In other words, if transaction costs were in fact 10 per cent, it would not have mattered whether the insurer traded or not; exactly the same result would have occurred in either case.

Ten per cent would seem to be an upper bound on the level of transaction costs for a seller of futures on October 19, because the true contemporaneous S&P 500 was surely much lower than its reported value. Given that transaction costs were almost certainly lower than 10 per cent, an insurer who *knew in advance* that the index was going to fall 20 per cent would have been taking the right step by selling futures. At the beginning of the day, however – and even near the end, with one hour of trading remaining, when the DJIA had dropped 300 points – it was far from obvious that the DJIA would end the day down 508 points. If, to take an extreme example, the index had reversed itself, the insurer who had not traded would have ended up outperforming the insurer who traded, not only because he would have avoided large whipsaw costs, but also because he would have been spared relatively high transaction costs. Balancing these considerations against each other, I would guess that, even if transaction costs were as little as $3\frac{1}{2}$ to 4 per cent, very little trading would have been advisable. Of course, after the fact, with the index down 20 per cent, anyone who had sold futures, even at high levels of transaction cost, would have realized superior performance.

A key issue in assessing the performance of portfolio insurance on October 19 is thus what the true level of transaction costs was for sellers of index futures. Studies of this question are currently under way, utilizing a time-stamped record of transactions in S&P 500 futures and constituent S&P 500 stocks. Such studies infer from the transaction prices of stocks that have traded information about the prices of other stocks that have been delayed in trading. Even after careful study of the available data, we may not be sure what transaction costs actually were on Black Monday.

Discontinuous markets

During the life of many portfolio insurance strategies, adjustments are made to compensate for unexpected shifts in the realized volatility of the underlying asset. Generally speaking, if volatility is higher than expected, the hedge is increased to make the strategy more conservative; if volatility is lower than expected, the hedge is reduced to make the strategy more aggressive. Given a required minimum rate of return, these adjustments prevent the strategy from stopping out and being forced completely and permanently into cash to guarantee delivery of the minimum return. While an insurance strategy that is forced to stop-out may still be able to deliver the minimum return, it will fail to capture any portion of subsequent upside movement in the underlying index.

Unfortunately, even for insurance strategies where some forethought was given to the possibility of stopping-out, the discontinuity in the markets and the sudden increase in volatility experienced on October 19 made it virtually impossible to prevent stop-out by making the usual adjustments. Indeed, the 7 per cent gap-down opening at the beginning of the day, and the last 200-point move in the DJIA, occurred so quickly that it was probably impossible to execute the requisite number of futures transactions during those times. As a result, although few insurers missed the minimum return, they were stopped-out and forced into cash for the remainder of the life of their policies. In effect, the volatility that had been expected to occur smoothly over the entire planned life of the policy instead occurred in one day.

Effects

The dependency of typical portfolio insurance strategies on preconditions of low transaction costs and market continuity should have been well-known to both those marketing the strategy and those using the strategy on their own portfolios. Even the most elementary understanding of the implementation of portfolio insurance would make this obvious. Because these preconditions were severely violated on Black Monday, it should not be surprising that portfolio insurance strategies, even though they typically did not violate the minimum return, did not in many cases perform as expected. What came as a shock to most participants was not that portfolio insurance performed poorly, given the market environment, but that the preconditions were so suddenly and strongly violated in the market.

The comparative performance of alternative portfolio insurers during the crash has been a topic of some interest. Despite the focus of attention on the amount of trading on October 19, I believe that differential performance depends primarily on the extent to which exchange-traded options were properly used to implement the insurance, the extent of the hedge already in place at the close of trading on October 16, and the extent to which it was possible to implement the insurance directly by trading stocks.

Although there were sound reasons not to implement portfolio insurance with options, policies properly relying on options instead of futures would nonetheless have been immune to the effects of high transaction costs and discontinuities. Once an option position is in place, it can be interpreted as providing the appropriate hedging adjustment automatically, without visible trading. Indeed, if purchased options were used to implement the strategy, with substantially expanding premiums resulting from the increase in perceived volatility, a portfolio insurer might even have shown a profit.

More importantly, conservative policies that started 50 per cent hedged, or originally aggressive policies that had become 50 per cent hedged because of the stock market decline over the previous two months, would have lost half as much as very aggressive policies just started with no hedge, even if they did no trading on October 19. The answer to the simple question, "How hedged were you going into Black Monday?" probably goes farther in explaining differential performance than any other factor.

Finally, insurers with access to the cash assets, even though they would have paid a large bid-ask spread in the stock market, could at least have avoided the additional unfavorable basis costs (if any) of using the futures market.

Ironically, the actions taken by a portfolio insurer in the futures market on Black Monday may have been of little importance by comparison. As we have seen, to the extent transaction costs were high, expected and to a large extent realized, losses may not have been greatly different whether one traded or not.

How Did Portfolio Insurance Strategies Affect the Crash?

Any investor who unexpectedly reduced his holdings of stock, shorted stock, covered long futures positions or increased open sold futures positions on October 19 contributed to the crash. Several regulatory agencies are currently gathering data in an attempt to align the amount of net sales with particular motivations. A proper analysis should focus on particular shifts in *net sold positions* as a percentage of the total shift in net sold positions in the stock and futures markets, rather than on an analysis of *trading volume*.

For example, an investor who began the day holding 1000 shares of stock and who bought 200 shares and sold 500 shares over the day, would have shifted his net position by 300 sold shares. To determine the total change in net sold stock positions over the day, these figures are value-weighted and added together across all investors selling shares on net during the day.

On Black Monday, about 162,000 S&P 500 futures contracts were traded for a total market value of about $22 billion. In addition, about 604,000,000 NYSE shares of stock were traded, with a market value of about $30 billion. Rough estimates of the dollar value of futures and stock sold by portfolio insurers on that day are $3.5 billion (26,000 contracts) and $2.5 billion, respectively. (I caution that these are very rough estimates, soon to become more accurate as the total size of portfolio insurance trades is made public.) Aggregating these figures together, portfolio insurers accounted for about 11½ per cent of the volume. Including trading on the American and regional exchanges and other index futures contracts, this figure may be reduced to about 9 per cent. If, say, three-quarters of the volume is accounted for by investors reducing their positions in stock and futures, then portfolio insurers would have accounted for about 12 per cent of the dollar change in net sold positions.

Is this "substantial"? It's difficult to say. It was well known from several sources that the amount of equities committed to portfolio insurance strategies was on the order of $60 to $80 billion before the crash. Therefore, one important mitigating factor is that much of the trading should have been anticipated by professional investors. Much more dangerous to the market are traders who unexpectedly revise their positions in the same direction, catching the market unprepared. Finally, it is well to remember that firms with portfolio insurance programs in place did not select these programs at random. For the most part, the programs were self-selected by the insurers' atypically strong desire to protect themselves against losses beyond a specified amount. Many of them might have been sellers during the week of the crash, even without a formal portfolio insurance strategy in place.

There is another important mitigating influence. As long as increases in transaction costs to portfolio insurers go hand-in-hand with rapid shifts in market values, these costs create a natural brake on the impact of portfolio insurance on market prices. A strong case can be made that transaction costs were very high on October 19. Under these conditions, a rational implementation of portfolio insurance would have stopped far short of implementing the full hedge that would have otherwise been called for. Indeed, this is precisely what happened.

We must also remember that the crash had many other potential causes that have been mentioned in the press. A partial list would include (1) the apparently unjustified and unprecedented rapid rise in market prices over the previous year, (2) the Dow's decline of 475 points during the two months previous to October 19, which left many investors poised to press the sell button, (3) fears of increasing interest rates and a resurgence of inflation, (4) dissatisfaction concerning the ability of Congress to control the federal deficit, (5) increasing protectionism in international trade, (6) fear of an increasing trade deficit, a fall in the dollar and a consequent withdrawal from U.S. markets of foreign investors, (7) reports of massive layoffs at securities brokerage firms during early October, (8) the apparent weakness of the executive branch of the federal government, as demonstrated by the Iran/Contra scandal and the failure to secure confirmation of Robert Bork to the Supreme Court, (9) fear of U.S. retaliation against escalating aggressive actions taken by Iran in the Persian Gulf, (10) proposed changes in the tax laws governing mergers and acquisitions, (11) fear that the mechanical structure of the market might fail going into October 19, and (12) observed failures of the structure during the crash.

This last concern was probably the most significant in precipitating the ensuing panic, as specialists closed trading in several large stocks because of order imbalances, as market-makers left the floors of the futures and options exchanges, as the capital of program traders dried up (uncoupling the futures and stock markets), as regulators considered trading halts, as the NYSE's SUPER DOT system for processing program trades experienced a massive mechanical failure because of system overload, as brokers throughout the country failed to answer phones and process clients' orders, as brokerage house and clearing firm failures became likely, and as banks became reluctant to extend loans to specialists and other traders.

The case that portfolio insurance was a substantial contributor to the market crash is also somewhat weakened by the fact that portfolio insurance currently plays a very small role in foreign markets, and yet the crash was international in scope. Finally, it is difficult to blame the subsequent prolonged increased volatility of the stock market on portfolio insurance. These observations strongly suggest that other, more important factors have been at work.

What Should be Done to Reduce the Probability of Crashes?

The continuing challenge to the design of securities markets has been to provide methods of liquid risk transfer among investors, while at the same time assuring the viability of the market mechanism permitting these transfers.

I am concerned that regulatory agencies will fall back on old remedies and fail to seek creative solutions to new problems. In recent years, it seems to me, our securities markets have undergone a significant change: Many large investors seem willing to buy or sell very large blocks of stock or index futures on short notice. Some of these may be portfolio insurers; most are investors attempting to shift their asset allocation for other reasons.

In large part, the willingness to make large trades can be attributed to reductions in the cost of trading. For example, in 1984 turnover on the NYSE reached 49 per cent, $2\frac{1}{2}$ times greater than in 1975, and block trades represented 50 per cent of traded shares, about three times greater than in 1975. In addition, the introduction of index futures in 1982 and index options in 1983, as well as new technology-based methods of programmed trading, have increased the ease with which portfolios of stocks can be traded as a group.

In this new environment, without a substantial expansion of the capitalization of specialists and market-makers, the possibility of exchanges becoming overwhelmed with orders on one side of the market is more likely. There are some proposals for changing the market mechanism, which would reduce this possibility and at the same time increase market liquidity. We should embrace any of these changes immediately.

Formalized voluntary "sunshine" trading

Suppose that, before the S&P 500 futures market opens, you plan to sell 5000 futures contracts at 11:00 if the index stays near its current level. If formal "sunshine" trading were allowed, you would be able to post these intentions on a bulletin board at the Chicago Mercantile Exchange before the opening of the market at 8:30; your trading intentions would also be carried via computer to broker-dealers all around the country. To prevent price manipulation, you would be required, as a sunshine trader, to carry out the trade if your stated conditions were met.

Many large traders, such as portfolio insurers, whose trades are not motivated by information may be attracted to sunshine trading as a way of creating a more orderly market to handle the other side of their trades. While the advisability for an investor of this form of trading is controversial among professionals, it should nonetheless be encouraged; voluntary advance disclosure of trading intentions can only enhance liquidity, compared with the alternative of suddenly surprising the market with a large order.

While the proposal submitted by the New York Futures Exchange to the CFTC concerning disclosure of trading intentions has not yet been approved, I believe the CFTC is likely to permit this type of trading in index futures when computer systems have been revised by data vendors to carry notification of sunshine trades. Unfortunately, vendors of prices may not voluntarily revise their software to carry such notification until there are sunshine trades to announce; so the proposal seems stymied at this juncture. I would hope that the parties involved would be encouraged to work together to make formalized sunshine trading a reality.

Sunshine trading should also be permitted on other markets. Many exchanges may actively resist sunshine trading proposals because such trading tends to lead to a matching of public orders with each other, thereby circumventing the inter-mediation role played by specialists and market-makers.

Periodic single-price auctions

The closest thing to an ideal single-price auction occurs at the opening on the NYSE. Supplies and demands are aggregated and executed at a single price – the lowest accepted bid and the highest accepted offer (which are the same). All market orders, limit orders to buy higher than that price, and limit orders to sell lower than that price are filled. If a trading imbalance occurs, the imbalance is announced and investors have a chance to change their orders.

Single-price auctions should be held at other times during the trading day, not just at the open. Like sunshine trading, single-price auctions take the pressure off the specialists or market-makers and reduce the damage to their capital during times of rapid price change in the same direction. Again, however, this is a proposal that may be resisted by exchanges because it also leads to circumvention of the normal intermediation services performed by specialists and market-makers.[3]

Side-by-side trading of related securities

Consider trading an underlying stock and its associated options contracts at the same physical location. Hedged positions would be easier to execute, economies of scale and the reduction of information trading should reduce transaction costs, and illegal trading practices would be more easily detected. Of course, the trading of options and stocks together would entail a major restructuring of those markets and would face considerable opposition from entrenched interests.[4]

Reduced margin for fully-hedged futures positions

There seems to be little reason to increase margin requirements for investors who are completely hedged, because these investors are already effectively 100 per cent margined.[5] For example, an investor who holds a diversified portfolio of common stocks should be able to sell futures covering a large portion of the value of the stock portfolio with very little, if any, required margin. Mechanisms should be in place that would allow that investor to pledge his stock portfolio as collateral and meet calls for variation margin by temporarily borrowing against that collateral, with the requirement that he liquidate his stock portfolio as needed in an orderly fashion.

During the week of October 19, several hedgers were forced to sell stock at a discount to raise variation margin due the next business day. Under this proposal, hedgers would be allowed to borrow temporarily to meet variation margin and to liquidate their stock to pay off the loan under the normal five-day stock-settlement procedure.

Alignment of margin requirements

I have wondered for some time why initial and maintenance margins on exchange-traded common stocks were 50 per cent and 30 per cent, respectively, while speculative maintenance margins in index futures contracts, prior to October 19, were about 7 per cent. Futures positions are resettled every day, but the marking-to-the-market of maintenance margins on stocks is quite similar. The typical individual stock is clearly more risky than a stock market index, but this relatively small differential in risks hardly justifies such a large differential in margin requirements. The truth is that margin requirements are to a large extent an accident of history, in part the result of the division of the regulation of financial instruments between the SEC and the CFTC.

Increases in speculative margin or capital requirements

The lower the level of speculative margin requirements, during times of normal market volatility, the easier it is for investors to take positions and the greater the liquidity of the market. During times of high volatility, however, investors with little margin may become overextended and be forced to sell or buy, compounding the problems that arise when the market has to absorb a lot of volume from one direction. Or investors such as specialists and market-makers may simply be forced to step aside because of inadequate capitalization. Ironically, as we have recently witnessed, the very provisions that lead to high liquidity in times of normal volatility can cause liquidity to dry up during periods of high volatility.

The level of initial speculative margin required for S&P 500 futures contracts was raised from $10,000 per contract before October 19 to its current level of $20,000 per contract, or to about 12 per cent of the value of the stock underlying the contract. Many individuals believe that this requirement is still too low. Should this requirement be raised?

Many products are purposely engineered with specific stochastic failure rates built in. For example, it simply does not pay to manufacture a car that will never break down. This same principle applies to the market for stocks. After over 50 years of more or less uninterrupted service, the market finally experienced two or three days when it failed to function as usual and came close to a total breakdown. Should we re-engineer the market to reduce further the probability of failure, or should we save costs during normal times and be content with the current built-in failure rate? The answer will depend both on the extent of the damage incurred during a failure and the expected frequency of failure.

In general, because speculative margin requirements should depend on the volatility of underlying assets, margin should be raised above normal levels during times of high volatility, such as we are now experiencing. This provides a case for temporarily increasing required margin for stocks as well as for unhedged options and futures. However, I believe it is a mistake to change margin requirements without ample warning, particularly during a period when the market is very vulnerable to sudden large changes in prices. Increasing requirements at these times can easily increase instability.

Although increases in speculative futures margins may be advisable, I suggest that forced sales by speculators in index futures to cover variation margin played a small role in the market crash. By contrast, sales by margined investors in the stock market almost surely played a much larger role, if for no other reason than that the market value of outstanding shares is far larger than the market value of the assets underlying the open interest in index futures.

Increasing speculative margin requirements obviously involves a tradeoff, in terms of liquidity, between low-volatility and high-volatility environments. Other proposals, such as the one described below, would reduce liquidity with little compensating benefit.

Price-move limits for index futures

Thirty-point limits were imposed on S&P 500 index futures contracts on October 23 and remain in force as of this writing. It has been argued that such limits (1) provide more time for investors to raise variation margin, (2) reduce the potential size of errors made by floor traders, thereby substantially reducing the likelihood in fast-moving markets of a floor trader bringing down his clearing firm to make up for his own bankruptcy, (3) provide time for clearing firms to reassess the credit they should extend to investors whose accounts they guarantee, (4) reduce the tendencies of investors who know they are in default to "double-up" their bets before they are forced to stop trading, (5) reduce the probability that an investor will voluntarily default on a futures position, (6) give the futures market time to adjust calmly to quickly moving prices and thereby reduce the magnitude of price whipsaws when investors are acting under panic, (7) prevent the index futures market from being blamed for abetting substantial declines in the stock market, and (8) represent an historically accepted way of controlling the magnitude of price changes in futures markets.

These arguments are far from compelling. No price-limit rule is going to be able to distinguish between a panicked reaction and a fundamentally justified price change. In the latter case, price limits trap investors into positions, substantially increasing their risk. A sequence of price-limit moves in the same direction can impose huge unavoidable losses. In the extreme, we have the infamous example of the Hong Kong Stock Exchange, which shut down trading for a week, thereby trapping many investors into untenable positions.

A further problem with limits is the tendency of the limit to act as a price magnet: As the futures price approaches the limit, the actions of investors, all fearful of being locked into their positions, drive the price even further toward the limit.

Finally, just as in the case of margins, I believe it is a mistake to impose or strengthen price limits during periods of sudden increases in market volatility. For example, in the first four days after October 19, the S&P 500 index futures price at the open gapped down 18.25 points, up 20.5 points, up 23.75 points and down 48.25 points in daily succession. It thus appeared that the 30-point limit imposed on the fifth day was very likely to be triggered (although, fortuitously, it was not). If the futures market had subsequently moved strongly up, we might have seen hedged investors with sold futures positions desperately buying back futures and selling stocks to meet variation margin. With the relative absence of program trading, this could have pushed futures prices toward their limit, while at the same time causing stock prices to fall.

How Will Portfolio Insurance Strategies be Modified?

In many cases, portfolio insurance strategies did not perform as expected during the market crash because of unexpected and sudden increases in transaction costs and large discontinuities in market prices. I believe it is prudent to presume that the probability of witnessing these kinds of markets again, at least for the near future, is much higher than one would have thought before the crash.

In addition, to providers of portfolio insurance, both index futures and options markets are for the time being much less useful than before the crash. Trading volume in both these markets has been cut in half, bid-ask spreads have widened, margin requirements for hedgers have been increased, price-move limits have been imposed on index futures, and the regulatory environment continues to be highly uncertain.

Even so, with the doubling of stock market volatility and the events of the week of October 19 so savagely imprinted on investors' minds, the demand continues for some form of portfolio insurance that can be delivered under current conditions.

The preference-based case for dynamic strategies remains unchanged. That is (in general terms), those who are sufficiently more concerned about downside risk than the average investor should attempt to buy insurance. Those who are sufficiently less concerned about downside risk than the average investor should attempt to sell insurance. All others should buy and hold.[6]

Those who proclaim the death of preference-based motivations for dynamic strategies are presupposing an implausible reformation of natural human desires. Nonetheless, the nature of the dynamic strategies investors will follow in the future will differ in several important ways from the strategies employed before the crash.

Alternative buying strategies

Even before the crash, it seemed that many investors who had attempted to buy portfolio insurance had selected policies containing "too much insurance." For example, an investor might choose a one-year policy with a minimum rate of return of zero. Although he might start out about 65 per cent invested in equities and 35 per cent invested in cash, as the expiration date approached he might soon find his portfolio either with almost nothing invested in equities (if the stock market fell) or with almost 100 per cent in equities (if the stock market rose). As this began to happen, most investors would find some reason to ratchet back to a more balanced position. After the crash, when many insured investors were completely in cash, and required by the initial policy to remain in cash for some time, these investors showed their true intentions by quickly "reinsuring" and moving to a more balanced position. It was not that these investors did not want insurance; rather, they wanted much less insurance than indicated by their initially stated intentions.

The extreme insurance policies selected by many investors could only be justified by a correspondingly extreme aversion to downside risk. As their subsequent actions revealed, a more appropriate policy for them would have been one that moved more slowly out of equities and into cash as the market fell (perhaps with a minimum exposure to equities of 25 per cent) and moved more slowly from cash into equities as the market rose (perhaps with a maximum exposure to equities of 85 per cent). I expect to see more strategies of this type in the future.[7]

In addition, I expect to see a greater emphasis by pension funds on "surplus" insurance rather than pension fund asset insurance.[8] This form of portfolio insurance typically requires much less trading than purely asset-based insurance.

Explicit selling of insurance

As the purchase of portfolio insurance became popular, it was surprising that few investors explicitly wanted to sell insurance. The other side of the market, to some extent supplied by rebalancers and investors following tactical asset allocation, was not well-organized.

Today, because of increased volatility, the apparent price of insurance is much higher than it was before the crash. Moreover, even when (if?) realized stock volatility falls back to more traditional levels, realistic pricing of insurance will probably be higher than before the crash. Under these circumstances, I believe, the market is likely to be better balanced, with explicit sellers as well as purchasers of insurance.

Transaction-cost-sensitive strategies

To the extent transaction costs increase, fewer investors should engage in dynamic strategies. Only investors with attitudes toward downside risk very different from those of the average investor should consider dynamic strategies, and the dynamic strategies they should select should require less trading. The minimum-and-maximum-exposure strategy, surplus insurance and insurance of balanced, rather than pure equity, portfolios have all reduced expected portfolio turnover. There will also be more implementation of portfolio insurance utilizing spot, rather than futures, markets, not only as a way of controlling the impact of the basis, but also in response to the reduced usefulness of the futures markets.

For some insurance strategies, higher transaction costs increase the barrier around the ideal hedge ratio until a trade is triggered. The size of this barrier is continually adjusted in an attempt to create an optimal tradeoff between the expected level of realized transaction costs and the accuracy of delivery of the target payoff pattern. This tends to reduce portfolio turnover during periods of high transaction costs. But this adjustment only goes partway toward reflecting the full impact of variable transaction costs, because it leaves the target payoff pattern unchanged. This target pattern was probably chosen under an assumption concerning the level of transaction costs. Insurers need to find a way to adjust the target as transaction costs change during the life of a policy.

Unfortunately, significantly variable transaction costs during the life of a policy substantially complicate the task of delivering a specified payoff pattern with accuracy. Both buyers and sellers of portfolio insurance, implemented either in the spot or futures markets, must learn to tolerate increased unpredictability of outcome.

Increased use of exchange-traded options

The second precondition of successful portfolio insurance using spot or futures markets is market price continuity. Listed options clearly provide a way around this problem. Protection against discontinuities may come at a price, but many insurers may find the benefits worth that price.[9]

Unfortunately, the size of an individual investor's (or group of investors') position in CBOE index options on the S&P 100 or S&P 500 on one side of the market is limited to 15,000 contracts in the near maturity.[10] This limit severely reduces the interest of the largest investors in implementation of portfolio insurance with options.

Implications

Under post-crash conditions, successful implementation of a systematic dynamic strategy is more difficult, requiring a mixture of trading in the underlying spot assets, in futures and in options. Uncertainty about the level of transaction costs, potential discontinuities in market prices and uncertainty in the regulatory environment increase the difficulty of predicting the outcome from any type of dynamic strategy. Understandably, the demand for portfolio insurance has fallen off. Moving forward, we are likely to see increased technological sophistication and a more balanced variety of dynamic strategies in the future.

Notes

The author thanks Tony Baker, Fisher Black, Michael Brennan, Larry Edwards, Jeremy Evnine, Bob Ferguson, Scott Grannis, Chris Hynes, Pete Kyle, Hayne Leland, Terry Marsh, Robert Merton, Merton Miller, David Modest, Girish Reddy, Richard Sandor and Andy Turner for their helpful conversations.

1. See M. Rubinstein and H. Leland, "Replicating Options with Positions in Stock and Cash," *Financial Analysts Journal*, July/August 1981, p. 66.
2. The capital of program traders able to take arbitrage positions by selling stock they already owned was for the most part absorbed by positions taken prior to the crash. Other program traders who rely on short selling were largely shut out by the short-sale up-tick rule. In addition, trading delays substantially increased the risk of arbitrage-related transactions.
3. For a much more detailed analysis of single-price auctions, see Steven Wunsch's discussion in Kidder, Peabody's *Stock Index Futures* commentary dated October 29, 1987.
4. See J. Cox and M. Rubinstein, *Options Markets* (Englewood Cliffs, NJ: Prentice-Hall, 1985), p. 86.
5. Prior to October 19, futures hedgers were required to deposit $5,000 per contract; now the requirement has been raised to $15,000 per contract.
6. Compared with investors who buy and hold, buyers (sellers) of insurance adopt strategies that systematically transfer wealth toward (away from) risky assets and away from (toward) less risky assets as the relative values of risky assets rise (fall), and do the opposite as risky asset values fall.
7. Well before the crash, investors were moving in this direction by selecting longer-term policies (which also tend to moderate trading in the early years of the policy), but even these investors would be faced with taking extreme positions near the end of the policy. Some insurance vendors have attempted to replicate these more complex policies with minimum and maximum exposures, but potential clients seemed to prefer the simplicity of the more extreme forms of insurance.
8. Surplus is defined as the difference or the ratio of the market values of the assets and liabilities of the pension fund.
9. In a Black-Scholes environment, options are priced as if investors are risk-neutral. But, by their assumption, price movements are continuous. In discontinuous markets, it is possible that options may be priced relative to their underlying assets with built-in risk premiums. This could raise the market prices of most options above their Black-Scholes values.
10. The limits are 25,000 contracts irrespective of maturity. However, longer-maturity options have poor liquidity, and positions greater than 15,000 contracts must be reduced to that number when the options become the nearest maturity contracts.

SECTION D

Over-the-counter Markets

18

The Role of Interest Rate Swaps in Corporate Finance

Anatoli Kuprianov

An interest rate swap is a contractual agreement between two parties to exchange a series of interest rate payments without exchanging the underlying debt. The interest rate swap represents one example of a general category of financial instruments known as derivative instruments. In the most general terms, a derivative instrument is an agreement whose value derives from some underlying market return, market price, or price index.

The rapid growth of the market for swaps and other derivatives in recent years has spurred considerable controversy over the economic rationale for these instruments. Many observers have expressed alarm over the growth and size of the market, arguing that interest rate swaps and other derivative instruments threaten the stability of financial markets. Recently, such fears have led both legislators and bank regulators to consider measures to curb the growth of the market. Several legislators have begun to promote initiatives to create an entirely new regulatory agency to supervise derivatives trading activity. Underlying these initiatives is the premise that derivative instruments increase aggregate risk in the economy, either by encouraging speculation or by burdening firms with risks that management does not understand fully and is incapable of controlling.[1] To be certain, much of this criticism is aimed at many of the more exotic derivative instruments that have begun to appear recently. Nevertheless, it is difficult, if not impossible, to appreciate the economic role of these more exotic instruments without an understanding of the role of the interest rate swap, the most basic of the new generation of financial derivatives.

Although the factors accounting for the remarkable growth of the swaps market are yet to be fully understood, financial economists have proposed a number of different hypotheses to explain how and why firms use interest rate swaps. The early explanation, popular among market participants, was that interest rate swaps lowered financing costs by making it possible for firms to arbitrage the mispricing of credit risk. If this were the only rationale for interest rate swaps, however, it would mean that these instruments exist only to facilitate a way around market inefficiencies and should become redundant once arbitrage leads market participants to begin pricing credit risk correctly. Thus, trading in interest rate swaps should die out over time as arbitrage opportunities disappear – a prediction that is at odds with actual experience.

Other observers note that the advent of the interest rate swap coincided with a period of extraordinary volatility in U.S. market interest rates, leading them to attribute the rapid growth of interest rate derivatives to the desire on the part of firms to hedge cash flows against the effects of interest rate volatility. The timing of the appearance of interest rate swaps, coming as it did during a period of volatile rates, seems to lend support to such arguments. Risk avoidance alone cannot explain the growth of the swaps market, however, because firms can always protect themselves against rising interest rates simply by taking out fixed-rate, long-term loans or by bypassing credit markets altogether and issuing equity to fund investments.

Recent research emphasizes that interest rate swaps offer firms new financing choices that were just not available before the advent of these instruments, and thus represent a true financial innovation. This research suggests that the financing choices made available by interest rate swaps may help to reduce default risk and may sometimes make it possible for firms to undertake productive investments that would not be feasible otherwise. The discussion that follows explains the basic mechanics of interest rate swaps and examines these rationales in more detail.

1. Fundamentals of Interest Rate Swaps

The most common type of interest rate swap is the fixed/floating swap in which a fixed-rate payer promises to make periodic payments based on a fixed interest rate to a floating-rate payer, who in turn agrees to make variable payments indexed to some short-term interest rate. Conventionally, the parties to the agreement are termed counterparties. The size of the payments exchanged by the counterparties is based on some stipulated notional principal amount, which itself is not paid or received.

Interest rate swaps are traded over the counter. The over-the-counter (OTC) market is comprised of a group of dealers, consisting of major international commercial and investment banks, who communicate offers to buy and sell swaps over telecommunications networks. Swap dealers intermediate cash flows between different customers, acting as middlemen for each transaction. These dealers act as market makers who quote bid and asked prices at which they stand ready to either buy or sell an interest rate swap before a customer for the other half of the transaction can be found. (By convention, the fixed-rate payer in an interest rate swap is termed the buyer, while the floating-rate payer is termed the seller.) The quoted spread allows the dealer to receive a higher payment from one counterparty than is paid to the other.

Because swap dealers act as intermediaries, a swap customer need be concerned only with the financial condition of the dealer and not with the creditworthiness of the other ultimate counterparty to the agreement. Counter-party credit risk refers to the risk that a counterparty to an interest rate swap will default when the agreement has value to the other party.[2] Managing the credit risk associated with swap transactions requires credit-evaluation skills similar to those commonly associated with bank lending. As a result, commercial banks, which have traditionally specialized in credit-risk evaluation and have the capital reserves necessary to support credit-risk management, have come to dominate the market for interest rate swaps (Smith, Smithson, and Wakeman 1986).

The discussion that follows largely abstracts from counterparty credit risk and the role of swap dealers. In addition, the description of interest rate swaps is stylized

and omits many market conventions and other details so as to focus on the fundamental economic features of swap transactions. For a more detailed description of
interest rate swaps and other interest rate derivatives, see Kuprianov (1993b).
Burghardt et al. (1991) and Marshall and Kapner (1993) provide more comprehensive treatments.

Mechanics of a fixed/floating swap

The quoted price of an interest rate swap consists of two different interest rates. In
the case of a fixed/floating swap, the quoted interest rates involve a fixed and a floating rate. The floating interest rate typically is indexed to some market-determined
rate such as the Treasury bill rate or, more commonly, the three-or six-month
London Interbank Offered Rate, or LIBOR.[3] Such a swap is also known as a
generic, or plain-vanilla, swap.

The basic mechanics of a fixed/floating swap are relatively straightforward.
Consider an interest rate swap in which the parties to the agreement agree to
exchange payments at the end of each of T periods, indexed by the variable $t = 1$,
$2, \ldots, T$. Let $\bar{r}^s$ denote the fixed rate and $r^s(t)$ denote the floating interest rate on
a fixed/floating swap. Payments between the fixed- and floating-rate payers commonly are scheduled for the same dates, in which case only net amounts owed are
exchanged. The net cost of the swap to the fixed-rate payer at the end of each
period would be $\bar{r}^s - r^s(t)$ for each \$1 of notional principal. If the swap's fixed rate
is greater than the variable rate at the end of a period (i.e., $\bar{r}^s > r^s(t)$), then fixed-
rate payer must pay the difference between the fixed interest payment on the notional principal to the floating-rate payer. Otherwise, the difference $\bar{r}^s - r^s(t)$ is
negative, meaning that the fixed-rate payer receives the difference from the floating-
rate payer. The net cost of the swap to the floating-rate payer is just the negative
of this amount. For the sake of notational convenience, the discussion that follows
assumes that all swaps have a notional principal of \$1, unless otherwise noted.

Uses of interest rate swaps – synthetic financing

Firms use interest rate swaps to change the effective maturity of interest-bearing
assets or liabilities. To illustrate, suppose a firm has short-term bank debt outstanding. At the start of each period this firm refinances its debt at the prevailing short-
term interest rate, $r^b(t)$. If short-term market interest rates are volatile, then the
firm's financing costs will be volatile as well. By entering into an interest rate swap,
the firm can change its short-term floating-rate debt into a synthetic fixed-rate
obligation.

Suppose the firm enters into an interest rate swap as a fixed-rate payer. Its resulting net payments in each period $t = 1, 2, \ldots, T$ of the agreement are determined
by adding the net payments required of a fixed-rate payer to the cost of servicing
its outstanding floating-rate debt.

Period t cost of servicing outstanding short-term debt	$r^b(t)$
+ Period t cost of interest rate swap payments	$\bar{r}^s - r^s(t)$
= Period t cost of synthetic fixed-rate financing	$\bar{r}^s + [r^b(t) - r^s(t)]$

Thus, the net cost of the synthetic fixed-rate financing is determined by the swap fixed rate plus the difference between its short-term borrowing rate and the floating-rate index.

Banks often index the short-term loan rates they charge their corporate customers to LIBOR. Suppose the firm in this example is able to borrow at LIBOR plus a credit-quality risk premium, or credit-quality spread, $q(t)$. Suppose further that the swap's floating-rate index is LIBOR. Then,

$$r^b(t) - r^s(t) = [\text{LIBOR}(t) + q(t)] - \text{LIBOR}(t)$$
$$= q(t).$$

The period t cost of synthetic fixed-rate financing in this case is just $\bar{r}^s + q(t)$, the swap fixed rate plus the short-term credit-quality spread $q(t)$.

Now consider the other side to this transaction. Suppose a firm with outstanding fixed-rate debt on which it pays an interest rate of $\bar{r}^b$ enters into a swap as a floating-rate payer so as to convert its fixed-rate obligation to a synthetic floating-rate note. The net period t cost of this synthetic note is just the cost of its fixed-rate obligation plus the net cost of the swap:

Period t cost of synthetic floating-rate note = $r^s(t) + (\bar{r}^b - \bar{r}^s)$.

The cost of synthetic floating-rate financing just equals the floating rate on the interest rate swap plus the difference between the interest rate the firm pays on its outstanding fixed-rate debt and the fixed interest rate it receives from its swap counterparty.

Thus, interest rate swaps can be used to change the characteristics of a firm's outstanding debt obligations. Using interest rate swaps, firms can change floating-rate debt into synthetic fixed-rate financing or, alternatively, a fixed-rate obligation into synthetic floating-rate financing. But these observations raise an obvious question. Why would a firm issue short-term debt only to swap its interest payments into a longer-term, fixed-rate obligation rather than just issue long-term, fixed-rate debt at the outset? Conversely, why would a firm issue long-term debt and swap it into synthetic floating-rate debt rather than simply issuing floating-rate debt at the outset? The next two sections explore the rationales that have been offered to explain the widespread use of interest rate swaps.

2. Interest Rate Swaps, Arbitrage, and the Theory of Comparative Advantage

The rapid growth of the swaps market in recent years strongly suggests that market participants must perceive significant benefits associated with the use of such instruments. The rationale most frequently offered by market participants is that interest rate swaps offer users an opportunity to reduce funding costs.[4] Bicksler and Chen (1986) present what is perhaps the best-known exposition of this viewpoint, which is based on the principle of comparative advantage. In international trade theory, the principle of comparative advantage explains the economic rationale for international trade by showing how different countries facing different opportunity costs in the production of different goods can benefit from free trade with other countries. According to Bicksler and Chen, differential information in different markets, institutional restrictions, and transactions costs create "some market imperfections and the presence of comparative advantages among different borrowers in these markets" (p. 646). These market imperfections, according to Bicksler and Chen, provide the economic rationale for interest rate swaps.

The quality-spread differential

All firms pay a credit-quality premium over the risk-free rate when they issue debt securities. These credit-quality premiums grow larger as the maturity of the debt increases. Thus, whereas a firm, call it firm A, might pay a credit-risk premium of 50 basis points over the risk-free rate on its short-term debt obligations, the credit-quality premium it is required to pay on longer-term debt, say, ten-year bonds, might rise to 100 basis points.

Not surprisingly, firms with good credit ratings pay lower risk premiums than firms with lower credit ratings. Moreover, the credit-quality premium rises faster with maturity for poorer credits than for good credits. Thus, if firm B has a poorer credit rating than firm A, it might pay a credit-risk premium of 100 basis points on its short-term debt while finding it necessary to pay 250 basis points over the risk-free rate to issue long-term bonds. The quality spread between the interest rate paid by the lower-rated firm and that paid by the higher-rated firm is only 50 basis points in the short-term debt market, but rises to 150 basis points at longer maturities. The quality-spread differential, the difference in the quality spread at two different maturities, is 100 basis points in this example. Firm A has an absolute cost advantage in raising funds in either the short- or long-term debt markets, but firm B has a comparative advantage in raising funds in short-term debt markets.

To explore this line of reasoning in more detail, suppose firms A and B both need to borrow funds for the next two periods, $t = 1, 2$. Let $r^f(t)$ denote the period t short-term (one-period) risk-free interest rate and r^J the long-term (two-period) fixed risk-free rate. The period t cost of short-term debt to firm A is the short-term risk-free rate plus the credit-quality spread $q_A(t)$. To issue long-term fixed-rate debt, firm A would be required to pay $r^J + \overline{q_A}$, where $\overline{q_A}$ denotes the long-term quality spread. Define $q_B(t)$ and $\overline{q_B}$ analogously. Assuming firm A has the better credit rating,

$$q_A(1) \leq q_B(1), \text{ and}$$

$$\overline{q_A} \leq \overline{q_B}.$$

An increasing quality spread means that

$$q_B(1) - q_A(1) < \overline{q_B} - \overline{q_A}.$$

Conditions necessary for arbitrage to be feasible

Under certain assumptions, both firms could lower their funding costs if firm A were to issue long-term debt, firm B were to issue short-term debt, and they swapped interest payments. To see how this would work, assume A and B enter into an interest rate swap with B as a fixed-rate payer and A as the floating-rate payer. As above, let $\bar{r}^s$ denote the fixed swap rate for a two-period agreement. To minimize the notational burden, assume that the swap floating rate is just the risk-free rate of interest, $r^f(t)$. The resulting period t ($t = 1, 2$) net cost of synthetic fixed-rate financing to firm B is:

Period t cost of servicing short-term, floating-rate debt	$r^f(t) + q_B(t)$
+ Period t cost of interest rate swap	$\bar{r}^s - r^f(t)$
= Period t cost of synthetic fixed-rate financing	$\bar{r}^s + q_B(t)$

The synthetic fixed-rate financing will be less costly for firm B than actual fixed-rate financing in each period t if and only if

$$\bar{r}^s + q_B(t) \le \bar{r}^f + \bar{q}_B,$$

which implies

$$\bar{r}^s - \bar{r}^f \le \bar{q}_B - q_B(t).$$

The term on the left-hand side of the last expression is the swap fixed-rate credit-quality spread, or risk premium, over the risk-free long-term interest rate. Thus, the quality spread associated with the swap fixed rate must be less than the increase in the credit-risk premium firm B would need to pay to issue long-term debt. Otherwise, synthetic fixed-rate financing will not be cheaper than actual fixed-rate financing.

Now examine the transaction from the vantage point of firm A, the floating-rate payer. The cost of synthetic floating-rate financing is determined by the cost of servicing fixed-rate debt plus the net cost of he swap:

Period t cost of servicing fixed-rate debt	$\bar{r}^f + \bar{q}_A$
+ Period t cost of swap	$r^s(t) - \bar{r}^s$
= Period t cost of synthetic floating-rate financing	$r^s(t) + (\bar{r}^f + \bar{q}_A - \bar{r}^s)$

Period t synthetic floating-rate financing will cost less than actual floating-rate financing for firm A if

$$r^s(t) + (\bar{r}^f + \bar{q}_A - \bar{r}_s) \le r^s(t) + q_A(t),$$

Which, in turn, requires that

$$\bar{q}_A - q_A(t) \le \bar{r}^s - \bar{r}^f.$$

That is, the increase in the credit-quality premium firm A must pay when issuing long-term fixed-rate debt must be smaller than the risk premium it receives from the swap's fixed-rate payer.

Combining results, firm A will have a comparative advantage in issuing long-term debt and firm B in issuing short-term debt if

$$\overline{q_A} - q_A(t) \leq \overline{r^s} - \overline{r^f} \leq \overline{q_B} - q_B(t), \qquad\qquad t = 1, 2.$$

For the floating-rate payer, synthetic floating-rate financing is cheaper than actual short-term financing if the interest rate swap quality spread (which the floating-rate payer receives) is greater than the added interest expense of long-term debt. For the fixed-rate payer, synthetic fixed-rate financing is less costly than issuing long-term bonds if the premium of the fixed swap rate over the two-period risk-free rate is less than the difference between its long-term and short-term quality spreads. Both parties will enjoy gains from trade if the swap floating-rate payer charges the fixed-rate payer a smaller credit-quality spread than the fixed-rate payer would be forced to pay in the bond market.

The astute reader will notice that the conditions outlined above require the parties to the agreement to know future values of $q_A(t)$ and $q_B(t)$. Both firms know their current short-term quality spreads along with $\overline{q_A}$ and $\overline{q_B}$ at the start of period 1. But it is unrealistic to assume that firms will know their future short-term quality spreads with certainty. Bicksler and Chen (1986) implicitly assume that firms expect the above relations to hold (at least on average) based on the past behavior of the quality-spread differential.

There is empirical evidence that long-term quality spreads for lower-rated counterparties are lower in the interest rate swap market than in credit markets (Sun, Sundaresan, and Wang 1993). Smith, Smithson, and Wakeman (1988) and Litzenberger (1992), among others, note that the expected loss to a swap counterparty in the event of a default is much less than that associated with holding a bond because interest rate swaps are not funding transactions and involve no exchange of principal. Moreover, swaps receive preferential treatment under the Bankruptcy Code in the event of a default. Under these conditions it may not seem surprising to find that quality spreads do not increase as rapidly in the swap market and that the cost of synthetic fixed-rate financing often seems lower than that of actual long-term financing. But while interest rate swaps might offer firms a way around paying increasing quality-spread differentials, synthetic fixed-rate financing does not offer firms the proverbial "free lunch." As the following discussion will show, the risks responsible for increasing quality-spread differentials do not disappear when firms use interest rate swaps.

Criticisms of the comparative advantage rationale

Smith, Smithson, and Wakeman (1986, 1988) argue that observed behavior in the swap market is not consistent with classic financial arbitrage of the type described by proponents of the comparative advantage rationale. The use of interest rate swaps to arbitrage quality-spread differentials, they argue, should increase the demand for short-term loans among firms with poor credit ratings while reducing demand for "overpriced" long-term loans. Eventually, such a process should reduce quality-spread differentials and therefore reduce demand for interest rate swaps. In fact, Bicksler and Chen (1986) did report evidence of declining quality-spread differentials as interest rate swaps came into widespread use. But trading activity in interest rate swaps has shown no sign of abating even as quality-spread differentials have declined. To the contrary, the market for interest rate swaps has grown exponentially since these instruments were first introduced in the early 1980s. According to the International Swap and Derivatives Association, the total notional principal amount of interest rate swaps outstanding has risen from $683 billion in 1987 to just over $3.8 trillion as of year-end 1992.

Smith, Smithson, and Wakeman (1986, 1988) observe that much of the apparent savings from the use of swaps can be attributed to the absence of a prepayment option on generic swaps. Fixed-rate bonds typically carry a prepayment option that allows the borrower to call and refund a debt issue should market interest rates fall. The cost of this option is incorporated into the interest rate the firm is required to pay on such bonds. In contrast, the generic interest rate swap carries no such prepayment option. Early termination of a swap agreement requires the value of the contract to be marked to market, with any remaining amounts to be paid in full. A borrower can buy a "callable" swap, which permits early termination, but must pay an additional premium for this option. Thus, to be fair, the cost of actual long-term debt should be compared to the cost of callable synthetic fixed-rate financing, which would reduce the measured cost advantage resulting from the use of interest rate swaps.

Another problem with the comparative advantage rationale, noted by Smith, Smithson, and Wakeman (1988), is that it does not address the underlying reason for the existence of quality-spread differentials between short- and long-term debt. Loeys (1985) notes that short-term creditors implicitly hold an option to refuse to refinance outstanding loans. He attributes the difference in quality spreads between short- and long-term debt to the value of that implicit option.[5] But while this option is valuable to lenders, it increases the risk of a future funding crisis to the borrowing firm, thereby increasing the risk of bankruptcy proceedings. The risk that lenders will refuse to refinance outstanding short-term debt is known as liquidity risk, or rollover risk. From the firm's perspective, added liquidity risk represents an implicit cost of short-term financing.

Bansal, Bicksler, Chen, and Marshall (1993) compare the cost of synthetic fixed-rate financing with the cost of actual fixed-rate financing when the hidden costs noted above are taken into account. They control for the cost of liquidity risk by adding in the expense of a bank standby letter of credit in which a bank guarantees that it will assume a firm's outstanding debt if the firm finds itself unable to roll over a commercial paper issue. To take account of the value of a prepayment option, they add the premium on a callable swap into the total cost of synthetic fixed-rate financing. Finally, they also take account of transactions and administrative costs. The cost advantage of synthetic fixed-rate financing disappears once these costs are taken into account. Bansal et al. conclude that "a significant part of the reputed gains from swaps . . . were illusory, stemming from the way the gains have been calculated in practice" (p. 91).

3. Alternative Explanations

Smith, Smithson, and Wakeman (1988) hypothesize that the rationale for interest rate swaps lies with their usefulness in creating new synthetic financial instruments

for risk management. The early 1980s brought unprecedented interest rate volatility, exposing firms to the risk of fluctuating funding costs. Rawls and Smithson
(1990) argue that these events led to an increased demand for risk-management
services on the part of firms. Smith, Smithson, and Wakeman (1988) argue that
the growth of the swaps market effectively increased market liquidity for forward
interest rate contracts, citing rapidly falling bid-ask spreads for interest rate swaps
as evidence.[6] Thus, they argue, trading in interest rate swaps has helped to complete
forward markets and to lower the cost to firms of managing their exposure to
interest rate risk.

The role for hedging in the theory of corporate finance

The foregoing discussion has focused on increased volatility in financial markets
as the major factor behind the growth of the derivatives market in recent years.
That firms would wish to hedge against the risk of such volatility simply has been
assumed. But as Smith, Smithson, and Wilford (1989) note, much of textbook
portfolio theory suggests that not hedging might be a firm's best policy. The well-
known Modigliani-Miller theorem states that a firm's financing decisions have
no effect on its market value when (1) a firm's management and outside investors
share the same information about the returns accruing to all investment projects; (2)
transactions costs are negligible; (3) a firm's tax bill is not affected by its financing
decisions; and (4) the costs of financial distress are inconsequential. Under these
assumptions, portfolio theory holds that individual investors can efficiently diver-
sify away volatility in individual firm profits at least as well as the firms themselves.
If so, there is no reason for firms to expend resources hedging against volatility in
future cash flows.

When these assumptions are relaxed, however, financing decisions may affect a
firm's value. First, a firm's managers can be expected to know more about the risks
and returns to different investment projects than outside investors. Second, the
existence of transactions costs makes some kinds of financing decisions more costly
than others. Third, a volatile cash flow stream can make a firm more susceptible to
financial distress and bankruptcy, which can be extremely costly as well as threat-
ening management with loss of control. Fourth, existing tax laws favor certain
forms of funding over others. Firms are permitted to treat interest payments on
debt as a tax-deductible expense, but not dividend payments to shareholders.
Moreover, tax laws sometimes favor the use of certain derivative instruments to
restructure cash flows. For all these reasons, firms will sometimes have incentives
to hedge their cash flows.

Agency costs as a rationale for interest rate swaps: incentives to undertake synthetic fixed-rate financing

Miller (1977) stresses the tax advantages of debt to explain why firms finance their
investments with a combination of debt and equity. As Jensen and Meckling (1976)
note, however, firms issued debt long before corporate income taxes came into
existence. As an alternative rationale for debt, Jensen and Meckling emphasize the
difficulty outside investors face in evaluating the performance of managers. As
defined by Jensen and Meckling, an agency relationship is "a contract under which

one or more persons (the principal(s)) engage another person (the agent) to perform some service on their behalf which involves delegating some decision making authority to the agent" (p. 308). If principals could always costlessly monitor the behavior of their agents, they could ensure that agents would always act in their best interests. Monitoring the behavior of agents is costly, however, and requires principals to expend resources. Thus, the agent might be required to incur certain bonding expenditures. Finally, if principals cannot ensure that agents will always act in their best interests despite monitoring and bonding, there may be some deadweight residual loss. Jensen and Meckling define "agency costs" as the sum of these expenditures. They show that debt finance can reduce overall agency costs for a firm, but their analysis does not consider the problem of interest rate volatility and the question of whether a firm should issue short-term or long-term debt.

Interest rate volatility would not affect the investment or financing decisions of firms if revenues were always perfectly correlated with changes in market interest rates, because revenues would vary along with debt servicing costs in this case. Revenues typically are not perfectly correlated with market interest rates, however. As a result, interest rate volatility can increase the risk of financial distress. If financial distress is costly (because of the administrative costs of bankruptcy proceedings), or if the firm's management values its right to exercise control over the affairs of the organization, management will have an incentive to mitigate such risks. Ideally, then, a firm would wish to schedule repayment of its capital financing costs to match the realization of revenues from its investments (Myers 1977). If a firm's revenues are completely uncorrelated with market interest rates, it could minimize the risk of future financial distress by funding long-term investments with long-term, fixed-rate debt and short-term investments with short-term debt.

Long-term lending carries substantial risks from an outside investor's viewpoint, however. A borrower's financial condition can deteriorate substantially over the term of the loan. Moreover, as Jensen and Meckling (1976) note, management has an incentive to take actions that benefit shareholders at the expense of creditors once a firm has received the proceeds of the loan. As an example, management can pursue high-risk strategies or otherwise attempt to dissipate the organization's assets by paying excessive dividends. Creditors could prevent such behavior if (1) they always knew as much about a firm's investment opportunities as its managers and (2) they could monitor management's behavior costlessly. But such actions are prohibitively costly for most creditors, if even feasible, for they would involve duplicating essentially all the functions of managements. For these reasons, bond-holders often demand loan covenants that limit management's discretion in deploying loan proceeds. Typically such covenants give creditors the right to exercise greater control over the firm when a condition of the loan is violated or in the event of a material deterioration in its financial condition. To be certain, enforcement of loan covenants still requires some monitoring on the part of creditors. Jensen and Meckling (1976) argue that these monitoring costs are ultimately borne by borrowers through higher interest rates.

Wall (1989) argues that the existence of agency costs is one reason that quality spreads widen with debt maturity. He notes that while established firms with good credit ratings and access to low-cost credit have incentives to limit risks, newer and smaller firms do not have the same incentives. Like Loeys (1985), Wall gives special emphasis to the influence creditors can exercise over borrowers when renegotiating short-term loans. Wall was among the first to observe that synthetic fixed-rate financing carries different incentives for borrowers than actual fixed-rate financing. To understand why this might be so, notice that the interest rate lenders charge a borrower when renewing a short-term loan can change for two reasons: (1) a change in market interest rates or (2) a change in the firm-specific credit-quality risk premium. Interest rate swaps compensate the borrower only for changes in market rates, and not for changes in the short-term quality spread. Thus, as noted earlier, the cost of synthetic fixed-rate financing is $\bar{r}^s + [r^b(t) - r^s(t)]$, the swap fixed rate plus the quality spread between the rate the firm pays on its short-term debt and the swap floating-rate index. A firm that chooses synthetic fixed-rate financing faces the risk that the quality spread $[r^b(t) - r^s(t)]$ might rise if lenders realize that management has increased the firm's riskiness. In extreme cases, the firm might even find itself unable to roll over its outstanding short-term debt and be forced into bankruptcy proceedings.

Wall's (1989) rationale for interest rate swaps lies with the observation that synthetic fixed-rate financing should discourage management from pursuing risky investment strategies.[7] According to this argument, interest rate swaps lower funding costs by controlling the adverse incentives a firm's management might have to increase the risk assumed by the firm to the detriment of creditors. Thus, interest rate swaps do make it possible for firms to reduce financing costs in Wall's theory. But the savings attributable to the use of swaps result from lower agency costs and do not constitute arbitrage in the sense that term is normally understood.

The problem of adverse selection: more incentives to borrow short and swap into fixed

Flannery (1986) and Diamond (1991) investigate the determinants of debt maturity by focusing attention on the incentives borrowers have to signal information to lenders about their financial condition. Their analysis is based on the assumption that outside investors have imperfect information about firms, and so are unable to discriminate perfectly between safe firms and relatively risky firms. If outside investors cannot perfectly discriminate between risky and safe firms, they will demand default-risk premiums on long-term debt that may appear excessively high to relatively safe borrowers. Conversely, the managers of a risky firm recognize that there is a high probability that the organization's financial condition will deteriorate, leading them to prefer long-term debt over short-term debt.

Firms that lenders can identify as risky borrowers have difficulty securing long-term loans and are forced to issue short-term debt that matures before the returns to an investment are realized. Often such firms must obtain their credit lines from banks, which specialize in credit evaluation and are well positioned to monitor the firm's activities. In the event that a firm's financial condition deteriorates, lenders can demand a higher interest rate upon refinancing, can further restrict the discretion of management, can engage in more intensive monitoring, can take some combination of these actions, or can even refuse to refinance outstanding debt. A firm that defaults on its outstanding debt obligations can be forced into bankruptcy proceedings.

If a firm's management believes that default premiums on long-term loans are excessive, it might choose a short-term funding strategy. By voluntarily taking on liquidity risk, management can signal that it does not expect the firm's condition to deteriorate in the future. Over time a firm that consistently demonstrates its ability to meet its financial obligations develops a reputation as a safe firm. Thus, a safe firm might employ a short-term funding strategy until it can convince creditors to extend long-term loans on better terms (Diamond 1991).

One drawback to such a strategy is that it can leave the firm's cash flows unhedged. Arak, Estrella, Goodman, and Silver (1988) stress that interest rate swaps are not redundant securities, but offer firms new financing choices that were not previously available in credit markets. Like Wall (1989), Arak et al. note that synthetic fixed-rate financing requires the borrower to bear the risk of changes in the short-term credit-risk premium. Their hypothesized rationale for interest rate swaps differs somewhat from that of Wall, however. They hypothesize that firms may have an incentive to bear rollover risk when management is more optimistic about a firm's future prospects than the market. If a firm's management is optimistic about its financial condition, it may choose to issue short-term debt in the expectation that the quality spread will fall in the future. In effect, the firm speculates on its own quality spread while using swaps to immunize itself against market risk.

Titman (1992) and Minton (1993a) derive conditions under which a firm's best strategy is to use interest rate swaps in conjunction with short-term financing. Like Flannery (1986) and Diamond (1991), Titman and Minton emphasize that firms may have an incentive to bear the liquidity risk associated with short-term debt finance as a means of signaling management's belief that the firm's financial prospects will improve. Titman finds conditions under with synthetic fixed-rate financing gives firms an incentive to undertake safer investments. Minton finds that giving firms the option of using interest rate swaps can reduce default risk and, in doing so, increase the capacity of firms to undertake productive long-term investment. Both Titman and Minton find plausible conditions under which interest rate swaps reduce financing costs, albeit not through the channels of financial arbitrage.

Notice that the basic logic of the adverse selection rationale runs closely parallel to that of Wall's (1989) agency cost rationale. While borrowers in Titman and Minton's models choose short-term financing to signal management's belief that the firm is creditworthy, the act of taking on short-term debt mitigates incentives to take on added risk once loan proceeds are received, just as Wall predicts.

Incentives to borrow fixed and swap into floating

The preceding discussion has focused on the incentives firms might have to enter into a swap as a fixed-rate payer. But every swap agreement must also have a floating-rate payer. Wall (1989) and Titman (1992) hypothesize that floating-rate payers share in the gains fixed-rate payers receive from synthetic fixed-rate financing. Litzenberger (1992) notes at least two reasons why highly rated firms may be able to lower funding costs by issuing callable fixed-rate debt and then swapping into synthetic floating-rate debt. First, like Wall and Titman, he hypothesizes that floating-rate payers essentially act as financial intermediaries that earn income in return for managing a diversified portfolio of risky contractual obligations. The total exposure resulting from this activity is small, he argues, because (1) the credit risk associated with an interest rate swap is much smaller than that associated with actual lending; (2) most swap agreements take place among parties with at least single A credit ratings (lower-rated counterparties are rejected or required to post collateral); and (3) a diversified swap portfolio has little risk of a large credit loss.

Second, Litzenberger also notes that the highly rated AAA firms that typically become floating-rate payers often issue callable fixed-rate notes, and then sell the prepayment options on these notes by selling callable swaps to swap dealers. He argues that such transactions can create synthetic floating-rate financing at a modest savings in cost because the prepayment options attached to fixed-rate debt tend to be underpriced, probably because of a past history of non-optimal exercises on such options. Thus, Litzenberger attributes at least part of the incentive to become a floating-rate payer to arbitrage opportunities created by the mispricing of prepayment options for corporate bonds.

Smith, Smithson, and Wakeman (1988) emphasize that interest rate swaps can help to conserve on transactions costs. As an example, they note that it can be cheaper to sell an interest rate swap than to call and refund outstanding fixed-rate debt.

4. A Comparison of Interest Rate Futures and Interest Rate Swaps

A discussion of the economic role of interest rate swaps would not be complete without at least some mention of interest rate futures. Interest rate futures can be used to create synthetic fixed-rate debt in much the same way as interest rate futures. In particular, selling a "strip," or sequence, of Eurodollar futures with successive maturity dates can be compared to buying an interest rate swap.

To see how interest rate futures can substitute for an interest rate swap, recall that the buyer (fixed-rate payer) of an interest rate swap receives a net payment from the seller whenever the floating-rate index exceeds the swap fixed rate. In the case of a generic swap with a floating rate indexed to some maturity of LIBOR, the buyer receives the difference in interest on the notional principal amount whenever the specified maturity of LIBOR exceeds the swap fixed rate. When LIBOR is below the fixed rate, the buyer must pay the difference in interest to the seller.

Selling a strip of Eurodollar futures creates a similar pattern of returns and payments. The seller of a Eurodollar contract receives the difference in interest on the notional principal ($1 million) when the futures rate negotiated at the outset of the agreement turns out to be less than the value of three-month LIBOR prevailing on the contract maturity date. Otherwise, the seller must pay the difference in interest to the buyer. Thus, selling a strip of Eurodollar futures produces a return stream comparable to that of a generic interest rate swap. Because of this similarity, an implied swap rate can be derived from Eurodollar futures rates.[8] Minton (1993b) finds evidence that the behavior of swap market rates is closely related to this implied swap rate.

These observations suggest that much of the rationale for interest rate swaps discussed above must also apply to interest rate futures – in particular, to Eurodollar futures. The foregoing discussion has focused on interest rate swaps because the growth of trading in Eurodollar futures in recent years appears to have been driven by the growth of the swap market. Although trading in Eurodollar futures predates the advent of the interest rate swap, trading was limited to contracts extending two years into the future at the time of the first widely publicized interest rate swap in

1982. As a result, Eurodollar futures were not as well suited for use in creating synthetic long-term financing as were interest rate swaps. More recently, the Chicago Mercantile Exchange has begun listing Eurodollar futures for delivery as far as ten years into the future. Burghardt et al. (1991) attribute the recent expansion of trading in Eurodollar futures to the growth of the interest rate swap market. Swap dealers in particular often use Eurodollar futures to hedge their commitments. Thus, although interest rate futures contracts can substitute for interest rate swaps, it was the growth of the swap market that had the greatest effect on corporate finance.

Kawaller (1990) and Minton (1993b) discuss the factors influencing the choice between interest rate futures and interest rate swaps. Kawaller emphasizes transactions costs and other practical considerations of managing a futures position as key factors influencing the choice between interest rate futures and interest rate swaps. The main benefit of a swap is that it can be custom-tailored to the needs of an individual firm, so that managing an interest rate swap is relatively easy compared to managing a futures market position. A firm that enters into an interest rate swap faces a set schedule for receiving or making its payments. As long as nothing happens to change the firm's underlying exposure to interest rates – that is, as long as nothing has happened to change the reasons the firm decided to create synthetic fixed- or floating-rate financing in the first place – managing an outstanding swap position merely requires the firm's treasurer to make or collect scheduled payments.

The principal disadvantage of interest rate swaps relative to interest rate futures lies with counterparty credit risk. Exchange-traded instruments such as interest rate futures are backed by a system of margin requirements, along with the guarantee of the exchange clearinghouse (which, in turn, is jointly backed by the paid-in capital of the clearinghouse member firms). This system of safeguards removes virtually all risk of default in the futures market. In contrast, a counterparty to an interest rate swap is exposed to the risk that the other counterparty might default. To be certain, most interest rate swaps take place between relatively creditworthy counterparties. Nonetheless, credit risk is a greater concern with interest rate swaps than with futures contracts.

The very factors that make interest rate futures safer also make managing a futures position somewhat more challenging than managing a swap commitment, however. First, a party to a futures contract is required to post margin before being permitted to buy or sell a futures contract. Second, the futures exchanges mark all outstanding positions to market at the end of each trading session, adding any realized gains or subtracting any realized losses from each trader's margin account. While this procedure minimizes default risk, it exposes any party with an open futures position to the risk of margin calls. As a consequence, payments are less predicable in the short run with a futures position than with an interest rate swap. Third, futures contracts are standardized agreements. Contract standardization, along with the clearinghouse guarantee, facilitates trading in futures contracts. Futures markets tend to be more liquid than OTC markets (and actual cash markets for that matter) as a result, lowering transactions costs. But while contract standardization facilitates trading, it also means that an interest rate futures contract will almost never be perfectly suited to the needs of any one trader.[9] Thus, an interest rate futures position requires greater monitoring and can be more difficult to execute unless a firm maintains a staff devoted to trading futures contracts.

While the factors that determine the choice between interest rate futures and interest rate swaps is of great interest to practitioners, it has not received a great deal of attention in the academic finance literature. Minton's (1993a) model of the hedging behavior of firms is a noteworthy exception. Minton finds that relatively safe firms – firms that expect their future credit-quality spreads to fall – may have an incentive to choose swaps over futures contracts so as to avoid the cost of margin requirements.

5. Concluding Comments

The reasons for the extraordinary growth of the swap market in recent years are not yet fully understood. But there seems to be a consensus that the market has developed because interest rate swaps offer firms financing choices that were not available before the advent of these instruments. In this respect, interest rate swaps represent a true financial innovation.

The early rationale offered for the existence of the market – that firms used interest rate swaps to arbitrage credit market inefficiencies – cannot by itself explain the exponential growth of the market over the past decade. By the same token, it is unlikely that firms would use interest rate swaps if they did not lower financing costs in some way. Recent research suggests at least two reasons why firms use interest rate swaps. First, in cases where a firm's management expects its financial condition to improve, interest rate swaps make it possible for firms to hedge against changes in market interest rates while avoiding excessive fixed-rate quality-spread premiums. Second, interest rate swaps make possible financial arrangements that reduce the incentives of borrowing firms to take on added risk at the expense of creditors.

Conceived in the wake of unprecedented interest rate volatility brought about by a decade of accelerating inflation, the interest rate swap was born of necessity. In a period of low interest rate volatility, the choice between short-and long-term borrowing was primarily a choice between fixed and floating credit-quality spreads. With rising interest rate volatility, however, the ability to separate the effects of changes in market rates from changes in credit-quality spreads became more valuable, leading firms to experiment with alternative financing schemes. Based on the results of recent research, it appears that interest rate swaps have helped firms to weather the uncertainties of volatile financial markets by reducing default risk and facilitating increased productive investment.

Notes

The views expressed herein are those of the author and do not necessarily represent the views of either the Federal Reserve Bank of Richmond or the Board of Governors of the Federal Reserve System. The motivation for this article grew out of discussions with Douglas Diamond. Michael Dotsey, Jeff Lacker, Roy Webb, and John Weinberg provided thoughtful criticism and helpful comments.
1. For a review of these stated concerns, recent policy initiatives, and pending legislation, see Cummins (1994a, 1994b), Karr (1994), and Rehm (1994).

2. An increase in market interest rates, for example, increases the value of a swap agreement to the fixed-rate payer, who will subsequently receive higher interest rate payments from the floating-rate payer.
3. The London Interbank Offered Rate is the rate at which major international banks with offices in London stand ready to accept deposits from one another. See Goodfriend (1993) or Burghardt et al. (1991) for a detailed description of the Eurodollar market.
4. For example, see Rudnick (1987).
5. Wall and Pringle (1987) note that Loeys' hypothesis is only consistent with increasing quality-spread differentials if the ability of short-term debtholders to refuse to renew outstanding debt makes it easier to force reorganization of a financially distressed firm.
6. An interest rate swap can be viewed as a bundle of forward contracts (see Smith, Smithson, and Wakeman [1988]). Sun, Sundaresan, and Wang (1993) find that bid-ask spreads in the interest rate swap market are smaller than those in the underlying market for long-term, fixed-rate corporate debt.
7. Diamond (1984) makes a similar observation regarding the optimal hedging behavior of firms, although he does not discuss the rationale for interest rate swaps per se.
8. For more detailed expositions, see Burghardt et al. (1991) and Kawaller (1990).
9. For a more detailed description of futures exchanges and interest rate futures, see Kuprianov (1993a).

References

Arak, Marcelle, Arturo Estrella, Laurie S. Goodman, and Andrew Silver. "Interest Rate Swaps: An Alternative Explanation," *Financial Management,* Summer 1988, pp. 12–18.

Bansal, Vipul K., James L. Bicksler, Andrew H. Chen, and John F. Marshall. "Gains from Synthetic Financing with Interest Rate Swaps: Fact or Fancy?" Continental Bank *Journal of Applied Corporate Finance,* vol. 6 (Fall 1993), pp. 91–94.

Bicksler, James, and Andrew H. Chen. "An Economic Analysis of Interest Rate Swaps," *The Journal of Finance,* vol. 41 (July 1986), pp. 645–55.

Burghardt, Belton, Luce, and McVey. *Eurodollar Futures and Options.* Chicago: Probus Publishing Company, 1991.

Cummins, Claudia. "Gonzalez Moving Legislation on Derivatives to Front Burner," *American Banker,* May 4, 1994a.

——. "OCC Eyes Lid on Swaps," *American Banker,* April 21, 1994b.

Diamond, Douglas W. "Debt Maturity and Liquidity Risk," *The Quarterly Journal of Economics,* vol. CVI (August 1991), pp. 709–37.

——. "Financial Intermediation and Delegated Monitoring," *Review of Economic Studies,* vol. 51 (August 1984), pp. 393–414.

Flannery, Mark J. "Asymmetric Information and Risky Debt Maturity Choice," *The Journal of Finance,* vol. 41 (March 1986), pp. 19–37.

Goodfriend, Marvin, "Eurodollars," in Timothy Q. Cook and Robert K. LaRoche, eds., *Instruments of the Money Market,* 7th ed. Richmond: Federal Reserve Bank of Richmond, 1993, pp. 48–58.

Jensen, Michael C., and William H. Meckling. "Theory of the Firm: Managerial Behavior, Agency Costs and Ownership Structure," *The Journal of Financial Economics,* vol. 3 (October 1976), pp. 305–60.

Karr, Albert R. "Bank Regulator Signals Move on Derivatives: Comptroller Voics Concern over For-Profit Trades and Internal Oversight," *The Wall Street Journal,* April 21, 1994.

Kawaller, Ira G. "A Swap Alternative: Eurodollar Strips," in Carl R. Beidleman, ed., *Interest Rate Swaps.* Homewood, Ill.: Business One Irwin, 1990, pp. 390–404.

Kuprianov, Anatoli. "Money Market Futures," in Timothy Q. Cook and Robert K. LaRoche, eds., *Instruments of the Money Market*, 7th ed. Richmond: Federal Reserve Bank of Richmond, 1993a, pp. 188–217.

——— . "Over-the-Counter Interest Rate Derivatives," in Timothy Q. Cook and Robert K. LaRoche, eds., *Instruments of the Money Market*, 7th ed. Richmond: Federal Reserve Bank of Richmond, 1993b, pp. 238–65.

Litzenberger, Robert H. "Swaps: Plain and Fanciful," *The Journal of Finance*, vol. 47 (July 1992), pp. 831–50.

Loeys, Jan G. "Interest Rate Swaps: A New Tool for Managing Risk," Federal Reserve Bank of Philadelphia *Business Review*, May/June 1985, pp. 17–25.

Marshall, John F., and Kenneth R. Kapner. *Understanding Swaps.* John Wiley and Sons: New York, 1993.

Miller, Merton H. "Debt and Taxes," *The Journal of Finance*, vol. 32 (May 1977), pp. 261–75.

Minton, Bernadette. "Interest Rate Derivative Products and Firms' Borrowing Decisions: The Case of Interest Rate Swaps and Short-Term Interest Rate Futures Contracts." Manuscript. University of Chicago, December 1993a.

——— . "An Empirical Examination of U.S. Dollar Swap Spreads." Manuscript. University of Chicago, November 1993b.

Myers, Stewart C. "Determinants of Corporate Borrowing," *Journal of Financial Economics*, vol. 5 (November 1977), pp. 147–75.

Rawls, S. Waite III, and Charles W. Smithson. "The Evolution of Risk Management Products," *Journal of Applied Corporate Finance*, reprinted in Robert J. Schwartz and Clifford W. Smith, Jr., eds., *The Handbook of Currency and Interest Rate Risk Management*. New York: New York Institute of Finance, 1990.

Rehm, Barbara A. "Trio of Heavyweights Sees No Swaps Crisis," *American Banker*, May 11, 1994.

Rudnick, Linda T. "Discussion of Practical Aspects of Interest Rate Swaps," in *Conference on Bank Structure and Competition*. Chicago: Federal Reserve Bank of Chicago, 1987, pp. 206–13.

Smith, Clifford W., Charles W. Smithson, and Lee Macdonald Wakeman. "The Market for Interest Rate Swaps," *Financial Management*, vol. 17 (1988), pp. 67–73.

——— . "The Evolving Market for Swaps," *Midland Corporate Finance Journal*, vol. 3 (Winter 1986), pp. 20–32.

Smith, Clifford W., Charles W. Smithson, and D. Sykes Wilford. "Financial Engineering: Why Hedge?" *Intermarket*, vol. 6 (1989), pp. 12–16.

Sun, Tong-Sheng, Suresh Sundaresan, and Ching Wang. "Interest Rate Swaps: An Empirical Investigation," *Journal of Financial Economics*, vol. 34 (August 1993), pp. 77–99.

Titman, Sheridan. "Interest Rate Swaps and Corporate Financing Choices," *Journal of Finance*, vol. 47 (September 1992), pp. 1503–16.

Wall, Larry D. "Interest Rate Swaps in an Agency Theoretic Model with Uncertain Interest Rates," *Journal of Banking and Finance*, vol. 13 (May 1989), pp. 261–70.

——— , and John J. Pringle. "Alternative Explanations of Interest Rate Swaps," in *Conference on Bank Structure and Competition*. Chicago: Federal Reserve Bank of Chicago, 1987, pp. 186–205.

19

A Tale of Two Bond Swaps

Andrew Kalotay
and Bruce Tuckman

I. The Swaps

The NWB transaction evolved as follows. Morgan Stanley & Co. purchased $42.675 million face amount of the utility's debt for about $34.5 million through open market and privately negotiated transactions. Table 1 provides some details on these bonds. NWB subsequently exchanged $42.883 million face amount of newly issued 7 3/4 percent bonds due 5/1/30 and a cash payment of $408,000 for the $42.675 principal amount of bonds purchased by Morgan Stanley. Finally, Morgan Stanley sold the new bonds to the public for $34.28 million. Figure 1 schematically illustrates the transaction.

Had Morgan Stanley acted as agent for NWB, purchasing the old bonds for NWB's account, the difference between each bond's basis[1] and its market price would have been taxable income to NWB. But the tax law at the time allowed for tax-free exchanges so long as the principal amount of the new issue was about the same as the principal amount retired.[2] Structuring the transaction as an exchange, therefore, allowed NWB to avoid taxes on its debt retirement. Section III shows that neither of the transactions would have proved profitable if taxes had to be paid on book gains. MST structured its exchange in the same way. Table 2 lists the retired bonds and Figure 2 depicts the rest of the swap.

II. Tax-induced Valuation Differences

As will be shown, when the corporate tax rate exceeds the marginal investor's tax rate, corporations value their outstanding discount debt[3] above market and their par debt at about market. Consequently, if the book gain on the extinguishment of discount debt were not taxed, corporations could profit by repurchasing discount bonds and simultaneously issuing par bonds. When the gain is taxed, however, the tax bill usually swamps the tax-induced valuation differences and destroys the profitability of the refunding operation.[4]

By avoiding the tax on debt extinguishment, the exchange structure used by NWB and MST attempted to restore the profitably of retiring discounts. But to qualify for non-taxable status, the bonds offered in exchange had to have the same face value as the bonds retired. This constraint, along with the desire to avoid cash

Table 1   Bonds retired through the Northwestern Bell Telephone debt-for-debt swap (principal reported in millions of dollars)

Coupon	Maturity	Principal outstanding	Principal retired
4–7/8%	6/1/98	$45	$9.590
7–1/2	4/1/05	100	4.000
6–1/4	1/1/07	100	10.300
7	1/1/09	75	7.185
7–7/8	1/1/11	150	4.600
9–1/2	8/15/16	300	7.000
			Total: $42.675

Table 2   Bonds retired through the Mountain State Telephone and Telegraph debt-for-debt swap (principal reported in millions of dollars)

Coupon	Maturity	Principal outstanding	Principal retired
5–1/2%	6/1/05	$50	$9.24
6	8/1/07	85	14.80
7–3/8	11/1/11	125	11.00
7–3/4	6/1/13	250	20.00
			Total: $55.04

Figure 1   The Northwestern Bell Telephone exchange

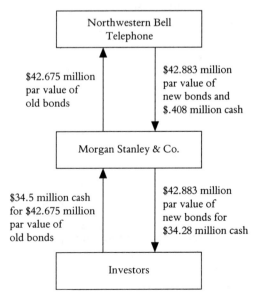

Figure 2   The Mountain States Telephone and Telegraph exchange

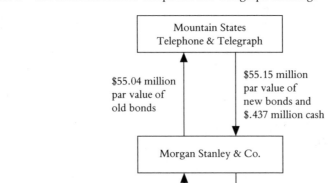

inflows or outflows,[5] forced the companies to offer new discount bonds in the exchanges.[6] Evidently, in order to profitably retire discounts, the companies had to sacrifice value by offering new discounts in exchange!

As shown below, the key to the profitability of the exchanges was that, for a given market value, the difference between the corporate and market valuation of discount bonds normally declines with maturity. Therefore, NWB and MST profited by exchanging their outstanding intermediate-term discounts for newly issued long-term discounts of the same market value. The benefit to the firms from extinguishing the intermediate-term discounts exceeded the losses from concomitantly offering the long-term discounts.

To begin the analytic demonstration, assume that (1) the investor tax rate is zero, (2) corporations pay taxes at a rate of τ_c, and (3) the yield curve is flat at rate y. Under these assumptions, the bond valuation equation is:[7]

$$V(c,N,y,\tau) = \sum_{t=1}^{N} c(1 - \tau)\,[1 + y(1 - \tau)]^{-t} + [1 + y(1 - \tau)]^{-N} \tag{1}$$

$$= c/y + (1 - c/y)[1 + y(1 - \tau)]^{-N}$$

where c is the annual coupon rate, N is the number of years to maturity, and τ is the relevant tax rate. Since this study concerns discount bonds, it is assumed throughout that $c < y$.

Say that a corporation considers exchanging outstanding bonds with a coupon of c_1, a maturity of N_1, and a face value of $1 for new bonds of equal market value with a coupon of c_2, a maturity of N_2, and a face value of $1.[8] Mathematically, the market value constraint takes the form:

$$c_2/y + (1 - c_2/y)(1 + y)^{-N_2} = V(c_1, N_1, y, 0) \tag{2}$$

Solving for c_2 and substituting into the bond valuation equation 1 gives a valuation function, $v(N, y, \tau)$, which incorporates the constraint that the market value of the new issue must equal the market value of the outstanding issue.[9] In other words, $v(N_2, y, \tau)$ does not depend on a coupon level because, for a given N_2, c_2 is adjusted to obey equation 2, the market value constraint. Some algebra reveals that:

$$v(N_2, y, \tau) = \frac{V(c_1, N_1, y, 0) - (1 + y)^{-N_2}}{1 - (1 + y)^{-N_2}} + \frac{[1 + y(1 - \tau)]^{-N_2}[1 - V(c_1, N_1, y, 0)]}{1 - (1 + y)^{-N_2}} \tag{3}$$

The goal of this section is to analyze $v(N_2, y, \tau_c) - v(N_2, y, 0)$, the difference between the corporate and market valuations of a discount bond. Showing that this difference is positive establishes that a corporation gains value when repurchasing discounts but loses value when offering discounts in exchange. Claim 1 proves this result. Showing that this difference decreases in N_2 establishes that a corporation gains more by extinguishing relatively short-term discounts than it loses by offering relatively long-term discounts in exchange, i.e., that these exchanges will prove profitable. Claim 2 gives sufficient conditions for this result.

Claim 1: $v(N_2, y, \tau_c) - v(N_2, y, 0) > 0$.

Proof: The difference $v(N_2, y, \tau_c) - v(N_2, y, 0)$ equals:

$$\int_0^{\tau_c} \frac{\partial v}{\partial \tau} d\tau \tag{4}$$

Therefore, establishing that $\partial v/\partial \tau > 0$ is sufficient for the valuation difference to be positive. This follows immediately from differentiating equation 3 with respect to τ:

$$\frac{\partial v}{\partial \tau} = y N_2 [1 + y(1 - \tau)]^{-N_2 - 1} \frac{1 - V(c_1, N_1, y, 0)}{1 - (1 + y)^{-N_2}} > 0 \tag{5}$$

The inequality follows since, for discount bonds, $V < 1$.

Claim 2: Two sufficient conditions for $v(N_2, y, \tau_c) - v(N_2, y, 0)$ to decrease in N_2 are $\tau_c \leq 1 - [(1 + y)^{1/2} - 1]/y$, and $\tau_c \leq .5$.

Proof: By equation 4, establishing that $\partial^2 v/\partial \tau \partial N_2 < 0$ for $\tau \leq \tau_c$ is sufficient for the valuation difference to decrease in N_2. The following lemma, proved in the appendix, signs $\partial^2 v/\partial \tau \partial N_2$ and completes the proof.

Lemma: If $\tau \leq 1 - [(1 + y)^{1/2} - 1]/y$, then $\partial^2 v/\partial \tau \partial N_2 < 0$ for all $N_2 > 0$. In particular, if $\tau \leq .5$ then, $\partial^2 v/\partial \tau \partial N_2 < 0$ for all N_2, $y > 0$.

Figures 3 and 4 illustrate the interpretation of Claim 2 in the context of a discount debt refunding. Assume that the yield curve is flat at 12 percent and that

Figure 3   Coupon rate required so that bonds of various maturities will sell for 80 in the market (the yield curve is assumed flat at 12 percent)

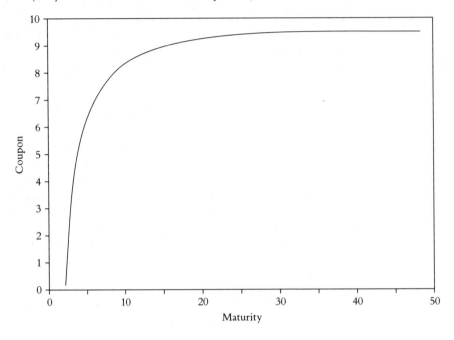

Figure 4   Corporate valuation of bonds priced by investors at 80 as a function of maturity (the yield curve is assumed flat at 12 percent)

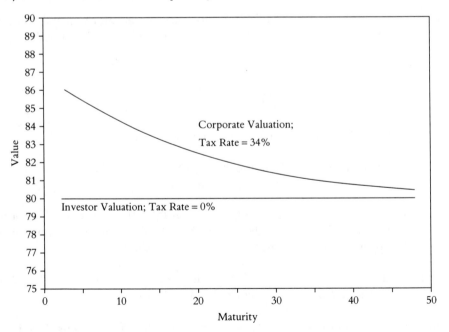

τ_c = 34 percent. The corporation's outstanding bonds carry a coupon of 9.32 percent, mature in 20 years, and, given the 12 percent yield, command a market price of $80 for each $100 in face value. The corporation wishes to swap these bonds for a new issue which can be sold at $80. Given this constraint, the coupon of the new issue must lie on the curve of Figure 3. For example, 9.57 percent bonds maturing in 40 years can be sold for $80. Figure 4 contrasts the corporate valuation of bonds which sell for $80 with the market valuation of $80. Notice that the corporation values its outstanding 9.32 percent, 20-year bonds at $82.55 while it values the 9.57 percent, 40-year bonds at $80.74. Therefore, swapping $100 face value of the 9.32 percent bonds for $100 of the 9.57 percent requires no cash outlay but generates a present value gain of $82.55 − $80.74 = $1.81. Figure 4 reveals that maturity extension creates these present value gains.

Claims 1 and 2 assumed that the investor tax rate is zero. Since the goal of this study is to show that corporations can profitably swap at least some of their discount bonds and since a sizable fraction of corporate bonds are held by investors with zero tax rates,[10] this assumption seems reasonable and allows for analytic proofs. However, the assumption can be substantially weakened. Corporations could profit from valuation differences with the market as long as a large enough set of investors in corporate bonds pay taxes at rates below τ_c. The current level of individual tax rates and the workings of clientele effects which attract relatively low-taxed investors to the corporate bond market virtually guarantee that this weakened assumption holds.[11]

In the case of a sloping yield curve, it is difficult to derive an analogue to Claim 2 analytically. First, the yield at which investors with marginal rates of zero discount cash flows no longer equals the pre-tax yield at which the corporation should discount flows. Second, both yields are functions of the new bond's maturity, N_2. Extensive numerical work reveals that the difference between corporate and investor valuation falls with maturity as long as any downward-sloping yield curve is not unrealistically steep.

III. Analysis of the NWB and MST Exchanges

Table 3 presents the gains of NWB and MST from their exchanges. The first two columns of each panel describe the retired and newly issued bonds. The third and fourth columns list market yields to maturity and prices, the source of which will be described shortly. Using τ_c = 34 percent and the yield in column three,[12] the fifth column computes bond values to the utilities from equation 1. The sixth column lists the face amount retired. The seventh column reports the gain from each issue, i.e., the difference between the utilities' valuation of the bond and its market price multiplied by the face value retired. The bottom lines of each panel report present value gains, costs, and net gains. The costs were defined as proceeds from the distribution of the new issue minus the cost of acquiring the old bonds plus the cash payment plus any miscellaneous expenses. Miscellaneous expense data were included in the prospectuses of the new issues.[13]

The market prices of the new bonds were reported in the press at the time of issue. While the aggregate amount Morgan Stanley paid for the bonds it purchased was reported in the exchange circulars, the prices of individual issues were not

Table 3   Present value gains from the Northwestern Bell Telephone and Mountain States Telephone and Telegraph exchanges

Panel A: The Northwestern Bell Telephone exchange

Coupon	Maturity	Market yield	Market price	Corporate value	Principal retired	PV gain
4.875%	6/1/98	9.30%	75.23	81.60	$9.590	.611
7.50	4/1/05	9.42	84.77	87.79	4.000	.121
6.25	1/1/07	9.45	73.39	78.29	10.300	.506
7.00	1/1/09	9.54	78.03	81.73	7.185	.266
7.875	1/1/11	9.53	85.14	87.45	4.600	.106
9.5	8/15/16	9.78	97.34	97.66	7.000	.023
7.75	5/1/30	9.80	79.54	80.72	42.833	−.508

Total present value gain:	$1.125 million
Costs of doing the exchange:	.248
Net gain:	$ .877 million

Panel B: The Mountain States Telephone and Telegraph exchange

Coupon	Maturity	Market yield	Market price	Corporate value	Principal retired	PV gain
5.50%	6/1/05	9.54%	68.04	74.29	$9.24	.577
6.00	8/1/07	9.59	70.01	75.35	14.80	.791
7.375	11/1/11	9.57	81.16	83.11	11.00	.324
7.75	6/1/13	9.51	83.67	85.95	20.00	.456
7.375	5/1/30	9.80	75.79	77.19	55.15	−.773

Total present value gain:	$1.376 million
Costs of doing the exchange:	.292
Net gain:	$1.084 million

Prices and values are as a percentage of face amount. Principal and present value gain are in millions of dollars. Corporate value computations use a corporate tax rate of 34 percent.

reported. In order to discount each bond's cash flows by the most applicable rate, data on the spread between the yields of the various issues were collected from *Moody's Bond Record*. The yield level was chosen to equate the market value of the old bonds with Morgan's expenditure.[14] It should be noted that the present value gains are quite robust to yield assumptions.

According to Table 3, the exchange allowed NWB to lower the present value of its outstanding debt by $1.125 million at a cost of $.248 million. MST gained $1.376 million at a cost of $.292 million.

As noted earlier, had the extinguishment of discount debt been taxable, the transactions would have proved unprofitable. According to the table, the book gains amount to $8.17 and $12.84 million, implying potential tax liabilities of $2.78 and

$4.37 million, respectively. The magnitudes of these liabilities would eclipse profits from the valuation differences.

The analysis of this section might be questioned along the following lines. Assume that the utilities plan to borrow through the maturity of the newly issued bonds, i.e., through 2030. It follows that, in the absence of the swaps, they would refinance their maturing bonds by issuing par bonds maturing in 2030. Why aren't those bonds incorporated in the analysis? The answer emerges by observing that investors and corporations differ little in their valuation of par bonds. Therefore, the value of the future refunding operation is near zero and may be ignored when analyzing the swaps.[15]

Unlike the refundings analyzed in the academic literature, these exchanges do not preserve after-tax debt service.[16] The swaps extend maturity and, therefore, increase the duration of the firms' debt. Consequently, if interest rates fall dramatically, the utilities would wish that they had left their intermediate-term debt outstanding. Of course, if desired, they could at least partially hedge against falling rates with financial futures. Furthermore, because regulatory lag delays the pass-through of the benefits of lower borrowing costs to consumers, utilities may be naturally hedged against falling rates.[17]

Recognition of the interest rate risk of the exchanges leads to another consideration. In the absence of transaction costs, firms would execute exchanges as soon as it were profitable to do so. In the presence of transaction costs, however, firms might postpone a profitable exchange in the hopes that rates will rise further and allow for an even more profitable exchange. While this implicit option has not been studied here, Mauer and Lewellen (1987) have studied a similar option in the context of premium debt refundings.

The analysis to this point has ignored the call features of the repurchased bonds. (The new issues are not callable.) This simplification comes at little cost. First, apart from the NWB 9.5's of 2016, the call features of bonds currently selling from 68 percent to 85 percent of face value will not be worth very much. Second, the market yields used to construct the fourth and fifth columns of the table incorporate the value of the call options. Therefore, the table neglects only the differences between the company's valuation of the call options and the marginal investor's valuation of the call options. While the omission of this effect does overestimate the profit from the exchanges,[18] the overestimation should be quite small.

IV. Conclusion

This paper has shown that by exchanging outstanding intermediate-term discount bonds for newly issued, long-term discount bonds, NWB and MST capitalized on the tax-driven difference between corporate valuation and market price. While management was motivated by these present value gains, it appears that it was also concerned with the accounting implications of the exchanges.

Shortly after these transactions were completed, NWB called and refunded $56.7 million of 13.5 percent bonds at 110.77 percent and, in the process, incurred a book loss of $6.11 million. MST called and refunded $60.8 million of 11⅝ percent bonds at 107 percent and $39.9 million of 12¼ percent bonds at 110.16 percent, for a total book loss of $8.31 million. Before 1988, FCC regulation allowed multi-state telephone companies to amortize such losses over the life of the refunding issue.[19] After 1988, these losses had to be recognized immediately. Reluctant to show such losses, NWB and MST were pleased to engage in exchanges which generated sufficient accounting gains to cancel the book losses resulting from the high-coupon redemptions.

The NWB and MST transactions provide an effective illustration of how financial innovation may be motivated by tax arbitrage and accounting considerations. The companies executed the swaps "just in time." Were it not for the exchanges, FCC accounting rules would have forced the companies to recognize large losses from the calls of their premium debt. Furthermore, had the companies waited to act, new laws[20] would have taxed the gains from discount debt extinguishment, making the exchanges unprofitable.

The swaps analyzed here are the latest in a series of innovations to escape the taxation of gains from discount debt repurchases.[21] Before 1981, some firms could, in lieu of paying taxes on the gains, reduce the basis of non-depreciable assets by the amount of the gains. The Bankruptcy Act of 1980 required firms to reduce the basis of depreciable assets, thus restoring taxability. Investment banks responded by creating equity-for-debt swaps: the bank bought an issuer's discount bonds, swapped them with the company for shares, and then sold the shares. The tax-free treatment of these swaps again enabled companies to avoid taxes when retiring discounts. Congress, in turn, responded with the Tax Reform Act of 1984, canceling the tax-free status of these swaps except for firms in bankruptcy. Enter the NWB and MST debt-for-debt swaps, followed by the Omnibus Budget Reconciliation Act of 1990. This act made debt-for-debt exchanges taxable events, except for companies in bankruptcy. Presumably the search is on for yet another means of escaping the tax.

There remain, perhaps, two unanswered questions. First, why didn't the companies repurchase more of each issue and possibly other discount issues as well? Second, why hadn't many other companies done the same?

An answer to the first question may be that Morgan Stanley could not buy many more bonds at the same, advantageous prices. This price pressure effect may be due to investor transaction costs and to the existence of investors, like insurance companies, who are extremely reluctant to sell bonds at a book loss. Another answer might be that the telephone companies were concerned that large book gains might induce regulators to reduce allowed revenues.

As to why other companies had not followed the lead of NWB and MST *en masse*, there are three possible explanations. First, understanding the transactions requires considerable financial sophistication. Second, at the time of the exchanges there were few deep discount bonds outstanding. Third, the legality of avoiding tax through these exchanges had not been definitively established. Firms may have been waiting on the sidelines to observe the response of the IRS and the courts. In short, innovators, almost by definition, are the few.

Appendix

Proof of lemma

Lemma: If $\tau \leq 1 - [(1 + y)^{1/2} - 1]/y$, then $\partial^2 v/\partial t \partial N_2 < 0$ for all $N_2 > 0$. In particular, if $\tau \leq .5$ then, $\partial^2 v/\partial t \partial N_2 < 0$ for all N_2 and $y > 0$.

Proof: Equation 5 can be rewritten as:

$$\frac{\partial v}{\partial \tau} = \frac{k_0 N}{k_1^N - k_2^N} \tag{A.1}$$

where $k_0 = \gamma(1 - V(c_1, N_1, \gamma, 0)/[1 + \gamma(1 - \tau)]$, $k_1 = 1 + \gamma(1 - \tau)$, $k_2 = k_1/(1 + \gamma)$, and $N = N_2$. Since only discounts are being considered, $V < 1$ and $k_0 > 0$. Furthermore, since $\tau \in (0,1)$, $k_1 > 1 \geq k_2 > 0$.

This proof analyzes $\partial v/\partial \tau$ as a function of N in four steps. First, the limits are computed as N tends to 0 and as N tends to infinity. Second, the limit of $\partial^2 v/\partial \tau \partial N$ as N tends to 0 is computed. Third, it is shown that $\partial^2 v/\partial \tau \partial N$ decreases in N. From the three steps one can draw two possible shapes for the function $\partial v/\partial \tau$. Fourth, the necessary and sufficient condition for $\partial^2 v/\partial \tau \partial N < 0$ is derived.

Step 1: Using l'Hopital's rule, it can be easily seen that:

$$\lim_{N \to 0} \frac{\partial v}{\partial \tau} = \frac{k_0}{\log k_1 - \log k_2} > 0$$

and that:

$$\lim_{N \to \infty} \frac{\partial v}{\partial \tau} = 0$$

Step 2: Differentiating equation A.1 with respect to N gives:

$$\frac{\partial^2 v}{\partial \tau \partial N} = k_0 \frac{k_1^N - k_2^N - N[k_1^N \log k_1 - k_2^N \log k_2]}{(k_1^N - k_2^N)^2} \tag{A.2}$$

Applying l'Hopital's rule twice reveals that:

$$\lim_{N \to 0} \frac{\partial^2 v}{\partial \tau \partial N} = \frac{-k_0 \log(k_1 k_2)}{2 \log(k_1/k_2)} \tag{A.3}$$

which is non-positive when $k_1 k_2 \geq 1$ and positive when $k_1 k_2 < 1$.

Step 3: Differentiating the numerator of equation A.2 with respect to N and using the fact that $k_1 > k_2$ reveals that the numerator falls in N. Differentiating the denominator with respect to N and using the two facts $k_1 > k_2$ and $k_2 < 1$ reveals that the denominator increases in N. Hence, $\partial^2 v/\partial \tau \partial N$ decreases in N.

From these three steps, $\partial v/\partial \tau$ will rise and then fall in N if $k_1 k_2 < 1$. The function will monotonically fall in N if $k_1 k_2 > 1$.

Step 4: Reverting to the notation in the text, it is easy to show that $k_1 k_2 \geq 1$ if and only if:

$$\tau \leq 1 - \frac{(1 + \gamma)^{1/2} - 1}{\gamma} \tag{A.4}$$

The right-hand side of equation A.4 increases in y. The limit as y tends to 0 is .5. Therefore, if $\tau \leq .5$, then $\partial v / \partial \tau$ declines in N_2.

Notes

1. From the issuer's perspective, the basis of a bond equals the original issue price minus unamortized underwriting expenses. Therefore, bonds sold at par carry a basis very close to face value.
2. This is a sufficient condition. The principal amount of the new bonds could have also exceeded the principal amount of the old bonds. This point will be discussed further in endnotes 6 and 8.
3. Throughout this paper, "discount debt" means debt that was issued at or close to par but, because of a rise in rates, is now selling below par. Original issue discount debt is not being considered.
4. See Kalotay (1978).
5. The difference between the market value of the old bonds and the market value of the new bonds was just $.22 million in the NWB exchange and $.19 million in the MS exchange.
6. The new issue also sells at a discount when its principal amount exceeds that of the old issue. As mentioned in footnote 2, such a structure also qualifies as a non-taxable exchange.
7. For arguments in support of discounting debt-equivalent, after-tax cash flows by the after-tax rate of interest, see Brealey and Myers (1991), pp. 470–74, and Ruback (1986).
8. The text assumes that the face value of both issues are the same because the corporation will choose to match principal. The reasoning is as follows: In matching market value, a corporation may choose a new issue with either a low coupon and a high face value or with a high coupon and a low face value. It is easy to show that the corporate valuation of the bond falls as coupon increases. Therefore, it will opt to offer bonds with a high coupon and a low face value. But, as mentioned in endnote 2, the lowest face value which preserves the exchange's non-taxable status is the face value of the old securities.
9. This procedure implicitly invokes the assumption that the yield curve is flat. Otherwise, it would be incorrect to assume that the investor discount rates are the appropriate pre-tax rates for the corporation.
10. At year end 1989, about 23 percent of corporate bonds were held by pension and retirement funds. Another 5 percent were held by mutual funds which may very well invest as if the relevant tax rate were zero.
11. Capital gains taxation will, of course, enter into the determination of the price at which investors will part with their bonds. Formally modelling the effect of capital gains taxation on the difference between corporate and investor valuations would require an analysis of optimal tax-trading, as in Constantinides and Ingersoll (1984), and of tax-clienteles, as in Schaefer (1982).
12. The use of the market yield as the pre-tax yield appropriate for corporate valuation can be justified in two ways. First, the sloping yield curve effect, mentioned in endnote 9, is quite small. Second, the yield curve at the time of the exchanges was rather flat. In the beginning of May 1990, 30-year Treasury bonds were yielding 8.85 percent while 1-year Treasury bills were yielding 8.55 percent.
13. Miscellaneous expenses amounted to $60,000 for NWB and $40,000 for MS. Since these expenses are amortized over the life of the issue, the value of the resulting tax deductions is quite small and has been ignored in the analysis.

14. Using *Moody's* yield directly, gross gains differ little from those reported in the text. But, using those yields, the market value of the securities retired appears to exceed the market value of the new securities plus the cash payments, i.e., Morgan Stanley appears to have lost money and the costs to the utilities appear negative!

15. This argument does not depend on the refinancing bonds being issued at par. Under current tax law, any new issue has nearly the same pre-tax and after-tax value.

16. See, for example, Mauer and Lewellen (1987) and Finnerty (1986) for premium and discount debt refundings, respectively.

17. For a discussion of a similar point, see Kalotay (1979).

18. See Boyce and Kalotay (1979) who show that corporations value call options more than investors when the corporations are taxed at the higher rate. This means that corporations would use a higher yield than implied by market prices when computing callable bond values.

19. Prior to 1975, these losses could be amortized over the life of the outstanding issue.

20. See Hilder (1990).

21. See, for example, Finnerty (1988) and Kalotay (1982).

References

Boyce, W. and A. Kalotay, "Tax Differentials and Callable Bonds," *Journal of Finance*, September 1979, pp. 825–38.

Brealey, R., and S. Myers, *Principles of Corporate Finance*, 4th ed., McGraw-Hill, 1991.

Constantinides, G. and J. Ingersoll, "Optimal Bond Trading with Personal Taxes," *Journal of Financial Economics*, March 1984, pp. 65–89.

Eades, K., P. Hess, and E. H. Kim, "On Interpreting Security Returns During the Ex-Dividend Period," *Journal of Financial Economics*, March 1984, pp. 3–34.

Elton, E. and M. Gruber, "Marginal Stockholders' Tax Rates and the Clientele Effect," *Review of Economics and Statistics*, February 1970, pp. 68–74.

Finnerty, J., "Refunding Discounted Debt: A Clarifying Analysis," *Journal of Financial and Quantitative Analysis*, March 1986, pp. 95–106.

Finnerty, J., "Financial Engineering in Corporate Finance: An Overview," *Financial Management*, Winter 1988, pp. 14–33.

Harris, J., R. Roenfeldt, and P. Cooley, "Evidence of Financial Leverage Clienteles," *Journal of Finance*, September 1983, pp. 1125–32.

Hilder, D., "Provision in Major Tax Plans Appears to Make Debt Restructurings More Costly," *The Wall Street Journal*, October 16, 1990, p. A6.

Kalay, A., "The Ex-Dividend Behavior of Stock Prices: A Re-examination of the Clientele Effect," *Journal of Finance*, September 1982, pp. 1059–70.

Kalotay, A., "On the Advanced Refunding of Discounted Debt," *Financial Management*, Summer 1978, pp. 14–18.

Kalotay, A., "Bond Redemption Under Rate Base Regulation," *Public Utilities Fortnightly*, March 1979, pp. 68–9.

Kalotay, A., "On the Structure and Valuation of Debt Refundings," *Financial Management*, Spring 1982, pp. 41–2.

Kim, E., W. Lewellen, and J. McConnell, "Financial Leverage Clienteles: Theory and Evidence," *Journal of Financial Economics*, March 1979, pp. 83–110.

Litzenberger, R., and K. Ramaswamy, "The Effects of Dividends on Common Stock Prices: Tax Effects or Information Effects?" *Journal of Finance*, May 1982, pp. 429–44.

Litzenberger, R., and J. Rolfo, "Arbitrage Pricing, Transaction Costs, and Taxation of Capital Gains," *Journal of Financial Economics*, 1984, pp. 337–51.

Long, J., "The Market Valuation of Cash Dividends: A Case to Consider," *Journal of Financial Economics*, June/September 1978, pp. 235–64.

Mauer, D., and W. Lewellen, "Debt Management under Corporate and Personal Taxation," *Journal of Finance*, December 1987, pp. 1275–91.

Miller, M., and M. Scholes, "Dividends and Taxes: Some Empirical Evidence," *Journal of Political Economy*, December 1982, pp. 1118–41.

Poterba, J., "The Market Valuation of Cash Dividends: The Citizens Utilities Case Reconsidered," *Journal of Financial Economics*, March 1986, pp. 395–406.

Ruback, R., "Calculating the Market Value of Risk-Free Cash Flows," *Journal of Financial Economics*, March 1986, pp. 323–39.

Schaefer, S., "Tax-Induced Clientele Effects in the Market for British Government Securities," *Journal of Financial Economics*, 1982, pp. 121–59.

20

Over-the-counter Financial Derivatives: Risky Business?

──────────────── Peter A. Abken

Their continuing rapid growth – and some spectacular, well-publicized losses by a few users – has gained financial derivatives a lot of attention in recent years. In late 1993 a U.S. subsidiary of the German conglomerate Metallgesellschaft AG lost $1.8 billion in oil futures and forward contracts. Its poorly conceived derivatives hedges nearly bankrupted the company. In 1992 senior managers at Showa Shell, the Japanese affiliate of Royal Dutch/Shell, wiped out 82 percent of shareholders' equity by taking a $6 billion position in yen/dollar futures, effectively wagering five dollars for every dollar they hedged. Their futures position turned out to be a disastrous bet when the yen sharply appreciated against the dollar (Richard C. Breeden 1994 and William Falloon 1994). Several major so-called hedge funds, which are private investment partnerships that leverage their investments using derivatives of all kinds as well as bank loans, lost enormous sums through derivatives positions. One lost $600 million speculating on the yen in two days, and another, $1 billion – a quarter of the funds under its management – since the beginning of 1994 (Michael R. Sesit and Laura Jereski 1994; Brett D. Fromson 1994). (On the other side of the coin, these funds made billions in 1992 speculating on European currencies.) The rapid, huge sales of bonds in order to cover derivatives losses and reduce exposures reportedly roiled bond markets around the world, causing concern about the disruption of financial markets from their trading.[1]

Also a source of anxiety are derivative instruments more exotic than these examples generally involve. A large consumer products firm recently announced a $157 million pretax loss on some leveraged swaps designed to bet on the direction of change in U.S. and German interest rates (Steven Lipin, Fred R. Bleakley, and Barbara Donnelly Granito 1994). This and other recently reported cases of losses have focused attention on the risks of these more complex derivatives. Aside from their complexity, the largely unregulated character of the over-the-counter (OTC) derivatives markets sets them apart from other financial markets, as has their extremely rapid growth and fast pace of innovation. This article examines the current structure of the OTC markets and recent recommendations for improved monitoring and perhaps broader regulation of their operation.

Over-the-counter derivatives are financial claims that derive their value from the level of an underlying price, price index, exchange rate, or interest rate. Some of the more common of these instruments include interest rate swaps, forward rate agreements, caps, collars, floors, options, and their foreign exchange equivalents. In recent years OTC derivatives have become a mainstay of financial risk management and are expected to continue growing in importance as more financial managers become more familiar with their use.

Exchange-traded derivatives, such as futures contracts, are similar to OTC instruments in terms of their risk management applications. They differ in a number of important respects, however – a key difference being that OTC instruments are intermediated by financial institutions, which design or tailor an instrument to the needs of the end user. OTC contracts are negotiated bilaterally – between two counterparties – and thus are essentially private transactions, unlike exchange-traded instruments, which are arranged openly through an organized futures or options exchange. Another key distinction is the largely unregulated nature of OTC derivatives trading, whereas exchange-traded derivatives are extensively regulated by federal government agencies.

The history of derivatives in the United States is long and checkered. Derivatives trace back to the founding of the Chicago futures exchanges in the mid-nineteenth century. The markets' modern history starts with the trading of financial and foreign exchange futures on the International Monetary Market of the Chicago Mercantile Exchange (CME) in 1972 and with standardized stock option contracts on the Chicago Board Options Exchange in 1973. With the emergence of the interest rate and currency swap market in the early 1980s, over-the-counter derivatives gained prominence.

Activity in derivatives markets is often characterized by a somewhat overly simplistic dichotomy between speculators and hedgers. Speculation and its putative association with excess price volatility have been a rationale for regulation both historically and currently.[2] However, concerns about derivatives today extend beyond price stability to market stability. In particular, financial regulators want to minimize systemic risk – the possibility that the failure of one firm as a result of derivatives trading would trigger the failures of other firms.

Most observers would agree that the use of derivatives carries risks, both to individual firms and to financial markets. From an economic perspective, it is the proposition that the derivatives markets do not internalize the social costs of their activities that supports the case for (further) regulation. Even when firms safeguard themselves individually in conducting derivatives operations, such measures may be inadequate to insulate the public from picking up the costs of a systemic crisis that could spread from the failure of one or more key derivatives players. The threat of such a so-called market failure, in which private and social costs diverge, is a classic reason for regulatory intervention (Stephen Schaefer 1992, 3). For U.S. depository institutions engaged in derivatives transactions, a further concern is that misuse of derivatives – for example, taking large speculative bets on interest rates – could endanger the deposit insurance safety net. Regulations span a wide array of actions and costs.[3]

Because of their perceived riskiness and their relatively unregulated status, the OTC derivatives markets have been under increasing scrutiny. Industry organizations as well as government regulators have conducted several comprehensive studies of the markets. The salient observations and recommendations of these studies are considered below.

An Overview of Derivatives Markets

Derivative instruments fall into four basic market groups: interest rate contracts, foreign exchange contracts, commodity contracts, and equity contracts. The first two groups are the dominant and older segments of the market. The instruments themselves consist of two basic types, those with linear payoffs and those with nonlinear payoffs.[4]

Linear payoff contracts are those whose value at maturity moves one-for-one with the level of the underlying price, price index, exchange rate, or interest rate (hereafter simply referred to as price). Forward contracts and swaps, which are sequences of forwards with successively longer maturities, are the primary linear payoff contracts. Forward contracts fix a price on an asset for delivery at a specified future date. These contracts are typically priced so that they cost nothing to initiate, but as the underlying price fluctuates away from the price that prevailed at initiation, they become assets or liabilities to the counterparty. This one-for-one movement makes these contracts well suited for hedging the underlying asset or liability because the future appreciation of the derivative can offset the loss on the asset or liability, or vice versa.

As an example, consider a simple, "plain vanilla" interest rate swap. A typical use of such a swap is in converting interest rate payments on floating-rate debt into fixed-rate payments. The swap obligates a counterparty to pay a fixed interest rate payment, determined by the stipulated swap rate, at semiannual intervals and simultaneously to receive a floating interest rate payment, typically indexed to LIBOR.[5] Only the net difference between the fixed- and floating-rate payments is exchanged. The combination of floating-rate debt and swap synthesizes a fixed-rate bond. As LIBOR rises above the fixed swap rate, the net swap payment offsets higher payments on the underlying debt; conversely, as LIBOR falls below the swap rate, interest saving on the debt is forgone as the counter-party makes a net swap payment to the other swap counterparty. Thus, a swap locks in a fixed interest rate, analogous to a forwards' fixing a price or exchange rate.

Nonlinear payoff contracts have payoffs that do not move one-for-one with the underlying price at expiration. Option contracts have the simplest and most common type of nonlinear payoff. For example, if the price is above a call option's strike price (the price at which the optionholder is entitled to purchase the asset), the payoff moves one-for-one, but if it is below the price, the payoff is zero. Prior to expiration, the value of an option is a smooth, convex function rather than a kinked function of the underlying price. As another example, a digital or binary option – a type of exotic option – has a payoff at expiration that jumps from zero to a fixed amount if the underlying price falls within a specified range. (In general, exotic options have relatively complicated contingencies that determine their payoffs. See William C. Hunter and David W. Stowe 1993a, 1993b.) The key point in the context of derivatives regulation is that nonlinear payoff contracts are more difficult to value than swaps and forwards. Regardless of type, options are assets to their purchasers and liabilities to their sellers or writers.

Size of the markets

The standard way to judge the size of OTC derivatives markets is by reference to the notional amount outstanding for particular types of derivatives. The notional amount is the face value of the principal of the underlying contract on which a derivative instrument is based. (With the important exception of currency swaps, principal is usually not exchanged in a swap transaction.) Notional principal is a misleading indicator of the size of derivatives transactions because most cash flows

Chart 1   Swaps outstanding: year-end notional amounts, 1987–92

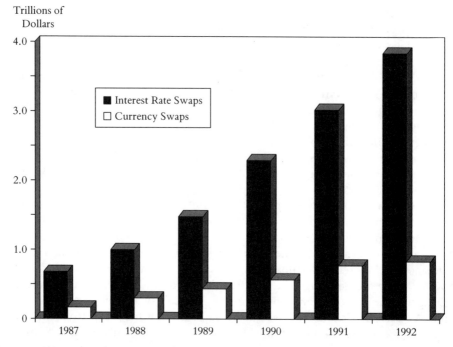

Source: CFTC, using data from the Bank for International Settlements and the International Swap and Derivatives Association.

arising from such transactions are small compared with notional principal. However, notional principal is useful as a measure of the relative importance of one type of derivative compared with another or as a measure of the growth in activity for one instrument.

One of the difficulties in studying OTC derivatives markets is that data on market activity are somewhat sketchy. Interest rate and currency swap activity has been surveyed by a trade association, the International Swaps and Derivatives Association, since the mid-1980s. Chart 1 shows the worldwide growth in notional principal for interest rate and currency swaps from 1987 to 1992. Interest rate swaps denominated in a single currency grew at a compound annual rate of 33.4 percent to a year-end 1992 notional amount of $3.9 trillion; currency swaps grew at 29.4 percent to a year-end notional amount of $860 billion over the same period. During this period, the notional value of exchange-traded interest rate and currency futures in the United States rose at a 22.0 percent compound annual rate, reaching a year-end 1992 combined level of $1.35 trillion (Commodity Futures Trading Commission [CFTC] 1993a, 24).

With the exception of forward foreign exchange contracts and forward rate agreements or FRAs (essentially one-period interest rate swaps), the other segments of the OTC derivatives markets are much smaller than the swaps market. Year-end 1992 dollar and non-dollar caps, collars, and floors were $468 billion, and options on swaps (swaptions) were $108 billion.

The volume of new swaps originated during 1992, in terms of notional principal, stood at $3.12 trillion (105,000 contracts), whereas the volume in global exchange-traded futures and options trading in 1992 totaled $140 trillion in notional value (600 million contracts).[6] Clearly, the exchange-traded futures and options are traded in more active markets in the sense that contract turnover is much higher. One reason for this activity is that the average maturity of futures and options contracts is less than one year; in fact, most trading involves contracts with maturities of one month or less. On the other hand, roughly 60 percent of interest rate swaps fall within a one- to three-year maturity band, about 30 percent within three to seven years, and 10 percent, more than seven years. Currency swaps are skewed toward even longer maturities. The long maturities of swap contracts affect the riskiness of swap portfolios.

Dealers

Most swap and other OTC derivatives trading takes place through dealers, which are primarily the largest money-center banks, investment banks, and insurance companies.[7] Worldwide, 150 dealers are members of the International Swap Dealers Association (ISDA). They run derivatives portfolios or "books" that contain various swap and other derivatives positions they have with their customers, who may be end users or other dealers. Dealers typically seek to hedge their books against changes in interest rates (and other market factors). Matching a swap of a counterparty that exchanges fixed-for-floating interest rate payments with another counterparty that exchanges floating-for-fixed payments is a standard method of insulating a swap portfolio from interest rate movements. (This risk is discussed more fully below.) Dealers also hedge or "lay off" risk using exchange-traded futures and options contracts – for example, Eurodollar futures contracts.

In addition to a commission, compensation for dealers' intermediation takes the form of a spread between the fixed rate they receive from a counterparty to a swap (the ask or offer rate) and the fixed rate they pay to another (the bid rate). The swap ask rate is a few basis points (hundredths of a percentage point) higher than the bid rate. Dealers quote different bid-ask spreads for each instrument in which they "make markets." Less active markets – exotic options markets, for instance – command larger dealer spreads. Dealers bear more risk and greater costs in hedging these derivatives. Larger spreads may also represent economic rents for offering unique derivative instruments.

No aggregate statistics on dealer activity are available. The dominant dealers in the United States are the largest commercial banks. Federal Reserve statistics from the Consolidated Financial Statements for Bank Holding Companies (FR Y-9C) give a glimpse of the largest bank holding companies' (BHC) dealer activity. The top ten BHCs' positions as of June 30, 1993, are reported in Table 1. More than 90 percent of the dealer derivatives business is concentrated in these largest institutions; relatively little is conducted in the next 205 BHCs. The total size of derivatives positions as measured by notional principal is typically a large multiple of the total assets of each institution, but, as mentioned earlier, this figure enormously exaggerates the scale of this business and its risks. Forwards are the main areas of bank dealer activity, followed by swaps and options.

Table 1 Ten holding companies with the most derivatives contracts (*June 30, 1993, Notional Amounts, $ Millions*)

Rank	Holding company name	State	Assets	Total derivatives	Total Futures and forwards	Total swaps	Total options
1	Chemical Banking Corporation	NY	145,522	2,117,385	1,245,500	554,257	317,628
2	Bankers Trust New York Corporation	NY	83,987	1,769,947	816,740	355,597	597,610
3	Citicorp	NY	216,285	1,762,478	1,207,132	264,811	290,535
4	J. P. Morgan & Co., Incorporated	NY	132,532	1,550,680	572,897	579,219	398,563
5	Chase Manhattan Corporation	NY	99,085	1,125,075	666,150	258,086	200,839
6	Bankamerica Corporation	CA	185,466	899,783	581,034	229,926	88,823
7	First Chicago Corporation	IL	49,936	452,780	276,790	100,666	75,324
8	Continental Bank Corporation	IL	22,352	170,052	61,058	52,953	56,041
9	Republic New York Corporation	NY	36,205	164,979	81,707	45,504	37,768
10	Bank of New York Company, Inc.	NY	41,045	91,434	65,128	12,200	14,106
	Top 10 Holding Companies			10,104,592	5,574,136	2,453,219	2,077,236
	Other 205 Holding Companies			617,374	247,461	227,278	142,574
	Total Notional Amount for All Holding Companies			10,721,965	5,821,597	2,680,497	2,219,811

Note: Table includes data for companies with total assets of $150 million or more or with more than one subsidiary bank.
Source: U.S. Congress (1993), using data from the Board of Governors of the Federal Reserve System Consolidated Financial Statements for Bank Holding Companies (FR Y-9C).

In ten years of derivatives trading, trading revenues amounted to $35.9 billion, whereas cumulative losses came to merely $19 million. Moody's and Standard and Poor's, which provide credit risk ratings for corporate bonds, have never downgraded a firm strictly on the basis of its derivatives activities. Both firms regard derivatives as sources of profit and income stability for commercial banks.[8] No commercial bank has failed because of derivatives activities.[9]

The Risks of Derivatives

Derivatives risk stems from a variety of sources. This section discusses each of the following categories of risk that arise in derivatives markets: market risk, credit risk, legal risk, settlement risk, operating risk, and systemic risk.

Market risk

Market risk refers to any market-related factor that changes the value of a derivatives position. The relevant exposure is the unhedged portion of a derivatives portfolio. Changes in the underlying price cause a change in the current market value of a derivative. This change in value is referred to as delta risk. For example, as the level of interest rates rises, the value of a plain vanilla swap falls for a counterparty that receives a fixed rate of, say, 8 percent on a swap. If the swap rate on a newly originated floating-for-fixed swap is now 9 percent, another counterparty would be willing to take over the existing swap and receive 8 percent payments only if compensated for the lower present value of the cash flows from that swap.[10] This situation is analogous to the capital loss realized on a fixed-rate coupon bond when interest rates rise. Conversely, a counterparty paying an 8 percent fixed rate would realize a capital gain on the swap upon closing it out before maturity. The net cash flows from a swap portfolio can be similarly analyzed.

The market risk of nonlinear payoff contracts – options and other derivatives with option features – is more difficult to assess. The entire "probability distribution" of the underlying price may be relevant to valuation. For example, as the volatility or dispersion of the price increases, option prices rise because of the greater likelihood that the contract will yield a payoff at maturity. This characteristic is known in the market jargon as volatility risk or vega risk. It is conceivable, and in fact not uncommon, for the price of the underlying contract to remain unchanged while its volatility shifts. Volatility risk is most effectively hedged using other option contracts.

A payoff's nonlinearity implies that the sensitivity of an option's price to changes in the underlying price varies with the underlying price. For example, a call option's price becomes increasingly sensitive to the underlying contract's price the farther in the money the option becomes (that is, the higher the price moves above the strike price). (In the extreme, the price of an option that has no chance of finishing out of the money moves one-for-one with the underlying price.) This risk, known as convexity or gamma risk, though predictable (unlike volatility shifts), complicates the hedging of options portfolios. Hedges need to be dynamic, meaning frequently adjusted, rather than static, as in the hedging of linear payoff contracts like swaps and forwards.[11]

Credit risk

Because OTC derivatives are entered into bilaterally, performance on a contract depends on the financial viability of the opposite counterparty. Should the opposite counterparty become insolvent and go bankrupt, a counterparty has to attempt to recover the value of a derivative contract in bankruptcy court or, in the case of depository institutions, through the institution's conservator or receiver (the Federal Deposit Insurance Corporation for banks or the Resolution Trust Corporation for savings and loans). This position contrasts with exchange-traded derivatives that have an exchange clearinghouse as the opposite counterparty. The credit exposure is to the clearinghouse – effectively all clearing members of an exchange – rather than to an individual counterparty.

According to an ISDA survey conducted at the end of 1991, the cumulative losses on derivative contracts among participating ISDA members (representing 70 percent of the market) over a ten-year period was $358 million (Group of Thirty 1993b, 43). Somewhat more than half this amount was attributable to defaults triggered by a legal technicality, which will be discussed in the next subsection. A recent survey of fourteen major U.S. OTC derivatives dealers revealed that cumulative, combined losses from 1990 through 1992 amounted to $400 million (with $250 million occurring in 1992). This loss represents only 0.14 percent of the dealers' gross credit exposure, which is a worst-case measure of losses if all contracts defaulted (U.S. General Accounting Office [GAO] 1994, 55, and Appendix III). Although actual losses experienced have been rather small historically, derivatives dealers are clearly cognizant of the credit risks derivatives pose, and evolving market practice continually refines safeguards against credit losses.

The credit risks of linear payoff contracts are different from nonlinear payoff contracts because the former can be either an asset or a liability to a counterparty, depending on the future evolution of the underlying price. A counterparty would not default on a swap that is an asset. Unwinding that swap by marking it to market and closing it out would result in a cash payment from the opposite counterparty.[12] Default occurs when the counterparty is insolvent and the swap is a liability. In fact, conceptually the credit risk of a swap or forward contract may be viewed and analyzed in terms of options.[13]

The current exposure of a derivative is its mark-to-market value or its replacement cost. The future exposure is the potential loss on a derivative as market rates and prices change. This exposure is difficult to quantify and generally requires sophisticated simulation analyses. The future exposure of an interest rate swap traces a dome-shaped curve that rises and then falls from the time of its origination to the time of its expiration. The reason is that early on there is relatively little uncertainty about movement in market rates. The dispersion of rates or prices away from current levels increases over time, elevating future exposure. On the other hand, derivatives have fixed maturities, so the number of remaining future payments falls with the passage of time. These two effects offset each other. By the last payment date there is no uncertainty and no future exposure. In contrast, currency swaps have future exposure profiles that rise steadily because the final exchange of principal is the dominant cash flow, which swamps the amortization effect of earlier periodic cash flows.

Converting derivatives exposures into expected losses requires an assessment of the probability that a counterparty will default. Intuitively, the credit exposure to a counterparty may be large in the near term – say, three months – but the expected loss during this interval could be negligible for a financially strong counterparty because insolvency is highly unlikely. The likelihood of default rises over progressively more distant time horizons as current information about a firm's financial condition has less and less predictive value and relevance. For example, currency swaps generally have larger expected credit losses compared with interest rate swaps because the greatest probability of default coincides with the greatest total credit exposures, both coming at the end of a currency swap's life.

The analysis of credit risk becomes more complex in moving from considering the credit risk of individual derivatives to portfolios of derivatives. Simulation analysis is again needed to handle the interrelationships of a portfolio's derivatives. One issue is the extent to which individual derivatives in a portfolio with the same counterparty may be netted against one another. That is, a dealer or end user may owe payments on some derivatives while simultaneously receiving payments on others, all with the same counterparty. If only the net amount is paid, then the total cash flow is generally much smaller. It is becoming increasingly common practice to bundle individual derivatives into so-called master agreements that provide for netting of payments.

A related concept is close-out netting in the event of counterparty bankruptcy. Through a master agreement, the amount a defaulting counterparty owes upon termination of its outstanding contracts with another counterparty would be limited to the net amount of the mark-to-market values. In the absence of a master agreement, the sum of the gross amounts of contracts with negative replacement value would be owed. The credit exposure is generally much larger without netting arrangements in place. The practice of bilateral netting and the use of master agreements are becoming more widespread. Legal uncertainties pose the greatest obstacles to broader application of bilateral netting.

Chart 2 shows the gross replacement costs relative to the book value of assets of commercial bank derivatives dealers from 1990 to 1992. These are disaggregated into interest rate and foreign exchange derivatives. The gross replacement costs or current exposures amount to less than 10 percent of assets. These measures exaggerate exposures because they ignore the fact that many derivatives contracts with a single counterparty are included in bilateral netting arrangements, which have been estimated to reduce counterparty exposures by 40 percent to 60 percent (Group of Thirty 1993b, 135). Furthermore, all derivatives counterparties are highly unlikely to default simultaneously – the expected loss is considerably smaller than the gross exposure – and recoveries in the event of default are likely to be greater than zero. Chart 3 shows the corresponding gross replacement costs for bank nondealers, who as a group have current exposures relative to assets about a tenth the size of bank dealers'.

Gross credit exposures appear larger when measured against the equity capital of an institution. In a recent survey conducted by the General Accounting Office, the derivatives gross credit exposure of thirteen major U.S. derivatives dealers in 1992 amounted to 100 percent or more of equity capital for ten of the thirteen dealers. However, another perspective emerges in considering the same exposures relative to loans for seven of the dealers that are commercial banks. Whereas the derivatives exposures ranged from 100 percent to 500 percent of equity capital, the commercial loan exposures ranged from about 350 percent to 1200 percent (GAO 1994, 53–55),

Chart 2   Commercial bank derivatives positions – dealers: replacement costs relative to book assets

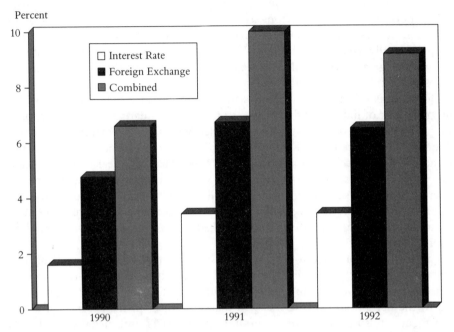

Source: CFTC, using data from the Board of Governors of the Federal Reserve System FR Y-9C Reports.

with loan exposures being a multiple of the derivatives exposures at each bank, except for one.

Legal risk

The derivatives markets span industrialized nations all over the globe. Each nation of course has different securities and bankruptcy laws, and uncertainty about how derivatives contracts are treated in different legal jurisdictions stands as one of the major challenges to the derivatives business. Another level of complexity is that many laws that affect OTC derivatives were legislated before the advent of OTC derivatives trading. Derivatives counterparties risk losses because of legal actions that render their contracts unenforceable.

The most notorious case is that of the London borough of Hammersmith and Fulham. In 1991 the U.K. House of Lords nullified swap contracts that this London municipality had established during the mid-1980s on the grounds that derivatives transactions were "beyond its capacity" – that is, the municipality did not have the legal authority to enter into the contracts. This decision was far-reaching and voided contracts between 130 government entities and 75 of the world's largest banks (Group of Thirty 1993b, 46). On the basis of consultations with regulators and lawyers, participants in these swaps had assumed prior to the ruling that the municipalities had the right to engage in swaps. Over half of the realized losses from defaults (as of year-end 1991) stemmed from the Hammersmith and Fulham decision.

Chart 3 Commercial bank derivatives positions – non dealers: replacement costs relative to book assets

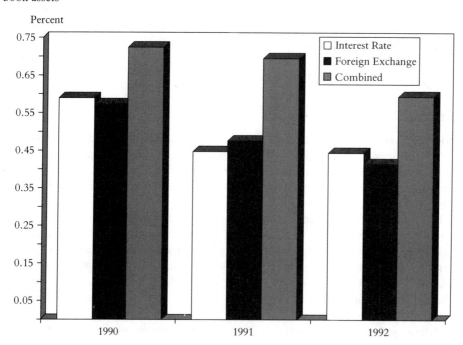

Percent

Legend:
- □ Interest Rate
- ■ Foreign Exchange
- ▦ Combined

Source: CFTC, using data from the Board of Governors of the Federal Reserve System FR Y-9C Reports.

The question of capacity is also an issue in jurisdictions outside of the United Kingdom as well as for other kinds of swap counterparties. A recent Group of Thirty survey disclosed that, besides municipalities, derivatives market participants are also concerned about entering into contracts with sovereigns (that is, national governments), pension funds, and, to a lesser degree, with unit investment trusts and insurance companies (Group of Thirty 1993b, 47).

Another major area of concern regarding legal risks is how derivatives are handled in the case of early termination as a result of the bankruptcy, insolvency, or liquidation of a counterparty. Market participants have serious doubts about how bankruptcy courts may treat master agreements with bilateral close-out netting provisions. First, there is the risk that a particular bankruptcy proceeding could result in netting provisions not being recognized, leaving a creditor counterparty with a higher exposure than anticipated. Second, even if respected, an automatic stay on terminating contracts (and transferring funds) that is typical in bankruptcy proceedings contributes to uncertainties about exposures and the eventual recovery of funds from a bankrupt counterparty.

The United States is ahead of many other jurisdictions in resolving these legal uncertainties because of the general consistency among the Bankruptcy Code (for nonfinancial entities) and the two laws governing financial institutions – the Financial Institutions Reform, Recovery, and Enforcement Act (FIRREA) of 1989 and the Federal Deposit Insurance Corporation Improvement Act (FDICIA) of 1991.[14]

Through its authority under FDICIA, the Federal Reserve Board in February 1994 expanded the definition of a financial institution to encompass all large-scale OTC derivatives dealers. In particular, certain affiliates of broker-dealers and insurance companies were not included in the definition prior to the ruling, which now accords legal certainty to netting arrangements that involve these institutions. The Federal Reserve Board advocates developing a single standard regarding the netting of obligations (U.S. Congress 1993, 353–54).

Settlement risk

Settlement risk is the risk of default during the period, usually less than twenty-four hours, when one counterparty has fulfilled its obligation under a contract and awaits payment or delivery of securities from the other counterparty. Owing to differences in time zones and other factors, most exchanges are not made simultaneously (doing so would eliminate settlement risk).

The classic case of settlement risk is the failure of the Bank Herstatt, a German bank, on June 26, 1974. As of the close of business that day, the German banking authorities permanently closed Herstatt, after it had received marks from New York banks for its foreign exchange transactions but had not yet paid the counterparty banks in dollars (R. Alton Gilbert 1992, 10). (The dollar payments were scheduled to be made after the close of business in Germany.) Settlement risk is now sometimes called Herstatt risk.

Bilateral payments netting through master agreements is one mechanism that reduces settlement risk. The fact that many contracts, such as interest rate swaps, do not involve exchanges of principal also mitigates this risk. The greatest settlement risks lie in cross-currency derivatives, for which notional amounts are exchanged in different currencies. However, the settlement risks of derivatives, excluding forward foreign exchange contracts, are small compared with those stemming from spot and forward foreign exchange contracts. In 1992 worldwide average daily net cash flows were $0.65 billion and $1.9 billion for interest rate and currency swaps, respectively, whereas the net worldwide cash flows for spot and short-dated forward foreign exchange transactions were $400 billion and $420 billion (Group of Thirty 1993a, 50).[15]

Operating risk

Operating risk is exposure to loss as a result of inadequate risk management and internal controls by firms using derivatives. This risk category encompasses a wide variety of nuts and bolts operations that are central to the use of derivatives, either as a dealer or as an end user. At the broadest level, lack of involvement or understanding by a firm's senior management or board of directors is an operating risk. The example cited earlier – Showa Shell, a subsidiary firm speculating on foreign currency – is an extreme case in point. There is a consensus between derivatives practitioners and regulators that an independent group within a dealing firm be responsible for overseeing risk management. For example, the oversight of a firm's derivatives positions needs to be uncolored by pressures to generate trading profits or by other conflicting objectives. End users with extensive derivatives involvement should adopt similar practices.

At a more mundane level, inadequacies in documentation, credit controls, limits on positions, and types of instruments approved for use can expose a firm to risk of loss. Related to these considerations is the functioning of the back-office operation, which handles trade confirmations, documentation, payments, and accounting. Errors anywhere along the line of processing trades or maintaining positions are potentially sources of loss. Systems have to be in place for allowing internal audits by the risk management group to monitor derivatives activity within the firm. Computer or communications hardware breakdowns could leave an organization open to losses because of the inability to conduct business. This danger is present for any business, but particularly for derivatives, which require frequent portfolio adjustments to hedge exposures and so forth.

Backlogs in documenting transactions can be a source of legal risk. During the beginning years of the OTC derivatives markets, severe backlogs were not uncommon and oral agreements were often the only contract binding counterparties. Because of rapidly changing rates and prices, it is standard practice in financial markets to make a transaction orally, followed by a written contract. The risk is that if too much time elapses, a counterparty holding a losing position could deny the existence of an oral agreement or dispute the terms of that agreement. Though a continuing concern, derivatives documentation backlogs are reportedly much less severe today (Group of Thirty 1993b, 45).

Personnel in derivatives operations are also sources of risk. As in any business, human error can be costly if not caught in time. The same is true of outright fraud. A more subtle problem is the reliance on one or a few highly specialized individuals. The loss of an individual or group of individuals could wreak havoc on an operation if no one else knows the specialists' jobs. For example, if the manager of a derivatives portfolio were to leave the firm for a better offer elsewhere, others might be hard pressed to understand the composition and risks of that portfolio or to be able to liquidate or unwind the portfolio in the event of a crisis.[16]

Systemic risk

The influential Promisel Report of the Group of Ten central banks defines systemic risk as "the risk that a disruption (at a firm, in a market segment, to a settlement system, etc.) causes widespread difficulties at other firms, in other market segments or in the financial system as a whole" (Group of Thirty 1993a, 61). As noted earlier, defaults have been relatively rare occurrences in derivatives markets. There has not been a systemic crisis.[17] However, the markets' global scope and interconnections as well as their relatively unregulated structure have raised concerns among regulators and legislators.

A major concern about derivatives markets is their lack of transparency. Accounting and disclosure of derivatives positions is widely regarded as inadequate. Accounting standards lag well behind financial innovation. An April 1993 survey of derivatives dealers and end users by the Group of Thirty revealed that only 60 percent of dealers and 30 percent of end users disclose their accounting policies for derivatives in their public financial statements, and 40 percent of dealers and 60 percent of end users have inconsistent accounting policies for derivatives and underlying assets. Other pertinent information about the risks and profitability, like credit exposures and unrealized gains and losses, of derivatives activities was available publicly from only a fraction of the survey respondents (Group of Thirty 1994, 80, 129). As of the survey date, 85 percent of dealers mark all derivatives positions to market for internal management purposes while only 41 percent of end users do so. These percentages are much lower for external financial statements – 67 percent and 28 percent, respectively.

Even if these deficiencies in disclosure were remedied, the fast-changing nature of derivatives positions would always create uncertainties for outsiders about current positions and exposures. In times of hectic market conditions, there will be less agreement among market participants about the equilibrium value of derivatives, particularly options and contracts containing embedded options. Traders may be uncertain about the appropriate volatility to use in pricing options. Furthermore, the financial condition of counterparties may be difficult to evaluate. As a result, market liquidity may be reduced so that buying or selling derivatives causes bigger price moves than during ordinary trading, reflecting a reluctance to trade. If a major derivatives player were suspected to be in difficulty, it might have problems hedging its positions or obtaining funding to finance them, which would tend to compound its solvency problems. Under such conditions, should the institution fail, the firm or its regulators could have a hard time closing out or assigning its derivatives positions to other counterparties. In fact, as a precautionary measure, counterparties may reduce their exposure limits with other counterparties in times of market turbulence.

Despite the relatively good – albeit brief – track record of the OTC derivatives practitioners, there is simply no way to guarantee that a systemic crisis will not occur. Any of the previous sources of risk individually or in combination could precipitate a systemic crisis. Federal Reserve Bank of New York president William J. McDonough states the regulator's perspective succinctly: "It may appear that central banks are unduly preoccupied with low-probability scenarios of possible systemic disruptions. However, it is precisely because market participants may only take minimal precautions for events in the tails of probability distributions that central banks must be vigilant" (James A. Leach and others 1993, 17). Implicit in this view is that the private sector may lack the incentive to internalize the costs of safeguarding markets against systemic risk. In other words, regulation may be necessary to compel participants to take additional measures to protect the stability of derivatives (and other) markets. Few observers of derivatives markets would deny that systemic risk is potentially a concern; the controversy is over measures to minimize that risk.

Recommendations for Safeguarding the Derivatives Markets

Derivatives markets have come under scrutiny by a number of derivatives industry groups and regulators – both in the United States and abroad. Each has made recommendations for improving industry practice to reduce the chance of firm-level losses as well as systemic risk. This section discusses the key recommendations of four of these groups whose views are particularly influential. The purpose here is to highlight the salient points and not to give a comprehensive review.

The studies and proposals to be considered are the following, in order of their publication:[18]

1. Basle Committee on Banking Supervision (April 1993):
   - "The Supervisory Recognition of Netting for Capital Adequacy Purposes"
   - "The Supervisory Treatment of Market Risks"
   - "Measurement of Banks' Exposure to Interest Rate Risk"
2. Group of Thirty (July 1993), "Derivatives: Practices and Principles"
3. House Committee on Banking, Finance, and Urban Affairs Minority Staff (November 1993), "Financial Derivatives"
4. U.S. General Accounting Office (May 1994), "Financial Derivatives: Actions Needed to Protect the Financial System"

The Basle Committee on Banking Supervision, established in 1975, consists of senior representatives of bank supervisory authorities and central banks from the Group of Ten countries.[19] The Group of Thirty comprises senior financial markets practitioners, regulators, and academics and largely corresponds to the private sector's perspective. The Minority Staff report, prepared under the direction of James Leach, the ranking minority member of the House Committee on Banking, Finance, and Urban Affairs, was submitted as part of the proceedings related to the committee's *Hearings on Safety and Soundness Issues Related to Bank Derivatives Activities* (U.S. Congress 1993). The U.S. General Accounting Office report was prepared at the request of members of several House committees that frame legislation affecting financial markets.

Among the organizations that have examined derivatives activity (see note 18 for other derivatives studies), there is a general consensus that the first line of defense rests with senior management and the board of directors at individual firms involved with derivatives. They need to establish internal controls and audit procedures necessary to monitor a firm's derivatives positions and exposures. This emphasis is reflected in bank regulators' oversight of bank derivatives activity. The examination of bank holding companies and state member banks by the Federal Reserve and of national banks by the Office of the Comptroller of the Currency (OCC) has been aided by new guidelines and instructions for examiners in evaluating a banking organization's derivatives operations. The OCC issued Banking Circular 277, "Risk Management of Financial Derivatives," in October 1993, and the Federal Reserve implemented "Examining Risk Management and Internal Controls for Trading Activities of Banking Organizations" in December 1993. These guidelines are largely consistent with the Group of Thirty's recommendations. However, this kind of regulatory oversight does not extend to all participants in derivatives markets, such as unregistered securities affiliates (like Drexel's derivatives affiliate mentioned in note 17) and insurance companies. As a matter of sound business practice, derivatives practitioners must self-regulate their activities – the message that is the tenor of the Group of Thirty's recommendations.

The Group of Thirty

In July 1993, the Group of Thirty published a list of twenty recommendations for dealers and end users that are intended as a "benchmark against which participants can measure their own practices" (Group of Thirty 1993a, 7). The clear implication is that alternative practices may be equally effective or superior (and the Group of Thirty points out that some of the recommendations were not unanimously endorsed by all of its members). A fundamental criticism of the Group of Thirty report is that derivatives dealers and end users may lack the incentive to adopt the recommended practices, particularly because of the costs of implementation. Of course, a powerful incentive in favor of heeding the recommendations is concern about government regulatory efforts, which also impose costs. An additional four recommendations are expressly for the consideration of legislators, regulators, and supervisors. Indeed, all of the recommendations have proved useful in framing many of the issues that legislators, regulators, and supervisors have been deliberating. The recommendations address each of the sources of derivatives risk sketched in the previous section.

The first recommendation stresses the integral role of senior management in understanding and controlling derivatives operations. Even among derivatives dealers, 51 percent of respondents to the April 1993 Group of Thirty survey rated the insufficient understanding of derivatives by senior management as being of serious concern (15 percent) or some concern (Group of Thirty 1994, 11). The next eight recommendations pertain to valuation and market risk management. One of these stresses the importance of having an independent group within the firm monitor market risk. Another emphasizes the need for daily marking to market of derivatives positions, which, in fact, most major dealers practice but less than half of end users do. A related recommendation advocates using a portfolio valuation approach known as value at risk. This statistical technique determines the change in the value of a derivatives portfolio resulting from adverse market movements (of any risk factor, such as price or volatility) during a fixed time period. The Group of Thirty advises using one day as the time horizon, consistent with its mark-to-market interval. The value at risk would be computed for a given confidence interval – that is, the probability of suffering a loss in excess of the value at risk would be quantified as 2.5 percent or some other small bound. (For a 2.5 percent probability, the actual daily loss would be expected to exceed the daily value at risk one trading day in every forty.) The Group of Thirty also advocates the use of portfolio stress tests, which focus on changes in portfolio value during periods of extreme volatility as well as illiquidity.

Although these last two are sound recommendations, both value-at-risk calculations and stress tests are demanding exercises. They should be conducted under conservative assumptions because there is little consensus about the best valuation models for complex interest rate derivatives. For example, there is no agreement about the best type of term structure model in the current academic literature. Such a model is one of the building blocks of simulation analyses. Current models generally fail to capture statistically the episodic bursts of volatility that occur in actual markets (see, for example, Thomas F. Cooley 1993). Also, in times of abnormal market conditions, liquidity is usually substantially reduced (see the earlier discussion of systemic risk), which would have to be recognized in stress tests as well as in value-at-risk evaluations. The challenges of simulation are compounded further when considering portfolios rather than individual instruments because of the need to estimate correlations and other interdependencies among instruments, which are also likely to be less predictable during periods of market stress.[20]

Another five recommendations address credit risk measurement and management. The Group of Thirty endorses using a probability analysis analogous to the one for measuring market risk exposure. Credit exposure, as mentioned earlier, is measured in terms of current and potential exposures. The evaluation of potential exposure (future replacement costs) requires all of the tools and sophistication that go into market risk calculations. In addition, the probability of counterparty default needs to be assessed. This is a much more challenging task because reliable statistical methods for predicting insolvency are not available and more judgmental approaches must be employed. Of course, financial institutions – especially commercial banks – are in the business of making credit evaluations and, presumably, have the expertise to monitor their counterparties. The Group of Thirty stresses the need for an independent group within the firm to evaluate credit standards and risks and to set credit limits vis-à-vis individual counterparties.

Credit enhancements of several types can reduce credit risks in derivatives transactions. The Group of Thirty recommends that dealers and end users evaluate the costs and benefits of such methods. One commonly used method is the posting of collateral, typically in the form of government securities, if the counterparty in a losing position has a mark-to-market value that exceeds a specified threshold, such as $1 million. This posting could be based on periodic marking-to-market or on a net risk limit, beyond which collateral would be transferred. Dealers generally resist being subject to collateralization provisions, but recently collateral has been requested in deals involving even triple-A banks. In transactions between dealers, it is more common for swap coupons to be reset so that credit exposures are periodically reduced to near zero (Lillian Chew 1994, 36–37). (The dealers effectively transact a new swap at current market rates.) Another method of credit enhancement is the establishing of separately capitalized derivatives subsidiaries or the use of third-party credit enhancements such as guarantees or letters of credit, which are discussed below.

The Group of Thirty strongly encourages the use of a single master agreement with each counterparty that provides for bilateral payments and close-out netting. This position is combined with a call for continuing efforts to ensure the legal enforceability of existing and future derivative contracts. The success of netting arrangements depends on the legal certainty of derivative contracts.

The remaining four recommendations to dealers and end users pertain to the adequacy of back office systems, to the high standards of expertise of derivatives professionals, to the line of authority for committing to derivative transactions, and finally to accounting and disclosure. The Group of Thirty seeks international harmonization of accounting standards and particularly urges consistency in the way income is recognized between derivatives and the assets or liabilities being hedged. With regard to public disclosures, the "financial statements of dealers and end users should contain sufficient information about their use of derivatives to provide an understanding of the purposes for which transactions are undertaken, the extent of the transactions, the degree of risk involved, and how the transactions have been accounted for" (Group of Thirty 1993a, 21). As noted earlier, the poor quality of information in public financial disclosures is a major area for improved industry practice.

An additional four recommendations are directed toward legislators, regulators, and supervisors. Two urge the international recognition of bilateral payments and close-out netting arrangements as well as efforts to resolve other legal and regulatory uncertainties, particularly issues concerning the legal enforceability of contracts. Many tax laws need amendment so that better consistency can be achieved between the taxation of gains and losses from derivative contracts and those from the under-lying instruments being hedged. Uncertainties and inconsistencies about the tax treatment of income flows impede wider use of derivatives in risk management. Finally, authorities responsible for setting accounting standards need to work to harmonize standards across jurisdictions and modernize these standards in accord with current derivative's risk management.

None of the Group of Thirty recommendations deals with capital adequacy. Capital is the cushion against losses for a financial institution. Regulators gener-ally seek to establish minimum prudential standards, not optimal levels. Implicitly, however, the value-at-risk and credit exposure assessments discussed above are relevant to determining how much capital a firm should hold to cover market and credit risks. The provision of capital to support derivatives activities is an issue properly included in a consideration of best practices and principles. Indeed, some major derivatives dealers have their own systems, similar to value-at-risk, for allo-cating capital internally to different activities, such as swaps trading or government bond trading (see "International Banking Survey" 1993).

As another example, unregistered broker-dealers of U.S. securities firms fall outside the scope of capital requirements imposed on registered broker-dealers by the Securities and Exchange Commission. Most OTC derivatives transactions of these firms are conducted by unregistered broker-dealers, which deal in derivat-ives, especially interest rate and currency swaps, that are not classified as securities by the SEC. One of the reasons for this segregation of activities is that secur-ities firms consider the SEC's net capital rule to be antiquated and excessive in its capital requirements.[21] (The net capital rule governs capital levels at the registered broker-dealers, and, in particular, requires that 100 percent of unrealized profits on derivatives positions be deducted from net capital.) As things stand now, capital supporting unregistered securities affiliates is determined by the discretion of man-agement, not regulators. The determination of appropriate capital levels is not just a worry of the regulators.

Some of these unregistered securities dealers have been restructured as "enhanced derivatives products companies" (DPCs) that have capital segregated in the sub-sidiary in order to gain the highest credit risk ratings (CFTC 1993b, Working Paper 6). The intention is that counterparties would be more willing to enter into derivatives transactions with the highly capitalized enhanced DPC than with the lower-rated parent company. (The enhanced DPC is presumed to be insulated from the bankruptcy of the parent company.) Some insurance companies have set up DPCs that are not separately capitalized but carry guarantees from the parent that confer a triple-A credit rating. These restructurings of the derivatives dealers are market-based responses to market participants' concerns about the capital adequacy of their counterparties.

Minority Staff report

The 900-page Minority Staff report assembles a wealth of information about derivatives markets. It reprints and summarizes much that is contained in earlier studies and gives further background information as well. In addition, the Minority Staff solicited responses from federal banking and securities regulators on a range of issues, including the Group of Thirty recommendations. (The regulators are the

Federal Deposit Insurance Corporation, the Office of Thrift Supervision, the Federal Reserve, the Office of the Comptroller of the Currency, the Securities and Exchange Commission, and the Commodity Futures Trading Commission.) The Minority Staff gives thirty recommendations of its own for stronger regulatory standards. Many of these recommendations reflect the federal regulators' perspectives on the derivatives markets, and many are consistent with those of the Group of Thirty. The Minority Staff's recommendations are intended to "suggest areas where the regulators may take action to implement prudential safeguards concerning derivatives activities."[22] They are presented as points for regulators and legislators to consider rather than as detailed suggestions.

Several recommendations deal with strengthening capital requirements and protecting the deposit insurance safety net. "Bank and thrift regulators should retain a strong leverage capital standard to generally guard against risks at insured financial institutions, including risks posed by derivative instruments" (Recommendation 1). The leverage capital standard is in addition to risk-based measures for credit and market risks. The leverage standard is based on the ratio of total assets (not risk-adjusted) to capital and serves as a backup for the risk-based standard. To the extent that the latter may imperfectly measure risks, the leverage ratio would place a ceiling on overall exposures. (For example, a bank could have relatively conservative assets – like Treasury securities that currently receive no capital charge – and consequently have a very low capital cushion against interest rate shocks. In the absence of a leverage ratio, a bank with federally insured deposits could expand its balance sheet by issuing liabilities and buying Treasuries and thereby raise its exposure to interest rate risk.) Furthermore, the regulators should evaluate the need for increasing capital, particularly for potential future credit exposures, above the current standard (Recommendation 11). Then, regulators should "adopt capital, accounting and disclosure standards based on a 99 percent confidence interval (3 standard deviations)" (Recommendation 13), which is much more conservative than the 95 percent confidence interval commonly in use by derivatives dealers and end users.

There are two areas in which the Minority Staff's recommendations go beyond previous proposals for improved derivatives practice and regulation. The first is greater coordination among federal banking and securities regulators. An interagency commission would be "established by statute to consider comparable rules related to capital, accounting, disclosure and suitability for dealers and end users of OTC derivative products" (Recommendation 4). One of the purposes of this commission would be to bring uniform rules to all participants, including those outside the oversight of federal regulators, like insurance companies. The central thrust of this approach is that regulation would be applied by product type rather than by institution, as in the current system. (Recommendation 2 emphasizes this point.) Consultations among federal regulators, which are now less structured and informal, would be formalized through the mechanism of an interagency commission. (A less formal structure is the Working Group on Financial Markets, which consists of the heads of the Federal Reserve, Treasury, CFTC, and SEC. The Working Group, formed in the wake of the October 1987 stock market crash, was reconvened earlier this year to examine issues regarding derivatives. In its report, the CFTC has proposed an interagency council to improve communication among regulators and to coordinate regulation. The OCC has a similar, though narrower, proposal for an interagency task force on U.S. bank activity in derivatives.) For the federal banking agencies, this coordination extends to joint examinations of bank holding companies and banks involved in derivatives as well as coordinated training programs for examiners.

The other area that gets particular attention in these recommendations is the protection of "less sophisticated" participants. Derivatives dealers would be required to judge the suitability of derivatives positions for their customers. (OCC Banking Circular 277 includes such a standard for its examiners in evaluating dealers affiliated with nationally chartered banks; the SEC requires broker-dealers to consider suitability when dealing with customers.) Counterparties, especially "less sophisticated" end users, would have to be informed about the "specific costs and risks of derivative instruments in varying interest rate or other market change scenarios" (Recommendation 23). Mutual funds that hold derivatives or securities with embedded derivatives should be subject to enhanced disclosures of risks for the benefit of their customers (Recommendation 26). Another recommendation directs regulators to set minimum prudential practices for municipalities and pension funds (Recommendation 25). The federal bank regulators would design and run programs to educate end users about the risks and benefits of derivatives (Recommendation 24).

GAO report

The GAO report echoes the Minority Staff report's call for congressional legislative action to improve uniformity of federal regulation and, in particular, to make insurance company derivatives affiliates and unregistered broker-dealers subject to federal regulation. They go further and also recommend that Congress reconsider the entire structure of the federal financial regulatory system, with the aim of modernizing it. However, the immediate need is to broaden federal regulatory authority. The banking system currently has the most stringent federal oversight because of its access to federal deposit insurance and the Federal Reserve's discount window, but the GAO argues that the failure of a nonbank derivatives dealer could also require federal involvement to stem systemic repercussions. "Existing differences in the regulation of derivatives dealers limit the ability of the federal government to anticipate or respond to a crisis started by or involving one of these institutions [securities and insurance affiliates]" (GAO 1994, 124).

The GAO report covers much of the same ground surveyed in earlier studies. Its accent is on a stronger hand of government regulators on derivatives users. The GAO endorses the Group of Thirty recommendations but sees the need for regulations to compel compliance with best practices standards. Currently, large insured depository institutions have to follow the corporate governance provisions mandated by FDICIA.[23] The GAO would have all major derivatives dealers adopt these provisions.

Even for the banking system, where regulation is now most comprehensive, much more could be done to improve the risks of derivatives. These steps would include "(1) gathering consistent information on large counterparty credit exposures and sources and amounts of derivatives-related income, and maintaining the information in a centralized location accessible to all regulators; (2) revising capital requirements to ensure that all derivatives risks are covered and that legally enforceable netting agreements are recognized; and (3) increasing emphasis on the identification and testing of key internal controls over derivatives activities" (GAO, 124).

The GAO does not believe that the April 1994 proposal by the Federal Financial Institutions Examinations Council for expanded bank reporting of derivatives activity goes far enough to be useful to regulators. The GAO wants more information on the sources of income by activity, whether from executing customer orders or from proprietary trading, and by derivative product. The proposed reporting requirements contain information that is still too aggregated to reveal potential future problems at individual banks.

Two areas that the GAO examines in some depth are accounting principals for derivatives and the state of international regulatory cooperation. As other groups have noted, accounting and disclosure practices for derivatives have many deficiencies. This shortcoming is particularly true for end users, which typically do not mark derivatives positions to market but rather account for positions at historical cost. These users can often apply so-called hedge accounting rules, which the GAO faults as being inconsistent and contradictory. Deferral hedge accounting allows the gains and losses on a derivative to be deferred and reported at the same time as the income from the instrument being hedged. A potential for manipulation of financial reports exists because hedge accounting can mask wide swings in values of derivatives that, after the fact, may prove not to have correlated well with the value of the hedged position and would not have qualified for this accounting treatment if the actual low correlation had been known (GAO, 98). Another area of concern is the use of hedge accounting in situations in which anticipated positions in an instrument are being hedged by derivatives, such as an anticipated purchase of a mortgage-backed security.

The Financial Accounting Standards Board has been improving disclosure requirements in financial statements through the adoption of several Statements of Financial Accounting Standards related to off-balance-sheet positions, but the current standard still leaves firms with much discretion about the amount of detail to reveal regarding derivatives positions. The solution, according to the GAO, is to move to a market-value accounting standard. Derivatives dealers have to apply market-value accounting to their trading positions. If all derivatives users were subject to this standard, the transparency of derivatives activity would be substantially improved.

The GAO report gives a thorough overview of the state of international regulatory coordination. The most successful area of international cooperation is in the regulation of bank capital, which is taken up in the next section. There is less agreement on capital adequacy for international securities firms. Wide differences in accounting and disclosure standards exist internationally. As noted above, laws regarding derivatives activity, especially netting, also vary considerably from one country to another.

The GAO has identified clear weaknesses in the oversight of derivatives activities within the management of firms and within the regulatory structure. Many of these problems were also cited in the earlier Group of Thirty report. The most serious shortcoming of the GAO's assessment of the OTC derivatives markets is a failure to weigh the costs and benefits of increased regulation and disclosure requirements. The GAO's argument for further regulation rests largely on the presumed need to eliminate the risk of failure of a major derivatives dealer. The benefit of avoiding that risk evidently outweighs the explicit costs imposed by more regulation and the implicit costs of less hedging (less risk-sharing) by intermediaries and end users because of the higher costs of such transactions. This issue deserves closer and more careful examination. The vulnerability of the financial system has not been established, despite the hundreds of pages of studies that have recently been devoted to the topic.

As part of its two-year study, the GAO conducted a survey of fifteen major U.S. OTC derivatives dealers and received fourteen responses (from seven banks, five securities firms, and two insurance company affiliates). Given the concern about "global involvement, concentration, and linkages" in this report (page 7), a surprising fact is that the weighted-average net credit exposure of the derivative dealer respondents to other U.S. dealers was 11 percent at year-end 1992 (GAO, 157). This exposure is slightly lower than it had been in the 1990 and 1991 GAO surveys. The exposure to non-U.S. dealers was 27 percent. (For the responding dealers, about 75 percent of their contracts were subject to netting agreements [GAO, 58].) Furthermore, among the world's largest derivatives dealers, none had more than a 10 percent market share of any particular derivative product (GAO, 41). Eight of the dealers who responded derived an average of 15 percent of their pretax income from derivatives acivity (GAO, 73). This and other information from the survey indicates that derivatives activity is not the dominant source of income; the major dealers appear to be well diversified. On balance, a convincing case has not been made that derivatives markets dangerously concentrate risks among a small number of participants.

Basle Committee proposals

The Basle Committee proposals of April 1993 would incorporate market risks into a risk-based capital standard for banks. For banks with international dealings, the Basle Capital Accord of 1988 established minimum capital adequacy standards that were fully implemented in the G-10 countries and many other countries by year-end 1992. The basic procedure entails weighting both on- and off-balance-sheet items by credit riskiness, using weights prescribed by the capital accord, and then maintaining capital against these risk-weighted balance sheet items at or above mandated levels. The minimum core capital ratio is 4 percent of core capital to risk-weighted balance sheet items, and the total capital ratio is 8 percent of core plus supplementary capital.[24]

The proposal on netting is intended to amend the 1988 capital standard to permit bilateral netting of credit risks under well-specified conditions. The market risk proposal would assess specific capital charges on open positions (that is, unhedged positions) for debt and equity trading portfolios as well as foreign exchange positions. Derivative securities are included in the coverage of all these portfolios. The proposal focuses on trading portfolios, in which positions change rapidly, as opposed to investment portfolios, in which positions are longer-term and relatively static. The trading portfolio contains proprietary positions taken to execute trades with customers, to speculate on short-term security price movements and arbitrage security price discrepancies, and to hedge other positions in the trading account. The investment portfolios would continue to be subject to the provisions of the 1988 Capital Accord. The interest rate risk proposal would cover the entire bank, but at its current stage of development, the proposal is advancing a measurement system rather than a procedure for assessing capital charges. Derivatives, including those outside of trading accounts, figure into the measurement scheme.

The Basle Committee proposes a new class of capital to help satisfy the capital charges against market risks in trading portfolios: "Capital requirements for market risk . . . tend to be far more volatile than those for credit risk and a more flexible source of capital may be considered appropriate" (Basle Committee 1993c, 9). (The other types of capital would also have to be allocated to back the trading portfolio activities.) Banks will be able to issue short-term subordinated debt for the sole purpose of meeting this capital requirement. Among other stipulations, the debt would have a lock-in feature that prevents the payment of principal or interest in the event a bank falls below 120 percent of the required market risk-based capital.

Under the capital accord, the only type of netting recognized is netting by novation, which is highly restrictive. Netting by novation entails combining contracts that are denominated in the same currency and have the same value dates (dates on which repricing occurs) into a new contract with a counterparty. The capital accord uses two methods to calculate credit equivalent amounts for off-balance-sheet items: current exposure and original exposure.[25] Capital requirements are based on risk weights applied to positions in on-balance-sheet items, like loans and government securities, and to credit-equivalent off-balance-sheet positions. Using the current exposure method, the total credit exposure for a derivative is its current replacement cost and a so-called add-on that represents the future exposure of the instrument, determined by a schedule of scale factors applied to the notional amount of the security. This schedule depends on the type of instrument and its time to maturity. (For example, currency swaps have higher add-ons than interest rate swaps, and longer-dated instruments have higher factors than shorter-dated ones.) The computation is performed for all contracts with positive current replacement value for which counterparty default would cause a credit loss, and then all of these credit equivalent amounts are totaled. This procedure is very conservative because any offsetting cash outflows from negative value contracts with the same counterparty reduce credit exposure but are ignored in determining the current exposure.

The netting proposal would base the current replacement cost on the net amount of the current exposure to a counterparty. The conditions under which this procedure would be permitted are restrictive. For example, the enforceability of the netting scheme must be clearly established in all relevant jurisdictions, and derivative contracts cannot contain "walkaway clauses" (discussed in note 12). The add-on amount, however, would be computed without considering netting, as it has been under the 1988 Capital Accord. The Basle Committee "has not yet identified any evidence suggesting that the need for add-ons declines appreciably in [a netting] environment" (Basle Committee 1993a, 4). They estimate that the capital charge would drop by 25 percent to 40 percent using the new procedure. However, some in the industry believe that the add-on treatment is excessive, but no satisfactory alternative method consistent with this framework has been proposed (Chew 1994, 38–39).

The proposal on market risks sets forth an elaborate system for measuring market risks of on- and off-balance-sheet items. Only interest rate derivatives positions will be considered here. For the purpose of capital determination, derivatives positions are converted into notional security positions. These positions are then grouped into thirteen maturity time bands, each of which has its own risk weight. The risk weight represents the sensitivity of that notional position at a given maturity to a given change in the interest rate risk factor. (The size of the change is a two-standard-deviation shift in interest rates. Separate factors are assigned to specific risks and general risks, for which only the latter usually apply to interest rate and foreign exchange derivatives. Specific risk reflects credit-related and liquidity risks of the underlying security.)

The conversion of a fixed-for-floating interest rate swap is relatively straight-forward. The swap is viewed as a combination of fixed- and floating-rate government securities with coupon payment dates and maturities matching the value dates and maturity of the swap. Receiving a fixed rate from a swap is equivalent to receiving a fixed coupon from a bond. The notional fixed-rate bond is slotted into the appropriate maturity time band in the capital calculation. Paying a floating rate on a swap is equivalent to having issued (or being short) a short-term bond that gets rolled over or repriced at the next value date. This bond gets slotted as a short-term instrument, say a three-month maturity.

Interest rate options and forward contracts are more complicated. Interest rate forward contracts are treated as combined long and short notional positions in government securities.[26] Options are similar but require conversion to notional amounts using delta equivalent values. (Delta is the sensitivity of the option price to a small change in the underlying security price and is evaluated using a particular option pricing model. Options can be hedged against small changes in the underlying price by taking an opposite position in the underlying price adjusted by [multiplied by] the delta value.) The separate long and short notional securities get slotted into the time bands.

The proposal then allows for further adjustments that reflect the offsetting impacts of different types of positions. Perfectly matched positions drop out from further consideration and do not affect capital. For example, a swap in a portfolio to pay fixed and receive floating together with an identical swap with the same counterparty, swap rate, and currency to receive fixed and pay floating would be exempt from inclusion in the capital charge computation. Full offsetting is also permitted for closely matched positions that meet a number of specified conditions.

Consolidated long and short positions within each maturity band are multiplied by risk weights, and then the weighted positions are offset to give a net weighted position. Because the included securities do not actually fully offset each other – there are differences in maturity within each band as well as differences in instruments of the same maturity – a vertical disallowance factor is introduced to compensate for the so-called basis risks. The disallowance, which is added to the net weighted position, is 10 percent of the smaller of the weighted gross long or short positions. A horizontal disallowance serves a similar purpose in adjusting for offsetting positions across different time bands. This calculation adjusts for the imperfect correlation of interest rate movements across maturity time bands. (Initially offsetting long and short positions across time bands will not change in value by perfectly offsetting amounts as the term structure of interest rates shifts and twists.) The overall net weighted open position plus the vertical and horizontal disallowances would constitute the net open position against which a market risk-based capital charge would be assessed.

Public comments on the Basle Committee proposals were extremely critical of the market risk-based capital standard. The fundamental problem is that the procedure for measuring market risks is at variance with industry practice. Derivatives dealers expressed doubts about the regulatory treatment of market risks in the April 1993 Group of Thirty survey. In response to the issue of "inappropriate treatment or proposed treatment by regulators of market risk in derivatives," 33 percent indicated serious concern and another 48 percent, some concern. This survey slightly predated the public release of the Basle proposals, but the general regulatory approach involving capital based on risk-adjusted balance sheet values is well known. Many comments on the market risk capital standard stressed that a portfolio approach is the appropriate way to measure risk. A basic deficiency in the regulators' approach is that risk is treated as though it can be evaluated separately by security type and maturity and then aggregated to give a portfolio exposure. Stephen Schaefer observes that "the connection between this and a modern portfolio theory approach is, at best, tenuous since it is well known that risk does not aggregate in the linear manner implied by [the regulators' approach]" (Schaefer 1992, 12). Hugh Cohen (1994) demonstrates that the error in measuring interest rate risk exposures using the regulators' approach, even for balance sheets consisting of nothing but easily valued government bonds, is unacceptably large.

ISDA argues that the Basle Committee market risk proposal would actually increase systemic risk because it could create perverse risk management incentives. The proposal penalizes some standard hedging methods by assessing horizontal or vertical disallowances for standard hedging methods. For example, it discourages hedging a swap with an offsetting position in a Treasury security or Treasury bond futures contract. This combination would be subject to a horizontal disallowance. The disallowance seems excessive in view of the small basis risk (that is, imperfect correlation). As another example, so-called duration-based bond hedges would be subject to a vertical disallowance.[27]

ISDA offers an alternative portfolio-based approach that recognizes the risk reduction possible through diversification of securities that have "imperfectly correlated risk factor subcategories" (Joseph Bauman 1993, 6). The subcategories they propose are parallel shift risk, term structure risk, basis risk, volatility risk, and convexity risk. The risk factors to which the subcategories apply include interest rates, foreign exchange spot rates, equity indexes, commodity prices, and others. The risk-factor sensitivity approach is akin to the value-at-risk measurement advocated by the Group of Thirty.

Needless to say, this is a demanding procedure. It is probably within the means of large derivative dealers to perform this kind of analysis, but it is less likely to be easily implemented by smaller participants. Still more demanding – and more accurate – are simulation approaches, also endorsed by ISDA. The evaluation of the precision of such analyses would come under the purview of the independent risk management group.

For establishing capital levels, ISDA would have the regulators specify the performance guidelines for each firm's internal risk model. For example, the regulators would decide the size of the confidence interval that applies to potential trading losses. The regulators would also have the discretion to evaluate the suitability of the internal risk model.

Following the requirements of FDICIA, the Federal Reserve, the OCC, and the FDIC issued a proposal (a "Notice of Proposed Rulemaking") for public comment in September 1993 that would establish a risk-based capital standard for interest rate risk, including derivatives positions, as well as fuller disclosures of off-balance-sheet items. The proposed method for measuring is very similar to that in the earlier Basle Committee proposal and shares many of its defects.[28] However, the Fed-OCC-FDIC proposal stipulates that examiners from the U.S. banking agencies could require firms to use their own internal models rather than the supervisory model of the proposal.

Clearly, the task of measuring capital and establishing capital requirements is one of the most challenging issues facing private sector participants and government regulators. The regulators have attempted to develop procedures that will set minimum prudential standards for capital without making the costs of compliance excessive. Another challenge is inconsistency in standards from one country to another – the lack of a level playing field for similar institutions. The Basle Committee seeks to achieve "regulatory convergence" across jurisdictions and expects that supervisors of other types of financial institutions will adopt its standards. However, since the release of the Basle proposals, international regulators have been unable to agree in their consultations on prudent capital standards (U.S. Congress 1993, 457).[29]

Conclusion

The central policy issue in derivatives regulation is whether further federal regulation is appropriate or whether the existing structure can oversee these markets. The six federal banking and securities regulators believe that the current regulatory structure is capable of supervising the OTC derivatives markets. Policy-makers need to be cautious about changing regulatory structures because such alterations often bring unintended and unforeseen consequences. Indeed, one leading academic observer argues that government regulation is "the sand in the oyster" that stimulates much financial innovation (Merton H. Miller 1986, 470). It is by now a truism that financial innovation outpaces the regulatory and legislative process.

Regulations that are deemed too onerous drive business into unregulated entities or offshore. An example of the former is the SEC's net capital rule for broker-dealers, which is currently under review for amendment. As noted above, this rule, in place long before the advent of OTC derivatives, was a principal reason that securities firms set up unregistered dealers to conduct most types of OTC derivatives transactions. As another example, because of uncertainties about the legality of commodity swaps (which the CFTC almost ruled to be illegal off-exchange commodity futures contracts), much of this business was transacted in London in its early years, until the passage of the Futures Trading Practices Act of 1992. (This act exempted swaps from the provisions of the Commodity Exchange Act of 1936 and its later amendments.) There are many other examples.

The regulation of capital is a specific area where ill-designed rules can be counterproductive. Different kinds of institutions are likely to have different requirements and thus a uniform standard may be inappropriate. Different institutions, such as banks and securities firms, may pose different systemic risks and therefore ought to face different capital requirements (Schaefer 1992). As pointed out above, risk-based capital standards, though an improvement over simpler standards, may mismeasure risk exposures. Consequently, firms may manage risks in suboptimal ways if better means are rendered too costly by additional capital charges. These sorts of considerations imply that rigid standards ought to be avoided because they may actually increase systemic risk by changing behavior to circumvent regulations or even by actions that comply with regulations. The current system of on-site examination, in which a degree of examiner discretion comes into play, coupled with minimum prudential standards mitigates the problems associated with fixed rules.

Systemic risk is the largest risk posed by OTC derivatives and at the same time the most ill-defined one. Diffuse fears of derivatives market calamities are shaky grounds for broader regulation. The key intermediaries in these markets are well diversified and highly capitalized. It is also important to note that those intermediaries not under federal regulation still face market discipline, as do other intermediaries. The recent creation of separately capitalized derivatives product companies is evidence of market pressures to limit credit risks. Collateralization and coupon resetting of swaps are other commonly used methods of reining in credit risks.

An issue to consider is that regulatory actions that might constrain derivatives activity might also exacerbate systemic problems elsewhere. Hedging should reduce the risk of failure. The breakdown in September 1992 of the European Exchange Rate Mechanism, which had narrowly aligned major European exchange rates, is a recent example of how derivatives performed under turbulent conditions. The following assessment comes from the Board of Governors of the Federal Reserve System, the FDIC, and the OCC: "The markets for some derivative instruments reportedly experienced reduced liquidity during the European currency crisis. This complicated hedging strategies and heightened market risks for some intermediaries during this period. Nevertheless, it is unlikely that the underlying markets would have performed as they did in September without the existence of related derivatives markets that enabled currency positions to be managed, albeit with some difficulty in some instruments" (1993a, 18). The colorful descriptions of derivatives activity in the popular press tend to overlook the market's stabilizing influence. There is little arguing with the contention that derivatives are risky business, but so are the underlying positions of intermediaries and end users.

Notes

1. Regulators subsequently testified that hedge fund activity was not a major cause of volatility (Harlan 1994).
2. Gramm and Gay (1994) point out that from the advent of futures trading through 1920, at least 160 bills were introduced in Congress to restrain or eliminate futures trading. Much of the impetus for such bills came from agricultural price declines attributed to futures trading. For the same reason, trading in commodity options was banned in 1934 by the Code of Fair Competition for Grain Exchanges under the National Industrial Recovery Act. Trade in onion futures was banned by Congress in 1958 (see Gray 1983). Hedge funds are now being considered for tougher regulation (Fromson 1994).
3. A broad overview of U.S. and international regulatory frameworks is given in Commodity Futures Trading Commission (1993b, Working Paper 3).
4. *Financial Derivatives: New Instruments and Their Uses* (1993) contains articles that discuss and analyze many derivatives contracts in detail. The dichotomy in terms of linear versus nonlinear payoffs is somewhat arbitrary because some linear payoff contracts, such as swaps, may contain embedded options. However, the basic distinction is useful.

5. LIBOR is the acronym for the London Interbank Offered Rate, which is the rate received by large banks for short-term time deposits in the interbank market. The fixed swap rate is determined by the term structure of LIBOR rates (and extrapolated to longer maturities using government securities).

6. These figures imply that the average swap contract size has a notional value 127 times larger than the average futures and options contract.

7. Two U.S. insurance companies act as dealers in the derivatives markets (U.S. Congress 1993).

8. See U.S. Congress (1993, 670–71). The trading revenue and losses data derive from Keefe, Bruyette & Woods. Inc. No dates are indicated for the period of the survey. However, the losses figure has probably risen somewhat after the market turbulence of early 1994.

9. To put trading losses in perspective, consider that the fifty largest commercial banks incurred cumulative loan charge-offs (losses) of almost $90 billion from 1985 to 1991 (Corrigan 1992, 12).

10. More precisely, the up-front payment would be equal to the present discounted value of the difference between the stream of 9 percent payments and the 8 percent payments.

11. A comprehensive list of risks that require hedging appears in Group of Thirty (1993a), 43–45.

12. Some swap agreements contain a so-called walkaway or limited two-way payment clause that gives a counterparty who owes a payment on a swap the right to terminate the agreement in the event the opposite counterparty becomes bankrupt. This is a case in which a solvent counterparty may withhold payment on a swap that has positive value to a bankrupt counterparty. Limited two-way payments were intended to give creditors extra leverage in negotiating with failed counterparties (specifically on other contracts with the failed counterparty with positive replacement value to the creditor). The ISDA and others have been advocating swap agreements with full two-way payments in the interest of establishing smooth-functioning netting agreements.

13. Abken (1993) and Hull (1989) take this approach to modeling default-risky derivatives.

14. See U.S. Congress (1993, especially 698 and 793–96), for further detail on the legal aspects of netting arrangements. Other areas of legal concern are discussed in depth in Group of Thirty (1993b, Section 3), as well as in U.S. Congress (1993, 695–700).

15. The text does not clarify whether the swap cash flows are gross or net. Presumably they are net to be comparable with the foreign exchange cash flows.

16. See Strauss (1993) for an example of extraordinary efforts by senior management to understand the risks being taken by a derivatives subsidiary.

17. The bankruptcies of Drexel Burnham Lambert in 1990 and the Bank of New England (BNE) in 1991 both required unwinding of the derivatives books of these institutions. These failures had the potential to have systemic repercussions, but both were closely managed by regulators. Reportedly, swap and other contracts were closed out or assigned to other counterparties smoothly, without significant losses to any counterparties. The FDIC took over BNE and temporarily acted as counterparty for the bank's derivatives. Similarly, the SEC unwound Drexel's derivatives portfolios, except for its swap book, which was under control of Drexel's unregistered broker-dealer affiliate. Nonetheless, the swap book was also closed out in an orderly fashion, without market disruption. Each of these institutions had derivatives books that were large, about $30 billion in notional size, but not of the size of major derivatives dealers. See U.S. Congress (1993, 798–800).

18. Two other major studies made at the request of Congress are Board of Governors (1993a) and CFTC (1993a). Other studies and recommendations have been made by the Institute of International Finance, the Bank of England, and the International Monetary Fund. See U.S. Congress (1993, 802–9) for summaries. The U.S. securities and banking

regulators also have a number of narrower proposals, which are listed in U.S. Congress (1993, 53–54).

19. The Basle Committee members come from Belgium, Canada, France, Germany, Italy, Japan, Luxembourg, the Netherlands, Sweden, Switzerland, the United Kingdom, and the United States. The group usually meets at the Bank for International Settlements in Basle, Switzerland, to frame common prudential standards for member countries.

20. See Odier and Solnik (1993) for evidence about the instability of correlations, particularly during market downturns. Asset price movements tend to become more synchronized internationally during volatile periods, reducing the benefits of diversification.

21. The SEC has proposed modifications to the net capital rule. See U.S. Congress (1993, 771–77).

22. See James A. Leach, letter to the House Committee on Banking, Finance, and Urban Affairs, November 22, 1993, 8, of U.S. Congress (1993).

23. FDICIA was enacted to protect the deposit insurance safety net and to limit systemic risk in the banking system. It contains so-called prompt-corrective-action provisions that enable regulators to intervene in problem banks before problems threaten the Bank Insurance Fund (see Wall 1993).

24. See Wall, Pringle, and McNulty (1993) for the definitions of core and supplementary capital.

25. Wall, Pringle, and McNulty (1993) give a detailed discussion and examples of the Basle Accord and example computations.

26. A security held in a long position is one that is purchased, often in the expectation of price appreciation. One in a short position is borrowed and sold in the expectation that an identical security can be purchased at a lower price.

27. A duration-based hedge insulates a bond portfolio from changes in value from interest rate fluctuations.

28. In particular, see Cohen (1994), for a critique of the measuring scheme in the Fed-OCC-FDIC proposal.

29. The CFTC and the SEC recently concluded an agreement with their U.K. counterpart, the Securities and Investments Board (SIB), to coordinate information sharing and promote improved industry practice in many of the areas cited by the Group of Thirty and others (Reed 1994).

References

Abken, Peter A. "Valuation of Default-Risky Interest-Rate Swaps." In *Advances in Futures and Options Research*, edited by Don M. Chance and Robert R. Trippi, vol. 6. Greenwich, Conn.: JAI Press, Inc., 1993.

Basle Committee on Banking Supervision. "The Prudential Supervision of Netting, Market Risks, and Interest Rate Risk." Preface to Consultative Proposal, April 1993a.

——. "The Supervisory Recognition of Netting for Capital Adequacy Purposes." Consultative Proposal, April 1993b.

——. "The Supervisory Treatment of Market Risks." Consultative Proposal, April 1993c.

——. "Measurement of Banks' Exposure to Interest Rate Risk." Consultative Proposal, April 1993d.

Bauman, Joseph. "Comment on 'Consultative Proposal by the Basle Committee: Capital Adequacy for Market Risk.'" International Swaps and Derivatives Association, Inc., December 28, 1993.

Board of Governors of the Federal Reserve System, Federal Deposit Insurance Corporation, and Office of the Comptroller of the Currency. "Derivative Product Activities of Commercial Banks." January 27, 1993a.

——. "Examining Risk Management and Internal Controls for Trading Activities of Banking Organizations." SR 93–69, December 20, 1993b.

Breeden, Richard C. "Directors, Control Your Derivatives." *Wall Street Journal*, March 7, 1994, A14.

Chew, Lillian. "Protect and Survive." *Risk* 7 (March 1994): 36–42.

Cohen, Hugh. "Data Aggregation and the Problem in Measuring a Bank's Interest Rate Exposure." Federal Reserve Bank of Atlanta working paper, 1994.

Commodity Futures Trading Commission. "OTC Derivative Markets and Their Regulation." October 1993a.

——. "OTC Derivative Markets and Their Regulation: Working Papers." October 1993b.

Cooley, Thomas F. "Comment on an Equilibrium Model of Nominal Bond Prices with Inflation-Output Correlation and Stochastic Volatility." *Journal of Money, Credit, and Banking* 25 (1993): 666–72.

Corrigan, E. Gerald. "Painful Period Has Set Stage for Banking Rebound." *American Banker*, February 3, 1992, 12–13.

Falloon, William. "From Bad to Worse." *Risk* 7 (April 1994): 7–8.

Financial Derivatives: New Instruments and Their Uses. Research Division, Federal Reserve Bank of Atlanta, 1993.

Fromson, Brett D. "Tougher Rules on Hedge Funds Sought." *Washington Post*, March 15, 1994, D1.

Gilbert, R. Alton. "Implications of Netting Arrangements for Bank Risk in Foreign Exchange Transactions." Federal Reserve Bank of St. Louis *Review* 74 (January/February 1992): 3–16.

Gramm, Wendy L., and Gerald D. Gay. "Scams, Scoundrels and Scapegoats: A Taxonomy of CEA Regulation over Derivative Instruments." *Journal of Derivatives* 1 (1994): 6–24.

Gray, Roger W. "Onions Revisited." In *Selected Writings on Futures Markets: Basic Research in Commodity Markets*, edited by Anne E. Peck, vol. 2, 319–22. Chicago: Board of Trade, 1983.

Group of Thirty, Global Derivatives Study Group. "Derivatives: Practices and Principles." July 1993a.

——. "Derivatives: Practices and Principles, Appendix I: Working Papers." July 1993b.

——. "Derivatives: Practices and Principles, Appendix III: Survey of Industry Practice." March 1994.

Harlan, Christi. "Regulators Believe Hedge-Fund Activity Wasn't Major Cause of Market Volatility." *Wall Street Journal*, April 14, 1994, A2.

Hull, John. "Assessing Credit Risk in a Financial Institution's Off-Balance Sheet Commitments." *Journal of Financial and Quantitative Analysis* 24 (1989): 489–501.

Hunter, William C., and David W. Stowe. "Path-Dependent Options." In *Financial Derivatives: New Instruments and Their Uses*, 167–72. 1993a. (First published in Federal Reserve Bank of Atlanta *Economic Review* 77 [March/April 1992]: 29–34.)

——. "Path-Dependent Options: Valuation and Applications." In *Financial Derivatives: New Instruments and Their Uses*, 173–86. 1993b. (First published in Federal Reserve Bank of Atlanta *Economic Review* 77 [July/August 1992]: 30–43.)

"International Banking Survey." *The Economist*, April 10, 1993, 3–38.

Leach, James A., William J. McDonough, David W. Mullins, and Brian Quinn. "Global Derivatives: Public Sector Responses." Group of Thirty, Occasional Paper 44, Washington, 1993.

Lipin, Steven, Fred R. Bleakley, and Barbara Donnelly Granito. "Just What Firms Do With 'Derivatives' Is Suddenly a Hot Issue." *Wall Street Journal*, April 14, 1994, A1, A7.

Miller, Merton H. "Financial Innovation: The Last Twenty Years and the Next." *Journal of Financial and Quantitative Economics* 21 (1986): 459–71.

Odier, Patrick, and Bruno Solnik. "Lessons for International Asset Allocation." *Financial Analysts Journal* 49 (March/April 1993): 63–77.

Office of the Comptroller of the Currency. "Risk Management of Financial Derivatives." Banking Circular 277, October 27, 1993.

Reed, Nick. "Connect and Survive." *Risk* 7 (April 1994): 10, 12.

Schaefer, Stephen. "Financial Regulation: The Contribution of the Theory of Finance." London Business School, IFA Working Paper 157–92, 1992.

Sesit, Michael R., and Laura Jereski. "Hedge Funds Face Review of Practices." *Wall Street Journal*, February 28, 1994, C1, C11.

Strauss, Cheryl Beth. "The Shadow War at AIG." *Investment Dealer's Digest*, September 6, 1993, 14–18.

U.S. Congress. House. Committee on Banking, Finance, and Urban Affairs. *Hearings on Safety and Soundness Issues Related to Bank Derivatives Activities.* Part 3 (Minority Report). 103d Cong., 1st sess., October 28, 1993. Serial 103–88.

U.S. General Accounting Office. "Financial Derivatives: Actions Needed to Protect the Financial System." GAO/GGD-94–133, May 1994.

Wall, Larry D. "Too-Big-to-Fail after FDICIA." Federal Reserve Bank of Atlanta *Economic Review* 78 (January/February 1993): 1–14.

Wall, Larry D., John J. Pringle, and James E. McNulty. "Capital Requirements for Interest Rate and Foreign Exchange Hedges." In *Financial Derivatives: New Instruments and Their Uses*, 226–38. 1993. (First published in Federal Reserve Bank of Atlanta *Economic Review* 75 [May/June 1990]: 14–28.)

Sources

Kawaller, Ira G., "Determining the ?elevant Fair Value(s) of S&P 500 Futures: A Case Study Approach," CME Financial Strategy Paper, (Chicago: Chicago Mercantile Exchange, 1991).

Kawaller, Ira G. and T. Koch, "Cash–and–Carry Trading and the Pricing of Treasury Bill Futures," *The Journal of Futures Markets*, 4:2, Summer 1984, pp. 115–123.

Black, Fischer, "How to Use the Holes in Black and Scholes," *Journal of Applied Corporate Finance*, 1:4, Winter 1989, pp. 67–73.

Abken, Peter A., "Beyond Plain Vanilla: A Taxonomy of Swaps," Federal Reserve Bank of Atlanta *Economic Review*, March/April 1991, pp. 12–29.

Marshall, John F. and Kenneth R. Kapner, "The Pricing of Swaps," Chapter 8 of Kapner, Kenneth R. and John F. Marshall, *The Swaps Handbook*, (New York: New York Institute of Finance), 1990, pp. 319–350.

Kuprianov, Anatoli, "Over-the-Counter Interest Rate Derivatives," Federal Reserve Bank of Richmond, *Economic Quarterly*, 79:3, Summer 1993, pp. 65–94.

Hunter, William C. and Stowe, David W., "Path-Dependent Options," Federal Reserve Bank of Atlanta, *Economic Review*, March/April 1992, pp. 29–34.

Hunter, William C. and Stowe, David W., "Path-Dependent Options: Valuation and Applications," Federal Reserve Bank of Atlanta, *Economic Review*, July/August 1992, pp. 30–43.

Gastineau, Gary, "An Introduction to Special-Purpose Derivatives: Path Dependent Options," *The Journal of Derivatives*, 1:2, Winter 1993, pp. 78–86.

Smith, Jr., Clifford W., Charles W. Smithson, and D. Sykes Wilford, "Managing Financial Risk," *Journal of Applied Corporate Finance*, 1:4, Winter 1989, pp. 27–48.

Kolb, R. and R. Chiang, "Improving Hedging Performance Using Interest Rate Futures," *Financial Management*, 10:4, 1981, pp. 72–79.

Kolb, R. and G. Gray, "Immunizing Bond Portfolios with Interest Rate Futures," *Financial Management*, 11:2, Summer 1982, pp. 81–89.

Kawaller, Ira G., "Interest Rate Swaps versus Eurodollar Strips," *CME Financial Strategy Paper*, (Chicago: Chicago Mercantile Exchange, 1987).

O'Brien, T., "The Mechanics of Portfolio Insurance," *Journal of Portfolio Management*, 14:3, Spring 1988, pp. 40–47.

Rubinstein, M., "Alternative Paths to Portfolio Insurance," *Financial Analysts Journal*, 41:4, July–August 1985, pp. 42–52.

Santoni, G. J., "The October Crash: Some Evidence on the Cascade Theory," Federal Reserve Bank of St. Louis, *Review*, May/June 1988, pp. 18–33.

Rubinstein, Mark, "Portfolio Insurance and the Market Crash," *Financial Analysts Journal*, 44:1, January/February 1988, pp. 38–47.

Kuprianov, Anatoli, "The Role of Interest Rate Swaps in Corporate Finance," Federal Reserve Bank of Richmond, *Economic Quarterly*, 80:3, Summer 1994, pp. 49–68.

Kalotay, Andrew and Tuckman, Bruce, "A Tale of Two Bond Swaps," *The Journal of Financial Engineering*, 1:3, December 1992, pp. 325–343.

Abken, Peter A., "Over-the-Counter Financial Derivatives: Risky Business?" Federal Reserve Bank of Atlanta, *Economic Review*, 79:2, March/April 1994, pp. 1–22.

Practical readings in
financial derivatives